Tenth Edition

CONTEMPORARY LOGISTICS

PREFACE

This edition of *Contemporary Logistics* reflects a business landscape that is characterized by a dizzying pace of technological advancement, a worldwide economic and financial crisis of historic proportions, and continuing geopolitical tensions in various parts of the world. Although these and other events present both challenges and opportunities for logistics managers, the logistics discipline still remains fun, exciting, and dynamic—characteristics that are reflected in our revision.

WHAT'S NEW IN THIS EDITION?

The tenth edition reflects input from reviewers, adopters, and other interested parties in terms of structure, presentation, and content. Specific modifications include:

- Part I consists of four chapters in the tenth edition, versus three chapters in the ninth edition.
  - Chapter 3, "Strategic and Financial Logistics," is brand new in this edition and reflects the increasing strategic and financial impact of the logistics discipline.
  - Chapter 4, "Organizational and Managerial Issues in Logistics," consists of material that appeared as Chapters 13 and 14 in *Contemporary Logistics*, ninth edition.
- Part II, "Supply Chain Management," is new to this edition and consists of two chapters, "The Supply Chain Management Concept" and "Procurement." Although these two chapters appeared in the ninth edition, their grouping as a separate section reflects the continuing evolution of the supply chain management discipline.
- Although Part III of this edition, "Elements of Logistics Systems," contains the same eight chapters as the ninth edition, the ordering of some chapters has been changed to reflect adopter and reviewer feedback. For example, because the effectiveness and efficiency of warehousing operations can be greatly influenced by packaging and materials handling considerations, the "Packaging and Materials Handling" chapter now immediately follows the "Warehousing Management" chapter.
- Each of the holdover chapters from the ninth edition has been revised to incorporate new examples and references, and several chapters have been retitled as well.
- New content has been added throughout the tenth edition. For example, Chapter 2, "Logistics Information Technology," now includes a section that discusses information technology challenges. Chapter 5, "The Supply Chain Management Concept," now discusses a third supply chain management framework, the Process Classification Framework. Chapter 9, "Distribution Center, Warehouse, and Plant Location," has added a section that looks at the strategic importance of facility location. Several new sections, including macroenvironmental influences on international logistics and the Logistics Performance Index, now appear in Chapter 14, "International Logistics."
- Tables and Figures containing country and industry data have either been revised or updated. Examples include Figure 10-3, "Workplace Safety Issues"; Table 12-1, "Infrastructure Statistics in Several Countries"; and Table 14-1, "Beginning Dates for the Chinese New Year 2011–2018."
- New tables and figures have been added in the tenth edition, such as Table 1-1, which presents logistics costs as a percentage of gross domestic product for selected countries; Table 4-2, which presents the 12 required items for the Importer Security Filing rule; Figure 5-4, which outlines the Process Classification Framework; and Table 13-1, which presents an example of the Class Rate System.

- The end-of-chapter Suggested Readings in the tenth edition have been revised, and the majority of them have been published since 2005.

SUPPLEMENTS FOR INSTRUCTORS

Available online to instructors only at our Instructor Resource Center (www.pearsonshighered.com/irc), supplements to accompany this text include:

Instructor's Manual: The Instructor's Manual features the solutions to the end-of-chapter questions and cases, examination questions with page references, and teaching suggestions.

PowerPoint Presentation: The PowerPoint Presentation includes basic chapter outlines and key points from each chapter, plus art from the text.

The current edition of *Contemporary Logistics* has been prepared by Paul Murphy, and he welcomes your comments and suggestions at drmurphy@jcu.edu. Paul gratefully acknowledges the substantial contributions that the late Donald F. Wood, James C. Johnson, and Daniel L. Wardlow made to earlier editions.

ACKNOWLEDGMENTS

Thanks go out to the following individuals, whose help and support made possible the writing of this and previous editions: Glen Adams, Standard Oil Company; Fred Altstadt, Four-phase System; Scott A. Ames, Logistics Associates; Folger Athearn, Jr., Athearn & Company; Can Atli; Donald W. Baldra, Schering Corporation; Charles L. Ballard, Hudson Valley Community College; Carl Bankard, York College of Pennsylvania; James H. Barnes, University of Georgia; Tayfun Tugberk Bekiroglu; Warren Blanding, Marketing Publications, Inc.; James F. Briody, Fairchild Camera and Instrument Company; Hank Bulwinkel, Towson State University; Frank Burinsky; W. R. Callister, Del Monte Corporation; Neil D. Chaitin, Challenge Equipment Corporation; W. M. Cheatham, Specialty Brands; Carolyn Coggins; Bill Cunningham, Memphis State University; Bob J. Davis, Western Illinois University; Patricia J. Daugherty, University of Oklahoma; Rick Dawe, Fritz Logistics Institute; George Derugin; Gary Dicer, University of Tennessee; John R. Doggett, *Warehousing Review*; W. R. Donham, Cambridge Plan International; A. J. Faria, University of Windsor; Joseph Garfall; Donald C. Garland, Zellerbach Paper; Navneet Gill; Stanley Groover, Towson State University; Carl Guelzo, Towson State University; Mark Haight, University of Wisconsin Center at Barron County; Jay Hamerslag, Hamerslag Equipment Company; Gerald Hampton; Lowell Hedrick, Phillips Petroleum Company; Weldon G. Helmus, Hewlett-Packard; Lynn Hill, Heublein, Inc.; Stephen G. Hill, Dole Packaged Foods Company; Stanley J. Hille, University of Missouri at Columbia; Donald Horton, American Warehousemen's Association; Rufus C. Jefferson; Creed Jenkins, Consolidated Distribution Services; J. M. Johnson, Johnson & Johnson; J. Richard Jones, Memphis State University; Robert E. Jones, F. E. Warren Air Force Base; Henry M. Karel, Shelby State Community College; R. L. Kemmer, GTE Service Corporation; Bob Kingston, Kaiser Permanente Medical Care Program; David Kupferman; Tibi Lacatus, Sertapak; C. John Langley Jr., University of Tennessee; Art LaPlant, Schlage Lock Company; Joseph R. Larsen, CIBA Pharmaceutical Company; Sean Laughlin; Ron Lennon, Towson State University; Douglas Long; Harry Loomer, University of Wisconsin Center at Barron County; Christopher Low; Irving C. MacDonald; Ernest Y. Maitland, British Columbia Institute of Technology; Don Marsh, United Airlines Maintenance Operations; Darwyn Mass, Rocky Mountain Motor Tariff Bureau; Frank McDonald; Michael McGinnis, Pennsylvania State University; Chinnubbie McIntosh, Warren Petroleum Company; Jim Meneley, American Honda Motor Company; Henry Metzner, University of Missouri–Rolla; Edward J. Meyers, Pacific Gas & Electric Company; Donald D. Mickel, Sacramento Army Depot; Lowell S. Miller; Rory K. Miller, California Maritime Academy; Joseph F. Moffatt, University of Southwestern Louisiana; Paul R. Neff, Boeing Company; Donald P. Nelson, National Distribution Agency; David Norton, Nabisco; Thomas Paczkowski, Cayuga Community College; Taeho Park, San Jose State University; Donald Pefaur, Trammell Crow Distribution Corporation; Ray Perin, Perin Company; Andru M. Peters, Andros, Inc.; Robert R. Piper; Lee Plummer, North Carolina State University; Ira Pollack; Ruby Remley, Cabrini College; Richard L. Rickenbacher, Safeway Stores; Dale S. Rogers, University of Nevada, Reno; Frank R. Scheer, University of Tennessee; Karl Schober; Skip Sherwood, California State University at Fresno; Charles S. Shuken, Metropolitan Warehouse Company; Melvin Silvester; David A. Smith, State University of New York at Buffalo; Jerome V. Smith, Consolidated Freightways; Michael Smith, Christian Brothers University; R. Neil Southern, University of Memphis; F. J. Spellman; Jack M. Starling, North Texas State University; Joseph J. Stefanic, Agrico Chemical Company; Wendell M. Stewart, Kearney Management Consultants; Stephen Stover; T. M. Tipton, USCO Services, Inc.; Teddy N. Toklas, Oakland Naval Supply Center; Lee Totten, Western New England College; Frances Tucker, Syracuse University; Roy Dale Voorhees, Iowa State University; Peter F. Walstad; Bill Walton, Pacific American Warehousing & Trucking Company; Boyd L. Warnick, Utah Technical College; Mary Margaret Weber, Missouri Western State College; Marcus A. Weiss-Madsen; Terry C. Whiteside, Montana State Department of

Agriculture; Lynn Williams, Logisticon; Kenneth C. Williamson, James Madison University; Warren Winstead, George Washington University; Doreen Wood; Suzan C. Woods, Logisticon; Jean Woodruff, Western New England College; Ronald S. Yaros; Mark Zborowski; James Ziola, Consolidated Freightways; and Howard Zysman, Morada Distribution, Inc.

At Pearson Prentice Hall, Paul extends thanks to Clara Bartunek, Melissa Sabella, Kierra Bloom, and Karin Williams and at Integra Software Services Pvt. Ltd., to Chitra Sundarajan.

Paul R. Murphy, Jr.
University Heights, Ohio

Tenth Edition

CONTEMPORARY LOGISTICS

PART I

OVERVIEW OF LOGISTICS

Part 1 of *Contemporary Logistics* introduces the many dimensions of the complex and dynamic subject of logistics. Chapter 1 presents an overview of logistics and introduces you to what logistics is and why it is important. The chapter covers the economic impact of logistics and discusses how logistics interacts with other functions, such as marketing, in an organization.

Chapter 2 provides an overview of the general types of information management systems that are applicable across each business function and examples of how these general types of information systems are specifically applied in logistics management. Chapter 2 also explores the Internet's influence on logistics and looks at some of the challenges associated with information technology.

Chapter 3 is new to this edition and discusses the strategic financial outcomes influenced by logistics decisions. It uses the strategic profit model to highlight how logistics activities influence the key corporate financial measures of net income, capital employed, and return on capital employed.

Chapter 4 examines organizational and managerial issues in logistics. The chapter begins by looking at organizational structure and organizational design for logistics. Chapter 4 also discusses select managerial issues in logistics such as productivity, theft and pilferage, and the impact of terrorism on logistics systems.

1 | AN OVERVIEW OF LOGISTICS

Key Terms

- Cost trade-offs
- Disintermediation
- Economic utility
- Form utility
- Landed costs
- Logistics
- Marketing channels
- Mass logistics

- Materials management
- Physical distribution
- Place utility
- Possession utility
- Postponement
- Power retailer
- Sorting function
- Stock-keeping units (SKUs)

- Stockouts
- Sustainable products
- Systems approach
- Tailored logistics
- Time utility
- Total cost approach

Learning Objectives

- To understand the economic impacts of logistics
- To learn what logistics is
- To learn about the increased importance of logistics
- To understand the systems and total cost approaches to logistics

- To expose you to logistical relationships within the firm
- To learn about marketing channels
- To provide a brief overview of activities in the logistics channel
- To familiarize you with logistics careers

ECONOMIC IMPACTS OF LOGISTICS

At this point, you may have limited awareness of, and knowledge about, logistics—the subject matter of this textbook. However, if that is the case, you're really not very different from lots of other people who inhabit this planet, and it might come as a surprise to you that logistics tends to have significant economic impacts. From a macroeconomic perspective, Table 1-1 presents logistics costs in relation to gross domestic product (GDP) for a select group of countries. Although absolute and relative logistics costs in relation to GDP vary from country to country, logistics is most definitely an important component in any country's economy.

More specifically, logistics can play an important role in a nation's economic growth and development. For example, a poor transportation infrastructure and high levels of inventory are two key drawbacks that have limited the expansion of Vietnam's economy.[1] In a similar fashion, both the government and the private sector in China have recognized that as China's labor cost

---

[1] No author, "High Logistics Costs Stifle Vietnam's Economic Growth," *EyeforTransport*, February 24, 2009.

TABLE 1-1	The Cost of the Business Logistics System in Relation to a Country's Gross Domestic Product

Country	Logistics as a Percentage of GDP
United States	9.4
Brazil	12.6
India	13.0
South Africa	15.9
Thailand	19.0
Finland	19.8
People's Republic of China	21.6
Vietnam	22.5

Sources: http://www.mb.com.ph/node/198686; http://www.business-standard.com/ india/news/logistics-cost-savings-to-have-big-impactgdp-kpmg/372434/; http://www. imperiallogistics.co.za/userfiles/file/PR030409_5thSOL.pdf; www.cepd.gov.tw/ dn.aspx?uid=4721; http://www.3plwire.com/2007/02/21/chinas-logistics-inefficiencies- could-hamper-growth/; http://www.latinamericanlogistics.org/articles/latin-american- a-strategic-concern-for-the-chinese.htm; Finland State of Logistics 2009, Ministry of Transport and Communication Finland; 20th Annual Sate of Logistics Report, Council of Supply Chain Management Professionals, 2009.

advantage shifts to other countries (such as Vietnam), logistics efficiency becomes an essential component to fueling an economy that has been expanding at between 8 and 10 percent per year.[2]

Apart from the previous examples of macro-level economic impacts, the economic impacts of logistics can affect individual consumers such as you. These impacts can be illustrated through the concept of **economic utility**, which is the value or usefulness of a product in fulfilling customer needs or wants. The four general types of economic utility are possession, form, time, and place. Logistics clearly contributes to time and place utilities.

Possession utility refers to the value or usefulness that comes from a customer being able to take possession of a product. Possession utility can be influenced by the payment terms associated with a product. Credit and debit cards, for example, facilitate possession utility by allowing the customer to purchase products without having to produce cash or a cash equivalent. Likewise, automotive leases allow customers to take possession of a more desirable model than would be possible with conventional automotive loans.

Form utility refers to a product's being in a form that (1) can be used by the customer and (2) is of value to the customer. Although form utility has generally been associated with production and manufacturing, logistics can also contribute to form utility. For example, to achieve production economies (i.e., lower cost per unit), a soft-drink company may produce thousands of cases of a certain type of soft drink (e.g., diet cola). You're not likely to purchase diet cola by the thousands of cases (unless you're having a really big social event!) but rather in smaller lot sizes, such as a six- or twelve-pack. Through *allocation*, logistics can break the thousands of cases of diet cola into the smaller quantities that are desired by customers.

Place utility refers to having products available *where* they are needed by customers; products are moved from points of lesser value to points of greater value. Continuing with the diet cola example, place utility is increased by moving the soda from a point of lesser value (e.g., stored in a warehouse) to a point of greater value (e.g., on a supermarket shelf).

Closely related to place utility is **time utility**, which refers to having products available *when* they are needed by customers. It's important to recognize that different products have different sensitivities to time; three-day late delivery of perishable items likely has more serious consequences than three-day late delivery of nonperishable items.

---

[2] Peter Tirschwell, "In China, Full Speed Ahead," *Journal of Commerce*, April 17, 2006, 38.

Note that simultaneous achievement of possession, form, place, and time utility goes a long way toward facilitating—but not guaranteeing—customer satisfaction. Consider the experience of a former student who used an online service to order Valentine's Day flowers for his out-of-state girlfriend. The online service facilitated possession utility by allowing for a secured payment by credit card. A healthy arrangement of the correct bouquet (form utility) arrived at the girlfriend's residence on Valentine's Day (place and time utility). The problem: The greeting card that accompanied the flowers had a wrong name for the girlfriend (but the right name for the boyfriend)!

LOGISTICS: WHAT IT IS

Now that you have a better understanding of the economic impacts of logistics, it's important to define what logistics is. Since approximately 1980, tremendous—and rapid—change has occurred in the business logistics field. One consequence of this rapid change is that business logistics has been referred to by a number of different terms, each having slightly different meanings. In recent years, some of the terms used to refer to business logistics have included (but are not limited to) the following:

- Business logistics
- Distribution
- Industrial distribution
- Logistics
- Logistics management
- Marketing logistics
- Physical distribution
- Supply chain management

In essence, each of these terms is associated with managing the flows of goods and information from a point of origin to a point of consumption.

Although the aforementioned terms are similar, they aren't the same; from a managerial perspective, this poses a potential problem of comparing apples to oranges as opposed to comparing apples to apples or oranges to oranges. For example, suppose that one organization defines logistics to include two activities—transportation and inventory management—whereas a second organization defines logistics to include three activities—transportation, inventory management, and warehousing. It seems reasonable that the second organization's total cost of logistics would be higher than that of the first organization (because the second organization's logistics encompasses more activities). However, it would be a mistake to conclude that, because of the higher total costs, the second organization is less effective or efficient with respect to logistics because the two organizations have different definitions of logistics.

In an effort to avoid potential misunderstanding about the meaning of logistics, this book adopts the current definition promulgated by the Council of Supply Chain Management Professionals (CSCMP), one of the world's most prominent organizations for logistics professionals. According to the CSCMP, "Logistics management is that part of Supply Chain Management that plans, implements, and controls the efficient, effective forward and reverse flow and storage of goods, services, and related information between the point of origin and the point of consumption in order to meet customers' requirements."[3]

Let's analyze this definition in closer detail. First, logistics is part of supply chain management. We'll talk about supply chains and supply chain management in greater detail in

---

[3] *www.cscmp.org.*

Chapter 5, but the key point for now is that logistics is part of a bigger picture in the sense that the supply chain focuses on coordination among business functions (such as marketing, production, and finance) within and across organizations. The fact that logistics is explicitly recognized as part of supply chain management means that logistics can affect how well (or how poorly) an individual firm—and its associated supply chain(s)—can achieve goals and objectives.

The CSCMP definition also indicates that logistics "plans, implements, and controls." Of particular importance is the word *and*, which suggests that logistics should be involved in all three activities—planning, implementing, and controlling—and not just one or two. Some suggest, however, that logistics is more involved in the implementation than in the planning of certain logistical policies.[4]

Note that the CSCMP definition also refers to "efficient and effective forward and reverse flows and storage." Broadly speaking, effectiveness can be thought of as, "How well does a company do what they say they're going to do?" For example, if a company promises that all orders will be shipped within 24 hours of receipt, what percentage of orders are actually shipped within 24 hours of receipt? In contrast, efficiency can be thought of as how well (or poorly) company resources are used to achieve what a company promises it can do. For instance, some companies use premium or expedited transportation services—which cost more money—to cover for shortcomings in other parts of their logistics systems.

With respect to forward and reverse flows and storage, logistics has traditionally focused on forward flows and storage, that is, those directed *toward* the point of consumption. Increasingly, however, the logistics discipline has recognized the importance of reverse flows and storage (*reverse logistics*), that is, those that *originate* at the point of consumption. Although the majority of the discussion in this book focuses on forward logistics, the relevance and importance of reverse logistics continue to grow as more companies recognize its tactical and strategic implications.[5] Reverse logistics is also likely to gain attention in the future as more companies recognize it as an opportunity for competitive advantage.[6]

The CSCMP definition also indicates that logistics involves the flow and storage of "goods, services, and related information." Indeed, in the contemporary business environment, logistics is as much about the flow and storage of information as it is about the flow and storage of goods. The importance of information in contemporary logistics is captured by Fred Smith, CEO and chairman of FedEx (a leading logistics service provider), who believes that "information about the package is as important as the package itself."[7]

Finally, the CSCMP definition indicates that the purpose of logistics is "to meet customer requirements." This is important for several reasons, with one being that logistics strategies and activities should be based on customer wants and needs, rather than the wants, needs, and capabilities of other parties. Although a customer focus might seem like the proverbial no-brainer, one implication of such a focus is that companies actually have to communicate with their customers to learn about their needs and wants. It suffices to say that, even today, some companies continue to be hesitant about communicating with their customers.

A second reason for the importance of meeting customer requirements is the notion that because different customers have different logistical needs and wants, a one-size-fits-all logistics

---

[4] Paul R. Murphy, Richard F. Poist, and Charles D. Braunschwieg, "Role and Relevance of Logistics to Corporate Environmentalism: An Empirical Assessment," *International Journal of Physical Distribution and Logistics Management* 25, no. 2 (1995): 5–19; Paul R. Murphy and Richard F. Poist, "Socially Responsible Logistics: An Exploratory Study," *Transportation Journal* 41, no. 4 (2002): 23–35.

[5] M. Jose Alvarez-Gil, Pascual Berrone, F. Javier Husillos, and Nora Lado, "Reverse Logistics, Stakeholders' Influence, Organizational Slack, and Managers' Posture," *Journal of Business Research* 60, no. 5 (2007): 463–473.

[6] James Stock, Thomas Speh, and Herbert Shear, "Many Happy (Product) Returns," *Harvard Business Review* 80, no. 7 (2002): 16–17.

[7] Jonathan Reiskin, "Carriers Invest in Web Sites, Software, Networks," *Transport Topics*, May 8, 2006, 10.

approach (**mass logistics**)—in which every customer gets the same type and levels of logistics service—will result in some customers being overserved while others are underserved. Rather, companies should consider **tailored logistics** approaches, in which groups of customers with similar logistical needs and wants are provided with logistics service appropriate to these needs and wants.[8]

The principles in this textbook are generally applicable not only to for-profit organizations but also to the workings of governmental and nonprofit entities. From a governmental perspective, logistics is quite germane to the armed forces, which shouldn't be surprising, given that logistics was first associated with the military. Consider, for example, the potential consequences of excessive inventory—a challenge faced by a number of for-profit organizations—in a war zone. Excessive inventory can slow down troops because there's more inventory to move when the troops are changing locations.[9]

Moreover, a community food bank provides one example of the relevance of logistics to nonprofit organizations. As an example, the Food Bank of New York City is responsible for delivering nearly 50 million pounds of food annually to more than 1,000 food assistance programs such as homeless shelters and food pantries. From a logistical perspective, the Food Bank of New York City is responsible for collecting, storing, repacking, and distributing food from its 90,000 square-foot warehouse.[10]

THE INCREASED IMPORTANCE OF LOGISTICS

The formal study of business logistics, and predecessor concepts such as traffic management and physical distribution, has existed since the second half of the twentieth century. Quite frankly, from approximately 1950 to 1980, limited appreciation was shown for the importance of the logistics discipline. Since 1980, however, increasing recognition has been given to the topic, and several key reasons are discussed next.

A Reduction in Economic Regulation

During the 1970s and the 1980s, widespread reductions in economic regulation (commonly referred to as *deregulation*) relaxed government control of carriers' rates and fares, entry and exit, mergers and acquisitions, and more. These controls were particularly onerous in the U.S. transportation industry in the sense that price competition was essentially nonexistent, and customers were pretty much forced to accept whatever service the carriers chose to provide. This meant that logistics managers had relatively little control over one of the most important cost components in a logistics system.

Reductions in economic regulation in the U.S. airfreight, railroad, and trucking industries allowed individual carriers flexibility in pricing and service. This flexibility was important to logistics for several reasons. First, it provided companies with the ability to implement the tailored logistics approach discussed earlier, in the sense that companies could specify different logistics service levels, and prices could be adjusted accordingly. Second, the increased pricing flexibility allowed large buyers of transportation services to reduce their transportation costs by leveraging large amounts of freight with a limited number of carriers.

Although the preceding discussion has focused on lessened economic regulation in the United States, it appears that deregulation has had similar effects in other countries. For example, lessened economic regulation of transportation among European countries has resulted in lower

---

[8] Joseph B. Fuller, James O'Conor, and Richard Rawlinson, "Tailored Logistics: The Next Advantage," *Harvard Business Review* 71, no. 3 (1993): 87–98.
[9] David Parera, "Running Lean," *Government Executive* 39, no. 8 (2007): 42–49.
[10] *www.foodbanknyc.org.*

prices for truck shipments in these countries.[11] Likewise, privatization of water ports has been found to improve their operational efficiency.[12]

Changes in Consumer Behavior

A common business adage suggests that "change is the only constant." Although changes in consumer behavior are commonly the purview of the psychology and marketing disciplines, such changes have important logistical implications as well. Several examples of changes in consumer behavior (market demassification, changing family roles, and rising customer expectations) and their possible logistical implications are discussed next.

The concept of *market demassification* suggests that, in contrast to mass markets, an ever-increasing number of market segments leads to distinct preferences. One way to address market demassification is through mass customization, which refers to the ability of a company to deliver highly customized products and services that are designed to meet the needs and wants of individual segments or customers. In mass customization, one size does not fit all needs, and this means that logistics systems must be flexible rather than rigid. To this end, logistics service providers such as FedEx and UPS offer a variety of delivery options to prospective customers. For example, next-day service—which used to mean delivery sometime during the next business day—can now be purchased in terms of delivery by the end of the next business day, delivery by midafternoon of the next business day, delivery by midmorning of the next business day, and delivery by early morning of the next business day. As a general rule, the earlier the delivery time, the more expensive the transportation cost.

In terms of *changing family roles,* 50 years ago less than 30 percent of U.S. adult women were in the workforce; today, by contrast, approximately 60 percent are in the working world.[13] One consequence of this has been an increasing emphasis on the convenience associated with a family's shopping experiences. This convenience is manifested in various ways to include extended store hours, home delivery of purchased items, and ready-to-eat–ready-to-cook foods, and each of these has logistics-related implications.

With extended store hours—some stores are now open 24 hours—retailers must address issues such as the optimal delivery times for replenishment trucks and when to replenish merchandise. For example, it wouldn't be a good idea for a 24-hour grocery store to replenish its shelves when its stores are crowded with customers. Although home delivery certainly adds to the purchaser's convenience, one challenge is the coordination of delivery times with the purchaser's ability to receive the item(s). In addition, the logistics associated with home delivery of grocery items is so challenging that even the *best operators* are only marginally profitable.[14] Finally, the growth in ready-to-eat–ready-to-cook foods means that some food processors have added high-volume cooking systems at their production facilities. In addition, ready-to-eat–ready-to-cook foods have different packaging requirements, such as reusable bags.[15]

As for *rising customer expectations,* it should come as no surprise that customer expectations tend to increase through time, which means that a satisfactory level of performance in the past might not be considered as so today. Consider that a made-to-order, direct-to-consumer personal computer was unheard of until the mid-1980s. Today, this concept, pioneered by Dell Computer, has become ubiquitous in the personal computer industry and has profoundly changed distribution channels and supply chains in the sense that make-to-order has much

---

[11] Francine LaFontaine and Laura Malaguzzi Valeri, "The Deregulation of International Trucking in the European Union: Form and Effect," *Journal of Regional Economics* 35, no. 1 (2009): 19–44.

[12] Jose Tongzen and Wu Heng, "Port Privatization, Efficiency, and Competitiveness: Some Empirical Evidence from Container Ports (Terminals)," *Transportation Research—Part A* 39, no. 5 (2005): 405–424.

[13] Philip Kotler and Gary Armstrong, *Marketing Principles,* 11th ed. (Upper Saddle River, NJ: Prentice Hall, 2006), Chapter 1.

[14] Eliot Swiebach, "Supervalu Deletes Delivery," *Supermarket News,* April 20, 2009, 1, 54.

[15] L. Patrick, "Cooked Products Ring the Register," *High-Volume Cooking,* March 2006, 12–13.

different production and inventory requirements than does make-to-stock. Moreover, Dell was able to produce made-to-order, direct-to-customer computers in a very short period of time, and its time-compressed, high-customization model has raised consumer expectations in other industries as well.

Technological Advances

Prior to the start of every academic year, Beloit College (Wisconsin) releases an annual survey concerning what members of the incoming freshmen class know about the year of their birth. From a technology perspective, if you were born during or after the late 1980s, you may not remember a world without personal computers, cell (mobile) phones, digital cameras, or global positioning satellite navigation systems. In addition, you probably haven't used (and may have never seen, except in pictures) a self-correcting electric typewriter. We're not trying to take a stroll down memory lane; rather, our point is that tremendous technological advances—in the course of your lifetime—have had profound influences for business management and, by extension, for business logistics.

From a logistical perspective, some of the most important technological advances have involved computer hardware and software in the sense that management of logistics involves a tremendous amount of data. The sheer magnitude of these data makes manual analysis a difficult and time-consuming process; technological advances in computer hardware, software, and capacity have allowed logisticians to make faster, more informed, and more accurate decisions with respect to customer service, transportation, inventory management, and other logistics activities.

The Internet—virtually unknown and unused until the mid-1990s—has also proved to be a powerful tool for improving logistical effectiveness and efficiency. Although Internet applications can be used for many logistical activities, research suggests the heaviest use of the Internet involves purchasing or procurement and transportation. Typical purchasing-related Internet applications include checking vendor price quotes and vendor negotiations, whereas claims management and pickup and delivery are common transportation uses.[16] With respect to pickup and delivery, for example, UPS drivers now carry wireless handheld computers that instantaneously warn if a mistake (such as picking up an incorrect shipment) is about to occur. UPS estimates that this system is saving over 75,000 miles of travel per day to correct pickup and delivery errors.[17]

The Internet has also profoundly influenced channel design by allowing companies to offer an alternate distribution channel (or alternate distribution channels) to already existing channels. In some cases, this alternate channel is direct (i.e., no intermediaries between the producer and final customer) in nature because the final customer orders directly from the producer rather than through an intermediary. The removal of intermediaries between producer and consumer—called **disintermediation**—can clearly affect the design of logistics systems in the sense that there could be changes in both the number and location of fixed facilities such as warehouses and distribution centers.

The Growing Power of Retailers

Another influence on logistics involves the emergence of **power retailers** such as Wal-Mart, Home Depot, and Best Buy that often wield greater power than the companies that supply them. Power retailers, which can be found in various retail formats (e.g., mass merchandisers, category killers), are characterized by large market share and low prices. Furthermore, power retailers are

---

[16] Richard A. Lancioni, Michael A. Smith, and Hope J. Schau, "Strategic Internet Application Trends in Supply Chain Management," *Industrial Marketing Management* 32, no. 3 (2003): 211–217.

[17] Reiskin, *Transport Topics*, 2006.

often the largest customers for some of their suppliers; for example, Wal-Mart accounts for over 15 percent of Procter & Gamble's annual sales.[18]

Many power retailers explicitly recognize superior logistics as an essential component of their corporate strategies, and because of this, their logistical practices are often viewed as a barometer for emerging logistics trends. In the 1990s, for example, Wal-Mart and Warner-Lambert were the first two companies to explore collaborative planning, forecasting, and replenishment (CPFR), a practice in which trading partners share planning and forecasting data to better match up supply and demand. Since then, there have been hundreds of successful (e.g., increased sales, reduced inventory levels) CPFR initiatives, although to be fair, not all CPFR initiatives have been successful.

Power retailers have also been logistical trendsetters with respect to focusing on improved inventory turnover (the number of times inventory sells in one year). This emphasis on inventory turnover forces suppliers to be more efficient in the sense that they should focus on providing those products that will be bought by consumers, as opposed to supplying slower-moving products that sit on store shelves for extended periods of time. In fact, the worldwide economic woes that began in late 2007 have seen some power retailers place an even greater emphasis on inventory turnover, with a particular focus on the elimination of slow-selling brands supplied by lesser-known manufacturers.[19]

Globalization of Trade

Although countries have traded with each other for thousands of years, globalization's impact is greater today than ever before. Consider that world trade grew at an average annual rate of approximately 6 percent between 1997 and 2007. Although recessionary economic conditions, record energy prices, and geopolitical uncertainties depressed world trade in 2008 and 2009, world trade is projected to bounce back in 2010.[20]

Many factors, such as rising standards of living and multicountry trade alliances, have contributed to the growth of global trade, and it's safe to say that logistics has played a key role, too. Having said this, one should recognize that international logistics is much more challenging and costly than domestic logistics. With respect to challenges, the geographic distances between buyers and sellers are often greater (which may translate into longer transit times), and monitoring logistics processes is sometimes complicated by differences in business practices, culture, and language. As for costs, the greater geographic distances tend to result in higher transportation costs, and documentation requirements can be quite costly as well.[21]

THE SYSTEMS AND TOTAL COST APPROACHES TO LOGISTICS

Logistics is a classic example of the systems approach to business problems. From a companywide perspective, the **systems approach** indicates that a company's objectives can be realized by recognizing the mutual interdependence of the major functional areas of the firm, such as marketing, production, finance, and logistics. One implication of the systems approach is that the goals and objectives of the major functional areas should be compatible with the company's goals and objectives. This means that one logistics system does not fit all companies because goals and objectives vary from one firm to another.

A second implication is that decisions made by one functional area should consider the potential implications on other functional areas. For example, one consequence of pursuing the

[18] Jagmohan Raju and Z. John Zhang, "Channel Coordination in the Presence of a Dominant Retailer," *Management Science* 24, no. 2 (2005): 254–262.

[19] Jack Neff, "Dial Fights Recession by Stepping up Spending," *Advertising Age*, May 18, 2009, 6.

[20] "Global Economic Prospects 2009 Forecast Update," *www.worldbank.org*, March 30, 2009.

[21] Donald F. Wood, Anthony P. Barone, Paul R. Murphy, and Daniel L. Wardlow, *International Logistics,* 2nd ed. (New York: AMACOM, 2002).

marketing concept, which focuses on satisfying customer needs and wants, is often a marked increase of the number of **stock-keeping units (SKUs)** or line items of inventory (each different type or package size of a good is a different SKU) offered for sale by many companies. An increased number of SKUs provides customers with more choices, which today's customer often wants.

Alternatively, from a logistics perspective, the proliferation of SKUs creates challenges such as more items to identify, more items to store, and more items to track, which increases the chances of mistakes—which today's customers don't like. An instance of misidentification occurred when a consumer products company that mistakenly assigned the *same product code* to a three-pack, six-pack, and twelve-pack of a particular product it sold. Imagine the reaction of the customer who ordered a three-pack of the product, only to receive a six-pack or a twelve-pack of it!

Just as the major functional areas of a firm should recognize their interdependence, so too should the various activities that comprise the logistics function (what we'll call *intrafunctional logistics*). The logistics manager should balance each logistics activity to ensure that none is stressed to the point where it becomes detrimental to others.

This can be illustrated by referring to Figure 1-1, which indicates that business logistics is made up of **materials management** (movement and storage of materials into a firm) and **physical distribution** (storage of finished product and movement to the customer). Intrafunctional logistics attempts to coordinate materials management and physical distribution in a cost-efficient manner that supports an organization's customer service objectives. Figure 1-2, an advertisement for Cargill salt, shows how a company can differentiate a commodity product (salt) by stressing a dependable logistics system.

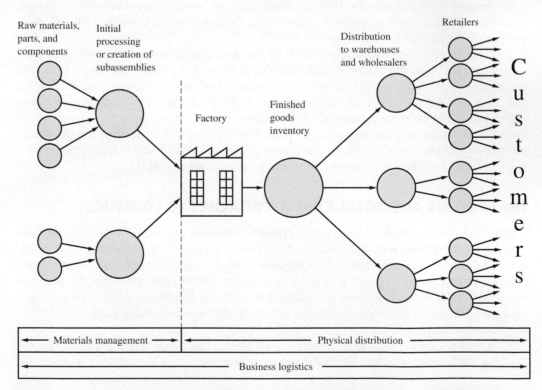

FIGURE 1-1   Control Over the Flow of Inbound and Outbound Movements

In this drawing, the circles represent buildings where inventories are stored, and the lines with arrows represent movement performed by carriers, a stop-and-start process. Current thought deals more with flows, possibly in different volumes and at different speeds, but without the inventory standing still. The supply chain extends to both the left and right of this diagram and includes the suppliers' suppliers and the customers' customers.

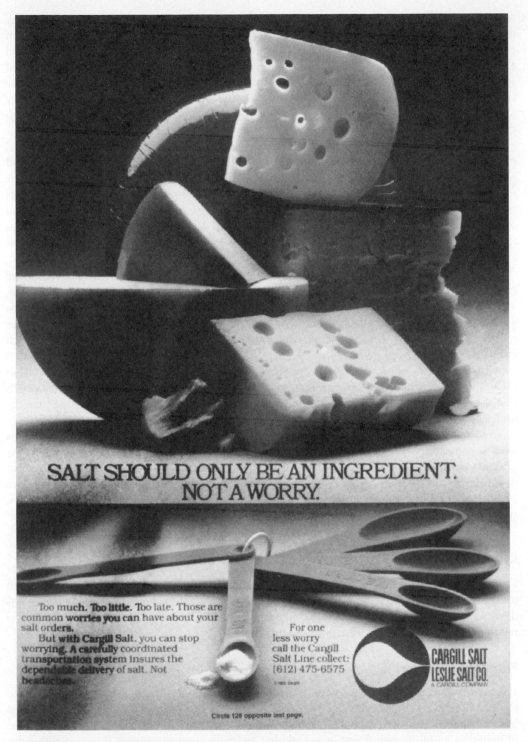

FIGURE 1-2   The Utilization of Logistics Service as a Major Selling Point
Source: Reproduced with permission of Cargill, Incorporated.

Materials management and physical distribution can be coordinated in many ways. One way is by using the same truck to deliver materials and component parts and to pick up finished goods. Although this may appear to be little more than common sense—and *common sense is one of the keys to being an effective logistics manager*—consider the case of the company that used the same trucking company to deliver materials and parts to one of its production plants as well as to take finished products from the facility. Unfortunately, one truck would arrive early in the morning to deliver the materials and components, and another truck would arrive in the late afternoon to pick up the finished products. How could this happen? Quite simply: The inbound logistics group and the outbound logistics group were unaware that they were using the same trucking company—the two groups never communicated even though they worked in the same building!

Logistics managers use the **total cost approach** to coordinate materials management and physical distribution in a cost-efficient manner. This approach is built on the premise that all relevant activities in moving and storing products should be considered as a whole (i.e., their total cost), not individually. Use of the total cost approach requires an understanding of **cost trade-offs**; in other words, changes to one logistics activity cause some costs to increase and others to decrease. Importantly, an understanding of logistical cost trade-offs recognizes that the costs of certain logistical activities generally move in opposite directions. As an example, a decrease in transportation costs is often associated with an increase in warehousing costs.

The key to the total cost approach is that all relevant logistical cost items are *considered simultaneously* when making a decision. For example, expedited transportation, such as airfreight, will increase a company's transportation costs. At the same time, expedited transportation leads to a faster order cycle, which allows the receiving company to hold lower levels of inventory, thus reducing both its inventory carrying costs and warehousing costs. The total cost approach evaluates if the decreased inventory and warehousing costs are greater than the increased costs of expedited transportation. If so, the company might consider using expedited transportation (assuming that customer satisfaction isn't negatively impacted), because the total logistics costs (consisting, in this example, of transportation, inventory, and warehousing costs) are less than the total costs of the existing system.

When used in the logistics decision-making process, the total cost concept approach forms what is commonly called the *total logistics concept*. This concept is unique not because of the activities performed but because of the integration of all activities into a unified whole that seeks to minimize distribution costs in a manner that supports an organization's customer service objectives. The total logistics concept can be extended to include a firm's suppliers and customers, such as in supply chain management, which will be covered in Chapter 5.

LOGISTICAL RELATIONSHIPS WITHIN THE FIRM

From a companywide perspective, the system and total cost approaches to logistics require an understanding of logistics and its relationships with other functional areas. Because Chapter 6 is devoted specifically to procurement (purchasing), our discussion here focuses on logistical relationships with finance, production, and marketing.

Finance

The finance staff is often charged with the responsibility of allocating the firm's limited funds to projects desired by the various operating departments. As such, the finance department is often instrumental in approving capital budgeting decisions that affect logistics, such as the acquisition of materials handling equipment (e.g., forklifts) and packaging equipment (e.g., a shrink-wrap machine). In such situations, finance personnel may decide between purchasing and leasing the relevant equipment, assuming they have approved the decision to acquire it.

Inventory is another area where finance and logistics can interact. A basic challenge for the two areas is that the finance department often measures inventory in terms of its cost or value in dollars, whereas logistics tends to measure inventory in terms of units. The differing ways of measuring inventory can create potential friction between the two groups, as illustrated in the following example. From a cash flow perspective, the finance department might prefer to sell two boxes of hair dryers worth $1,000 than to sell 15 boxes of hair shampoo worth $850. Alternatively, from a productivity perspective such as the number of boxes handled per worker, the logistics department might prefer selling the 15 boxes of hair shampoo rather than the two boxes of hair dryers.

In addition, in times of inflation, identical items added to inventory at different times means that each unit has a different cost, and even though inventory levels are not affected, it makes a difference whether an organization uses historic cost or current value as an indicator of the inventory's total value. Or, consider the concept of depreciation, which reduces the monetary value of inventory by a certain amount per period of time, even though the actual quantity of inventory may be unchanged. Both authors have consulting experiences with companies that showed a particular SKU to be fully depreciated, with an accounting value of $0—while the companies' warehousing facilities contained several hundred units of physical inventory of the particular SKU.

Production

One of the most common interfaces between production and logistics involves the length of production runs. In many cases, the production people favor long production runs of individual products because this allows the relevant fixed costs to be spread over more units, thus resulting in a lower production cost per unit. Having said this, long production runs generate large amounts of inventory, and it is often a logistics staff responsibility to store and track the inventory. It's generally much easier to store and track 5 units of a product than it is to store and track 500 units of the product.

Another consideration with long production runs is that sometimes excess inventory for particular products occurs because of limited (or no) demand for them. At a minimum, these products add to a company's inventory carrying costs and also take up space that could be used to store other products. Slow-selling (or nonselling) products may also increase a company's handling costs, as illustrated by a situation in which forklift drivers would periodically move 150 refrigerators from one warehouse area to another, just to ensure that the warehouse managers would not see the refrigerators sitting in the same place for an extended period of time! You may find it difficult to believe that these 150 refrigerators were moved throughout the warehouse for nearly five years before managers were alerted to the behavior.

Increasing utilization of the **postponement** concept (the delay of value-added activities such as assembly, production, and packaging until the latest possible time[22]) also influences the interface between production and logistics. More specifically, some value-added activities (e.g., case packing, case labeling) that were traditionally performed at a production plant are now performed in warehousing facilities. As a result, warehousing facilities are adding new types of equipment and being configured differently to allow specific value-added activities to take place.

Marketing

Contemporary marketing places a heavy emphasis on customer satisfaction, and logistics strategies can facilitate customer satisfaction through reducing the cost of products, which can translate into lower prices as well as bringing a broader variety of choices closer to where the customer wishes to buy or use the product. Logistics strategies offer a unique way for a company to differentiate itself among competitors, and logistics now offers an important route for many firms to create marketing superiority. The following discussion about the interactions between logistics and marketing focuses on the marketing mix, sometimes referred to as the *four Ps* of marketing (place, price, product, and promotion).

---

[22] John J. Coyle, Edward J. Bardi, and C. John Langley, *The Management of Business Logistics: A Supply Chain Perspective*, 7th ed. (Mason, OH: South-Western, 2003).

PLACE DECISIONS

One important marketing concern is place, and decisions regarding place involve two types of networks: logistics and the marketing channel (which is discussed in greater detail later in this chapter). Logistics decisions concern the most effective way to move and store the product from where it is produced to where it is sold. An effective logistics system can provide positive support by enabling the firm to attract and utilize what it considers to be the most productive channel and supply chain members. Channel members are frequently in a position to pick and choose which manufacturer's products they wish to merchandise. If a manufacturer is not consistently able to provide a certain product at the right time, in the right quantities, and in an undamaged condition, the channel members may end their relationship with the supplier or cease active promotion of the supplier's product.

From a marketing perspective, place decisions may also involve new strategies for reaching customers. A popular retailing strategy in recent years involves a branding alliance that allows customers to purchase products from two or more name-brand retailers at one store location. Yum! Brands, for example, is the parent company of A&W All American Food, KFC, Long John Silver's, Pizza Hut, Taco Bell, and Wing Street, and you may have eaten at a site where several of these brands are available under one roof. From a marketing perspective, branding alliances (1) offer potential customers convenience (satisfying multiple needs in one place) (2) increase customer spending per transaction, and (3) boost brand awareness.[23] Logistical challenges with branding alliances include the costs and timing of product delivery. Yum! Brands has addressed these issues by scheduling one delivery per location, which requires coloading trailers with products for all six chains.

PRICE DECISIONS

A key price-related decision for marketers involves how a product's transportation costs should be reflected in its selling price. One alternative is for a company to base the suggested selling price on a product's landed costs, which refers to the price of a product at the source plus transportation costs to its destination. On the one hand, a selling price that is based on a product's landed cost allows the seller to offer "free" delivery of the product to prospective customers, because the transportation costs associated with delivery are captured in the landed cost. On the other hand, a selling price that is based on a product's landed cost could result in a substantial increase in a product's selling price, and a higher selling price tends to decrease buyer demand for most products.

In addition to transportation considerations, logistics managers may play an important role in product pricing. They are expected to know the costs of providing various levels of customer service and therefore must be consulted to determine the trade-offs between costs and customer service. Because many distribution costs produce per unit savings when larger volumes are handled, the logistics manager can also help formulate the firm's quantity discount pricing policies.

PRODUCT DECISIONS

A number of potential interfaces are possible between marketing and logistics in terms of product decisions. For example, as noted earlier, the marked increase in product offerings—which allows for more customer choice—creates logistical challenges in terms of identification, storage, and tracking.

Another product interface between marketing and logistics involves the amount of particular SKUs to hold. Marketers often prefer to carry higher quantities of particular items because this reduces the likelihood of stockouts (being out of an item at the same time there is demand

---

[23] Rhonda Bauer, "Co-branding: Growing Family or Family Feud?" *Franchising World*, May–June 2002, 22–23.

for it). However, from a logistics perspective, higher quantities of inventory (1) necessitate additional storage space and (2) increase inventory carrying costs.

Product design, which is often the purview of marketers, can also have important implications for logistical effectiveness and efficiency. For example, long-necked glass beverage containers might be more distinctive than aluminum cans; however, from a logistics perspective, long-necked bottles take up more space and are more likely to be damaged than aluminum cans.

In addition, marketers' growing emphasis on offering sustainable products—products that meet present needs without compromising the ability of future generations to meet their needs—can also impact logistical decisions. Consider, for example, *fair trade products,* or those that guarantee a better deal for producers in the developing world through fair and stable prices as well as teaching farming methods that are environmentally sustainable.[24] From a logistical perspective, an organization's commitment to selling fair trade products, such as coffee or chocolate, may result in changed sourcing requirements for the necessary raw materials.

PROMOTION DECISIONS

Many promotional decisions require close coordination between marketing and logistics. One important situation concerns the availability of highly advertised products, particularly when a company is running pricing campaigns that lower the price of certain items. Few things are more damaging to a firm's goodwill than being stocked out of items that are heavily promoted in a sales campaign. In addition, in some instances imbalances of product supply and demand can be viewed as *bait and switch tactics*—that is, enticing customers with the promises of a low-priced product, only to find that it is unavailable, but that a higher-priced substitute product is readily available.

Moreover, once a decision is made to promote the introduction of a new product, the logistics staff assumes responsibility for having the product in place on the scheduled release date— not earlier, not later. The complexity of so doing is well illustrated by looking at some of the activities associated with the release of *Harry Potter and the Deathly Hallows,* the final book in the Harry Potter series, which went on sale at midnight on July 21, 2007. The book's author, J. K. Rowling, finished writing *Harry Potter and the Deathly Hallows* in Edinburgh, Scotland in early 2007. Mark Seidenfeld, who was in charge of bringing the manuscript to New York to begin the publishing process, made sure the manuscript was safe by *sitting on it* during his airplane flight to the United States! Barnes and Noble, a large book retailer, hired an outside security firm to guard the padlocked trucks that contained its copies of the *Deathly Hallows.*[25]

MARKETING CHANNELS

Another concept that is useful to studying the marketing relationships between and among firms is to look at **marketing channels**, which refer to "a set of institutions necessary to transfer the title to goods and to move goods from the point of production to the point of consumption and, as such, which consists of all the institutions and all the marketing activities in the marketing process."[26]

The principal, traditional institutions in the marketing channel are the manufacturer, the wholesaler, and the retailer. Each in turn assumes ownership of the inventory of goods. Each also assumes risks associated with temporary inventory ownership. The channel members in this arrangement, carrying out this task, can also be referred to as the *ownership channel.* The same or related parties also get together in other channel arrangements, and these channels are called the *negotiations channel*, the *financing channel*, the *promotions channel*, and the *logistics channel.* Let us

---

[24] Derek Townsend, "Fair Trade Future?" *Food Service*, June 2008, 27.

[25] Lev Grossman, Andrea Sachs, Kristine Dell, and Laura Fitzpatrick, "Harry Potter and the Sinister Spoilers," *Time*, July 9, 2007, 49–52.

[26] American Marketing Association Dictionary, *www.marketingpower.com.*

look more closely at how the three traditional parties—the manufacturer, the wholesaler, and the retailer—interact in each of the five mentioned channels.

The *ownership channel* covers movement of the title to the goods. The goods themselves might not be physically present or even exist. If a good is in great demand, one might have to buy it before it is produced, such as a commissioned piece of art or a scarce new consumer product. Sometimes, a product will not be made until there are sufficient financial commitments, which is often the case with new models of commercial airplanes. The party owning the good almost always has the right to trade or sell it and bears the risks and costs associated with having it in inventory. Also, while owning the good, one can use it as collateral for a loan, although this may place some restrictions on its use or movement.

The *negotiations channel* is the one in which buy and sell agreements are reached. This could include transactions face to face or by telephone, e-mail, electronic data interchange, or almost any other form of communication. In many situations, no actual negotiations take place; the price for the product is stated, and one either buys at that price or does not. In some trades, auctions are used; in others, highly structured, organized trading takes place, such as markets for some commodities. One part of the negotiations covers how activities in the other channels are to be handled. For example, each buying party will specify the point and time of delivery and the point and time of payment. Even packaging design may be negotiated. (An old Henry Ford story is that suppliers of some parts were directed to ship in wooden crates built of good lumber and to very exacting specifications. It turned out that the empty crates were then partially disassembled and became floorboards in Ford Model Ts.)

The *financing channel* handles payments for goods. More importantly, it handles the company's credit. The multiple participants in the channel have different financial strengths, and often one must help another to keep the entire channel alive. For example, a newly opened retail store may have some of its goods placed on consignment, meaning that the wholesaler, not the store, owns them. The retailer will reimburse the wholesaler only for goods sold; the wholesaler bears nearly all the financial risks. Sometimes, in an effort to develop what it believes is a necessary new product line, a wholesaler will assist the manufacturer by putting up cash in advance along with an order. Alternatively, the wholesaler will place a large, guaranteed order, and the manufacturer can take that order to a bank and use it as a basis for receiving a loan. Credit is important to all parties in the channel, who frequently receive or extend it, and credit becomes an integral part of the negotiations. If bills are not paid when due or if credit is overextended, collection becomes a financing channel function.

The *promotions channel* is concerned with promoting a new or an existing product and can be related to the financing channel because monetary allowances are often part of the promotion effort. In addition, the promotions channel and the logistics channel are linked in several ways. First, there may be special advertising materials, such as coupon books, floor advertising posters, or displays, which must be distributed with the promoted product. Second, some of the cartons or consumer packs may have special labeling, and their placement at retailers must coincide with other promotional efforts. Third, because logistics personnel handle order processing, they have instantaneous records of actual sales, which indicate the initial success of the promotional efforts.

As mentioned previously, the *logistics channel*, its components, and its functioning are the main topics of this book. The most significant contribution that the logistics channel makes to the overall channel process is the **sorting function**, which bridges "the discrepancy between the assortment of goods and services generated by the producer and the assortment demanded by the consumer."[27] The sorting function has four steps, and these are important to understanding the concept of goods flowing through the logistics channel:

- *Sorting out* is sorting a heterogeneous supply of products into stocks that are homogeneous.
- *Accumulating* is bringing together similar stocks from different sources.

---

[27] Ibid.

- *Allocating* is breaking a homogeneous supply into smaller lots.
- *Assorting* is building up assortments of goods for resale, usually to retail customers.

These steps take place between the manufacturer and the consumer, which means that they are performed by the wholesaler, the retailer, or specialist intermediaries.

In addition to the major actors or primary participants in a logistics channel, many less-well-known actors, called *facilitators* or *channel intermediaries*, play minor but essential roles. Intermediaries make the entire system function better and should only be used when they add value to a transaction. They spring up and flourish in areas where communications and other interactions between major parties are not well meshed. In international transactions, for example, translators may be an important intermediary. Intermediaries also function in areas needing orderly routines, such as order processing, and in searching, for example, when customers are looking for products or producers are looking for customers. Intermediaries fill niches, are very well focused, and serve as buffers between various channel members. Usually, they do not take an ownership position in the products or goods being handled.

The five channels discussed previously show where intermediaries function and fit. For example, in the ownership channel, a common intermediary is the bank or finance company, which may assume temporary or partial ownership of goods as part of an ongoing transaction. Often, this is a condition for the extension of credit. Banks routinely loan funds to all parties in a channel, making it possible for goods to be manufactured, marketed, and sold.

Brokers, who are associated with the negotiation channel, are independent contractors paid to arrange a particular transaction. A broker can be used by either a buyer or seller and is often used to arrange truck transportation for either the buyer (shipper/receiver) or seller (trucker). A broker can add value for a trucker in the sense that an individual trucker believes that his or her time is more profitably spent driving, rather than being on the phone or Internet trying to negotiate for the next load. In a similar fashion, a broker adds value for a shipper/receiver because of the broker's knowledge of potential transportation options.

Banks and finance companies are prominent intermediaries in the financing channel, and both parties supply the credit necessary for a deal to be finalized. For big-ticket items, such as ships or warehouses, the buyer almost always borrows money to finance part of the purchase. Sometimes insurance is also a requirement in the agreement, so insurance companies may also serve as intermediaries.

The promotions channel has intermediaries that aid with promotions, such as firms that design, build, and transport product exhibits for display at trade shows. Advertising agencies can handle the preparation and media placement of advertising materials, and firms often use public relations agencies to represent them to the news media. Some companies choose to outsource their personal selling functions by hiring an intermediary to provide them with a contract sales force. These promotion efforts handled by intermediaries must be coordinated with the firm's overall marketing communication activities.

The logistics channel has many intermediaries, and many are mentioned in this book. A commonly used intermediary is the freight forwarder, whose function is to assemble small shipments into larger shipments and then tender them in truckload or railcarload quantities to truck lines or to railroads. In international logistics, intermediaries abound, and more than a hundred different types could be listed. One example is cargo surveyors who specialize in coffee; these specialists examine and arbitrate damage claims involving shipments of coffee beans.

ACTIVITIES IN THE LOGISTICAL CHANNEL

To successfully apply the systems and total cost approaches to logistics, it is essential to understand the various logistics activities. Keep in mind that because one logistics system does not fit all companies, the number of activities in a logistics system can vary from company to company. Activities that are considered to be logistics related include, but are not limited to, the following:

Customer service   Demand forecasting
Facility location decisions   International logistics
Inventory management   Materials handling
Order management   Packaging
Procurement   Reverse logistics
Transportation management   Warehousing management

Customer Service

There can be many definitions of *customer service*, such as "keeping existing customers happy." Customer service involves making sure that the right person receives the right product at the right place at the right time in the right condition and at the right cost. Customer service is discussed in greater detail in Chapter 7.

Demand Forecasting

Demand forecasting refers to efforts to estimate product demand in a future time period. The growing popularity of the supply chain concept has prompted increasing collaboration among supply chain partners with respect to demand forecasting. Such collaboration can enhance efficiency by reducing overall inventory levels in a supply chain. We discuss demand forecasting in Chapter 7.

Facility Location Decisions

It's often said that the success of a retail store depends on three factors: location, location, and location. It can also be said that the success of a particular logistics system is dependent on the location of the relevant warehousing and production facilities. Facility location decisions are increasingly important as the configuration of logistics systems is altered due to the impacts of multinational trade agreements. Facility location decisions are covered in Chapter 9.

International Logistics

International logistics, which refers to the logistics activities associated with goods that are sold across national boundaries, is much more costly and challenging than domestic logistics. We'll take a closer look at international logistics in Chapter 14.

Inventory Management

Inventory refers to stocks of goods that are maintained for a variety of purposes, such as for resale to others, as well as to support manufacturing or assembling processes. When managing inventory, logisticians need to simultaneously consider three relevant costs: the cost of carrying (holding) product, the cost of ordering product, and the cost of being out of stock. Chapter 8 provides further discussion concerning inventory management.

Materials Handling

Materials handling refers to the short-distance movement of products within the confines of a facility (e.g., plant, warehouse). Because materials handling tends to add costs (e.g., labor costs, product loss, and product damage) rather than value to logistics systems, managers pursue cost-efficiency objectives such as minimizing the number of handlings and moving the product in a straight line whenever possible. Materials handling considerations are presented in Chapter 11.

Order Management

Order management refers to management of the activities that take place between the time a customer places an order and the time it is received by the customer. As such, order management is a logistics activity with a high degree of visibility to customers; order management is discussed in Chapter 7.

Packaging

Packaging can have both a marketing (consumer packaging) and a logistical (industrial packaging) dimension. Industrial (protective) packaging refers to packaging that prepares a product for storage and transit (e.g., boxes and crates), and packaging has important interfaces with the materials handling and warehousing activities. As such, Chapter 11 discusses packaging in conjunction with materials handling.

Procurement

Procurement refers to the raw materials, component parts, and supplies bought from outside organizations to support a company's operations.[28] Procurement's direct link to outside organizations means that its strategic importance has increased as the supply chain management philosophy has become more popular. Procurement is discussed in more detail in Chapter 6.

Reverse Logistics

Products can be returned for various reasons, such as product recalls, product damage, lack of demand, and customer dissatisfaction. The challenges associated with reverse logistics can be complicated by the fact that returned products often move in small quantities and may move outside forward distribution channels. Reverse logistics is examined in Chapter 4.

Transportation Management

Transportation can be defined as the actual physical movement of goods or people from one place to another, whereas transportation management refers to the management of transportation activities by a particular organization. Transportation can account for up to 50 percent of a firm's total logistics costs and thus represents the most costly logistics activity in many organizations. The transportation system is discussed in Chapter 12, and transportation management is discussed in Chapter 13.

Warehousing Management

Warehousing refers to places where inventory can be stored for a particular period of time. As noted previously, important changes have occurred with respect to warehousing's role in contemporary logistics and supply chain systems. Warehousing is discussed in Chapter 10.

LOGISTICS CAREERS

The logistics manager has a highly complex and challenging position, in part because the logistician needs to be both a generalist and specialist. As a generalist, the logistician must understand the relationship between logistics and other corporate functions, both within and outside the firm. As a specialist, the logistician must understand the relationships between various logistics activities and must have some technical knowledge of the various activities.

---

[28] Donald J. Bowersox, David J. Closs, and M. Bixby Cooper, *Supply Chain Logistics Management* (Boston, MA: McGraw-Hill Irwin, 2002).

Despite the worldwide economic slowdown that began in 2007, the job market for logisticians continues to be strong at both the undergraduate and MBA levels. Indeed, the magazine *U.S. News & World Report* highlighted "logistician" as one of the 50 best careers for the year 2010 and predicted that logistics employment should increase by 20 percent through 2018.[29]

Logistics-related jobs include, but are not limited to, logistics analyst, consultant, customer service manager, purchasing manager, transportation manager, and warehouse operations manager.[30] Unlike 20 to 30 years ago, career paths in logistics can lead to the executive suite; in fact, the two most recent CEOs of Wal-Mart, the world's largest retailer, had worked in logistics and distribution during their Wal-Mart careers. Compensation levels for entry-level positions requiring an undergraduate degree in logistics can range from the upper $30K to the mid-$50K level.

Because of the growing importance of logistics, a number of professional organizations are dedicated to advancing the professional knowledge of their members. The rationale for these professional associations is that the state of the art is changing so rapidly that professionals must educate and reeducate themselves on a regular basis. Some of the more prominent professional logistics organizations are summarized in the appendix to this chapter.

Summary

This chapter introduced the topic of logistics, which the CSCMP defines as "that part of Supply Chain Management that plans, implements, and controls the efficient, effective forward and reverse flow and storage of goods, services, and related information between the point of origin and the point of consumption in order to meet customers' requirements."

The economic impacts of logistics were discussed, along with reasons for the increased importance of logistics since 1980. Systems and total cost approaches to logistics were discussed, as were logistical relationships within a firm, with a particular focus on various interfaces between marketing and logistics. A short description of a number of logistics activities was presented, and the chapter concluded with a brief look at logistics careers.

Questions for Discussion and Review

1. Did it surprise you that logistics has such an important economic impact? Why or why not?
2. Distinguish between possession, form, time, and place utility.
3. How does logistics contribute to time and place utility?
4. How can a particular logistics system be effective but not efficient?
5. Explain the significance of the fact that the purpose of logistics is to meet customer requirements.
6. Explain how an understanding of logistics management could be relevant to your favorite charitable organization.
7. How has a reduction in economic regulation contributed to the increased importance of logistics?
8. Discuss the logistical implications associated with the increased emphasis on the convenience associated with a family's shopping experience.
9. Explain how power retailers are logistical trendsetters.
10. What is the systems approach to problem solving? How is this concept applicable to logistics management?
11. Distinguish between materials management and physical distribution.
12. Explain what is meant by the total cost approach to logistics.
13. Define what is meant by a cost trade-off. Do you believe that this concept is workable? Why or why not?
14. What are several areas in which finance and logistics might interface?
15. Discuss the postponement concept as it relates to the production and logistics interface.
16. Define what is meant by a landed cost and explain its relevance for pricing decisions.
17. Discuss several possible interfaces between marketing and logistics in terms of product decisions.

---

[29] Liz Woglemuth, "The 50 Best Careers of 2010," *U.S. News & World Report*, December 28, 2009.
[30] *www.cscmp.org.*

18. Briefly discuss the ownership, negotiations, financing, promotions, and logistics channels.

19. Discuss five activities that might be part of a company's logistics department.

20. *Logistics managers must be both generalists and specialists.* Why is this true? Does this help to explain why there tends to be an imbalance in the supply of, and demand for, logistics managers?

Suggested Readings

Davis-Sramek, Beth, and Brian S. Fugate. "State of Logistics: A Visionary Perspective." *Journal of Business Logistics* 28, no. 2 (2007): 1–34.

Fawcett, Stanley E. "An Update on the State of Supply Chain Education." *Supply Chain Management Review* 13, no. 6 (2009): 36–42.

Genchev, Stefan E. "Reverse Logistics Program Design: A Company Study." *Business Horizons* 52, no. 2 (2009): 139–148.

Giminez, Christina, and Eva Ventura. "Logistics-Production, Logistics-Marketing and External Integration: Their Impact on Performance." *International Journal of Operations and Production Management* 25, no. 1 (2005): 20–38.

Larson, Paul D., Richard F. Poist, and Arni Halldosson. "Perspectives on Logistics vs. SCM: A Survey of SCM Professionals." *Journal of Business Logistics* 28, no. 1 (2007): 1–24.

Lowe, David. *Dictionary of Transport and Logistics.* (London: Kogon Page, 2002).

Lynch, Jacqueline, and Linda Whicher. "Do Logistics and Marketing Understand Each Other? An Empirical Investigation of the Interface Activities between Logistics and Marketing." *International Journal of Logistics: Research & Applications* 11, no. 3 (2008): 167–178.

Mentzer, John T., Soonhong Min, and Michelle L. Bobbitt, "Toward a Unified Theory of Logistics." *International Journal of Physical Distribution & Logistics Management* 34, no. 8 (2004): 606–627.

Murphy, Paul R., and Richard F. Poist. "Skill Requirements of Senior-Level Logisticians: A Longitudinal Assessment." *Supply Chain Management: An International Journal* 12, no. 6 (2007): 423–431.

Periatt, Jeffrey A., and Subra Chakrabarty. "Using Personality Traits to Select Customer-Oriented Logistics Personnel." *Transportation Journal* 46, no. 1 (2007): 22–37.

Wu, Yen-Chun Jim. "Contemporary Logistics Education: An International Perspective." *International Journal of Physical Distribution & Logistics Management* 37, no. 7 (2007): 504–528.

CASE

CASE 1-1   Kiddieland and the Super Gym

KiddieLand is a retailer of toys located in the Midwest. Corporate headquarters is in Chicago, and its 70 stores are located in Minnesota, Wisconsin, Michigan, Illinois, Indiana, Ohio, Iowa, and Kentucky. One distribution center is located in Columbus (for Kentucky, Indiana, Michigan, and Ohio) and one in Chicago (for Illinois, Iowa, Minnesota, and Wisconsin).

KiddieLand markets a full range of toys, electronic games, computers, and play sets. Emphasis is on a full line of brand-name products together with selected items sold under the KiddieLand brand. KiddieLand's primary competitors include various regional discount chains. The keys to KiddieLand's success have been a comprehensive product line, aggressive pricing, and self-service.

Donald Hurst is KiddieLand's logistics manager. He is responsible for managing both distribution centers, for traffic management, and for inventory control. Don's primary mission is to make sure all stores are in stock at all times without maintaining excessive levels of inventory.

One morning in late January, while Don was reviewing the new year's merchandising plan, he discovered that starting in March, KiddieLand would begin promoting the Super Gym Outdoor Children's Exercise Center. Don was particularly interested that the new set would sell for $715. In addition, the Super Gym is packaged in three boxes weighing a total of 450 pounds. "Holy cow!" thought Don. "The largest set we have sold to date retails for $159 and weighs only 125 pounds."

"There must be some mistake," thought Don as he walked down the hall to the office of Olga Olsen, KiddieLand's buyer for play sets. Olga was new on her job and was unusually stressed because both of her assistant buyers had just resigned to seek employment on the West Coast.

As soon as Olga saw Don, she exclaimed, "Don, my friend, I have been meaning to talk to you." Don knew right then that his worst fears were confirmed.

The next morning Don and Olga met with Randy Smith, Don's transportation manager; A. J. Toth, general manager for KiddieLand's eight Chicago stores; and Sharon Rabiega, Don's assistant for distribution services. Because the previous year had been unusually profitable, everyone was in a good mood because this year's bonus was 50 percent larger than last year's.

Nevertheless, A. J. got to the point: "You mean to tell me that we expect somebody to stuff a spouse, three kids, a dog, and 450 pounds of Super Gym in a small sedan and not have a conniption?"

Randy chimed in, "Besides, we can't drop ship Super Gyms from the manufacturer to the consumer's address because Super Gym ships only in quantities of 10 or more."

Olga was now worried. "We can't back out of the Super Gym now," she moaned. "I have already committed KiddieLand for 400 sets, and the spring–summer play set promotion went to press last week. Besides, I am depending on the Super Gym to make my gross margin figures."

"What about SUVs?" asked Toth. "They make up half the vehicles in our parking lots. Will the three packages fit inside them?"

By now the scope of the problem had become apparent to everyone at the meeting. At 3 P.M. Don summarized the alternatives discussed:

1. Purchase a two-wheeled trailer for each store.
2. Find a local trucking company that can haul the Super Gym from the KiddieLand store to the customer.
3. Stock the Super Gym at the two distribution centers and have the truck that makes delivery runs to the retail stores also make home deliveries.
4. Charge for delivery if the customer cannot get the Super Gym home.
5. Negotiate with the Super Gym manufacturer to ship directly to the customer.

When the meeting adjourned, everyone agreed to meet the following Monday to discuss the alternatives. On Thursday morning a record-breaking blizzard hit Chicago; everyone went home early. KiddieLand headquarters was closed on Friday because of the blizzard. By Wednesday, the same group met again.

Don started the meeting. "Okay," Don began, "let's review our options. Sharon, what did you find out about buying trailers for each store?"

"Well," Sharon began, "the best deal I can find is $1,800 per trailer for 70 trailers, plus $250 per store for an adequate selection of bumper hitches, and an additional $50 per year per store for licensing and insurance. Unfortunately, bumpers on the newest autos cannot accommodate trailer hitches."

"Oh, no," moaned Olga, "we only expect to sell 5.7 sets per store. That means $368 per Super Gym for delivery," she continued as she punched her calculator, "and $147 in lost gross margin!"

Next, Randy Smith summarized the second option. "So far we can get delivery within 25 miles of most of our stores for $38.21 per set. Actually," Randy continued, "$38.21 is for delivery 25 miles from the store. The rate would be a little less for under 25 miles and about $1.50 per mile beyond 25 miles."

A. J. Toth chimed in, "According to our marketing research, 85 percent of our customers drive less than 25 minutes to the store, so a flat fee of $40 for delivery would probably be okay."

Randy continued, "Most delivery companies we talked to will deliver twice weekly but not daily."

Sharon continued, "The motor carrier that handles shipments from our distribution centers is a consolidator. He said that squeezing an 18-wheeler into some subdivisions wouldn't make sense. Every time they try, they knock down a couple of mailboxes and leave truck tracks in some homeowner's lawn."

Olga added, "I talked to Super Gym about shipping direct to the customer's address, and they said forget it. Whenever they have tried that," Olga continued, "the customer gets two of one box and none of another."

"Well, Olga," Don interrupted, "can we charge the customer for delivery?"

Olga thought a minute. "Well, we have never done that before, but then we have never sold a 450-pound item before. It sounds like," Olga continued, "our choice is to either absorb $40 per set or charge the customer for delivery."

"That means $16,000 for delivery," she added.

"One more thing," Don said. "If we charge for shipping, we must include that in the copy for the spring–summer brochure."

Olga smiled. "We can make a minor insert in the copy if we decide to charge for delivery. However," she continued, "any changes will have to be made to the page proofs—and page proofs are due back to the printer next Monday."

Questions

1. List and discuss the advantages and disadvantages of purchasing a two-wheeled trailer for each store to use for delivering Super Gyms.
2. List and discuss the advantages and disadvantages of having local trucking companies deliver the Super Gym from the retail stores to the customers.
3. List and discuss the advantages and disadvantages of stocking Super Gyms at the distribution centers, and then having the truck that makes deliveries from the distribution center to the retail stores also make deliveries of Super Gyms to individual customers.
4. List and discuss the advantages and disadvantages of charging customers for home delivery if they are unable to carry home the Super Gym.
5. Which alternative would you prefer? Why?
6. Draft a brief statement (catalog copy) to be inserted in the firm's spring–summer brochure that clearly explains to potential customers the policy you recommended in Question 5.
7. In the first meeting, A. J. asked about SUVs, but there was no further mention of them. How would you follow up on his query?

APPENDIX 1

Logistics Professional Organizations

APICS—The Association for Operations Management (*www.apics.org*)

APICS "builds knowledge and skills in operations management professionals to enhance and validate abilities and accelerate careers." APICS helps its "members and their organizations successfully compete and build a stronger global economy." APICS offers four certification programs: Certified in Integrated Resource Management (CIRM), Certified in Production and Inventory Management (CPIM), Certified Fellow in Production and Inventory Management (CFPIM), and Certified Supply Chain Professional (CSCP).

American Society of Transportation and Logistics (AST&L) (*www.astl.org*)

AST&L was founded by industry leaders "to ensure a high level of professionalism and promote continuing education in the field of transportation and logistics." It offers one certification program, Certified in Transportation and Logistics (CTL), and has added a new entry-level designation, Professional Designation in Logistics and Supply Chain Management (PLS).

Council of Supply Chain Management Professionals (*www.cscmp.org*)

Formerly known as the Council of Logistics Management, the CSCMP is a nonprofit professional organization whose vision is "to lead the evolving supply chain management profession by developing, advancing, and disseminating supply chain knowledge and research."

Delta Nu Alpha (DNA) (www.deltanualpha.org)

DNA is an "international organization of professional men and women in all areas and at all levels of transportation and logistics." Its primary focus is on education, financial assistance, and mentoring for students.

International Society of Logistics (SOLE) (*www.sole.org*)

The International Society of Logistics, formerly the Society of Logistics Engineers, is a "non-profit international professional society composed of individuals organized to enhance the art and science of logistics technology, education and management." It has several certification programs:

the Demonstrated Logistician (DL) Program, the Certified Professional Logistician (CPL) Program, and the Certified Master Logistician (CML) Program.

Supply Chain & Logistics Association Canada (SCL) (*www.sclcanada.org*)

SCL is a "non-profit organization of business professionals interested in improving their logistics and supply chain management skills through a comprehensive program of education, research and networking opportunities."

The Chartered Institute of Logistics and Transport in the UK—CILT (UK) (*www.ciltuk.org.uk*)

CILT (UK) "is the professional body for everyone in the logistics, passenger transportation, transport planning and related industries and is dedicated to supporting, developing, and representing all specialisms at all stages of career development."

Warehousing Education and Research Council (WERC) (*www.werc.org*)

WERC "offers resources that help distribution professionals stay at the leading edge including educational events, performance metrics for benchmarking, practical research, expert insights, and peer-to-peer knowledge exchange."

2 | LOGISTICS AND INFORMATION TECHNOLOGY

The logistics discipline has been through many changes since the first edition of this book was published in the mid-1970s. The first edition, for example, primarily focused on physical distribution management, and the corresponding definition emphasized the *movement and storage of goods.* The current edition of this book, by contrast, is focused on logistics and its role in supply chain management. Moreover, the corresponding definition of logistics (see Chapter 1) mentions the *flows and storage of goods, services, and related information.*

The effective and efficient utilization of information can be quite beneficial to logistics and supply chain management, and four of the more prominent benefits include the following:

- Greater knowledge and visibility across the supply chain, which makes it possible to replace inventory with information
- Greater awareness of customer demand via point-of-sale data, which can help improve planning and reduce variability in the supply chain
- Better coordination of manufacturing, marketing, and distribution through enterprise resource planning (ERP) tools
- More streamlined order processing and reduced lead times enabled by coordinated logistics information systems.[1]

---

[1] Stephen M. Rutner, Brian J. Gibson, Kate L. Vitasek, and Craig G. Gustin, "Is Technology Filling the Information Gap?" *Supply Chain Management Review,* March/April 2001, 58–63.

In short, the effective and efficient use of information allows organizations to simultaneously reduce their costs and improve customer satisfaction in the sense that organizations stock the inventory that will be demanded by customers. For example, several U.S.-based grocery chains have carefully studied Hispanic consumers and learned that they place greater emphasis on fresh produce than do other ethnic groups. As such, grocery stores located in heavily Hispanic areas often stock more fresh produce than do grocery stores located in other areas.

Before proceeding further, it's important to distinguish between data and information: "data are simply facts—recorded measures of certain phenomena—whereas information is a body of facts in a format suitable for decision making."[2] Advances in technological hardware and software now allow contemporary logisticians access to abundant amounts of data in relatively short periods of time. In attempting to manage this data, contemporary logisticians and supply chain managers must first determine which data are relevant for their purposes. Next, the data need to be organized and analyzed; once analyzed, managers should make the appropriate decision or decisions. In the contemporary business environment, these actions must be completed in as short a time period as possible.

The next section of this chapter will provide an overview of general types of information management systems that are applicable across each business function. In addition, examples of how these general types of information systems might be specifically applied in logistics management are provided. This will be followed by a discussion of the Internet's influence on logistics, and the chapter will conclude with a look at select information technology challenges.

GENERAL TYPES OF INFORMATION MANAGEMENT SYSTEMS

Professor Steven Alter has identified six different types of information systems that are applicable to every business function.[3] These six categories, summarized in Figure 2-1, form the basis of the discussion in this section.

Office Automation System

Office automation systems provide effective ways to process personal and organizational business data, perform calculations, and create documents.[4] Included in office automation systems are general software packages—word processing, spreadsheet, presentation, and database management applications—that most of you probably learned in an introductory computer class.

The most relevant general software package for logisticians is the spreadsheet. Whereas early spreadsheet programs for personal computers were little more than speedy calculators, today's spreadsheets have a multitude of capabilities that allow managers to solve a variety of business problems relatively quickly and inexpensively.

Indeed, logistics spreadsheet applications into the early 1990s tended to reflect the rather limited capabilities of the existing software packages. For example, representative topics included economic order quantity (EOQ) calculations, warehouse sizing, transportation modal and carrier decisions, production planning, and center-of-gravity location decisions, among others.[5] As we moved through the 1990s, increased spreadsheet capabilities allowed organizations to analyze issues that had traditionally been solved by specially designed computer programs. In this vein, the classic issue of transportation cost minimization—transporting products from multiple sources to multiple destinations, at a minimum transportation cost—could be analyzed using

---

[2] William G. Zikmund and Michael d'Amico, *Marketing*, 7th ed. (Cincinnati, OH: South-Western, 2001), p. 125.
[3] The framework in this section is adapted from S. Alter, *Information Systems*, 4th ed. (Upper Saddle River, NJ: Prentice Hall, 2002).
[4] Alter, *Information Systems*, p. 191.
[5] John E. Tyworth and William L. Grenoble, "Spreadsheet Modeling in Logistics: Advancing Today's Educational Tools," *Journal of Business Logistics* 12, no. 1 (1991): 1–25.

System type	Logistics examples
Office automation system: provides effective ways to process personal and organizational business data, to perform calculations, and to create documents	Spreadsheet applications to calculate optimal order quantities, facility location, transport cost minimization, among others
Communication system: helps people work together by interacting and sharing information in many different forms	Virtual meetings via computer technology Voice-based order picking
Transaction processing system (TPS): collects and stores information about transactions; controls some aspects of transactions	Electronic data interchange Automatic identification technologies such as bar codes Point-of-sale systems
Management information system (MIS) and executive information system (EIS): converts TPS data into information for monitoring performance and managing an organization; provides executives information in a readily accessible format	Logistics information system
Decision support system (DSS): helps people make decisions by providing information, models, or analysis tools	Simulation Application-specific software such as warehouse management systems Data mining
Enterprise system: creates and maintains consistent data processing methods and an integrated database across multiple business functions	Logistics modules of enterprise resource planning systems

FIGURE 2-1   **General Types of Information Management Systems**

Source: Taken from Steven Alter, *Information Systems*, 4th ed. (Upper Saddle River, NJ: Prentice Hall, 2002), p. 191.

spreadsheet software.[6] More recently, spreadsheets have been used to construct an ammunition requirements model for the Canadian Army.[7]

Communication System

Communication systems help various stakeholders—employees, suppliers, customers—work together by interacting and sharing information in many different forms.[8] From a logistical perspective, the importance of well-defined and well-executed communication systems was highlighted by the events of September 11, 2001, especially for companies that use or provide airfreight services. Because of the total shutdown of the U.S. aviation system for several days following the terrorist attacks, many air shipments were diverted onto trucks, thus delaying many deliveries. As such, airfreight providers such as FedEx worked feverishly to inform customers when their shipments would be arriving.[9]

---

[6] Brian J. Parker and David J. Caine, "Minimizing Transportation Costs: An Efficient and Effective Approach for the Spreadsheet User," *Transport Logistics* 1, no. 2 (1997): 129–137.

[7] W. J. Hurley and Mathieu Balez, "A Spreadsheet Implementation of an Ammunition Requirements Model for the Canadian Army," *Interfaces* 38, no. 4 (2008): 271–280.

[8] Alter, *Information Systems*, Chapter 5.

[9] Kristen S. Krause, "FedEx's 9–11 Response," *Traffic World*, September 9, 2002, 12–13.

Many advances in telecommunication technology—such as fax machines, personal computers, electronic mail, cellular phones, and smart phones, among others—have occurred since the first edition of this book was published in the 1970s. As recently as the 1990s, some of these technologies were considered workplace "luxuries." Today, by contrast, many of these technologies are essential for enabling the contemporary logistician to perform in the workplace.

Electronic data interchange (EDI) (to be discussed in the next section), was viewed by many experts as the measuring stick for logistics information technology in the 1990s. By contrast, **wireless communication** emerged as the measuring stick during the first decade of the twenty-first century.[10] For our purposes, wireless communication refers to communication without cables and cords and includes infrared, microwave, and radio transmissions, among others.

Although wireless communication has many logistical applications, we'll take a look at one of the more popular types, namely, global positioning systems. Global positioning systems, or GPS, refer to a network of satellites that transmits signals that pinpoint the exact location of an object. You might be familiar with GPS in the form of personal navigation devices that provide maps or voice instructions as you drive your automobile.

GPS have become quite valuable to the transportation component of logistics because of high fuel costs and the relentless pressure to improve efficiency and productivity. Indeed, transportation companies that have implemented GPS have reported an increase in worker productivity, reduced operating costs, and improved customer relations. More specifically, one study found that GPS implementation allows transportation companies to recapture nearly one hour per day of their drivers' time, which translates into labor savings of approximately $5,500 per employee. The same study also reported that GPS implementation allows companies to reduce vehicle travel by about 230 miles per week, for an annual fuel savings of approximately $52,000.[11]

Continuing advances in hardware and software have resulted in dramatic cost reductions for wireless communication, and one implication is that the technology is no longer limited to those companies with the deepest financial resources. Moreover, hardware and software cost reductions have shortened the relevant investment payback period and GPS systems can pay for themselves within one year.[12]

Transaction Processing System (TPS)

A *transaction processing system* collects and stores information about transactions and may also control some aspects of transactions. The primary objective of a TPS is the efficient processing of transactions, and to this end, organizations can choose to do batch or real-time processing.[13] With batch processing, data are collected and stored for processing at a later time, with the later time perhaps being based on schedule (e.g., process every six hours) or volume (e.g., process once 25 transactions have accumulated) considerations. Real-time processing, not surprisingly, means that transactions are processed as they are received. Although batch processing might be somewhat out of step with the contemporary emphasis on speed and time reduction, it can be quite effective when real-time processing is not necessary. Moreover, in comparison with real-time systems, batch processing tends to be less costly and easier for employees to learn.

A prominent example of a logistics-related TPS is EDI, the computer-to-computer transmission of business data in a structured format. Because EDI provides for the seamless transmission of data across companies (assuming technological compatibility), it can facilitate the integration of, and coordination between, supply chain participants. Thus, firms with strong

---

[10] Roger Morton, "Working Without a Wire," *Logistics Today*, February 2005, 29–33.
[11] Bridget McCrea, "The Golden Age of Wireless," *Logistics Management*, October 2008, 47–50.
[12] No author, "Remote Asset Management Worth the Cost," *GPSWorld*, January 2009, 27.
[13] Alter, *Information Systems*, Chapter 5.

EDI links to both suppliers and customers might have a substantial advantage over supply chain arrangements without such implementations. Common uses of EDI include invoicing, purchase orders, pricing, advanced shipment notices, electronic funds transfer, and bill payment.

EDI has a number of benefits, including reductions in document preparation and processing time, inventory carrying costs, personnel costs, information float, shipping errors, returned goods, lead times, order cycle times, and ordering costs. In addition, EDI may lead to increases in cash flow, billing accuracy, productivity, and customer satisfaction. Potential drawbacks to EDI include a lack of awareness of its benefits, high setup costs, lack of standard formats, and incompatibility of computer hardware and software.

Despite these drawbacks and a perception that EDI is an "old" technology,[14] EDI continues to be an important logistics technology tool in the twenty-first century. Moreover, while the Internet was viewed by some as a possible replacement or substitute for EDI, time has shown that the Internet can serve as a complement to, rather than a replacement or substitute for, EDI. For example, Wal-Mart was one of the first companies to adopt Internet-based EDI (I-EDI) in place of value-added network (VAN)-based EDI. Importantly, I-EDI's significantly lower setup costs than VAN-based EDI make I-EDI more affordable for smaller companies, thus expanding EDI's scope.[15]

Automatic identification technologies, another type of logistics-related TPS, include optical character recognition (which can read letters, words, and numbers), machine vision (which can scan, inspect, and interpret what it views), voice-data entry (which can record and interpret a human voice), **radio-frequency identification (RFID)** (which can be used where there is no line of sight between scanner and label), and magnetic strips.

Automatic identification systems are an essential component in point-of-sale (POS) systems; the idea behind POS systems is to provide data to guide and enhance managerial decision making. Operationally, POS systems involve scanning Universal Product Code (UPC) labels, either by passing the product over an optical scanner or recording it with a handheld scanner. The UPC is read and recorded into a database that supplies information such as the product's price, applicable taxes, whether food stamps can be used, and so on. The specific price of each product and its description are also flashed on a monitor screen positioned near the counter. When all the products have been recorded, the customer receives verification that lists the products purchased, the price of each article, and the total bill.

Bar code scanners currently remain the most popular automatic identification system in use. They work to integrate suppliers and customers along the supply chain because all parties read the same labels; in addition, the transfer of goods between parties can be recorded by simple electronic means. Traditionally, laser scanners have been used to read bar codes. The scanners record inventory data and may be directly attached to a computer that uses the data to adjust inventory records and track product movement.

RFID technology is another automatic identification technology that has received considerable attention in the first part of the twenty-first century. Conceptually, RFID involves the use of radio frequency to identify objects that have been implanted with an RFID tag. Operationally, RFID consists of three components: a scanning antenna, an RFID tag (chip) that conveys the relevant data, and a transceiver that interprets the data. As an RFID tag passes within the scanning antenna's range, the tag's data are picked up by the scanning antenna and interpreted by the transceiver. Compared to bar codes, RFID (1) does not require clear line of sight between an object and RFID hardware, (2) can store much larger quantities of data, and (3) can offer both read and write capabilities.

---

[14] Malcolm Wheatley, "A Question of Standards," *Automotive Logistics*, September/October 2008, 60–64.
[15] Zhenyu Hang, Brian D. Janz, and Mark N. Frolik, "A Comprehensive Examination of Internet-EDI Adoption," *Information Systems Management* 25, no. 3 (2008): 273–286.

A major catalyst for RFID usage in logistics was a Wal-Mart mandate that by January 1, 2005, its top 100 suppliers deploy RFID tags on shipments into one particular Wal-Mart distribution center in Texas. Wal-Mart's mandate jumpstarted a technology that had existed since the 1940s but that had not been widely used by organizations.

A number of benefits have been reported by adopters of RFID technology. For example, dramatic reductions (between 20 and 50 percent) in inventory stockouts have been reported by Wal-Mart and some its suppliers.[16] In addition, RFID reduced the time needed to count inventory by 80 percent and improved the accuracy of inventory counts at one clothing retailer.[17] Despite the potential benefits associated with RFID, various challenges must be addressed before the technology becomes more widely used in logistics. A major drawback to more widespread RFID adoption involves the costs of installing the related hardware and software, which can range from $100,000 for smaller companies to $20 million for larger companies. Some suggest that widespread adoption of RFID will only occur when the price for read-only tags, which at the time of publication are between 7 and 10 cents, drops to 2 cents.[18]

Another drawback to RFID involves privacy concerns, such as the inappropriate use of the technology. For example, a major retailer embedded RFID chips into a particular line of cosmetic products, and consumers who selected this product from the store shelf were videobeamed, via webcam, to the manufacturer's headquarters![19] Yet another drawback is that data accuracy can be lower in items with high moisture content, such as fruits and vegetables.

Management Information System (MIS) and Executive Information System (EIS)

These systems convert TPS data into information for monitoring performance and managing an organization, with the objective of providing managers and executives with the information they really need.[20] To this end, a **logistics information system (LIS)** can be defined as "the people, equipment, and procedures to gather, sort, analyze, evaluate, and distribute needed, timely, and accurate information to logistics decision makers."[21]

As shown in Figure 2-2, an LIS begins with a logistics manager requesting information and ends with the manager receiving regular and customized reports. For logistics managers to receive *needed* information, it's important that they be fairly specific when submitting requests. For example, a logistics manager who wants information about a specific warehouse or distribution center needs to request information on, say, "the Chicago warehouse," rather than information on "corporate warehouses."

Timely information would appear to be incumbent on the effectiveness and efficiency of a company's particular LIS and timely information can encompass several dimensions. On the one hand, *timely* can refer to the up-to-date status of information, which can be influenced by a company's collection and analysis procedures. Information collection should emphasize both internal and external sources; unfortunately, internal sources of logistics information are not always as plentiful as desired. Indeed, research into the business value attributable to logistics discovered that "logistics measurement is happening much less frequently than one might imagine."[22] External sources focus on information from outside the company and include

[16] John S. Webster, "Wall-Mart's RFID Revolution a Tough Sell," *Network World*, September 15, 2008, 34–36.

[17] Alan M. Field, "Tag, You're It!" *Florida Shipper*, October 13, 2008, 10–11.

[18] Webster, "Wall-Mart's RFID Revolution a Tough Sell."

[19] Tom Andel, "Big Brother in Aisle Five?" *Paperboard Packaging*, February 2006, 4.

[20] Alter, *Information Systems*, Chapter 5.

[21] Adapted from a definition of "marketing information system" provided by Philip Kotler and Gary Armstrong, *Principles of Marketing*, 11th ed. (Upper Saddle River, NJ: Prentice Hall, 2006), Chapter 4.

[22] James S. Keebler, Karl B. Manrodt, David A. Durtsche, and D. Michael Ledyard, *Keeping Score: Measuring the Business Value of Logistics in the Supply Chain* (Oak Brook, IL: Council of Logistics Management, 1999), Chapter 2.

FIGURE 2-2   Structure and Function of a Logistics Information System
Source: Adapted from Michael Etzel, Bruce Walker, and William Stanton,
Marketing, 14th ed. (New York: McGraw-Hill Irwin, 2007), p. 172.

information about customers, competitors, and suppliers, along with information about economic, technological, political, legal, and sociocultural environments.

Timely can also refer to how quickly managers receive the information requested; this is affected by each company's retrieval and dissemination procedures. A manager's ability to quickly receive information can be influenced by technology hardware and software, and faster and more powerful technology has helped to reduce retrieval and dissemination times. Alternatively, retrieval and dissemination can be slowed by hardware and software glitches, including incompatible hardware or software, power outages, system crashes, and computer viruses.

Accurate information may also reflect the effectiveness and efficiency of a company's logistics information system. As such, an LIS must be concerned with the nature and quality of the relevant data; for instance, although the Internet can provide access to tremendous amounts of external information at a very low cost, the validity of some Internet information is suspect. Keep in mind the *GIGO*—garbage in/garbage out—principle: Information that is erroneous, misrepresented, or unclear will likely result in poor decisions by logisticians.

Decision Support Systems (DSS)

Decision support systems help managers make decisions by providing information, models, or analysis tools,[23] and they can be widely applied and used by logisticians. Specific uses of DSS in logistics include, but are not limited to, vehicle routing issues, inventory control decisions, developing automatic order picking systems, and optimization models for buyer–seller negotiations. Several of the more prominent logistics-related DSS techniques are discussed in the following paragraphs.

Simulation is a technique that models a real-world system, typically using mathematical equations to represent the relationships among the system's components. Simulation reliability is achieved by making the model as akin to the real world as possible, and as Figure 2-3 illustrates, very little business behavior cannot be simulated. Although simulation can be a powerful analytic tool, a poorly constructed simulation involving bad data or inaccurate assumptions about the relationships among variables can deliver suboptimal or unworkable solutions to logistics problems.

The primary advantage of simulation is that it enables the firm to test the feasibility of proposed changes at relatively little expense. In addition, it prevents firms from experiencing the public embarrassment of making a major change in their logistics system that might result in a deterioration of customer service levels or an increase in total operating expense.

---

[23] Alter, *Information Systems*, Chapter 5.

*"It can't actually think, but when it makes a mistake,
it can put the blame on some other computer."*

FIGURE 2-3   **Computers Can Simulate Many Forms of Business Behavior**
Source: Reproduced by permission of the artist and the Masters Agency.

A second type of DSS is what can be broadly labeled as **application-specific software**, which has been developed to help managers deal with specific logistics functions or activities. Traditionally, application-specific software often involved customers purchasing a particular software package and then having the software installed (i.e., so-called "purchase and install") on their computer(s). The purchase and install option was (is) quite expensive in the sense that the software costs can approach $500,000, while implementation costs can run into the several millions of dollars. Figure 2-4 provides a humorous glimpse of some application-specific software packages that are available to logistics managers.

An increasingly popular option for application-specific software is **on-demand software** (also referred to as **software-as-a-service**), or "software that users access on a per-use basis instead of software they own or license for installation."[24] A major advantage of on-demand vis-à-vis purchase and install software is that on-demand's pay-per-use model allows customers to avoid high capital investment costs (we'll look more closely at on-demand software later in the chapter).

Transportation management systems (TMSs) and **warehouse management systems (WMSs)** are two prominent examples of logistics-related application-specific software. Indeed, an annual software survey conducted by *Logistics Management* magazine has consistently found that TMS and WMS software are the most likely applications to be purchased or upgraded.[25] Due to their importance as logistical DSS, we'll take a brief look at TMSs and WMSs.

---

[24] David Hannon, "On-Demand Brings Spend Control to the Masses," *Purchasing*, March 2, 2006, 40–42.
[25] Bridget McCrea, "Scrutiny Rules the Day," *Logistics Management*, April 2009, 38–40.

FIGURE 2-4   **There May Be an Overabundance of Logistics-Related Software Packages**
Source: Used with the permission of Material Handling Management, copyright Penton Media, Inc.

A TMS is a software package that automates the process of building orders, tending loads, tracking shipments, audits, and payments,[26] and Table 2-1 presents a representative list of 15 tasks that might be performed by a TMS package. Organizations that have implemented TMS software have reported decreases in empty vehicle miles, reduced fuel consumption, and reduced transportation expenditures.

WMSs are software packages that "control the movement and storage of materials within an operation."[27] Activities that can be controlled by a WMS include inventory management,

TABLE 2-1 Transportation Management Systems Task Capabilities	
Task Capability	**Task Capability**
Asset tracking	Carrier selection
Claims management	Driver management
Freight payment	Load planning
Load tendering	Order or shipment visibility
Package delivery verification	Package pickup tracking
Pickup scheduling	Rating
Real-time route reporting	Route optimization
Shipment consolidation	—

Source: "Transportation Management Systems Solution Selector," *Logistics Today*, September 2004, 76–80.

---

[26] Amy Zuckerman, "Transportation Management Systems Give Shippers Power to Make Smarter Trucking Choices," *World Trade*, January 2008, 34–38.
[27] Dave Piasecki, "Warehouse Management Systems," *www.inventoryops.com*.

product receiving, determination of storage locations, order selection processes, and order shipping. Potential benefits to WMS include dramatic reductions in data entry errors as well as dramatic reductions in the travel distances for order picking. Other benefits to WMS include reduced operating expenses, fewer stockouts, increased inventory accuracy, and improved service to customers. Figure 2-5 shows what might happen to a company that doesn't use a WMS.

Because of the many different TMS and WMS options that are available to a logistics manager, it's important that an organization utilizes a software package that best suits its

FIGURE 2-5   Stock Controls Are Necessary

If papayas (a tropical fruit) are kept too long, they attract insects. This cartoon accompanied the text of an advertisement for a computerized warehouse inventory control system.   *Source:* Courtesy of Logisticon Inc., Flexible Material Management Systems. Santa Clara, CA.

needs, as opposed to one from a "name" provider or one that offers many unneeded options. Moreover, the installation of a TMS or WMS can cause organizational upheaval in the sense that the organization will change its established approach to managing transportation and warehousing, and current employees will need varying degrees of training to become proficient with the new system.

Data mining, which can be defined as "the application of mathematical tools to large bodies of data in order to extract correlations and rules,"[28] is a DSS technique that has grown in popularity in recent years. Data mining utilizes sophisticated quantitative techniques to find "hidden" patterns in large volumes of data; these patterns allow managers to improve their decision-making abilities as well as enhance their organization's competitive advantage. Although data mining has been characterized as a "fishing expedition" of sorts—in the sense of applying sophisticated quantitative techniques merely to find relationships, whether meaningful or not—data mining, in reality, should follow a well-defined methodology.[29]

Efficient data mining is dependent on **data warehouses**, that is, a central repository for all the relevant data collected by an organization. Wal-Mart, which is acknowledged to have one of world's foremost data warehouses, and its vendors make extensive use of data mining to improve logistical effectiveness and efficiency. For example, data mining has allowed Wal-Mart to discover that when hurricanes are projected to hit the state of Florida, demand dramatically increases for two products, beer and Kellogg's Pop Tarts (a toasted pastry product)! So, when a hurricane is projected to hit Florida, Wal-Mart makes sure that additional stocks of beer and Pop Tarts are available in its stores there.

Enterprise System

Enterprise systems, the final general type of information management system to be discussed, create and maintain consistent data processing methods and an integrated database across multiple business functions.[30] The most prominent example of enterprise systems is probably **enterprise resource planning (ERP) systems**, which "lets a company automate and integrate the majority of its business processes, share common data and practices across the enterprise, and produce and access information in a real-time environment."[31] In theory, ERP systems (such as those offered by Oracle and SAP) allow all prospective users access to a single database when making decisions. The attractiveness of ERP systems comes from their potential for lower costs (such as inventory reductions), as well as increased productivity and customer satisfaction.

Although contemporary ERP systems encompass a firmwide perspective, their origins can be traced back to logistics and manufacturing in the form of inventory control and materials requirement planning programs.[32] Unlike these earlier programs, today's ERP systems (conceptually, at least) provide an opportunity for all functional areas within a firm to access and analyze a common database—which might not have been previously possible because (1) certain data were proprietary to a particular functional area and (2) of insufficient or slow computing capabilities.

One of the most frequently mentioned shortcomings of ERP systems involves the costs of installation. It's common knowledge that ERP software is relatively expensive; however, the software is only one part of ERP implementation costs. For example, the vast amounts of data necessary for ERP systems may necessitate new or upgraded computer hardware. Other hidden or frequently overlooked costs of ERP implementation include employee training, data conversion (converting existing data into a usable and consistent format), integrating and testing a new

[28] Sam Joseph and Daniel Scuka, "AI," *Japan Inc.*, November 2001, 20–28.

[29] Michael S. Garver, "Try New Data-Mining Techniques," *Marketing News*, September 16, 2002, 31–33.

[30] Alter, *Information Systems*, Chapter 5.

[31] Joel D. Wisner, G. Keong Leong, and Keah-Choon Tan, *Principles of Supply Chain Management: A Balanced Approach*, 2nd ed. (Mason, OH: South-Western Cengage Learning, 2008), p. 507.

[32] Kuldeep Kumar and Jos van Hillegersberg, "ERP Experiences and Evolution," *Communications of the ACM* 43, no. 4 (2000): 23–26.

system, maintenance costs, and consultant fees. Indeed, consultant fees can quickly ratchet up ERP implementation costs; there are suggestions that consultant fees may be three times more costly than the software itself.[33] When all relevant costs are factored in, ERP installation costs can easily reach up to the tens of millions of dollars, and installation costs in the hundreds of millions of dollars are not out of the question.

A second shortcoming is that implementation of ERP systems can be a very time-consuming process. Indeed, many of the hidden costs of ERP implementation mentioned in the previous paragraph are the result of hidden time associated with ERP implementation. For instance, employee training, data conversion, and integrating and testing the new system all require time beyond the installation of the ERP software itself. A general rule of thumb is that actual time to implement ERP systems may range from two to four times longer than the time period specified by the ERP vendor.

A third shortcoming of ERP systems is that they initially lacked strong application-specific logistical capabilities such as TMS or WMS. Many companies addressed this challenge by adding so-called "best of breed" (i.e., the best product of its type) logistical applications to their ERP programs, but the process associated with adding the respective software could be costly and time consuming. In recent years, however, ERP vendors have begun to provide high-quality application-specific logistical capabilities, particularly with respect to WMS.[34]

Given the preceding discussion on time and implementation costs, it is not surprising that some ERP installations do not go as smoothly as desired, and these ERP glitches occasionally have a logistical component to them. For example, ERP implementation problems at a leading manufacturer of home medical products caused the company to lower its revenue estimates for several time periods. From a logistical perspective, the ERP-related problems meant that the company missed shipment deadlines, could not respond to customer inquiries, and had limited information about order status. The order-related problems, in turn, resulted in a higher-than-normal level of returns associated with incorrect orders, and the missed shipment deadlines caused the company to spend more money for expedited transportation.[35]

THE INTERNET'S INFLUENCE ON LOGISTICS

Although the Internet may appear to be a ubiquitous technology today, the reality is that only about 25 percent of the world's population currently uses the Internet, up from approximately 5 percent of the world's population at the beginning of the twenty-first century.[36] Just as the Internet's usage continues to expand during the twenty-first century, so does its influence on the logistics discipline. While it's not possible to present a comprehensive discussion of the Internet's influence on logistics, this section will discuss three specific influences—online retailing, on-demand software, and electronic procurement—of the Internet on the logistics discipline.

Online Retailing

It should be noted that there are logistical similarities between online retailing and in-store retailing. For example, many logistical functions and activities—such as transportation, warehousing, materials handling, and order management—occur in both. Likewise, both may use the same type of equipment and materials, such as bar coding and WMSs.

Alternatively, powerful differences exist between online and in-store retailing with respect to the execution of logistics functions and activities. For example, the orders associated with online shopping tend to be more plentiful and in much smaller quantities than those

[33] Bob Violino, "Will a New Planning System Bust You?" *Baseline*, June 2005, 88.
[34] Bridget McCrea, "ERP: Gaining Momentum," *Logistics Management*, November 2008, 44–46.
[35] Marc L. Songini, "Faulty ERP App Results in Shortfall for Medical Firm," *Computerworld*, January 2, 2006, 8.
[36] *www.internetworldstats.com*.

associated with in-store retailing. As such, online retailing requires an order management system capable of handling high volumes of orders, and it's also essential that the information management system be capable of correctly transmitting each order so that it can be filled in a timely fashion.

In addition, because of smaller order quantities, online shopping is characterized by open-case, rather than full-case, picking; open-case picking is facilitated by materials handling equipment, such as totes and push carts. Moreover, open-case picking necessitates that products be slotted (placed) in locations that facilitate picking effectiveness and efficiency. Not surprisingly, online retailing's smaller order quantities have important packaging implications as well, in the sense that companies need containers—small cartons, envelopes, bags—that are well suited to holding small quantities of product.[37] Some companies that engage in both online and in-store retailing choose to outsource online's pick-and-pack activities because they are so different than for in-store retailing.[38]

Two other key logistical considerations for online retailing involve transportation and returned orders. The smaller order quantities occasioned by online retailing tend to favor transport companies with extensive delivery networks and expertise in parcel shipments. This, in turn, suggests that outbound shipments tend to be picked up at a loading dock by small-capacity vehicles, such as delivery vans. Moreover, many online retailers are challenged by "last-mile" considerations (those related to delivering product to the customer) such as congestion, frequent stops, and return trips if the customer is not available to accept the delivery.

Although returned orders are an issue in all types of retailing, the return rates associated with online shopping tend to be much higher than with other types of retailing; one estimate suggests 10 percent return rates for traditional forms of retailing, compared to approximately 30 percent for online purchases.[39] Because many of these returns are from individual customers, not businesses or organizations, online retailers should attempt to make the return process as painless as possible. As such, when online customers receive their orders, they might also receive information on how to return the order, a return label, as well as a return container such as an envelope or bag. A relatively smooth and painless return process not only improves return effectiveness and efficiency but can also be an effective way of building and maintaining customer loyalty.[40]

Furthermore, it's important to note that a "one size fits all" logistics strategy is not likely to facilitate the effectiveness and efficiency of online shopping. Rather, a variety of logistics strategies might need to be applied, and it's important to recognize the potential trade-offs associated with the different strategies. For example, one way of addressing the last-mile issue of customer unavailability would be to install some type of receptacle (e.g., a drop box) for the product at the customer's residence. However, these receptacles might not be feasible for large items (such as a refrigerator), perishable items (such as certain types of food), or extremely valuable items (such as jewelry). The challenges of implementing the appropriate logistics strategy, or strategies, for online shopping are exacerbated by the fact that (1) a particular customer may require vastly different levels of service depending on the product ordered and (2) a particular product may require vastly different levels of service depending on the customer ordering it.[41]

On-Demand Software

On-demand software (software as a service), which was mentioned earlier in this chapter, has experienced meteoric growth since the beginning of the twenty-first century. There are

---

[37] Norm Saenz, Jr., "Picking the Best Practices for E-fulfillment," *IIE Solutions* 33, no. 3 (2001): 37–40.
[38] William Hoffman, "One-Click Shopping," *Journal of Commerce*, February 20, 2006, 22–23.
[39] Saenz, "Picking the Best Practices."
[40] Tim Parry, "Many Happy Returns?" *Multichannel Merchant*, February 2006, 37.
[41] Alberto Grando and Marco Gosso, "Avoiding the E-Commerce Trap," *EBF*, Summer 2004, 48–51.

myriad logistics-related applications for on-demand software, including collaborative forecasting and inventory optimization, with TMSs emerging as the most popular on-demand application.[42]

One reason for on-demand's popularity is that its pay-per-use formula allows customers to avoid high capital investment costs, which speeds up return on investment for the software. In addition, because on-demand involves operational as opposed to capital expenditures, it becomes a viable option for many companies that could not afford to purchase, install, and maintain application-specific software such as TMSs and WMSs. Moreover, the worldwide economic slowdown that began in 2007 has caused many organizations to slash their information technology expenditures, thus benefitting on-demand applications. Other advantages of on-demand include faster and less-costly installation, a smaller information technology staff, and regular upgrades and updates from the software provider.[43]

Although on-demand software appears to be quite attractive, particularly from a financial perspective, it has several potential drawbacks. For example, the regular software upgrades and updates mentioned earlier can sometimes be *too numerous* and *too frequent*, and customers can struggle to keep up with them. Moreover, on-demand software allows for a limited amount of customization, meaning that customers need to fit what they're doing to what the software can achieve.[44] And, because the Internet is the primary transaction medium for on-demand software, security issues such as data protection have been identified as a key concern.

Electronic Procurement

Electronic procurement (also known as **e-procurement**) uses the Internet to make it easier, faster, and less expensive for an organization to purchase goods and services. The types of benefits that come from e-procurement include transactional benefits, compliance benefits, management information benefits, and price benefits. *Transactional benefits* measure the transactional benefits (e.g., a reduced invoice-to-payment time) associated with e-procurement. *Compliance benefits* focus on the savings that come from adherence to established procurement policies. *Management information benefits* encompass those that result from management information, customer satisfaction, and supplier satisfaction levels after implementation of e-procurement. *Price benefits* are those that are given as a result of adopting e-procurement. For example, the electronic processing of invoices can save a great deal of money in terms of postage and stationery, and these savings can be passed on to the buyer.[45]

Just as there are benefits to e-procurement, there are important drawbacks as well. One concern with electronic commerce in general, and e-procurement in particular, involves the security of information that is being transmitted; there is a risk that sensitive or proprietary information could end up in the wrong hands. Another concern is that e-procurement can be impersonal in the sense that human interaction is replaced by computer transactions. Moreover, despite substantial hype about the potential benefits of e-procurement, one study discovered that only about 25 percent of the responding companies mandate the use of e-procurement. The same study also found a dramatic drop in user confidence with respect to having the required skills and knowledge to use e-procurement tools.[46]

One activity that has been greatly facilitated by e-procurement is online reverse auctions. You might be familiar with traditional auctions in which multiple buyers bid on a particular product, with the product being sold to the highest bidder. By contrast, in a **reverse auction**, a buyer invites bids from multiple sellers, and the seller with the lowest bid is generally awarded the business. As reverse auctions have evolved, so too have their parameters; in some situations, a

---

[42] Bridget McCrea, "The State of On-Demand: Catching Fire," *Logistics Management*, January 2009, 43–45.
[43] John Fontana, "What's Behind On-Demand's Software Rise," *Network World*, December 12, 2005, 1, 14.
[44] Hannon, "On-Demand Brings Spend Control."
[45] David Eakin, "Measuring E-Procurement Benefits," *Government Procurement*, August 2002, 6–12.
[46] Maria Varmazis, "Buyers Become More Selective in Online Tools," *Purchasing*, September 15, 2005, 43–45.

buyer is exempted from accepting the lowest bid, whereas in other situations a buyer does not have to accept any of the bids.[47]

Buyers tend to like reverse auctions because they aim to generate low procurement prices, and the online nature of reverse auctions allows buyers to drill down to a seller's low price very quickly. Alternatively, sellers are critical of reverse auctions because their primary emphasis is low price. However, reverse auctions can provide sellers with valuable information such as the number of other bidders. This can be important in the sense that a large number of bidders will likely lead to a great deal of price competition.[48]

INFORMATION TECHNOLOGY CHALLENGES

Thus far, this chapter has presented various challenges associated with specific types of information technology. We conclude this chapter with a discussion of several macro-level information technology challenges, or those challenges that might be faced regardless of the type(s) of information technology being utilized.

One macro-level challenge is the recognition that information technology *is a tool* that can help managers to address organizational problems and *is not a panacea* or a be-all/end-all solution for organizational problems. This can be illustrated by the situation of a senior manager whose disorganization caused him to regularly miss scheduled meetings with various constituencies. The senior manager and his boss decided to "solve" the missed meeting problem by providing the manager with a smart phone that contained a calendar detailing the time and place of his various meetings. Unfortunately, the senior manager continued to miss regularly scheduled meetings because he occasionally failed to (1) carry the smart phone with him, (2) have the smart phone turned on, or (3) upload the meeting information into the smart phone's calendar. In this situation, the technological "solution" could not address—and may have actually exacerbated—the manager's disorganization.

Security concerns represent another macro-level information technology challenge, and these security concerns have many dimensions. For example, a 2006 study indicated that information security is the most important technology issue that companies face today.[49] Moreover, the theft of proprietary information for an "average" company is estimated to cost approximately $300,000 annually.[50] Moreover, increasing reliance on the Internet for logistics activities such as ordering and shipment tracking makes it essential that Web sites are as secure as possible from computer viruses or computer hackers that could compromise a customer's access to those Web sites.

Yet another security concern involves the decreasing size and increasing portability of technology devices such as laptop computers, flash drives, and smart phones. These smaller technology devices are more susceptible than larger technology devices to loss or theft and it's important to recognize that the loss or theft of small, portable technology devices cause an organization to lose both the device *and* the data stored on the device. A particularly noteworthy example involved an intern for the state of Ohio who had a laptop computer containing personal data on approximately one million residents of Ohio stolen from her car.

A third information technology challenge involves human resource issues. Importantly, people-related factors such as employee resistance have been identified as a major cause of information technology implementation failure.[51] Technology addiction, another human resource issue, is perhaps best exemplified by the term "CrackBerry," which describes a person who uses a BlackBerry smart phone addictively or obsessively.[52] Underscoring the potential seriousness of technology addiction is whether an employer can be held liable for an employee's technology addiction.

---

[47] Bridget McCrea, "Going Once, Going Twice," *Industrial Distribution*, July 2005, 30–32.
[48] Ibid.
[49] Paul Demery, "Safe Driving? Is Your Lap Strapped in?" *Accounting Technology*, September 2006, 45–49.
[50] Ray Zambroski, "Think Before You Send," *Communication World*, May–June 2006, 38–40.
[51] Tracey E. Rizzuto and Jennifer Reeves, "A Multidisciplinary Meta-Analysis of Human Barriers to Technology Implementation," *Consulting Psychology Journal: Practice and Research* 59, no. 2 (2007): 226–240.
[52] *www.dictionary.com*.

Summary

This chapter discussed key issues of logistics and information technology. Six general types of information management systems were examined, with a particular emphasis on relevant logistical applications. Topics discussed include GPS, EDI, application-specific software, and enterprise resource planning systems.

The chapter also looked at the Internet's influence on logistics in terms of three issues, online retailing, on-demand software, and e-procurement. A discussion of information technology challenges—such as the recognition that information technology is a tool and not a panacea—concluded the chapter.

Questions for Discussion and Review

1. In what ways can information be helpful in logistics and supply chain management?
2. List the six general types of information management systems, and give one logistics application for each one that you've named.
3. Do you view the spreadsheet as the most relevant general software package for logisticians? Why or why not?
4. How can communication systems facilitate logistics management in the aftermath of situations such as terrorist attacks and natural disasters?
5. What advances in telecommunications technology do you view as being most beneficial to logistics management? Why?
6. Discuss how global positioning systems have become quite valuable in transportation management.
7. Discuss the benefits and drawbacks of EDI.
8. Discuss the relationship between automatic identification technologies and point-of-sale systems.
9. Why are some companies hesitant to adopt RFID technology?
10. Discuss the importance of timely and accurate information to a logistics information system.
11. What benefits are associated with transportation management and warehouse management systems?
12. What is data mining? How might it be used in logistics?
13. Discuss advantages and disadvantages of enterprise resource planning systems.
14. Refer back to the logistical activities listed in Chapter 1; pick two that you're interested in and research how they have been influenced by the Internet. Are you surprised by your findings? Why or why not?
15. From a logistical perspective, what are some of the differences between online and in-store retailing?
16. Why is a "one size fits all" logistics strategy not likely to facilitate effective or efficient online shopping?
17. Discuss the advantages and disadvantages of on-demand software.
18. Discuss the benefits and drawbacks to electronic procurement.
19. What is an online reverse auction? Why do buyers like them?
20. What are some of the macro-level information technology challenges that managers face?

Suggested Readings

Fawcett, Stanley E., Paul Osterhaus, Gregory M. Magnan, and Amydee M. Fawcett. "Mastering the Slippery Slope of Technology." *Supply Chain Management Review* 12, no. 7 (2008): 16–25.

Hurley, W. J., and Mathieu Balez. "A Spreadsheet Implementation of an Ammunition Requirements Model for the Canadian Army." *Interfaces* 38, no. 4 (2008): 271–280.

Kerr, John. "Technology Outlook: Getting by Without the Big Buys." *Supply Chain Management Review* 13, no. 1 (2009): 14–19.

Lai, Fujun, Dahui Li, Qiang Wang, and Xiande Zhao. "The Information Technology Capability of Third-Party Logistics Providers: A Resource-Based View and Empirical Evidence from China." *Journal of Supply Chain Management* 44, no. 3 (2008): 22–38.

Leonard, Lori N. K., and Christine Clemons. "Supply Chain Replenishment: Before-and-After EDI Implementation."

Supply Chain Management: An International Journal 11, no. 3 (2006): 225–232.

Min, Hokey. "Application of a Decision Support System to Strategic Warehousing Decisions." *International Journal of Physical Distribution & Logistics Management* 39, no. 4 (2009): 270–281.

Moser, George, and Peter Ward. "Which TMS Is Right for You?" *Supply Chain Management Review* 12, no. 3 (2008): 50–56.

Parry, Glenn, and Andrew Graves. "The Importance of Knowledge for ERP Systems." *International Journal of Logistics: Research & Applications* 11, no. 6 (2008): 427–441.

Pearcy, Dawn H., and Larry C. Guinipero. "Using E-Procurement Applications to Achieve Integration: What Role Does Firm Size Play?" *Supply Chain Management: An International Journal* 13, no. 1 (2008): 26–34.

Savitske, Katrina. "Internal and External Logistics Information Technologies: The Performance Impact in an International

Setting." *International Journal of Physical Distribution & Logistics Management* 37, no. 6 (2007): 454–468.

Schoenherr, Tobias. "Diffusion of Online Reverse Auctions for B2B Procurement: An Exploratory Study." *International Journal of Operations & Production Management* 28, no. 3 (2008): 259–278.

White, Andrew, and Mark Johnson. "RFID in the Supply Chain: Lessons from European Early Adopters." *International Journal of Physical Distribution & Logistics Management* 38, no. 2 (2008): 88–107.

CASE

CASE 2-1   Just-in-Time in Kalamazoo

Jim Ballenger was president of a medium-size firm that manufactured mini motor homes in Kalamazoo, Michigan. The firm had expanded from a local Midwest market to a national one, including Southern California and New England. As markets had expanded, so too had sources of supply for the company, with major suppliers located in Southern California, the Pacific Northwest, and Michigan. The decision to found the company in Michigan had been made for two reasons: Jim's former associates in the auto industry were there, and the largest single component of the mini—the truck or van chassis on which the rest of the vehicle is built—was purchased from one of the U.S. light-truck makers.

Like others in the field, Jim's company actually manufactured very few of its components. Virtually the entire product was assembled from components purchased from outside vendors. There was, however, a well-defined order in which the components could most efficiently be installed in the vehicle. Recently, it had become clear to Jim that transportation and inventory costs contributed to a relatively large portion of his component parts expenses and that they might be ripe for a substantial reduction. He had been hearing about just-in-time (JIT) systems. According to some notes he had taken at a professional meeting, the JIT production system was developed by the Toyota Motor Company more than 50 years ago. It involves an approach to inventory that, in turn, forces a complementary approach to production, quality control, supplier relations, and distributor relationships. The major tenets of JIT can be summarized as follows:

1. Inventory in itself is wasteful and should be minimized.
2. Minimum replenishment quantity is maintained for both manufactured and purchased parts.
3. Minimum inventory of semifinished goods should be maintained—in this case, partially completed motor homes.
4. Deliveries of inputs should be frequent and small.
5. The time needed to set up production lines should be reduced to the absolute minimum.
6. Suppliers should be treated as part of the production team. This means that the vendor makes every effort to provide outstanding service and quality and that there is usually a much longer-lasting relationship with a smaller number of suppliers than is common in the United States.
7. The objective of the production system is zero defects.
8. The finished product should be delivered on a very short lead time.

To the U.S. inventory planner, vice president of logistics, and production planner, an operation run on the preceding principles raised a number of disturbing prospects. Jim Ballenger was very aware of the costs that might arise if a JIT production system were to be established. From the materials management standpoint, the idea of deliberately planning many small shipments rather than a few large ones appeared to ensure higher freight bills, especially from more distant suppliers, for which freight rates would make the most difference.

With regard to competition among suppliers, Jim often had the opportunity, in the volatile mini–motor home market, to buy out parts and component supplies from manufacturers that were going out of business. Those components could be obtained at a substantial savings, with the requirement that inventory in the particular parts be temporarily increased or that purchases from existing vendors be temporarily curtailed. Perhaps the greatest question raised by JIT, however, had to do with the probability of much more erratic production as a result of tight supplies of components. Both with suppliers' products and with his own, Jim operated with the (generally tacit) assumption that there would be some defective components purchased and that there would likely be something wrong with his product when it first came off the assembly line. For this reason, the Kalamazoo minis were extensively tested (their advertising said, "We hope you'll never do what we do to your Kalamazoo mini"), as were the components prior to installation. To the extent that only a few of a particular type of component were on hand, the interruption in the production schedule would be that much greater. It might entail expensive rush orders for replacement components or equally expensive downtime for the entire plant.

Jim was also concerned about his relationship with his suppliers, as compared, say, to a large auto manufacturer. In the mini–motor home business, generally the manufacturers are small and the component makers large. In this situation, it was somewhat more difficult to see the idea of the supplier as a part of the production team, in the sense that the supplier would be expected to make a special effort in either quality control or delivery flexibility on behalf of one of its almost miniscule accounts.

Despite these concerns, Jim was painfully aware that he was using a public warehouse near his plant that usually contained between $500,000 and $1,000,000 in inventory, on which he paid more than 1.5 percent per month for the borrowed funds used to buy it, as well as expenses relating to the use of the warehouse itself. In addition, his firm was now producing so many different models (one with a bath, one with a shower only) and

using so many different appliances (various types of radio, three varieties of refrigerator, and so forth) that the costs of a safety stock for each component were going up every day.

As an aid to making his decision on whether to try a JIT orientation at his plant, Jim's executive assistant, Kathy Williams, drew up a table that summarized the anticipated impacts of a JIT system (see Exhibit 2-A). The figures are based on random samples of inventory items. The major component of any mini–motor home—the chassis—would always be purchased on a one-at-a-time basis from Ford, Chevrolet, Dodge, or International. With rare exceptions, it would always be available on demand. It would be delivered through the local dealer. If the dealer did not have one in stock, one could easily be obtained from another area dealership.

Exhibit 2-A is a representative 10 percent sample of Ballenger's components inventory. It covers weekly use of each item, the current lot size purchased, and so on. Before figuring the total costs under the present and JIT systems, two additional facts must be noted. First, Ballenger's inventory carrying costs are assumed to be 20 percent per year on the average investment in inventory on hand, including its acquisition and transportation costs.

Second, under the current system, the number of units of each type of component kept in stock is calculated as follows: For those items purchased from vendors more

	Current System					Using JIT		
Item	Distance from vendor (in miles)	Average number of units used each week	Current lot size purchased	Unit cost	Average freight cost per unit	JIT lot size	Unit cost	Average freight cost per unit (surface)
Gas range	1,145	10	200	$100	$20	10	$105	$22
Toilet	606	10	240	80	18	10	100	18
Pump	26	56	125	16	3	7	15	4
Refrigerator (large)	22	6	120	110	20	6	113	25
Refrigerator (small)	22	7	15	95	15	1	85	15
Foam cushion	490	675	1,500	8	2	75	7	3
DVD Player (type D)	1,800	9	24	136	11	3	130	26
Dome lights	3	824	1,720	2	0	36	4	0
Awning brackets	48	540	1,200	4	1	60	5	1
Insect screens	159	570	1,240	7	1	50	7	2

EXHIBIT 2-A Ten Percent Random Sample of Component Inventory
Note: The plant operates 52 weeks per year and produces 10 mini motor homes per week.

than 500 miles away, a safety stock representing four weeks of use is maintained. For items from vendors between 100 and 500 miles away, a safety stock representing two weeks of use is maintained. For items from closer sources, a safety stock representing one week of use is maintained. In addition to safety stocks, the average inventory of any item is the current lot size purchased, divided by 2.

If you are familiar with Excel or other spreadsheet software, you might try using it here, although it is not necessary.

Questions

1. What is the total annual cost of maintaining the components inventory under the present system?
2. What would be the total annual cost of maintaining the components inventory under the JIT system (assuming no safety stocks)?
3. Should Ballenger take into account any other costs or benefits from the JIT system? If so, what are they?
4. If the JIT system is adopted, are there safety stocks of any item that should be maintained? If so, which ones and how much?
5. If the JIT system is adopted, what changes, if any, should occur in the relationships between Ballenger's firm and his suppliers of components? Discuss.
6. Assume that Ballenger has switched to the JIT system and that he receives a surprise phone call from a competitor who is going out of business. The competitor wants to sell Ballenger 7,000 dome lights of the type listed in Exhibit 2-A. Should Ballenger buy them? If so, at what price?
7. Carrying costs are 20 percent. Is there a level of carrying costs at which both Ballenger's present system and a JIT system have similar costs? If so, what is it?

3 | STRATEGIC AND FINANCIAL LOGISTICS

Key Terms

- Assets
- Asset turnover
- Balanced scorecard (BSC)
- Balance sheet
- Cost leadership strategy
- Current ratio
- Differentiation strategy
- Expenses (costs)
- Focus strategy
- Income statement
- Liabilities
- Net profit margin
- Owners' equity
- Return on assets (ROA)
- Revenues (sales)
- Strategic Profit Model (SPM)

Learning Objectives

- To appreciate how logistics can influence an organization's strategic financial outcomes
- To review basic financial terminology
- To understand how the Strategic Profit Model can demonstrate the financial impact of logistics activities
- To become aware of some of the more common measures of logistics performance

As was highlighted in Chapter 1, an effective and efficient logistics function holds a crucial role within most organizations. Research has continuously demonstrated that logistical activities can be an important consideration for achieving exceptional levels of customer service and ultimately contributing to firm financial performance.[1] As an example, depending on the industry and product type, reverse logistics costs as a percent of revenue can range between 3 and 6 percent.[2]

From a financial perspective, improvements to an organization's reverse logistics system could provide cost improvements and/or revenue enhancement opportunities. As an example, Estée Lauder (a manufacturer of cosmetics, skin care, and fragrances) made an investment of $1.3 million to build a system of scanners and other technologies to assist its reverse logistics efforts. With respect to cost improvements, this system enabled Estée Lauder to sharply reduce the percentage of returned goods that it dumped into landfills while also providing half a million dollars in labor cost savings. In terms of revenue enhancements, the system is a key part of a $250 million product line based on returned cosmetics. Estée Lauder collects items and then sells them to seconds stores or to retailers in developing countries.[3]

---

[1] Michael Tracey, "The Importance of Logistics Efficiency to Customer Service and Firm Performance," *International Journal of Logistics Management* 9, no. 2 (1998): 65–81.
[2] Sumantra Sengupta, "10 New Ideas for Generating Value," *Supply Chain Management Review* 13, no. 4 (2009): 20–25.
[3] Andrew O'Connell, "Improve Your Return on Returns," *Harvard Business Review* 85, no. 11 (2007): 30–34.

This chapter provides an overview of how an organization's strategic financial outcomes are influenced by logistics decisions. We begin with a discussion of the connection between functional logistics strategy and overall corporate strategy and ultimately financial performance. Next, a general overview of key financial terminology will be presented. This is followed by a description of how the strategic profit model can be used to highlight how logistics activities influence the key corporate financial measures of net income, capital employed, and return on capital employed. The chapter concludes with a description of the balanced scorecard and common logistics performance measures.

CONNECTING STRATEGY TO FINANCIAL PERFORMANCE

A recurring theme in the logistics research is that an organization's logistics capabilities need to be directly connected to objective (as opposed to subjective) firm performance measures. In addition, this research stream asserts that logistics managers must continue to find ways to effectively communicate how these logistics capabilities provide value and ultimately support corporate strategy and success in financial terms.[4] Strategy can be formulated at a corporate level, a business unit level, and a functional level. Corporate-level strategy is focused on determining the goals for the company, the types of businesses in which the company should compete, and the way the company will be managed. Typically, organizations strive to create value by effectively managing a portfolio of businesses and ensuring that each of these businesses is financially successful.

Strategy at a business unit level is primarily focused on the products and services provided to customers and on finding ways to develop and maintain a sustainable competitive advantage with these customers. Renowned strategist Michael Porter has identified three generic strategies that can be pursued by an organization, namely, cost leadership, differentiation, and focus. A cost leadership strategy requires an organization to pursue activities that will enable it to become a low-cost producer in an industry for a given level of quality. A differentiation strategy entails an organization developing a product and/or service that offers unique attributes that are valued by customers and that the customers perceive to be distinct from competitor offerings. Finally, a focus strategy concentrates an organization's effort on a narrowly defined market to achieve either a cost leadership or differentiation advantage.[5]

The functional level of the organization is where logistics resides. The strategic issues at this level are related to business activities that support the achievement of the higher-level goals set by the business unit and corporation. This *hierarch of strategy* entails the functional units of an organization providing input into the other levels of strategy formulation. This input could take the form of information on the resources and capabilities available to the organization. After the corporate-level and business unit strategies are developed, the functional units must translate these strategies into discrete action plans they must accomplish for the higher-level strategies to succeed.

Functional-level strategies will exist in such areas as marketing, finance, manufacturing, and logistics. Logistics strategy decisions involve issues such as the number and location of

---

[4] See, for example, Edward A. Morash, Cornelia L. M. Droge, and Shawnee K. Vickery, "Strategic Logistics Capabilities for Competitive Advantage and Firm Success," *Journal of Business Logistics* 17, no. 1 (1996): 1–22; Douglas M. Lambert and Renan Burduroglu, "Measuring and Selling the Value of Logistics," *International Journal of Logistics Management* 11, no. 1 (2000): 1–17; Edward A. Morash, "Supply Chain Strategies, Capabilities, and Performance," *Transportation Journal* 41, no. 3 (2001): 37–54; Jeff Hoi Yan Yeung, Willem Selen, Chee-Chuong Sum, and Baofeng Huo, "Linking Financial Performance to Strategic Orientation and Operational Priorities: An Empirical Study of Third-party Logistics Providers," *International Journal of Physical Distribution and Logistics Management* 36, no. 3 (2006): 210–230; and Kenneth W. Green Jr., Dwayne Whitten, and R. Anthony Inman, "The Impact of Logistics Performance on Organizational Performance in a Supply Chain Context," *Supply Chain Management: An International Journal* 13, no. 4 (2008): 317–327.

[5] Michael Porter, *Competitive Strategy: Techniques for Analyzing Industries and Competitors* (New York: The Free Press, 1980).

warehouses, the selection of appropriate transportation modes, the deployment of inventory, and investments in technology that support logistics activities. In addition to being influenced by the goals of the corporate and business unit strategies, logistics strategy is directly influenced by strategic decisions in the functional areas of marketing and manufacturing. Marketing goals in areas such as product availability, desired customer service levels, and packaging design directly influence logistics decisions that must be made to support achievement of these goals or to provide information for strategy formulation in these areas. Similarly, a strategic decision by manufacturing to implement a just-in-time system would affect logistics decisions in areas such as warehousing, transportation, and inventory management.

The ability of the logistics function to ultimately influence the overall financial success of an organization is based on the ability of logistics managers to develop and implement strategies that are aligned with the overall corporate strategy. Research has shown a positive effect of this alignment of functional-level strategies with higher-level strategies on financial performance.[6] Specifically, logistics strategy must be designed to optimally support the requirements of the business and the corporation in order to positively affect the financial outcomes of an organization. Thus, an appreciation for this interconnectedness and need for alignment of strategies is important for every logistics manager.

BASIC FINANCIAL TERMINOLOGY

Logistics managers in every organization are expected to use financial information to help them make decisions, allocate resources, and budget expenses. Having a basic understanding of financial terminology is important in assisting logistics managers to formulate intelligent questions for other functions as well as understanding how logistical activities can help improve their company's financial performance. Some of the more important financial terms are described in the following sections.

Income Statement

The **income statement** shows revenues, expenses, and profit for a period of time, and an example is presented in Figure 3-1. It can also be referred to as a profit and loss (P&L) statement. In general, the income statement measures the profitability of the products and/or service provided by a company. It reports the revenues generated by company activities during a given period of time, the expenses associated with achieving these revenues, and the profit or loss that is a result of these activities. **Revenues**, also referred to as sales, provide a dollar value of all the products and/or services an organization provides to its customers during a given period of time. **Expenses**, also referred to as costs, provide a dollar value for the costs incurred in generating revenues during a given period of time.

Logistics managers need to understand how logistics costs influence the profits or losses being incurred by their firm so that they can make appropriate decisions. While it is not likely for a logistics manager to directly correlate logistics service improvements with an increase in sales, superior logistics service can have a positive influence on an organization's financial performance.

---

[6] See, for example, Maheshkumar P. Joshi, Ravi Kathuria, and Stephen J. Porth, "Alignment of Strategic Priorities and Performance: An Integration of Operations and Strategic Management Perspectives," *Journal of Operations Management* 21, no. 3 (2003): 353–369; Paul D. Cousins, "The Alignment of Appropriate Firm and Supply Strategies for Competitive Advantage," *International Journal of Operations and Production Management* 25, no. 5 (2005): 403–428; and, Cristian Baier, Evi Hartmann, and Roger Moser, "Strategic Alignment and Purchasing Efficacy: An Exploratory Analysis of Their Impact on Financial Performance," *Journal of Supply Chain Management* 44, no. 4 (2008): 36–52.

Income Statement 2010		
Sales		$200,000
Cost of Goods Sold		$130,000
Gross Margin		$70,000
Transportation Cost	$6,000	
Warehousing Cost	$3,000	
Inventory Carrying Cost	$1,000	
Other Operating Costs	$30,000	
Total Operating Costs	$40,000	
Earnings before interest and taxes		$30,000
Interest		$11,000
Taxes		$6,000
Net Income		$13,000

FIGURE 3-1 Example Income Statement

More obvious direct correlations of logistics decisions occur across the expense categories of the income statement. Specifically, cost of goods sold may be influenced directly by procurement decisions and inbound transportation costs that are part of a product acquisition agreement. In addition, the potential to reduce several categories of operating costs associated with logistics can be significant. Because a large percentage of costs for a typical organization are driven by logistics decisions, many organizations spend considerable time focusing on this connection between logistics and financial performance.[7]

More efficient and effective decisions in the areas of transportation, warehousing, and inventory costs offer great potential for logistics managers to directly influence overall financial performance. Referring to Figure 3-1, a decrease in transportation, warehousing, and/or inventory costs (assuming no change in logistics service performance) translates into lower total operating costs and higher earnings before interest and taxes. In addition, the ability of logistics managers to do *more with less* in areas such as inventory, plant, and equipment can ultimately affect the interest and tax expense categories on the income statement. As can be seen in Figure 3-1, the ability to lower these costs will fall directly to the bottom line (i.e., higher net income).

Balance Sheet

The **balance sheet** reflects the assets, liabilities, and owners' equity at a given point in time. The balance sheet equates assets with liabilities plus owners' equity. **Assets** are what a company owns and come in two temporal forms: *current assets* that can be easily converted to cash (such as stock) and *long-term assets* that have a useful life of more than a year (such as a company-owned warehouse). **Liabilities** are the financial obligations a company owes to another party. Similar to assets, liabilities come in two temporal forms: *current liabilities*, which need to be paid in less than a year, and *long-term liabilities*, which are due over an extended period of time. **Owners' equity** is the difference between what a company owns and what it owes at any particular point in time.

Figure 3-2 is an example of a basic balance sheet. As is the case with the income statement, logistics can affect the balance sheet of an organization in several distinct ways. Order cycle time, order completion rate, and invoice accuracy can influence the speed with which one's customers pay their invoices, thus directly affecting the cash and accounts receivables categories on the balance sheet. Clearly, inventory management decisions that raise or lower

[7] Martin Christopher, *Logistics and Supply Chain Management*, 3rd ed. (Harlow, England: Financial Times/Prentice Hall, 2005).

Balance Sheet 2010	
Assets	
Cash	$20,000
Accounts Receivable	$35,000
Inventory	$15,000
Total Current Assets	$70,000
Net Fixed Assets	$80,000
Total Assets	$150,000
Liabilities	
Current Liabilities	$60,000
Long-term Debt	$30,000
Total Liabilities	$90,000
Shareholders' Equity	$60,000
Total Liabilities and Equity	$150,000

FIGURE 3-2   Example Balance Sheet

inventory levels show up in the inventory category. Expansion of company-owned warehouses and/or acquiring additional equipment to use in one's warehouses will flow through to the fixed assets category. In terms of liabilities, procurement's purchase order quantities are reflected in current liabilities, and financing options for inventory, plant, and equipment could impact long-term debt levels.[8]

STRATEGIC PROFIT MODEL[9]

Several general measures of performance reflect on an organization's financial results and should be understood by logistics managers. As was discussed in the income statement section, profit is a basic financial measure that represents the difference between revenues and expenses. While a raw number such as profit would seem to be adequate, there are issues with reporting financial figures without an appropriate context. Therefore, many financial measures are reported as ratios that indicate the relationship of one number to another. Ratios provide a point of comparison and can provide management with more information than raw numbers alone. For example, the **current ratio**, which is calculated by dividing *total current assets* by *total current liabilities*, measures how well an organization can pay its current liabilities by using only current assets.

Profitability analysis is an important means of assessing logistics activities and proposed changes to a firm's logistical systems. Profitability analysis goes beyond just focusing only on logistics costs by attempting to also include the revenue effect of logistical activities. For example, an improved level of service provided by higher levels of safety stock should bring about increased revenue as customers respond to improved in-stock availability. These revenue effects must be built into the analysis of logistics performance.

A common measure of organizational financial success is return on investment (ROI), which can be measured by return on net worth (RONW) or return on assets (ROA). RONW measures the profitability of the funds that have been invested in the business and is most likely

---

[8] Ibid.

[9] The material in this section is drawn from Drew Stapleton, Joe B. Hanna, Steve Yagla, Jay Johnson, and Dan Markussen, "Measuring Logistics Performance Using the Strategic Profit Model," *International Journal of Logistics Management* 13, no. 1 (2002): 89–107.

of primary interest to investors. ROA provides a more operational perspective by providing insight on how well managers utilize operational assets to generate profits. Thus, ROA becomes a key managerial tool for logistics profitability analysis.

Return on assets (ROA) indicates what percentage of every dollar invested in the business ultimately is returned to the organization as profit. Logistics managers are inherently concerned with assets such as inventory and equipment used to support logistics activities. While these types of assets will show up on the balance sheet, ROA will allow managers to understand how effective their organization is in using these assets to generate profit. The formula for ROA is as follows: ROA = net profit margin × asset turnover.

The **Strategic Profit Model (SPM)** provides the framework for conducting ROA analysis by incorporating revenues and expenses to generate net profit margin, as well as an inclusion of assets to measure asset turnover. **Net profit margin** measures the proportion of each sales dollar that is kept as profit, while **asset turnover** measures the efficiency of the capital employed to generate sales. Together, they form the basis for computing ROA. Figure 3-3 provides the general framework for how to develop an SPM to better understand how a logistics manager's decisions can impact net profit margin, asset turnover, and ultimately, ROA. Suppose, for example, that a logistics manager is able to eliminate some unnecessary inventory; this would reduce the value of current assets as well as total asset value. As a result, sales divided by total assets—asset turnover—would be higher, as would the organization's ROA.

The SPM has the advantage of assisting logistics managers in the evaluation of cash flows and asset utilization decisions. It provides a way for managers to examine how a proposed change to their logistics system influences profit performance and ROA. However, it fails to consider the timing of cash flows, is subject to manipulation in the short run, and fails to recognize assets that are dedicated to specific relationships.[10]

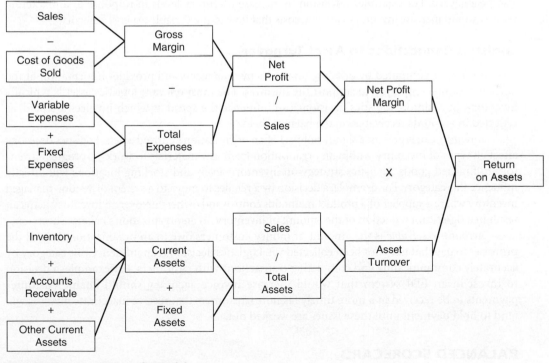

FIGURE 3-3   Strategic Profit Model

[10] Lambert and Burduroglu, "Measuring and Selling the Value of Logistics."

Logistics Connections to Net Profit Margin

Operationally, net profit margin is net profit divided by sales, and looking at net profit and sales as reported on the income statement suggests multiple ways in which net profit margin can be influenced by managerial decisions. The most relevant categories for logistics managers to consider are sales, costs of goods sold, and total expenses.

Sales are the dollar value of all the products or services an organization provides to its customers during a given period of time. The primary influence of logistics activities on sales would be through the improvement of customer service. For example, one logistics decision that could be made by an e-commerce company would be to provide overnight delivery to their customers at no cost. While this type of decision would need to consider the cost implications of providing this level of service, it would be expected that the move would have a positive influence on customer retention and sales.

Cost of goods sold is one category of expenses. It includes all the costs or materials and labor directly involved in producing a product or delivering a service. A significant part of this expense category is the cost of materials that are used to make a product. As such, logistics can influence these costs through procurement activities (e.g., purchasing at volume discounts, reverse auctions) or through any logistics-related efficiency improvements that enable labor to be more productive (e.g., enhanced materials handling processes on a production line).

Total expenses are made up of the variable and fixed costs that are not directly related to making the product or delivering a service. This expense category could include logistics-related activities in areas such as transportation, warehousing, and inventory. For example, a logistics decision to reduce the number of less-than-truckload shipments through a consolidation strategy would show up in the transportation costs category that is part of variable expenses. A decision to sell a company-owned warehouse could directly affect the fixed expenses of running the facility. In addition to understanding the financial effects of a logistics cost reduction, any potential cost increases should also be analyzed. For example, a decision to increase inventory levels in response to a marketing request would increase inventory carrying costs that flow to the variable expense category.

Logistics Connections to Asset Turnover

Asset turnover is computed by dividing total sales by total assets and provides information of the efficiency capital employed to support the business. The most relevant logistics asset is typically inventory. In addition, logistics decisions can influence the speed at which invoices are paid, as reflected in accounts receivable on the balance sheet.

Inventory can represent a significant part of an organization's current assets. Logistics decisions affect all types of inventory within an organization from raw materials to work-in-progress inventory to finished goods. Logistics strategy on inventory levels and stocking locations will directly influence this category. For example, a decision by a retailer to move to a system of vendor-managed inventory where a supplier of a product maintains control and ownership over an inventory item can result in a significant reduction of the amount of inventory on an organization's balance sheet.

Accounts receivable is the amount of money customers owe to an organization. It is all the promises to pay that have not been collected yet. Logistics decisions can influence this category by accurately communicating and completing transactions with customers. For example, a decision to invest in an EDI system that would increase invoice accuracy should enable customer payments to be received in a more timely fashion. Customers that receive inaccurate invoices will tend to hold payment until these issues are worked out.

BALANCED SCORECARD

The **balanced scorecard (BSC)** is a strategic planning and performance management system used extensively in industry, government, and nonprofit organizations. It is based on the belief that management should evaluate their business from four distinct perspectives: customers, internal business processes, learning and growth, and financial. Performance measures are developed to address particular goals or capabilities under one of these four perspectives. While there is no standard set of measures that firms should employee, using a concise, yet comprehensive, set of measures should provide an effective monitoring and management tool for an organization.[11]

When viewed from a logistics point of view, the BSC approach forces managers to look beyond traditional financial measures when conducting a strategic logistics analysis. While the financial perspective is still considered a good indicator of whether or not logistics strategy is being properly implemented and executed, the BSC pushes for a more holistic approach that includes the other three perspectives. To develop an effective logistics scorecard, management first defines the organization's vision and goals. Next, logistics strategies are designed to ensure achievement of this vision and goals. These strategies are then translated into specific tactical performance-enhancing activities, and, finally, appropriate measurements are established for each activity. The next section provides some common logistics measures that can be used in isolation or as part of a logistics BSC.

COMMON LOGISTICS MEASURES

Performance measures are critical for effectively managing logistics activities. A continuing challenge for logistics managers is to develop and maintain an effective set of measures to help make decisions and support the achievement of financial success. As detailed in our discussion of the BSC, both financial and nonfinancial measures should be leveraged. In addition, the measures can be at a strategic, tactical, or operational level.[12] While it is not possible to cover all potential logistics measures in this section, we will highlight some of the more common measures related to a few key areas of logistics management. The section will conclude by providing some guidance on how best to design and implement a system of logistics measures in an organization.

Logistics measurement systems have been traditionally designed to include information on five types of performance: (1) asset management, (2) cost, (3) customer service, (4) productivity, and (5) logistics quality.[13] Several measures are designed and implemented in each of these categories to manage logistics activities such as transportation, warehousing, and inventory management. Research suggests that leading-edge organizations are highly focused on performance measurement across these five areas, and this serves as a platform on which competitive position, value-adding capabilities, and supply chain integration can grow.[14]

Transportation Measures

The major transportation measures focus on such things as labor, cost, equipment, energy, and transit time. The diversity of equipment types, sizes, and products carried will complicate the performance measurement in this area of logistics. Measurements in this area include items such as ROI (investments in transportation equipment), outbound freight costs, transportation labor productivity, on-time deliveries, and in-transit damage frequency, to name a few.

---

[11] Matthew J. Liberatore and Tan Miller, "A Framework for Integrating Activity-Based Costing and the Balanced Scorecard into the Logistics Strategy Development and Monitoring Process," *Journal of Business Logistics* 19, no. 2 (1998): 131–154.

[12] A. Gunasekaran, C. Patel, and E. Tirtiroglu, "Performance Measures and Metrics in a Supply Chain Environment," *International Journal of Operations & Production Management* 21, no. 1–2 (2001): 71–87.

[13] Donald Bowersox and David Closs, *Logistical Management, The Integrated Supply Chain Process* (New York: McGraw-Hill, 1996); and Donald Bowersox, Patricia Daugherty, Cornelia Droge, Dale Rogers, and Daniel Wardlow, *Leading Edge Logistics: Competitive Positioning for the 1990's* (Oak Brook, IL: Council of Logistics Management, 1989).

[14] Stanley E. Fawcett and M. Bixby Cooper, "Logistics Performance Measurement and Customer Success," *Industrial Marketing Management* 27, no. 4 (1998): 341–357.

Warehousing Measures

The primary warehousing measures include such things as labor, cost, time, utilization, and administration. As was the case with transportation, the diversity of warehouse types, sizes, and products carried will complicate the performance measurement in this area. Some common measurements focused on warehouse activities include ROI (investments in warehousing facilities or equipment), warehouse order processing costs, warehouse labor productivity, and picking errors.

Inventory Measures

Inventory management measures tend to relate to the inventory service levels to customers as well as controlling inventory investment across an organization's logistics system. Some common performance measures include obsolete inventory, inventory carrying cost, inventory turnover, and information availability.

Design and Implementation of Measures[15]

While the number and types of measures to use can seem daunting to a logistics manager, several suggestions have emerged from research to provide some guidance. Some of the key things to consider when applying performance measures to logistics activities include the following:

1. Determination of the key measures should be tailored to the individual organization and level of decision making.
2. Data collection and analysis are a major part of a performance measurement system in logistics. This complexity is increased in global settings.
3. Behavioral issues should be considered when establishing and implementing a system of logistics measures. Top management support can help tremendously in this area.
4. Frequent communication and constant updating of the measures is a necessary condition for ensuring they are supporting the stated goals of the organization.

Summary

This chapter focused on the connection between logistics strategy and an organization's financial performance. Beginning with a discussion of the connection between corporate strategy and logistics strategy, the chapter provided an overview of key financial concepts as they relate to forming a better understanding of how logistics decisions can influence financial results.

The chapter also discussed key financial tools, such as the income statement, the balance sheet, the strategic profit model and the balanced scorecard. Various logistics performance measures were also presented. We also looked at some key considerations when implementing a performance measurement system focused on logistics activities.

Questions for Discussion and Review

1. Discuss the differences between corporate-level, business unit–level, and functional-level strategies.
2. Discuss the cost leadership, differentiation advantage, and focus strategies.
3. What are the two key components of an income statement?
4. What are the three key components of a balance sheet?
5. What are the key components of the Strategic Profit Model? How can it be used to examine the effect of logistics decisions?
6. Discuss how logistics decisions affect net profit margin in an organization.
7. Discuss how logistics decisions affect asset turnover in an organization.

---

[15] This section based on findings from Angappa Gunasekaran and Bulent Kobu, "Performance Measures and Metrics in Logistics and Supply Chain Management: A Review of Recent Literature (1995–2004) for Research and Applications," *International Journal of Production Research* 45, no. 12 (2007): 2819–2840.

8. Discuss some of the ways that inventory costs can be reduced in order to affect an organization's financial performance.

9. Do you agree or disagree that return on assets is a good way to examine operational efficiency? Why?

10. How does logistics strategy connect to overall corporate strategy? Is it a one-way or two-way connection?

11. Why is top management commitment necessary for establishing a successful logistics performance measurement system?

12. Most managers believe that while it is possible to connect logistics decisions to costs, the connection to revenue enhancement is difficult to impossible. Do you agree or disagree? Why?

13. Discuss the common logistics measures in transportation, warehousing, and inventory management.

14. Do you think corporate cultures are relevant for designing a logistics measurement system? Why or why not?

15. Why might performance measurement be more difficult in global logistics systems?

16. Discuss how logistics decisions might affect an organization's cost of goods sold.

17. Discuss the common types of information included in traditional logistics measurement systems.

18. What are the major parts of a balanced scorecard? Why are these parts needed?

19. Do you agree or disagree with the sentiment that logistics measurement systems need to include both financial and nonfinancial measures? Why?

20. Discuss some of the key considerations for a logistics manager who is designing and implementing a logistics measurement system in his or her organization.

Suggested Readings

Bhatnagar, Rohit, and Chee-Chong Teo. "Role of Logistics in Enhancing Competitive Advantage: A Value Chain Framework for Global Supply Chains." *International Journal of Physical Distribution & Logistics Management* 39, no. 3 (2009): 202–226.

Berman, Karen, and Joe Knight. *Financial Intelligence: A Manager's Guide to Knowing What the Numbers Really Mean* (Boston, MA: Harvard Business School Press, 2006).

Gunasekaran, Angappa, and Bulent Kobu. "Performance Measures and Metrics in Logistics and Supply Chain Management: A Review of Recent Literature (1995–2004) for Research and Applications." *International Journal of Production Research* 45, no. 12 (2007): 2819–2840.

Green Jr., Kenneth W., Dwayne Whitten, and R. Anthony Inman. "The Impact of Logistics Performance on Organizational Performance in a Supply Chain Context." *Supply Chain Management: An International Journal* 13, no. 4 (2008): 317–328.

Hult, G. Tomas M., David J. Ketchen, Jr., Garry L. Adams, and Jeannette A. Mena. "Supply Chain Orientation and Balanced Scorecard Performance." *Journal of Managerial Issues* 20, no. 4 (2009): 526–544.

Kaplan, Robert S., and David P. Norton. *The Balanced Scorecard: Translating Strategy into Action* (Boston, MA: Harvard Business Press, 1996).

Lambert, Douglas M., and Renan Burduroglu. "Measuring and Selling the Value of Logistics." *International Journal of Logistics Management* 11, no. 1 (2000): 1–17.

Morash, Edward A. "Supply Chain Strategies, Capabilities, and Performance." *Transportation Journal* 41, no. 1 (2001): 37–54.

Neely, Andy. *Business Performance Measurement: Unifying Theory and Integrating Practice.* 2nd ed. (Cambridge, UK: University Press, 2007).

Slone, Reuben E., John T. Mentzer, and J. Paul Dittmann. "Are You the Weakest Link in Your Company's Supply Chain?" *Harvard Business Review* 85, no. 9 (2007): 116–127.

Stapleton, Drew, Joe B. Hanna, Steve Yagla, Jay Johnson, and Dan Markussen. "Measuring Logistics Performance Using the Strategic Profit Model." *International Journal of Logistics Management* 13, no. 1 (2002): 89–107.

Toyli, Juuso, Lotta Hakkinen, Lauri Ojala, and Tapio Naula. "Logistics and Financial Performance: An Analysis of 424 Finnish Small and Medium-Sized Enterprises." *International Journal of Physical Distribution & Logistics Management* 38, no. 1 (2008): 57–80.

Zacharia, Zach G., Nancy W. Nix, and Robert F. Lusch. "An Analysis of Supply Chain Collaborations and Their Effect on Performance Outcomes." *Journal of Business Logistics* 30, no. 2 (2009): 101–124.

CASE

CASE 3-1   Brant Freezer Company

Located in Fargo, North Dakota, the Brant Freezer Company manufactures industrial freezers. These freezers come in one size and are distributed through public warehouses in Atlanta, Boston, Chicago, Denver, Los Angeles, Portland, and St. Louis. In addition, some space is used in the company's Fargo warehouse. Young Joaquin (J. Q.) Brant, with a fresh M.B.A. degree from the University of South Alabama, returned to the family firm, where he had once worked during summers. On his first day of work, J. Q. met with his father. His father complained that they were being "eaten alive" by warehousing costs. The firm's controller drew up a budget each year, and each warehouse's monthly activity (units shipped) and costs were tallied.

| | 2009 Figures | | | | 2010 Figures | | | |
| | Units Shipped | | Warehouse Costs | | Units Shipped | | Warehouse Costs | |
	12 Months January– December	5 Months through May 31	12 Months January– December	5 Months through May 31	Projected 12 Months January– December	Actual 5 Months May 31	Budgeted 12 Months January– December	Actual Costs through May 31
Atlanta	17,431	4,080	156,830	35,890	18,000	4,035	178,000	40,228
Boston	6,920	3,061	63,417	27,915	7,200	3,119	73,000	29,416
Chicago	28,104	14,621	246,315	131,618	30,000	15,230	285,000	141,222
Denver	3,021	1,005[a]	28,019	8,600[a]	3,100	1,421	31,000	14,900
Fargo	2,016	980	16,411	8,883	2,000	804	17,000	9,605
Los Angeles	16,491	11,431	151,975	109,690	17,000	9,444	176,000	93,280
Portland	8,333	4,028	73,015	36,021	9,000	4,600	85,000	42,616
St. Louis	5,921	2,331	51,819	23,232	8,000	2,116	56,000	19,191

EXHIBIT 3-A   Brant Freezer Warehouse Performance

[a]Denver warehouse closed by strike March 4–19, 2009

Exhibit 3-A shows actual 2009 figures for all warehouses, plus actual figures for the first five months of 2010. Projected 12-month 2010 budgets and shipments are also included. Exhibit 3-B shows the income statement for 2009. Exhibit 3-C is the 2009 balance sheet. If you are familiar with Excel or other spreadsheet software, you might try using it to answer the following questions.

Income Statement 2009		
Sales		$4,003,450
Cost of Goods Sold		$937,000
Gross Margin		$3,066,450
Transportation Cost	$657,322	
Warehousing Cost	$735,982	
Inventory Carrying Cost	$567,987	
Other Operating Costs	$345,876	
Total Operating Costs		$2,307,167
Earnings before interest and taxes		$759,283
Interest		$110,000
Taxes		$69,000
Net Income		$580,283

EXHIBIT 3-B   Brant Freezer 2009 Income Statement

Balance Sheet 2009

Assets	
Cash	$706,034
Accounts Receivable	$355,450
Inventory	$1,590,435
Total Current Assets	$2,651,919
Net Fixed Assets	$803,056
Total Assets	$3,454,975
Liabilities	
Current Liabilities	$1,678,589
Long-term Debt	$398,060
Total Liabilities	$2,076,649
Shareholders' Equity	$1,378,326
Total Liabilities and Equity	$3,454,975

EXHIBIT 3-C   Brant Freezer 2009 Balance Sheet

Questions

1. When comparing performance during the first five months of 2010 with performance in 2009, which warehouse shows the most improvement?
2. When comparing performance during the first five months of 2010 with performance in 2009, which warehouse shows the poorest change in performance?
3. When comparisons are made among all eight warehouses, which one do you think does the best job for the Brant Company? What criteria did you use? Why?
4. J. Q. is aggressive and is going to recommend that his father cancel the contract with one of the warehouses and give that business to a competing warehouse in the same city. J. Q. feels that when word of this gets around, the other warehouses they use will "shape up." Which of the seven should J. Q. recommend be dropped? Why?

5. The year 2010 is nearly half over. J. Q. is told to determine how much the firm is likely to spend for warehousing at each of the eight warehouses for the last six months in 2010. Do his work for him.
6. When comparing the 2009 figures with the 2010 figures shown in the table, the amount budgeted for each warehouse in 2010 was greater than actual 2009 costs. How much of the increase is caused by increased volume of business (units shipped) and how much by inflation?
7. Use the 2009 income statement and balance sheet to complete a Strategic Profit Model for J. Q.
8. Holding all other information constant, what would be the effect on ROA for 2010 if warehousing costs declined 10 percent from 2009 levels?

ORGANIZATIONAL AND MANAGERIAL ISSUES IN LOGISTICS

Key Terms

- "C-level" position
- Centralized logistics organization
- Container Security Initiative (CSI)
- Customs Trade Partnership Against Terrorism (C-TPAT)
- Decentralized logistics organization
- Excess capacity
- Flexibility
- Fragmented logistics structure
- Importer Security Filing (ISF) rule
- Logistics social responsibility
- Pilferage
- Productivity
- Relevancy
- Responsiveness
- Reverse logistics
- Tachograph
- Theft
- Transportation Worker Identification Credential (TWIC)
- Unified logistics structure

Learning Objectives

- To examine organizational structure for logistics
- To learn about traditional and contemporary organizational design for logistics
- To explore productivity issues in logistics
- To learn about ways to manage theft and pilferage
- To introduce you to the concept of logistics social responsibility
- To discuss issues associated with reverse logistics
- To expose you to programs designed to lessen the impact of terrorism on logistics systems

This chapter focuses on organizational and managerial issues in logistics, and with respect to organizational issues the degree to which logistics activities are fragmented or unified can play a key role in determining an organization's logistical effectiveness and efficiency. Likewise, logistical effectiveness and efficiency can be enhanced by successfully addressing the wide variety of managerial issues faced by today's logistician.

Chapter 4 first looks at organizing logistics within the firm, with a specific focus on organizational structure for logistics as well as organizational design for logistics. The chapter also looks at select managerial issues in logistics, with a particular emphasis on productivity, theft, social responsibility, reverse logistics, and terrorism.

ORGANIZING LOGISTICS WITHIN THE FIRM

The organization of logistics activities within a firm depends on a number of factors, including the number and location of customers, as well as an organization's size, among others.[1] For example, the number and location of customers might influence whether a firm adopts a

---

[1] David J. Bloomberg, Stephan LeMay, and Joe B. Hanna, *Logistics* (Upper Saddle River, NJ: Prentice Hall, 2002).

centralized or decentralized logistics organization (to be more fully discussed in the following section, "Organization Structure for Logistics"). A company's size might influence the organizing of logistics activities in the sense that there are limitations in the degree of specialization of managerial talents in small firms. In such situations, one consideration in organizing might be to even out the workloads of each manager. Thus, one manager might have transportation-related responsibilities, another manager might be responsible for ordering and inventory management, and a third manager might be assigned warehousing responsibilities.

It's not possible to present a comprehensive discussion of the many organizational topics associated with logistics. As a result, we'll focus on two key organizational topics, namely, organizational structure for logistics and organizational design for logistics.

Organizational Structure for Logistics

Two basic organizational structures are associated with logistics, namely, fragmented and unified. In a **fragmented logistics structure**, logistics activities are managed in multiple departments throughout an organization. For example, a company might assign outbound transportation, demand forecasting, warehousing management, and customer service to the marketing department, whereas procurement, inbound transportation, packaging, and materials handling might be assigned to the manufacturing department. A fragmented logistics structure might also see order management under the control of the accounting department, and inventory management might be under the auspices of the finance department.

Although the example in the previous paragraph suggests logistics activities that are spread across four separate departments, a fragmented logistics structure can come in all shapes and sizes. In a fragmented structure, it's possible for the various logistics activities to be managed in two, three, four, or more departments. Likewise, although our example assigns particular logistics activities to certain departments, there is no established template for which logistics activities are assigned to which departments. For example, an organization might divide inventory management into three categories—raw materials, work in process, and finished goods; raw materials and work-in-process inventories might be managed by the manufacturing department, whereas finished goods inventory might be the purview of the marketing department.

One problem with a fragmented logistics structure is that because logistics activities are scattered throughout the firm, they likely remain subservient to the objectives of the department (e.g., marketing, manufacturing) in which they are housed. Moreover, because effective and efficient logistics is predicated on a high degree of coordination among logistics activities, such coordination can become difficult when the logistics activities are spread throughout an organization.

In a **unified logistics structure**, multiple logistics activities are combined into, and managed as, a single department. The unified structure can be further classified based on the number and type of activities assigned to the department. A basic unified logistics structure might have responsibility for transportation, inventory management, and warehousing. A more progressive unified structure would include these basic activities plus several additional logistics activities such as order management and customer service. An advanced unified structure would include both the basic and progressive activities, along with several other logistics activities such as demand forecasting and procurement.

Regardless of how many, or what type, of logistics activities are managed, the unified logistics structure should be better positioned than the fragmented structure to achieve coordination across the various activities. For example, efficient and accurate communication among inbound and outbound transportation, warehousing, inventory management, procurement, and so on should be facilitated when they are combined into one department. Indeed, so-called leading-edge logistics companies—firms with demonstrably superior logistical capabilities—exhibit different logistics organizational structures than do other organizations. For example, leading-edge organizations are more likely to use a unified, as opposed to fragmented, logistics organizational structure. In addition, leading-edge companies tend to manage more types of logistics activities than do other companies, including less-traditional logistics activities such as demand forecasting and procurement.[2]

An important issue in organizational structure is whether the logistics department should be centralized or decentralized. A **centralized logistics organization** implies that the company maintains a single logistics department that administers the related activities for the entire company from the home office. A **decentralized logistics organization**, in contrast, means that logistics-related decisions are made separately at the divisional or product group level and often in different geographic regions.

There are advantages to both approaches, with a primary advantage of centralization being its relative efficiency, whereas a primary advantage of decentralization is its customer responsiveness. Centralization allows an organization to take advantage of the cost savings that can arise from volume-creating opportunities. Suppose, for example, that an organization has four distribution facilities that annually generate 125,000 pounds of outbound freight, for a total outbound volume of 500,000 pounds. A centralized logistics organization should be able to achieve lower transportation rates for 500,000 pounds of volume than the individual facilities could each achieve for 125,000 pounds of volume.

Advocates of decentralization question the ability of a centralized logistics unit to provide the required levels of customer responsiveness. Indeed, the contemporary marketplace is made up of heterogeneous customers who aren't necessarily well served by centralized logistics practices. For instance, an organization with a mixture of consumer and business-to-business product lines might benefit from decentralization because of differing logistical requirements of consumer and business-to-business segments. Likewise, many global firms need to decentralize operations because of geographic and time distances from the home office. As an example, the time difference between the United States and China (at least 12 hours depending on one's location in the United States) doesn't readily lend itself to timely resolution of issues if managed under a centralized approach. Figure 4-1 illustrates the decentralized organization of a multinational medical supply firm.

Another important issue in logistics organization structure is the job title or corporate rank (e.g., manager, director, vice president, chief) of the top logistics person; indeed, one attribute of leading-edge organizations is that logistics tends to be headed by senior-level (vice president, chief) personnel.[3] Although in recent years logistics has assumed greater importance in many organizations in the sense that the top logistics person holds a vice president title, to date logistics has generally been excluded from holding a **"C-level" position**, which refers to corporate officers such as a chief executive officer (CEO), a chief operating officer (COO), or a chief financial officer (CFO). In other words, there are few companies in which logistics is led by a chief logistics officer.

Organizational Design for Logistics[4]

Organizational design is much broader than the familiar series of boxes and lines that detail who reports to whom in an organization. Organizational design is also concerned with issues such as who makes work-related decisions and the appropriate communication channels between workers and managers, among others. Broadly speaking, three primary types of organizational design are used: hierarchical (also called functional), matrix, and network.

[2] Donald J. Bowersox, Patricia J. Daugherty, Cornelia Dröge, Dale B. Rogers, and Daniel Wardlow, *Leading Edge Logistics: Competitive Positioning for the 1990s* (Oak Brook, IL: Council of Logistics Management, 1989).
[3] Ibid.
[4] Much of the material in this section is drawn from G. Bruce Friesen, "Organization Design for the 21st Century," *Consulting to Management* 14, no. 3 (2005): 32–51.

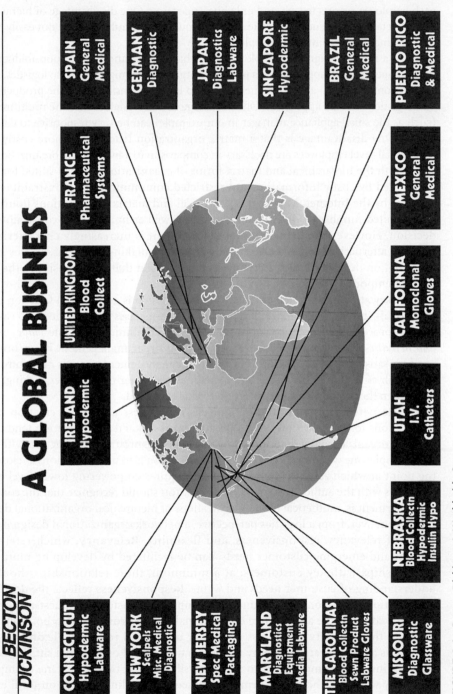

BECTON DICKINSON

A GLOBAL BUSINESS

CONNECTICUT
Hypodermic
Labware

NEW YORK
Scalpels
Misc. Medical
Diagnostic

NEW JERSEY
Spec Medical
Packaging

MARYLAND
Diagnostics
Equipment
Media Labware

THE CAROLINAS
Blood Collectn
Sewn Product
Labware Gloves

MISSOURI
Diagnostic
Glassware

NEBRASKA
Blood Collectn
Hypodermic
Insulin Hypo

UTAH
I.V.
Catheters

CALIFORNIA
Monoclonal
Gloves

IRELAND
Hypodermic

UNITED KINGDOM
Blood
Collect

FRANCE
Pharmaceutical
Systems

SPAIN
General
Medical

GERMANY
Diagnostic

JAPAN
Diagnostics
Labware

SINGAPORE
Hypodermic

BRAZIL
General
Medical

PUERTO RICO
Diagnostic
& Medical

MEXICO
General
Medical

FIGURE 4-1 Becton Dickinson's Worldwide Sources

Source: Courtesy of Becton Dickinson and Company.

59

Hierarchical, or functional, organizational design has its foundations in the command and control military organization, where decision making and communication often follow a top–down flow. One advantage to hierarchical design is flexibility in exercising command in the sense that no one manager commands more than a "limited" number (e.g., 10, 20, 25) of employees. In addition, each employee reports to one, and only one, supervisor. One disadvantage of hierarchical design is that societal changes, such as individuality and questioning authority, are not easily accommodated in a command and control philosophy.

In a matrix design, one employee might have cross-functional responsibilities. For example, the manager of small appliances at a particular organization might report to logistics, marketing, and production executives, and he or she would also have responsibility for the production, marketing, and logistics of small appliances. One advantage of this design is that the multifunction manager (such as the small appliance manager in our example) can be very responsive to customer requirements. One disadvantage is that a matrix organization tends to be more costly because more managerial-level employees are necessary in comparison to a hierarchical organization.

Both the hierarchical and matrix forms of organization are well suited for environments dominated by costly information and restricted communication—constraints that have been lessened by the Internet. Moreover, hierarchical and matrix organizations flourish when there are a limited number of decision alternatives as well as limited time constraints on making a decision. However, the contemporary environment is increasingly characterized by myriad decision alternatives and a shorter time window for making decisions. To this end, a network organization design attempts to create an organization that is responsive to the parameters of the contemporary business environment.

A key attribute of a network organizational design is a shift from function to process. In a functional—hierarchical philosophy, products and processes were divided into easy-to-complete tasks. A process philosophy, by contrast, focuses on combining tasks into *value-creating products and activities.* For example, effective and efficient order management is a process designed to produce satisfied and loyal customers, and order management consists of a number of different tasks such as order receipt, order entry, credit check, order triage, order picking, and so on. It's only when these tasks work in concert that value is created.

The network organization's emphasis on process and value creation has important implications for organization design. Because processes and value creation tend to be customer focused, organizational design should facilitate an organization's interaction with its customers. For example, one way to facilitate customer interaction is to move decisions as close as possible to the point at which action is required, which requires empowering lower-level employees and managers with the authority to make decisions. You should recognize that the concept of worker empowerment is antithetical to the specifications of hierarchical organizational design.

Moreover, from a logistics perspective, a network organizational design is manifested in terms of relevancy, responsiveness, and flexibility. **Relevancy**, which refers to satisfying current and emerging customer needs, can be facilitated by developing mutually beneficial relationships with key customers; at a minimum, these relationships should provide an understanding of customer needs and wants. **Responsiveness** reflects the degree to which an organization can accommodate unique or unplanned customer requests; responsiveness can be achieved when the appropriate decision makers are provided with both relevant information and the authority to address unique or unplanned requests. **Flexibility**, which can be defined as an organization's ability to address unexpected operational situations, is predicated on avoiding early commitment to an irreversible course of action. One example of logistics flexibility would be the postponement of assembly, labeling, and so on until exact customer requirements are known.[5]

---

[5] Donald J. Bowersox, David J. Closs, and Theodore P. Stank, *21st Century Logistics: Making Supply Chain Integration a Reality* (Oak Brook, IL: Council of Logistics Management, 1999), Chapter 3.

MANAGERIAL ISSUES IN LOGISTICS

The logistics discipline would be relatively easy if it entailed simply organizing a logistics system and then putting it into operation. However, well-run companies recognize that logistics systems must not only be organized but also be managed. Although the remaining chapters will discuss managerial issues associated with particular logistics activities (e.g., procurement-specific managerial issues and warehousing-specific managerial issues), the present discussion will look at overarching managerial issues, or those that are not function or activity specific.

Productivity

Productivity is an important managerial issue because it provides insight into the efficiency (or inefficiency) with which corporate resources are being utilized. At a basic level, **productivity** can be defined as the amount of output divided by the amount of input. An understanding of this relationship leads to the recognition that there are but three ways to improve productivity: reduce the amount of input while holding output constant, increase the amount of output while holding input constant, or increase output while at the same time decreasing input.

Understanding the three ways to improve productivity is important to the logistics manager because several logistics activities, particularly warehousing and transportation, are heavily dependent on human labor. For productivity purposes, human labor is considered an input (i.e., workers receive wages or salaries), and most humans are resistant to productivity suggestions that focus on reducing their wages or salaries (i.e., input). As such, productivity improvement efforts in logistics are often directed toward *increasing the amount of output while holding input constant*.

Moreover, in some geographic locations, logistics-operating employees (e.g., warehouse workers and truck drivers) are unionized, and the union contracts can provide a challenge to improving productivity. This is because union work rules are often very specific in the sense that job descriptions spell out in exacting detail the responsibilities associated with a particular job. Thus, if an order picker's forklift were to malfunction, the order picker might be prohibited from remedying the situation because forklift repairs are the responsibility of another group of workers. Although detailed job specifications help create additional employment opportunities, the relative lack of worker flexibility can potentially hinder productivity by increasing inputs (e.g., additional workers, hence additional labor costs) while also decreasing output. For example, the order picker with the malfunctioning forklift may have to delay order picking until the forklift is repaired or another forklift becomes available for use.

Many warehousing facilities have clearly articulated work rules that serve a number of purposes, the most important of which is to keep the workforce in general, and individual employees in particular, from engaging in unproductive and potentially destructive activities. Figure 4-2 shows one warehouse's set of work rules, but it's simply not enough to have a set of clearly articulated work rules—to be effective, the work rules must be enforced.

A distinction needs to be made between warehousing and trucking when discussing the management of labor productivity in logistics. In warehousing, supervisors can be physically present and are expected to be on top of nearly any situation. When a worker in a warehouse falls behind schedule, it is usually noticed relatively quickly, and corrective action can be taken in a timely fashion.

However, once on the road, truck drivers are removed from immediate supervision, and their work becomes more difficult to evaluate. Truck drivers can fall behind schedule or be delayed for a variety of reasons such as traffic conditions, a bottleneck at a loading dock, or perhaps too much time socializing with fellow drivers at a particular truck stop. Initially, a manager has little choice but to accept the driver's explanation for the delay. As such, it is necessary to have control mechanisms so that drivers who often encounter uncontrollable delays (e.g., traffic conditions) can be distinguished from those who encounter controllable delays (e.g., socializing with fellow drivers).

Technological considerations play an increasingly important role in managing truck drivers and their productivity. For example, some firms photograph or videotape drivers making pickups at their loading docks. Moreover, Figure 4-3 shows the printout of the activity recorded

Ours is a company that has been built on service to its customers. Our business has grown both in the number of customers and in the area which we serve. We are constantly striving to improve our service, because it is only through growth and progress that a company can give to its employees the good wages, increased benefits, and job security that everyone wants.

In order to meet these aims it is necessary to adhere to a set of rules. Whenever people work together they have certain rights and privileges. Along with these rights they have certain obligations and responsibilities. So that each employee will know what is expected of him we have drawn up a list of work rules which are necessary for the orderly and efficient operation of our business. By following these rules you contribute to the progress of the company and therefore to the stability of your own job. These rules therefore benefit you rather than hinder you. They are fair rules and to keep them fair to everyone they will be enforced in every required situation.

These rules are listed in two groups, by type of violation, and are as follows:

- Violations subject to discharge on the first offense.
- Violations subject to constructive discipline.

Violations Subject to Discharge on the First Offense

(1) The possession of, drinking of, or use of any alcoholic beverages or narcotic drugs on company property; or being on company premises at any time under the influence of alcohol, or drugs, or while suffering from an alcoholic hangover which materially affects work performance.

(2) The transportation of, or failure to notify the company of, unauthorized persons on company equipment or its property.

(3) Theft or misappropriation of company property or the property of any of its customers or employees.

(4) Deliberate or malicious damage to the company's equipment and warehouse facilities or to the merchandise and property of its customers.

(5) Intentional falsification of records in any form, including ringing another employee's time card, or falsifying employment application.

(6) Fighting while on duty or on company premises or provoking others to fight.

(7) Smoking in a building or van, or any restricted area, or while loading or unloading merchandise and other items.

(8) Immoral or indecent conduct which affects work performance or makes the employee unsuited for the work required.

(9) Unauthorized possession of, or carrying of, firearms or other weapons.

(10) Insubordination — refusal to perform assigned work or to obey a supervisor's order, or encouraging others to disobey such an order.

Violations Subject to Constructive Discipline

The rules printed below are subject to constructive discipline. This means that for the first offense you will be given a constructive reprimand. For a second offense you will receive a disciplinary layoff without pay, the length of which will depend upon the seriousness of the offense; subject to the terms of the collective bargaining agreement which may exist between employee and union. For a third offense you will be discharged, subject to the collective bargaining agreement.

If you have had a violation, followed by a record of no violations for a nine (9) month period, the original violation will be withdrawn from your record.

(1) Excessive tardiness regardless of cause. (Being tardy and not ready to perform work at the designated starting time may at the company's option result in the employee being sent home without pay.)

(2) Absenteeism without just cause and excessive absenteeism regardless of cause. If you must be absent for a justifiable reason notify the company in advance. Justified absence will be

FIGURE 4-2 Sample Warehouse Work Rules

Source: Courtesy of American Warehouse Association.

excused if the company is notified as soon as possible before the beginning of the shift; however, too many justified and excused absences may be grounds for constructive discipline as well as unjustified, unexcused absence. If you are absent from work for three consecutive work days without notification followed by failure to report for work on the fourth day you will automatically be removed from the payroll with the notification "quit without notice."

(3) Failure to work reasonable overtime.

(4) Unauthorized absence from assigned work location.

(5) Failure to observe proper break periods, lunch periods, and quitting times, unless otherwise directed by your supervisor.

(6) Disregard for common rules of safety, safe practices, good housekeeping and sanitation.

(7) Unauthorized or negligent operation or use of machines, tools, vehicles, equipment and materials.

(8) Loss or damage to the property of the company or its customers which could have been reasonably avoided.

(9) Failure to complete work assignments within a reasonable length of time or loafing on such assignments.

(10) Garnishments not satisfied prior to the hearing before the court issuing same.

(11) Gambling on company premises.

(12) Use of immoral, obscene or indecent language on company premises.

(13) Trying to persuade or organize other employees to disobey any of these rules and regulations. ∎

FIGURE 4-2 Continued

FIGURE 4-3 Printout from a Truck Tachograph

Source: Argo Instruments, Inc., Fleet Management Systems.

by a **tachograph**, a recording instrument that is installed inside a truck and produces a continuous, timed record of the truck's operations, its speed, and its engine speed. From the information on the tachograph chart, one can tell how efficiently the truck and driver are being used. If the driver works on a regular route, it may be possible to rearrange the stops so that the driver can avoid areas of traffic congestion. Bad driving habits, such as high highway speeds and excessive engine idling, can also be detected. In case of an accident, the tachograph chart is invaluable in reporting and explaining what occurred just prior to impact.

The interfaces involving wireless communications, global positioning systems (GPS), and graphical information systems (GIS) offer tremendous technology-related opportunities to improve driver productivity. GPS use satellites that allow companies to compute vehicle position, velocity, and time, whereas GIS allow companies to produce digital maps that can drill down to site-specific qualities such as bridge heights and customer locations. GPS and GIS are evolving toward a situation in which instant updates can be provided to GIS databases—data that can be leveraged to provide real-time route planning that can direct drivers away from accidents and other traffic bottlenecks.

Our discussion thus far has focused on worker productivity, but asset productivity is also an important consideration for logistics managers. One asset-related productivity concern involves space utilization, or the percent of available space that's actually being used. **Excess capacity**, or unused available space, can be unproductive because it may result in the purchase of additional equipment or facilities—a situation that adds to costs (input) but not necessarily to output, thus resulting in lower productivity.

Consider the example of a company that built an approximately 700,000 square foot warehouse as a replacement for a smaller storage facility. A review of the new warehouse one year after its opening revealed that approximately 55 percent of the available space was actually being utilized, and the company concluded (reluctantly) that it could have satisfied current and future demand with a 450,000 square foot facility. The 700,000 square foot facility caused the company to purchase additional real estate, incur higher construction costs, and incur higher materials handling costs (in the form of storage racks and forklifts) when compared to a 450,000 square foot facility. From a managerial perspective, the 700,000 square foot facility handled the same amount of product (output), at a higher cost (input), as could a 450,000 square foot facility, thus resulting in decreased productivity.

A second asset-related productivity concern focuses on improving the output from existing assets. Southwest Airlines, for example, is able to fly more trip segments per day with its airplanes than many of its competitors because Southwest's planes spend less time parked at airport gates. Another way of improving the output from existing assets involves extending their revenue-producing lifespan. For example, one of the authors worked for a trucking company that regularly utilized 25-year-old tractors to serve certain customers. From one perspective, the 25-year-old tractors were extremely productive in the sense that a fully depreciated asset was generating revenues. Having said this, the 25-year-old tractors lacked certain safety features found on newer-model tractors and were less fuel efficient than newer-model tractors.

Theft and Pilferage

Theft (stealing), which can be defined as the taking and removing of personal property with the intent to deprive the rightful owner of it,[6] is a managerial issue that confronts many organizations. Unfortunately, it is often difficult to accurately quantify the impact of theft, in part because some companies are hesitant to report this data—a reported theft serves as direct evidence of a logistics system shortcoming. Having said this, anecdotal evidence suggests that cargo theft increased as U.S. economic conditions began to deteriorate in late 2007.[7]

You might be wondering why logisticians would be concerned about theft, particularly because many organizations carry insurance to compensate themselves in cases of theft. However, even though insurance may reimburse an organization for the market value of the

---

[6] *www.m-w.com/dictionary*.
[7] Barry Tarnef, "Into Thin Air," *World Trade*, September 2008, 50–52.

stolen items, the time and costs (e.g., documentation) associated with theft tend not to be covered by insurance. A second logistical concern is that theft results in the planned flow of goods being interrupted and can lead to stockouts in the distribution channel.

In addition, theft can factor into the facility location decision in the sense that some organizations will avoid locating their facilities in areas characterized by high crime rates.[8] It's also possible for the stolen products to reappear in the market at a lower price to compete with products that have moved through traditional channels. Indeed, there are suggestions that approximately 2 percent of the products available on Internet auction sites are actually stolen goods.[9]

Pilferage, which refers to employee theft, cannot be eliminated, and both warehousing and transportation operations are especially vulnerable to pilferage. Managing pilferage can be challenging for the logistics manager, and the managing begins with the hiring process. In fact, one of the best ways to manage pilferage is to avoid hiring people who are predisposed to steal, such as people with credit, alcohol, or drug problems. Some organizations utilize psychological tests as part of the hiring process in an effort to identify prospective employees who might pilfer.

Organizations can better manage pilferage if they have clearly articulated and enforced pilferage-related policies. To this end, experts recommend that the best pilferage policy should be based on zero tolerance because problems inevitably arise for those companies that tolerate a "small amount" of pilferage. For example, there may be disagreement in terms of how to operationalize "amount"—are we concerned with the number of units or the dollar value of items? Once this has been established, then what is meant by "small"—does, say, five units or $75 qualify as "small"? Quite simply, a zero-tolerance policy means that pilferage exceeding zero units or zero dollars is unacceptable.

One of the most effective methods of protecting goods from theft or pilferage is to keep them moving through the system. Goods waiting in warehouses, in terminals, or to clear customs are more vulnerable to theft than goods that are moving. No list of methods of protecting goods is complete; determined thieves are likely to overcome almost any hindrance or barrier placed in their way. However, a few suggestions are offered here, mainly to reflect the breadth of measures that might be taken:

- Decals are required for autos in employee parking lots, and nonemployees may be required to park in designated areas as well as to register with a company receptionist. This makes it more difficult for outsiders to access an organization's facilities.
- Forklifts in warehouses are locked at night, making it difficult to reach high items or to move heavy items.
- Seals (small wirelike devices that once closed cannot be reopened without breaking) are used more and more, with dispatchers, drivers, and receiving personnel all responsible for recording the seal number and inspecting its condition. Figure 4-4 shows a seal used for truck trailer or container doors.
- Electronic tags or strips are embedded in products at the time of their manufacture, and they can activate alarms at warehouse or retail store doors.
- Organizations should take a proactive approach to theft; waiting until theft reaches "unacceptable" levels might mean that certain dysfunctional behavior has been permitted for so long that it has come to be viewed as typical or acceptable.
- Experts suggest that companies should facilitate an employee's ability to report theft and other aberrant behavior, such as through a hotline that guarantees anonymity as well as retribution from potential retaliation or retribution.

Note that many of the preceding suggestions are common sense in nature (e.g., decals, locked forklifts); indeed, common sense is viewed as a basic foundation for controlling theft. Importantly, commonsense approaches to system security are often no cost, or low cost, in nature.[10]

---

[8] Perry A. Trunick, "To Catch a Thief," *Logistics Today*, July 2005, 35–40.
[9] Julia Kuzeljevich, "The Seven Deadly Sins in Warehouse Security," *Canadian Transportation & Logistics*, April 2006, 44.
[10] Michael Imlay, "Off-Highway Robbery," *Off-Road Business*, November 2005, 55–57.

FIGURE 4-4   The Small Wire Shown on the Left Will Break if the Trailer Door Latch Is Opened.
The Plug at its Upper End Is Marked with a Unique Number
Source: CGM Security Solutions, Inc.

The discussion to this point has been primarily focused on domestic theft and pilferage. When goods move in international commerce, particularly by ship, they are much more vulnerable to theft and pilferage. Piracy attacks on ships have become a major concern in the twenty-first century, and unlike the somewhat romanticized pirates of movies and literature who wore eye patches and carried swords, contemporary pirates use speedboats, smart phones, GPS, and automatic weapons. In addition, approximately 20 percent of all pirate attacks in recent years have involved petroleum tankers, which is of concern because of the potential for an environmental accident as well as the fact that some tankers could be used as floating bombs.

To underscore the seriousness of pirate attacks for today's logistics manager, the International Maritime Bureau, an arm of the International Chamber of Commerce, reported 240 pirate attacks worldwide in the first six months of 2009 compared to 114 pirate attacks during the same time period in 2008.[11] Much of the 2009 increase was due to a surge in pirate attacks off the Somalian coast, and managerial responses to these attacks included outrunning the pirates, rerouting vessels away from Somalia, vehicle escort services, and armed professionals. The cost of these responses to pirate attacks—just for Somalia—has been estimated at approximately *$500 million annually!*[12]

Logistics Social Responsibility

The social responsibility concept suggests that an organization's obligations transcend purely economic considerations such as profit maximization. While the corporate social responsibility concept has existed since the early 1970s, the concept of **logistics social responsibility**, or corporate social responsibility issues that relate directly to logistics,[13] did not emerge until the mid-1990s.

Potential logistics social responsibility dimensions include the environment, ethics, diversity, safety, philanthropy, and human rights, among others, and myriad activities or practices can be used

---

[11] *www.ics-ccs.org.*
[12] Robert R. Frump, "Danger at Sea," *The Journal of Commerce*, February 16, 2009, 20–24.
[13] Craig R. Carter and Marianne M. Jennings, "Logistics Social Responsibility: An Integrative Framework," *Journal of Business Logistics* 23, no. 2 (2002): 145–180.

to assess each of these dimensions. In terms of the environment, for example, organizations might focus on reusing and recycling products, reducing the amount of packaging, improving energy efficiency, and reducing various types of pollution. Ethical considerations include improperly sharing information, as well as bribes and gift giving, whereas diversity might evaluate the use of minority and female suppliers. Safety-related activities or practices include the safe movement and storage of products, particularly those of a hazardous nature, preventive vehicle maintenance, and proper workplace equipment (e.g., hardhats and goggles). Philanthropic logistics activities might include the donation of excess or obsolete inventory to charitable organizations, and sweatshop labor continues to be a preeminent human rights consideration.

Energy efficiency is a prominent logistics social responsibility issue for many organizations, and we'll take a closer look at energy efficiency in the following paragraphs. Warehousing and transportation represent two logistics activities where most energy costs occur and where energy-saving measures should be focused. For instance, design, lighting, and roofing represent three possible energy control areas in warehousing. With respect to design, facilities might be positioned so that dock doors aren't placed on the north side of a building (most cold winds blow from the north). Lighting provides a variety of opportunities for managing energy consumption; skylights, large windows that incorporate solar energy, and high-efficiency lighting can reduce electricity usage between 20 and 60 percent. In addition, high-efficiency lighting generally provides better lighting quality and thus potentially improves workplace safety (another logistics social responsibility issue).

Roofing, which tends to be the largest exposed surface of a warehouse facility, is often overlooked as an area for energy control. White roof material, for example, tends to reflect sun-generated heat, while darker roof colors such as black and gray tend to absorb sun-generated heat, which results in increased electricity consumption for cooling the interior areas of a warehouse. Moreover, some warehousing facilities are being designed with grass roofs, which lower energy consumption during the summer months.

Transportation is a second logistics activity where considerable energy savings can take place, particularly because transportation is a primary consumer of energy. Indeed, transportation accounts for approximately two-thirds of all petroleum consumption in the United States. As a result, many transportation providers are actively searching for ways to reduce their fuel consumption, which in turn will reduce their fuel costs. The U.S. Environmental Protection Agency's Smart Way Transport Partnership, established in 2004, helps companies to address environmental challenges such as fuel consumption. Results have been promising, as illustrated by Kohl's Department Stores, which has reduced empty truck movements by nearly four million miles since joining the Partnership.[14]

Managing Reverse Logistics

You might be surprised to learn that the annual cost of **reverse logistics**, which refers to the process of managing return goods, exceeds $100 billion in just the United States. In addition, reverse logistics can be four to five times more expensive than forward logistics, and the reverse logistics process can take 12 times as many steps (assessing the returned product, repairing the returned product, etc.) as the forward logistics process.[15]

The reverse logistics process focuses on three critical factors—(1) why products are returned, (2) how to optimize reverse logistics, and (3) whether reverse logistics should be managed internally or outsourced to a third party[16]—and each will be discussed below. With respect to the first factor, products are returned for a variety of reasons, such as the customer making an error in ordering or the shipper making an error when filling an order. Goods may also be returned because of a product recall, which occurs when a hazard or defect is discovered in a manufactured or processed item, and its return is mandated by a government agency.

[14] Marianne Wilson, "Green Transport," *Chain Store Age*, January 2009, 55.
[15] David Blanchard, "Moving Ahead by Mastering the Reverse Supply Chain," *Industry Week*, June 2009, 58–59.
[16] John Paul Quinn, "Are There Ever Any Happy Returns?" *Logistics Management*, June 2005, 63–66.

Another reason for returned products is that in an age of increasingly sophisticated consumer products, customers sometimes cannot get whatever they bought to work. Products may also be returned simply because the buyer no longer wants, needs, or likes it, or because of damage in transit or in handling.

The second factor in managing returned goods, optimizing reverse logistics, involves a number of strategic and tactical considerations. One basic decision concerns the design of the reverse logistics system, such as whether return operations should be incorporated into existing warehousing and production facilities. If so, how will returned products be segregated from other products in an effort to reduce loss of returned product, prevent mixing returned and nonreturned goods, and prevent returned products from mistakenly being shipped out of the particular facility?[17]

Optimizing reverse logistics is incumbent on goods being carefully counted and the appropriate records (e.g., accounting, inventory) being adjusted accordingly. After a returned item has been counted and recorded, it is important to evaluate the item in terms of a series of questions:

- Is the product damaged and unsalable, or can it be refurbished and resold?
- Was it returned as part of an overstock arrangement with a retailer?
- Is it a product that is being recalled?
- Is the item in an unopened package that can go into inventory for immediate resale?
- Does the item need to undergo special testing?
- What is the item's worth?
- How do the company's returned goods policies apply to this item?[18]

The scope of the preceding questions indicates that returned goods should not be managed as an afterthought. This leads directly to the third critical factor in managing reverse logistics—whether reverse logistics should be managed internally or outsourced to a third party. If a company decides to internally manage returned goods, there must be recognition that one or more employees will have returned goods as their primary, if not only, job responsibility. Because reverse logistics can be so different (e.g., irregular flow of product and small shipments) from forward logistics, the outsourcing of reverse logistics continues to grow in popularity.[19] In fact, there are several third-party logistics companies, such as GENCO, whose primary expertise involves returns management.

Lessening the Impact of Terrorism on Logistics Systems

Terrorism can be defined as "the unlawful use or threatened use of force or violence by a person or an organized group against people or property with the intention of intimidating or coercing societies or governments, often for ideological or political reasons."[20] Although terrorism is often viewed through a political or ideological lens, it can have important implications for commerce and for managing logistics systems.

It's no exaggeration to state that the terrorist attacks in the United States on September 11, 2001, were a defining moment that brought terrorism considerations to the forefront of logistics management. The September 11 terrorist attacks have profoundly impacted logistics practices on a worldwide basis, and processes, procedures, and activities that might have been given minimal attention prior to September 11 are now viewed from an entirely different perspective.

Consider the storage and transport of hazardous materials, which prior to September 11 was primarily managed from a safety perspective. Today, although safety remains an important perspective, the storage and transport of hazardous materials is also managed with an eye to potential terrorist considerations. For example, there are continuing efforts to reroute rail shipments of hazardous materials—because of terror concerns—away from major U.S.

---

[17] Ibid.
[18] Ibid.
[19] Bob Trebilcock, "Outsourcing Reverse Logistics," *Modern Materials Handling*, June 2008, 18–20.
[20] Terrorism, *The American Heritage® Dictionary of the English Language*, 4th ed. (n.d.). Retrieved from Dictionary.com website: *http://dictionary.reference.com/browse/terrorism*.

population centers; we've already indicated in this chapter that oceangoing petroleum tankers have the potential to be mobile bombs.

One response to the September 11 attacks involved the creation of a new federal agency in the United States, the Department of Homeland Security (DHS); two of its major aims are to prevent terrorist attacks in the United States as well as to reduce the vulnerability of the United States to terrorism. A total of 22 separate U.S. government entities were incorporated into the DHS, with the Transportation Security Administration (TSA) and Customs and Border Protection (CBP) being two of the most important from a logistics perspective.

The TSA is responsible for the security of the U.S. transportation system. You might be familiar with the TSA because it is the agency that conducts the passenger screening at U.S. commercial airports. The TSA also plays a number of roles with respect to freight security, such as using dogs to screen airfreight. In addition, the TSA was responsible for developing a **Transportation Worker Identification Credential (TWIC)**, which is a common credential used to identify workers across all modes of transportation. One of the key attributes of TWIC is that the corresponding card contains both personal and biometric data, with the biometric data being used to exclude certain workers from secure areas at ports and terminals. The TWIC program became fully operational in early 2009, and while implementation has been relatively smooth, several problems, such as lengthly processing time for credentials, have surfaced.[21]

CBP is responsible for securing U.S. borders to protect the American people and the U.S. economy. One key CBP function is inspecting cargo, and a number of high-profile CBP initiatives have affected the management of logistics systems. The Trade Act of 2002, which required submission of advanced electronic data on all shipments entering and leaving the United States, is aimed at identifying high-risk shipments that might threaten U.S. safety and security. Table 4-1 summarizes the manifest times for inbound and outbound shipments involving air, rail, water, and truck.

In particular, oceangoing containers destined for the United States are receiving much greater scrutiny today than prior to September 11. One of the things learned after the 2001 terrorist attacks was that a relatively small percentage of containers that arrived at U.S. ports was scanned to learn about their actual contents. This alarmed some U.S. legislators, and the result was a series of proposals that culminated in legislation requiring 100 percent scanning of U.S.-bound containers by 2012.

TABLE 4-1 Timeline for Presenting Electronic Advance Manifest Information

Inbound to the United States

Mode	Timeline
Air and courier	Four hours prior to arrival in the United States, or "wheels up" from certain nearby airports
Rail	Two hours prior to arrival at a U.S. port of entry
Ocean vessel	Twenty-four hours prior to lading at foreign port
Truck	Free and Secure Trade (FAST): 30 minutes prior to arrival in the United States; non-FAST: one hour prior to arrival in the United States

Outbound from the United States

Mode	Timeline
Air and courier	Two hours prior to scheduled departure from the United States
Rail	Two hours prior to the arrival of the train at the border
Ocean vessel	Twenty-four hours prior to departure from U.S. port where cargo is laden
Truck	One hour prior to the arrival of the truck at the border

Source: Erlinda Byrd, "Rules for Improving Cargo Security," *Customs and Border Protection Today*, March 2004.

---

[21] R. G. Edmonson, "TWIC's Forgotten Few," *The Journal of Commerce*, April 20, 2009, 20.

This scanning, which is to be done prior to a container being loaded onto ships at non-U.S. ports, has the potential to be quite disruptive to international trade because a number of nondomestic ports currently do not have the technology required to inspect containers. These ports would have to acquire and install the relevant scanning technology (which is quite expensive), discontinue sending containers to the United States, or route containers through other nondomestic ports that are equipped with the relevant technology. However, in early 2009, DHS Secretary Janet Napolitano suggested that the 2012 scanning deadline probably would not be achieved, in part because of difficulties in achieving agreements with all nondomestic ports that ship containerized cargo to the United States.[22]

Another example of the CBP's emphasis on containerized shipments is the **Container Security Initiative (CSI)**, an agreement in which some of the world's ports agree to allow U.S. customs agents to identify and inspect high-risk containers bound for the United States before they are loaded onto ships. Approximately 60 international ports, including such major ports as Hong Kong, Singapore, Shanghai, and Rotterdam, currently participate in the CSI.

One of the best-known CBP programs enacted since September 11 is the **Customs Trade Partnership Against Terrorism (C-TPAT)**, in which public (CBP) and private (e.g., retailers and manufacturers) organizations work together to prevent terrorism against the United States through imports and transportation. Private organizations apply to CBP for C-TPAT certification, and the process involves demonstrating that organizations have improved the physical security of their containerized shipments as well as the ability to track people who have access to the containerized shipments. Although the government-provided benefits to C-TPAT certification include fewer security inspections of inbound containers along with faster processing time through customs, many companies have discovered that the C-TPAT process has also led to a reduction in cargo theft, pilferage, and loss.[23]

As if logistics managers aren't potentially overwhelmed by TWIC, CSI, C-TPAT, and other terrorism-related acronyms, CBP is also responsible for implementing and enforcing the **Importer Security Filing (ISF) rule**, also known as "10+2," which went into effect in early 2009. The "10+2" moniker refers to the fact that importers are required to file 10 pieces of information, and carriers two pieces of information, before cargo is loaded at non-U.S. water ports; Table 4-2 lists the "10+2" information requirements.

TABLE 4-2	Information Required for 10 + 2 Rule

Importer:
1. Manufacturer's name and address
2. Seller's name and address
3. Buyer's name and address
4. Ship to name and address
5. Scheduled container stuffing location
6. Consolidator's name and address
7. Importer of record
8. Consignee identification number
9. Country of origin
10. Harmonized tariff schedule at minimum six-digit level

Carriers:
1. Vessel stow plan
2. Container status message

Source: R. G. Edmonson, "10 + 2 = Now," *The Journal of Commerce*, June 1, 2009, 13.

---

[22] R. G. Edmonson, "DHS's New Boss," *The Journal of Commerce*, March 9, 2009, 16.
[23] Christine Blank, "Cruise through Customs," *Multichannel Merchant*, August 2006, 46–47.

The initial feedback on "10 + 2" suggests that while erroneous filings have declined from 30 percent to less than 5 percent, some importers struggle to get timely, accurate, and complete information for their 10 required pieces of information. In addition, importers are concerned with the costs of "10 + 2" compliance, which can include the cost of upgrading their information systems, the actual cost of filing the 10 pieces of information, and potential monetary penalties for erroneous information or failure to file the information.[24]

Summary

This chapter covered two primary topics, namely, organizational and managerial issues in logistics. With respect to the former, the chapter looked at organizational structure for logistics and discussed the fragmented and unified solutions as well as centralized and decentralized logistics organizations. Organizational design for logistics was also discussed, with a particular emphasis on network organizational design and its implications for logistics.

The chapter also looked at select managerial issues that are not function or activity specific, including productivity, theft, and pilferage, logistics social responsibility, managing reverse logistics, and terrorism. The terrorist activities of September 11, 2001, have profoundly affected the management of logistics systems, and select activities of the Transportation Security Administration and Customs and Border Protection were discussed.

Questions for Discussion and Review

1. Discuss several issues that influence the organization of logistics activities within a firm.
2. Compare and contrast the fragmented and unified logistics organizational structures.
3. What are the differences between a centralized and a decentralized logistics department?
4. Describe the hierarchical and matrix organizational design.
5. From a logistics perspective, how is network organizational design manifested in terms of relevancy, responsiveness, and flexibility?
6. Define productivity, and discuss the ways in which productivity can be improved.
7. In what ways can a unionized workforce be a challenge to improving worker productivity?
8. Discuss how technological considerations can help in managing truck drivers and their productivity.
9. What are some potential challenges to improving productivity by getting more output from existing assets?
10. Discuss the reasons why logisticians might be concerned with theft.
11. How can logistics managers attempt to control pilferage?
12. Explain how piracy attacks on ships are a serious issue for today's logistics manager.
13. Describe some potential logistics social responsibility dimensions.
14. How can warehouses control their energy usage in terms of design, lighting, and roofing considerations?
15. Discuss the reasons why products might be returned.
16. What questions should be asked after a returned item has been counted and recorded?
17. What are some ways in which the Transportation Security Administration is attempting to improve the security of the U.S. transportation system?
18. In what ways is the legislation requiring 100 percent scanning of U.S.-bound containers likely to be disruptive to international trade?
19. Discuss the Customs Trade Partnership Against Terrorism (C-TPAT).
20. What concerns have importers expressed with implementation of the Importer Security Filing rule?

Suggested Readings

Autry, Chad W., Zach G. Zacharia, and Charles W. Lamb. "A Logistics Strategy Taxonomy." *Journal of Business Logistics* 29, no. 2 (2008): 27–51.

Bernon, Michael, and John Cullen. "An Integrated Approach to Managing Reverse Logistics." *International Journal of Logistics: Research and Applications* 10, no. 1 (2007): 41–56.

Cantor, David E. "Workplace Safety in the Supply Chain: A Review of the Literature and Call for Research." *International Journal of Logistics Management* 19, no. 1 (2008): 65–83.

Ekwell, Daniel. "The Displacement Effect in Cargo Theft." *International Journal of Physical Distribution & Logistics Management* 39, no. 1 (2009): 47–62.

---

[24] R. G. Edmonson, "10 + 2 = Now," *The Journal of Commerce*, June 1, 2009, 10–13.

Gamelas, Theophilos, and Mark Johnson. "A Systems Approach to Transportation Security." *Journal of Transportation Law, Logistics and Policy* 74, no. 2 (2007): 156–180.

Kraska, James, and Brian Wilson. "Maritime Piracy in East Africa." *Journal of International Affairs* 62, no. 2 (2009): 55–68.

Kumar, Sameer, and Janis Verruso. "Risk Assessment for the Security of Inbound Containers at U.S. Ports: A Failure, Mode, Effects, and Criticality Analysis Approach." *Transportation Journal* 47, no. 4 (2008): 26–41.

Maloni, Michael J., and Michael E. Brown. "Corporate Social Responsibility in the Supply Chain: An Application in the Food Industry." *Journal of Business Ethics* 68, no. 1 (2006): 35–52.

Mollenkopf, Diane, and G. Peter Dapiran. "World-Class Logistics: Australia and New Zealand." *International Journal of Physical Distribution & Logistics Management* 35, no. 1 (2005): 63–74.

Spence, Laura, and Michael Bourlakis. "The Evolution from Corporate Social Responsibility to Supply Chain Responsibility: The Case of Waitrose." *Supply Chain Management: An International Journal* 14, no. 4 (2009): 291–302.

Stock, James R., and Jay P. Mulki. "Product Returns Processing: An Examination of Practices of Manufacturers, Wholesalers/ Distributors, and Retailers." *Journal of Business Logistics* 30, no. 1 (2009): 33–62.

Whitfield, Gwendolyn, and Robert Landeros. "Supplier Diversity Effectiveness: Does Organizational Culture Really Matter?" *Journal of Supply Chain Management* 42, no. 4 (2006): 17–29.

CASE

CASE 4-1   Red Spot Markets Company

The Red Spot Markets Company operates a chain of grocery stores in New England. It has a grocery distribution center in Providence, Rhode Island, from which deliveries are made to stores as far north as Lowell, Massachusetts, as far west as Waterbury, Connecticut, and as far northwest as Springfield, Massachusetts. No stores are located beyond the two northernmost points in Massachusetts. Stores to the west are supplied by a grocery warehouse located in Newburgh, New York. The Providence grocery distribution center supplies 42 Red Spot retail stores.

Robert Easter, Red Spot's distribution manager, is responsible for operations at the Newburgh and Providence distribution centers. By industry standards, both centers were fairly efficient. However, of the two, the Providence center lagged in two important areas of control: worker productivity and shrinkage. Warehouse equipment and work rules were the same for both the Newburgh and Providence centers, yet the throughput per worker hour was 4 percent higher for the Newburgh facility. Shrinkage, expressed as a percentage of the wholesale value of goods handled annually, was 3.6 percent for the Newburgh center and 5.9 percent for the Providence center. Jarvis Jason had been manager of the Providence distribution center for the past three years and, at great effort, managed to narrow the gap between the performance rankings of the two Red Spot facilities. Last week he requested an immediate reassignment, and Easter arranged for him to become the marketing manager for the Boston area, which would involve supervising the operations of 11 Red Spot markets. The transfer involved no increase in pay.

Easter needed a new manager for the Providence distribution center, and he picked Fred Fosdick for the task. Fosdick graduated from a lesser Ivy League college, where he majored in business with a concentration in logistics. He had been with Red Spot for two years and had rearranged the entire delivery route structure so that two fewer trucks were needed. As part of this assignment, he also converted the entire system to one of unit loads, which meant everything loaded on or unloaded from a Red Spot truck was on a pallet. Fosdick was familiar with the operations of both the Providence and Newburgh centers. He has been in each facility at least 50 different times. In addition, he spent two weeks at the Providence center when the loading docks were redesigned to accommodate pallet loading. Fosdick was surprised that Jason had requested his reassignment to a slot that did not involve an upward promotion. That was his first question to Easter after Easter asked whether he was interested in the Providence assignment.

"I'm sorry you started with that question," said Easter to Fosdick. "Now we'll have to talk about the troublesome aspects of the assignment first, rather than the positive ones. To be frank, Fred, one of the union employees there made so much trouble for Jason, he couldn't stand it."

"Who's the troublemaker?" asked Fosdick.

"Tom Bigelow," was Easter's answer.

Fosdick remembered Bigelow from the times he had been at the Providence center. Thomas D. Bigelow was nicknamed T. D. since his days as a local Providence high school football star. Fosdick recalled that during work breaks on the loading dock, Bigelow and some of the other workers would toss around melons as though they were footballs. Only once did they drop a melon. Fosdick recalled hearing the story that Bigelow had received several offers of athletic scholarships when he graduated from high school. His best offer was from a southern school, and he accepted it. Despite the fact that the college provided a special tutor for each class, Bigelow flunked out at the end of his first semester and came back to Providence, where he got a job in the Red Spot warehouse.

In the warehouse, Bigelow was a natural leader. He would have been a supervisor except for his inability to count and his spotty attendance record on Monday mornings. On Mondays, the day that the warehouse was the busiest because it had to replenish the stores' weekend sales, Bigelow was groggy, tired, and irritable. On Mondays, he would sometimes hide by loading a forklift with three pallets, backing into any empty bay, and lowering the pallets in position (which hid the lift truck from view), and he would fall asleep. The rest of the week Bigelow was happy, enthusiastic, and hardworking. Indeed, it was he who set the pace of work in the warehouse. When he felt good, things hummed; when he was not feeling well or was absent, work dragged.

"What did Bigelow do to Jason?" Fosdick asked Easter.

"Well, as I understand it," responded Easter, "about two weeks ago Jason decided that he had had it with Bigelow and so he suspended him on a Monday morning after Bigelow showed up late, still badly hung over. It was nearly noon, and he told Bigelow to stay off the premises and to file a grievance with his union shop steward. He also told Bigelow that he had been documenting Bigelow's Monday performance—or nonperformance—for the past six months and that Red Spot had grounds enough to fire Bigelow if it so chose. He told Bigelow to go home, sober up, and come back on Tuesday when they would discuss the length of his suspension. Bigelow walked through the distribution center on his way out, and I'm sure Jason felt he had control of the matter."

"However," continued Easter, "by about one o'clock, Jason realized he had a work slowdown on his hands. Pallet loads of bottled goods were being dropped, two forklifts collided, and one lift truck pulled over the corner of a tubular steel rack. At 4:00 P.M. quitting time, there were still three trucks to be loaded; usually they would have departed by 3:30. Rather than pay overtime, Jason let the workforce go home, and he and the supervisor loaded the last three trucks.

"On Tuesday, Bigelow did not show up, and the slowdown got worse. In addition, retail stores were phoning with complaints about all the errors in their orders. To

top it off, at the Roxbury store, when the trailer door was opened, the trailer contained nothing but empty pallets. Tuesday night somebody turned off the switches on the battery chargers for all the lift trucks, so on Wednesday, the lift-truck batteries were dying all day. I got involved because of all the complaints from the stores. On Wednesday, Jason got my permission to pay overtime, and the last outgoing truck did not leave until 7:00 P.M. In addition we had to pay overtime at some of our retail stores because the workers there were waiting for the trucks to arrive. While I was talking to Jason that afternoon, he indicated that he had fired Bigelow."

Easter lit his cigar and continued. "On Wednesday, I decided to go to Providence myself, mainly to talk to Jason and to determine whether we should close down the Providence center and try to serve all our stores out of Newburgh. This would have been expensive, but Providence was becoming too unreliable. In addition, we had a big weekend coming up. When I showed up in Providence, Jason and I had breakfast together in my hotel room Thursday morning, and he told me pretty much the same thing I've been telling you. He said he knew Bigelow was behind all the disruption and that today, Thursday, would be crucial. I've never seen Jason looking so nervous. Then we drove to the distribution center. Even from a distance, I could tell things were moving slowly. The first echelon of outgoing trucks, which should have been on the road, was still there. Another 20 of our trucks were waiting to be loaded. On the other end of the building, you could see a long line of arriving trucks waiting to be unloaded; usually there was no line at all. I knew that our suppliers would start complaining because we had established scheduled unloading times. However, I decided not to ask Jason whether he had begun receiving phone calls from them."

"Inside the center, the slowdown was in effect. Lift-truck operators who usually zipped by each other would now stop, turn off their engines, dismount, and carefully walk around each other's trucks to ensure there was proper clearance. Satisfied of this, they would then mount, start their engines, and spend an inordinate amount of time motioning to each other to pass. This was only one example. When we got to Jason's office, he had a message to phone Ed Meyers, our local attorney in Providence, who handles much of our labor relations work there. He called Meyers and was upset by the discussion. After he hung up, he told me that Meyers had been served papers by the union's attorney, charging that Wednesday's firing of Bigelow was unjustified, mainly because no provable grounds existed that Bigelow was behind the slowdown. Meyers was angry because, in firing Bigelow on Wednesday, Jason may have also blown the suspension of Bigelow on Monday. Jason and I started talking, even arguing. I talked so much that my cigar went out," said Easter, "so I asked Jason, who was sitting behind his desk, for a match. He didn't carry matches but looked inside his center desk drawer for one. He gasped, and I didn't know what was the matter. He got up, looking sick, and walked away from his desk. He said that a dead rat had been left in his desk drawer, and he wanted a transfer. He was in bad shape and the distribution center was in bad shape, so I had the opening in the Boston area and I let him have it. Actually, right now he and his family are vacationing somewhere in Eastern Canada. He needs the rest."

Fosdick was beginning to feel sorry that he knew all the details, but he persisted. "Then what?" he asked Easter.

"Well, I took over running the distribution center. I phoned Meyers again, and he and I had lunch. He thought that Jason had blown the case against Bigelow and that we should take him back. So on Friday, Meyers, Bigelow, the union attorney, the shop steward, Bigelow's supervisor, and I met. Jason, of course, was not there. It was a pleasant meeting. Everything got blamed on poor Jason. I did tell Bigelow that we would be documenting his performance and wanted him to know that Jason's successor, meaning you, was under my instructions to tolerate no nonsense. Bigelow was so pleasant that day that I could not imagine him in the role of a troublemaker. The amazing thing was that, when he went out into the center to resume work, a loud cheer went up and all the drivers started blowing their lift-truck horns. For a moment, I was afraid all the batteries would run down again. But I was wrong. They were plain happy to see Bigelow back. You know, the slowdown was still in effect when Bigelow walked onto the floor. I'd say it was 10:00 A.M. and they were an hour behind. Well, let me tell you what happened. They went to work! By noon we were back on schedule, and by the end of the shift we were a half-hour ahead of schedule. In fact, the last half-hour was spent straightening up many of the bins that had been deliberately disarranged during the slowdown. I tell you, Tom Bigelow does set the work pace in that warehouse!"

"So what do you suggest I do at the center?" asked Fosdick.

"Well, the key is getting along with Bigelow. Talk to Meyers about the kind of records you should keep in case you decide to move against Bigelow. Be sure to consult with Meyers before you do anything irreversible. Frankly,

I don't know whether Bigelow will be a problem. We never had trouble with him that I knew about before Jason was there. According to Bigelow and the union attorney, Jason had it in for Bigelow. If I were you, I'd take it easy with Bigelow and other labor problems. See what you can do instead about the inventory shrinkage."

On the next Monday morning, Fosdick showed up at the Providence distribution center. After gingerly looking in all his desk drawers, he had a brief meeting with his supervisors and then walked out to meet the entire workforce on a one-to-one basis. Many remembered Fosdick from his earlier visits to the facility. Because it was a Monday morning, he had not expected to encounter Bigelow, who was present, clear eyed, alert, and enthusiastic. Bigelow was happy to see Fosdick and shook his hand warmly. Bigelow then excused himself, saying he had to return to work. The truck dispatcher said that the workforce was ahead of schedule again: It was 11:00 A.M., and they were about 15 minutes ahead. Fosdick returned to his office, and there was a phone message from Ed Meyers. Meyers asked to postpone their luncheon for that day until Tuesday noon. Then Robert Easter called to ask how things were going on Fosdick's first day. Easter was pleased that things were going smoothly.

It was lunchtime. Fosdick decided to walk to a small café where he had eaten at other times. It was two blocks from the distribution center and on the side away from the office. So he walked through the center, which was quiet since it was closed down for lunch. He walked by the employees' lunchroom and heard the normal sounds of 50 people eating and talking. Just outside the lunchroom was one lift truck with an empty wooden pallet on it. As Fosdick watched, one of the stock clerks came out of the lunchroom with an opened case of sweet pickles from which three jars had been taken. Next came another stock clerk with an opened carton of mustard from which two bottles had been removed. One of the clerks suddenly saw Fosdick and said weakly, "We take these opened cases to the damaged merchandise room." Fosdick went into the lunchroom. There, on the center table were cases of cold meat, cheese, soft drinks, mayonnaise, and bread. All had been opened and partially emptied to provide the workers' lunches.

Bigelow was making himself a large sandwich when he saw Fosdick approach. "Don't get uptight," he said to Fosdick. "You've just come across one of the noncontract fringe benefits of working at the Red Spot Providence distribution center. May I make you a sandwich?"

Questions

1. How should Fosdick respond to the immediate situation?
2. What controls might have been used by Red Spot Markets to reduce or eliminate the problems discussed in the case?
3. What longer-range steps should Fosdick take to control the operations of the Providence distribution center?
4. What longer-range steps should Fosdick take to improve the Providence distribution center's productivity?
5. What longer-range steps can Fosdick take to reduce the distribution center's high rate of shrinkage?
6. Assume that Fosdick decides that the practice of free lunches from the opened cases of goods must be stopped. Develop and present the arguments he should give in a meeting with the union shop steward.
7. (This is a continuation of Question 6.) Assume, instead, that you are the union shop steward. Develop and present your argument that the free lunches represent a long-standing employee benefit enjoyed by the distribution center's employees and that management's attempt to stop them is a breach of an unwritten contract and will be resisted.
8. Much of the situation described in the case seems to evolve around the personality of T. D. Bigelow. How should he be treated? Why?

SUPPLY CHAIN MANAGEMENT

Because supply chain management and procurement are inextricably linked with logistics management, Part II of *Contemporary Logistics* takes a closer look at these two topics. Chapter 5 looks at the supply chain management concept, which connects the entities within one's supply chain. Also covered are concepts and entities that affect one's ability to integrate their network of relationships.

Chapter 6 examines procurement, a function for ensuring a reliable supply of materials. It will examine aspects of this essential linkage between suppliers and buyers and the mechanism that initiates the movement of materials into one's logistics system.

5 | THE SUPPLY CHAIN MANAGEMENT CONCEPT

Key Terms

- Agile supply chain
- Bullwhip effect
- Fast supply chain
- Fourth-party logistics (lead logistics provider)
- Global Supply Chain Forum (GSCF) model
- Leagility
- Lean supply chain
- Partnerships
- Perfect orders
- Process Classification Framework (PCF)
- Supply chain
- Supply chain analytics
- Supply chain collaboration
- Supply chain management (SCM)
- Supply Chain Operations Reference (SCOR) model
- Third-party logistics (logistics outsourcing; contract logistics)

Learning Objectives

- To learn about supply chains and their management
- To appreciate the attributes affecting supply chain management implementation
- To consider potential barriers to supply chain management implementation
- To examine supply chain integration

As pointed out in Chapter 1, contemporary thinking views logistics as part of **supply chain management (SCM)**, and there are many examples of the importance of the logistics function to SCM. Research on underperforming supply chains, defined as those exhibiting poor service, unproductive assets, or high variable operating costs, suggests that logistical considerations can be crucial to achieving desired levels of supply chain performance. For example, damaged goods resulting from shoddy materials-handling practices might result in poor service. Poor inventory turnover, an example of unproductive assets that can drag down firm performance, can be addressed by consolidating stocking points and eliminating slow-moving items. Finally, high transportation costs, one example of margin-reducing operating costs, call for an examination of modal or carrier selection policies as well as of transportation routing decisions.[1]

This chapter provides an overview of SCM and begins with a description of its evolution along with a discussion of three prominent models of SCM. This will be followed by an examination of key attributes that can affect a firm's ability to implement SCM, such as customer power and interorganizational collaboration. Next comes a discussion of select barriers to SCM implementation, and the chapter concludes with a look at supply chain integration.

---

[1] Foster Pinley and Chap Kistler, "Fixing an Underperforming Supply Chain," *Supply Chain Management Review* 9, no. 8 (2005): 46–52.

EVOLUTION OF SUPPLY CHAIN MANAGEMENT

SCM is a relatively new concept in the sense that it was rarely mentioned in either the academic or practitioner communities prior to 1990. According to Professor Mentzer and colleagues, "the supply chain concept originated in the logistics literature, and logistics has continued to have a significant impact on the SCM concept."[2] More specifically, a dominant logistical philosophy throughout the 1980s and into the early 1990s involved the integration of logistics with other functional areas of an organization in an effort to achieve the enterprise's overall success.[3] The early to mid-1990s witnessed a growing recognition that there could be value in coordinating the various business functions not only within organizations but *across* organizations as well—in what can be referred to as a SCM philosophy.

Since the early to mid-1990s academics, practitioners and industry associations have suggested a number of definitions for both supply chains and SCM. As was the case when defining logistics, it's important to have a common understanding of what is meant by *supply chain* and *supply chain management* in order to support management efforts in this area.

A **supply chain** "encompasses all activities associated with the flow and transformation of goods from the raw material stage (extraction), through to the end user, as well as the associated information flows."[4] Figure 5-1 presents illustrations of several generic types of supply chains, and it's important to note several key points. First, supply chains are not a new concept in that most organizations traditionally have been dependent on suppliers, and organizations traditionally have served customers. For example, Procter & Gamble (P&G), a prominent multinational company that produces consumer packaged goods, needed raw materials to make soap, as well as customers for the soap, when it was founded in 1837; today, P&G still needs raw materials to make soap—and still needs customers for its soap.

Supplier ⟷ Organization ⟷ Customer

Figure 1a—Direct supply chain

- -

Supplier's supplier ⟷ ... ⟷ Supplier ⟷ Organization ⟷ Customer ⟷ ... ⟷ Customer's customer

Figure 1b—Extended supply chain

- -

Ultimate supplier ⟷ ... ⟷ Supplier ⟷ Organization ⟷ Customer ⟷ ... ⟷ Ultimate customer

Third-party logistics supplier

Financial provider

Market research firm

Figure 1c—Ultimate supply chain

FIGURE 5-1 Different Supply Chain Configurations

Source: John T. Mentzer et al., "Defining Supply Chain Management," *Journal of Business Logistics* 22, no. 2 (2001): 1–25.

---

[2] John T. Mentzer et al., "Defining Supply Chain Management," *Journal of Business Logistics* 22, no. 2 (2001): 1–25.
[3] Richard F. Poist, "Evolution of Conceptual Approaches to Designing Business Logistics Systems," *Transportation Journal* 25, no. 1 (1986): 55–64.
[4] Robert B. Handfield and Ernest L. Nichols, Jr., *Introduction to Supply Chain Management* (Upper Saddle River, NJ: Prentice Hall, 1999).

Figure 5-1 also points out that some supply chains can be much more complex (in terms of the number of participating parties) than others, and coordinating complex supply chains is likely to be more difficult than doing so for less-complex supply chains. Moreover, complex supply chains may include "specialist" companies, such as third-party logistics (3PL) providers, to facilitate coordination among various supply chain parties. Note also that customers are an integral component in supply chains, regardless of their complexity.

With respect to SCM, the Council of Supply Chain Management Professionals (CSCMP) offers the following definition:

> Supply Chain Management encompasses the planning and management of all activities involved in sourcing and procurement, conversion, and all Logistics Management activities. Importantly, it also includes coordination and collaboration with channel partners, which can be suppliers, intermediaries, third-party service providers, and customers. In essence, Supply Chain Management integrates supply and demand management within and across companies.[5]

Moreover, although nearly any organization can be part of a supply chain(s), SCM "requires overt management efforts by the organizations within the supply chain."[6]

Successful SCM requires companies to adopt an enterprise-to-enterprise point of view, which can cause organizations to accept practices and adopt behaviors that haven't traditionally been associated with buyer–seller interactions (as will be seen in the following section). Moreover, successful SCM requires companies to apply the systems approach (previously mentioned in Chapter 1) across all organizations in the supply chain. When applied to supply chains, the systems approach suggests that companies must recognize the interdependencies of the decisions made in major functional areas within, across, and between firms. In turn, the goals and objectives of individual supply chain participants should be compatible with the goals and objectives of other participants in the supply chain. For example, a company that is committed to providing a high level of customer service might be out of place in a supply chain comprised of companies whose primary goal is cost containment.

While several SCM models have been proposed, three of the more prominent viewpoints are established by the Supply Chain Council [**Supply Chain Operations Reference (SCOR) model**], the Supply Chain Management Institute [**Global Supply Chain Forum (GSCF) model**], and the APQC (Process Classification Framework). The prominence of these models is attributable to the fact that they identify business processes in such a way that the processes can actually be implemented, and thus evaluated, by organizations; each of the models is also supported by major corporations.[7] The proposed models are briefly described next.

The SCOR identifies five key processes—*Plan*, *Source*, *Make*, *Deliver*, *Return*—associated with SCM (see Figure 5-2). Moreover, closer analysis of the five key processes, and their definitions, indicates the important role of logistics in SCM. It can be argued that logistics has some involvement in both sourcing and making; for example, with respect to making, recall the discussion in Chapter 1 about the concept of postponement resulting in value-added activities being performed in warehousing facilities. Alternatively, logistics can be heavily involved in delivering and returning; the definition of delivery specifically mentions the logistics components of order management, transportation management, and distribution management.

---

[5] *www.cscmp.org.*
[6] Mentzer et al., "Defining Supply Chain Management."
[7] Douglas M. Lambert, Sebastian J. Garcia-Dastugue, and Keely L. Croxton, "An Evaluation of Process-Oriented Supply Chain Management Frameworks," *Journal of Business Logistics* 26, no. 1 (2005): 25–51; and Christopher R. Moberg, Kate Vitasek, Theodore P. Stank, and Abre Pienaar, "Time to Remodal," *Supply Chain Quarterly* 2, no. 3 (2008): 32–44.

SCOR Process	Definitions
Plan	Processes that balance aggregate demand and supply to develop a course of action which best meets sourcing, production, and delivery requirements
Source	Processes that procure goods and services to meet planned or actual demand
Make	Processes that transform product to a finished state to meet planned or actual demand
Deliver	Processes that provide finished goods and services to meet planned or actual demand, typically including order management, transportation management, and distribution management
Return	Processes associated with returning or receiving returned products for any reason. These processes extend into post delivery customer support

FIGURE 5-2   Five Processes in the Supply Chain Operations Reference (SCOR) Model
Source: SCOR Model, Version 10.0, Pittsburgh: Supply Chain Council, Inc.

Eight relevant processes are identified in the GSCF model (see Figure 5-3)—*customer relationship management, supplier relationship management, customer service management, demand management, order fulfillment, manufacturing flow management, product development and commercialization,* and *returns management.* As is the case in the SCOR model, logistics also plays an important role in the processes associated with the GSCF model. For example, logistical considerations such as on-time pickup and delivery might be part of the customer service management process, whereas logistics can contribute to supplier relationship management (SRM) in terms of inbound material flow. Moreover, reverse logistics is a key logistical consideration for the returns management process.[8]

The **Process Classification Framework (PCF)** is organized around twelve cross-enterprise operating and management processes (see Figure 5-4). The operating processes include the following: *develop vision and strategy; design and develop products and services; market and sell products and services; deliver products and services;* and *manage customer service.* The management processes are the following: *develop and manage human capital; manage information technology; manage financial resources; acquire, construct, and manage property; manage environmental health and safety; manage external relationships;* and *manage knowledge, improvement, and change.* The PCF has several clear connections with logistics management activities, and these connections are most pronounced in the deliver products and services operating process where a distinct subprocess exists for managing logistics and warehousing. The PCF and SCOR model provide open-source benchmarking data for the logistics activities that are part of their established processes, while the GSCF model has an assessment tool that includes logistics-related items.

ATTRIBUTES AFFECTING SCM IMPLEMENTATION

A number of key attributes affect a firm's ability to implement SCM, including customer power, a long-term orientation, leveraging technology, enhanced communication across organizations, inventory control, interorganizational collaboration, and the use of supply chain facilitators.

---

[8] Douglas M. Lambert, "The Eight Essential Supply Chain Management Processes," *Supply Chain Management Review* 8, no. 6 (2004): 18–26.

GSCF Process	Definitions
Customer Relationship Management	Provides the structure for how relationships with customers are developed and maintained
Customer Service Management	Represents the company's face to customer
Demand Management	Balances customer requirements with supply chain capabilities
Order Fulfillment	Encompasses all activities necessary to define customer requirements, design a network, and enable a firm to meet customer requests while minimizing total delivered cost
Manufacturing Flow Management	Includes all activities necessary to obtain, implement, and manage manufacturing flexibility in the supply chain and to move products through the plants
Supplier Relationship Management	Provides the structure for how relationships with suppliers are developed and maintained
Product Development and Commercialization	Provides the structure for working with customers and suppliers to develop products and bring them to market
Returns Management	Manages activities associated with returns, reverse logistics, "gatekeeping," and return avoidance within the firm and across key members of the supply chain

FIGURE 5-3 Eight Processes in the Global Supply Chain Forum (GSCF) Model

Source: Douglas M. Lambert, "The Eight Essential Supply Chain Management Processes," *Supply Chain Management Review*, September 2004, 18–26.

PCF Process	Definitions
Develop Vision and Strategy	Defines the business concept and vision along with developing and managing the business strategy
Develop and Manage Products and Services	Involves the development and management of products and services
Market and Sell Products and Services	Includes understanding the markets, customers and capabilities in order to develop appropriate marketing strategies
Deliver Products and Services	Provides logistical support for the inbound and outbound materials to support produced or service delivery
Manage Customer Service	Development and management of a customer service strategy
Develop and Manage Human Capital	Recruitment, development and retention of employees
Manage Information Technology	Management of information technology resources
Manage Financial Resources	Involves accounting and financial activities in support of business operations
Acquire, Construct and Manage Property	Acquisition and management of productive and nonproductive assets
Manage Environmental Health and Safety (EHS)	Planning and management of EHS activities
Manage External Relationships	Management of external stakeholder and government relationships
Manage Knowledge, Improvement, and Change	Involves benchmarking and change management activities

FIGURE 5-4 Twelve Processes in the Process Classification Framework (PCF)

Source: Process Classification Framework, Version 5.1.0, Houston: APQC.

Although each of these is discussed in the following paragraphs as discrete entities, interdependencies exist among them. For example, advances in technology could facilitate enhanced communication across organizations, whereas a long-term orientation could facilitate interorganizational collaboration.

Customer Power

You're probably familiar with the adage that "information is power." In recent years, the customer has gained tremendous power over buying decisions, in large part because of greater access to information.[9] This access, largely fueled by the Internet, allows the consumer to become highly knowledgeable about an individual organization and its products—as well as also becoming highly knowledgeable about competing organizations and their products.

This increased power of customers has important implications for the design and management of supply chains. For example, because customer needs and wants can change relatively quickly, supply chains should be fast and agile, rather than slow and inflexible. A **fast supply chain** emphasizes a speed and time component, whereas an **agile supply chain** focuses on an organization's ability to respond to changes in demand with respect to volume and variety.[10] Failure to be fast and agile can result in decreased market share, reduced profitability, lower stock price, or dissatisfied customers for supply chain participants.

Furthermore, the customer power concept suggests that traditional factory-driven, push-oriented supply chains should be replaced by customer-centric, pull-oriented ones. And where traditional supply chains use metrics (measures) such as labor costs and freight costs, customer-centric supply chains are concerned with **perfect orders** (i.e., *simultaneous* achievement of relevant customer metrics such as on-time delivery and correct order quantity) and total SCM cost.[11]

However, it is important to design supply chains according to market needs. An agile supply chain may be most appropriate in contexts where demand is volatile, and the customer requirement for variety is high management cost.[12] In cases where customer demand is relatively stable and variety is low, establishing a **lean supply chain** may be a more appropriate goal. Lean supply chains are focused on eliminating all waste, including time, and to ensure a level schedule. Sometimes referred to as **leagility**, both of these paradigms have been combined in practice as a way to focus part of one's supply chain on a timely response to fluctuating customer orders and/or product variety and another part of the supply chain on leveling out the planning requirements to smooth production output.[13]

Long-Term Orientation

Well-run supply chains improve the long-term performance of the individual companies and the supply chain as a whole. This emphasis on long-term performance suggests that supply chains should employ a long-term orientation as opposed to a short-term orientation with the various participants—suppliers, customers, intermediaries, and facilitators. Importantly, a long-term orientation tends to be predicated on *relational exchanges*, whereas a short-term orientation tends to focus on *transactional exchanges*. For relational exchanges to be effective, a transactional "What's in it for me?" philosophy needs to be replaced by a relational "What's in it for us?" philosophy.

---

[9] Glen. L. Urban, "Customer Advocacy: A New Era in Marketing," *Journal of Public Policy and Marketing* 24, no. 1 (2005): 155–159.

[10] Martin Christopher, "The Agile Supply Chain," *Industrial Marketing Management* 29, no. 1 (2000): 37–44.

[11] Kevin O'Marah, "The Leaders' Edge: Driven by Demand," *Supply Chain Management Review* 9, no. 4 (2005): 30–36.

[12] Denis Towill and Martin Christopher, "The Supply Chain Strategy Conundrum: To be Lean or Agile or To be Lean and Agile," *International Journal of Logistics: Research and Applications* 5, no. 3 (2002): 299–309.

[13] J. Ben Naylor, Mohamed M. Naim, and Danny Berry, "Leagility: Integrating the Lean and Agile Manufacturing Paradigm in the Total Supply Chain," *International Journal of Production Economics* 62 (1999): 107–118.

Relational exchanges tend to be characterized by a far different set of attributes than are transactional exchanges, including—but not limited to—trust, commitment, dependence, investment, and shared benefits.[14]

At a minimum, relational exchange may result in individual supply chain participants having to rethink (and rework) their approaches to other supply chain participants. Commitment, for example, suggests that supply chain participants recognize the importance of maintaining the relationship that has been established, as opposed to regularly changing participants to take advantage of short-term bargains. Moreover, relational exchanges—and, by extension, SCM—cannot be successful without information sharing among various participants. However, this is much more easily said than accomplished, in part because the previously mentioned business adage, "Information is power," can make supply parties somewhat hesitant to share information, lest they jeopardize their competitive advantages or expose organizational shortcomings.

Partnerships, which can be loosely described as positive, long-term relationships between supply chain participants, are part and parcel of a relational exchange. Key characteristics of supply chain partnerships include, but are not limited to, high interdependence among supply chain participants, shared information, compatible goals, mutual trust, and buying decisions based on value as opposed to cost or price. Recent research has empirically demonstrated favorable relationships between supply chain partnerships and performance-related outcomes such as cost reduction, improved profits, and revenue growth.[15] Organizations should establish systematic processes for identifying, developing, implementing, and continuously improving the key relationships in their supply chain.[16]

Leveraging Technology

It is argued that technology has been at the center of changes taking place that affect the supply chain, and that two key factors—computing power and the Internet—have sparked much of this change.[17] With respect to the former, supply chains can be complex entities consisting of multiple organizations, processes, and requirements. As such, attempts at applying mathematical modeling techniques to supply chains in an effort to maximize shareholder wealth or minimize costs (1) were not very practical prior to the advent of computers and (2) took a great deal of time, even after computers were introduced. However, the introduction and continued development of the computer chip now allows for fast, low-cost mathematical solutions to complex supply chain issues.

Business futurists Joseph Pine and James Gilmore have referred to the Internet as "the greatest force of commodization known to man, for both goods and services."[18] With respect to supply chains, the Internet can facilitate efficiency and effectiveness by providing opportunities for supply chains to simultaneously improve customer service and reduce their logistics costs.[19]

It's important to recognize that the Internet has important implications for both business-to-consumer links and business-to-business links within supply chains. Indeed, the Internet can allow one supply chain party to have virtually instantaneous visibility to the same data as other parties in the supply chain. Such instantaneous visibility offers the opportunity for supply chains to become more proactive and less reactive, which can translate into lower inventories and improved profitability throughout the supply chain.[20]

---

[14] Robert M. Morgan and Shelby D. Hunt, "The Commitment—Trust Theory of Organizational Commitment," *Journal of Marketing* 58, no. 3 (1994): 20–38.

[15] Rachel Duffy and Andrew Fearne, "The Impact of Supply Chain Partnerships on Supplier Performance," *International Journal of Logistics Management* 15, no. 1 (2004): 57–71.

[16] Douglas M. Lambert and A. Michael Knemeyer, *Building High Performance Business Relationships* (Sarasota, FL: Supply Chain Management Institute, 2009).

[17] Barbara Rosenbaum, "The Technology-Enabled Supply Chain Network," *Industrial Management* 43, no. 6 (2001): 6–10.

[18] B. Joseph Pine and James H. Gilmore, *The Experience Economy* (Boston, MA: Harvard Business School Press, 1999).

[19] George Gecowets and Michael J. Bauer, "The Effect of the Internet on Supply Chain & Logistics," *World Trade* 13, no. 9 (2000): 71–80.

[20] Rosenbaum, "The Technology-Enabled Supply Chain Network."

Enhanced Communication Across Organizations

Because supply chains depend on huge quantities of real-time information, it is essential that this information can be seamlessly transmitted across organizations. For example, retail point-of-sale information can be transmitted directly to suppliers and translated into orders for replenishment of product. Alternately, vendors may allow customers to query vendor inventory records to determine what products are in stock and where the stocks are located. The enhanced communication across organizations is dependent on both technological capabilities and a willingness to share information (part of a long-term orientation). Figure 5-5 shows a handheld computer with radio-frequency connections used to communicate some real-time inventory information regarding a truck and its contents.

FIGURE 5-5   A handheld scanning machine transmits real-time shipment information.

Inventory Control

Another attribute of SCM involves various activities that can be lumped under the inventory-control rubric. For example, SCM attempts to achieve a smoother and better-controlled flow of inventory with fewer expensive inventory "lumps" along the way. In this situation, the focus is on reducing the so-called **bullwhip effect**, which is characterized by variability in demand orders among supply chain participants—the end result of which is inventory *lumps*.[21] In short, one aspect of inventory control in SCM is to move from a pattern of stops and starts to a continuous flow.

A second aspect of inventory control in SCM involves a reduction in the amount of inventory in the supply chain. Inventory can be reduced in a number of ways, such as smaller, more frequent orders; the use of premium transportation; demand-pull, as opposed to supply-push, replenishment; and the elimination or consolidation of slower-moving product, among others. However, prominent supply chain disruptions in the early part of the twenty-first century—terrorist attacks (such as September 11, 2001), natural disasters (such as the 2010 earthquake in Haiti and the 2005 hurricane that hit New Orleans), and health pandemics [such as sudden acute respiratory syndrome (SARS) and swine flu (H1N1)]—have caused some supply chains to reassess their emphasis on inventory reduction.

Interorganizational Collaboration

Because a primary objective of SCM is to optimize the performance of the supply chain as a whole, rather than optimizing the performance of individual organizations, collaboration among supply chain participants is essential. Collaboration within an organization (internal collaboration) can sometimes be problematic, so how can an organization successfully collaborate with other supply chain participants (external collaboration)?

A great deal has been written about supply chain collaboration in recent years, and a review of what's been written might leave the reader confused in the sense that some writings indicate that supply chain collaboration is currently more wishful thinking than practical reality, that few organizations engage in collaboration, and those that do haven't experienced much improvement in performance. Alternatively, other writings indicate that supply chain collaboration is widely applied, and participating organizations experience noticeable performance-related improvements. One reason for the widely divergent views of supply chain collaboration is that there are myriad definitions of it. For our purposes, **supply chain collaboration** will be defined as "cooperative, supply chain relationships—formal or informal—between manufacturing companies and their suppliers, business partners or customers, developed to enhance the overall business performance of both sides."[22]

In addition, some writers believe that supply chain collaboration is strategic in nature (a "narrower" view), whereas others view collaboration as ranging from transactional to strategic behaviors (a "broader" view). We'll take the broader view, which suggests that supply chain collaboration can be classified as transactional, tactical information sharing, or strategic in nature (summarized in Figure 5-6). According to this rubric, although transactional and tactical information sharing are currently the most prevalent types of collaboration, strategic collaborations are increasing and offer the best opportunity for improving supply chain performance.[23]

It is important to realize that interorganizational coordination of activities, functions, and processes can be a daunting task. A large part of the challenge of interorganizational coordination involves the tremendous amount of information to be transmitted across, and be available to, supply chain participants. To this end, supply chain software packages have been developed to

---

[21] Hau L. Lee, V. Padmanabhan, and Seungin Whang, "The Bullwhip Effect in Supply Chains," *Sloan Management Review* 38, no. 3 (1997): 93–102.
[22] John Matchette and Andy Seikel, "How to Win Friends and Influence Supply Chain Partners," *Logistics Today*, December 2004, 40–42.
[23] Ibid.

Relationship Type	Definition	Examples of Data Exchanged
Transactional	Integrate and automate the flow of information to align with product flow	Purchase orders; invoices
Tactical information sharing	Share information before or after a purchase is made	Order status; product prices
Strategic	Joint buyer/seller processes, decision making and measurement (often proprietary)	Forecasts; fulfillment processes

FIGURE 5-6 Levels of Supply Chain Collaboration

Source: John Matchette and Andy Seikel, "How to Win Friends and Influence Supply Chain Partners," *Logistics Today*, December 2004, 41.

address the data and informational needs of supply chain participants, and these packages run the gamut in terms of costs and problem-solving capabilities.

Software costs can range from $0 (e.g., *www.freightquote.com*) to tens of millions of dollars (e.g., enterprise resource planning installations). With respect to problem-solving capabilities, some software packages focus on specific functional areas, such as inventory management, reverse logistics, transportation management, or warehousing management. Other software packages focus on specific supply chain processes, such as collaborative planning, forecasting, and replenishment (CPFR), customer relationship management (CRM), or SRM. Still other packages attempt to simultaneously optimize supply chain processes across organizations. Regardless of which type of software package is chosen, it's important to keep in mind that many are developed for general applications, and buyers may need to modify the packages to address their specific needs, thus adding to the costs of the software.

Supply Chain Facilitators

In Figure 5-1, we saw that the ultimate supply chain contains several types of organizations (e.g., financial provider, 3PL supplier, market research firm), which exist to facilitate coordination among various supply chain participants. Because this is a logistics textbook, the most relevant facilitator for our purposes is the 3PL supplier, so it is especially relevant to examine its impact on logistics and supply chains.

Third-party logistics, also called logistics outsourcing or contract logistics, continues to be one of the most misunderstood terms in logistics and SCM. As we have seen with other supply chain concepts (e.g., collaboration, SCM), there is no commonly accepted definition of 3PL. Some definitions, for instance, take a "broad" perspective by suggesting that any logistics activity not performed in house is representative of 3PL. Other definitions, in contrast, emphasize that 3PL arrangements involve a long-term perspective between buyer and seller and that the parties have a relationship, as opposed to transactional, perspective.

Regardless of whether one takes a broad or narrow perspective, the general idea behind 3PL is that one company (say, a manufacturer) allows a specialist company to provide it with one or more logistics functions (e.g., warehousing, outbound transportation). Some well-known 3PL providers include Exel Logistics, FedEx Supply Chain Services, Kuehne and Nagle, Schenker Logistics, and UPS Supply Chain Solutions. A great deal of consolidation has occurred among 3PL providers in recent years (e.g., Deutsche Post acquired Exel), and this consolidation is expected to continue into the future. Although these consolidations could provide customers a broader range of supply chain services, consolidation could also lead to fewer competitive options.[24]

---

[24] Jeff Berman, "Recent Deals Drive Logistics Industry Consolidation," *Logistics Management*, January 2006, 14–16.

3PL customers can demand a number of different activities, with some of the most common involving inbound and outbound transportation, carrier negotiation and contracting, and freight consolidation.[25] Moreover, some 3PL providers have begun to offer so-called supplemental services—such as final product assembly, product installation, and product repair, among others—that are beyond their traditional offerings. These supplemental 3PL services can blur traditional distinctions among supply chain participants (e.g., product assembly has generally been performed by the manufacturing group). Importantly, however, this blurring of distinctions may actually facilitate supply chain integration, in that there is less emphasis on functional issues and more emphasis on cross-functional processes.[26]

The decision to use 3PL services can be driven by strategic considerations, in the sense that an organization believes that one or more aspects of its supply chain(s) need to be transformed. Alternatively, the decision to use 3PL services could be more tactical in nature; an organization might have an inefficient distribution network, an inability to control internal costs, a costly or inflexible workforce, outdated warehousing facilities, or outdated information systems. Whether strategic or tactical in nature, the use of 3PL services is driven by recognition that an organization does not have sufficient internal capabilities to address the issue, or issues, in question.[27]

Although logistics outsourcing has the potential to improve both the effectiveness and efficiency of supply chains, 3PL arrangements can easily result in failure (i.e., an inability for one party to provide what is expected by the other party). One common cause of 3PL failure is unreasonable and unrealistic expectations, generally from the user's perspective; for example, it might be unrealistic (and unreasonable) for a customer to expect a 3PL provider to cut the user's annual transportation expenditures by 50 percent. Another cause of failure in 3PL arrangements involves a lack of flexibility. Regardless of how thoroughly the provider and customer have prepared for a 3PL arrangement, unexpected issues and challenges are bound to arise. Has the arrangement been structured so that unexpected occurrences can be dealt with in a timely and satisfactory manner?[28]

One measure of the pervasiveness of outsourcing in SCM can be seen in the evolution of **fourth-party logistics (4PL)**, or the **lead logistics provider (LLP)**, concept, which emerged in the mid-1990s. Because 4PL/LLP is still relatively young, there is disagreement as to what it should be called as well as how it should be defined. With respect to the former, lead logistics provider appears to be emerging as the moniker of choice, but some providers, such as UPS Supply Chain Services, don't use either term to describe their services. And although an exact definition is elusive, for our purposes, 4PL/LLP will refer to a company whose primary purpose is to ensure that various 3PLs are working toward the relevant supply chain goals and objectives. Whatever one calls it, by one estimate, 4PL/LLP currently accounts for approximately 20 percent of total logistics outsourcing expenditures, and revenues are projected to continue growing in the future.[29]

BARRIERS TO SCM IMPLEMENTATION

Although implementation of SCM may sound attractive from a conceptual perspective, a number of barriers can block its effectiveness, and these are discussed in the following paragraphs.

[25] A. Michael Knemeyer, Thomas M. Corsi, and Paul R. Murphy, "Logistics Outsourcing Relationships: Customer Perspectives," *Journal of Business Logistics* 24, no. 1 (2003): 77–109.

[26] Remko I. van Hoek, "The Contribution of Performance Measurement to the Expansion of Third-Party Logistics Alliances in the Supply Chain," *International Journal of Operations & Production Management* 21, no. 1/2 (2001): 15–29.

[27] Brooks Bentz, "So You Think You Want to Outsource?" *Logistics Today*, May 2006, 24–27.

[28] James A. Tompkins, "The Business Imperative of Outsourcing," *Industrial Management*, January/February 2006, 8–12.

[29] David Biederman, "Inside the Supply Chain: Fourth-Party Logistics," *The Journal of Commerce*, June 6, 2005, 28–31.

Regulatory and Political Considerations

Several decades ago, many of the supply chain arrangements in use today would have been considered illegal under certain regulatory statutes. In the United States, for example, cross-business coordination was fostered by the passage of the National Cooperative Research and Development Act of 1984. Long-term commitments, which are one of the bedrocks of SCM, may stifle competition to the extent that they make it more difficult for others to enter particular markets. Although the overall global climate for business has shifted toward allowing more cooperation among firms, it still would be wise to seek sound legal advice before entering into future supply chain arrangements.

Political considerations such as war and governmental stability can also act as a barrier to SCM. With respect to war, the twenty-first century has witnessed ongoing tensions in the Middle East, ongoing tensions between Pakistan and India (both with nuclear weapon capabilities), wars in Iraq and Afghanistan, as well as civil and political unrest in various parts of Africa. These political uncertainties might cause some organizations to shy away from joining or developing supply chains that rely on companies located in warring countries. Governmental stability is also a key consideration, because SCM is so dependent on interorganizational coordination. Governmental policies that either discourage such coordination or discourage doing business with certain countries would obviously have a negative impact on supply chain efficiency.

Lack of Top Management Commitment

Top management commitment is regularly cited as an important component when individual companies attempt to initiate and implement new initiatives, programs, and products. Because of SCM's interorganizational focus, top management commitment is absolutely essential if supply chain efforts are to have any chance of success. Top management has the ability to allocate the necessary resources for supply chain endeavors and the power to structure, or restructure, corporate incentive policies to focus on achieving organizational and interorganizational (as opposed to functional) objectives.

Unfortunately, recent research presents a "mixed bag" of sorts with respect to top management commitment to SCM. More specifically, although senior management tends to be aware of SCM, actual senior management commitment to SCM occurs in only one of every three organizations.[30] Top management may be hesitant to fully commit to SCM because it is uncomfortable with (or does not understand) one or more of its underpinnings. For example, some companies may be uncomfortable with the concept of customer power in supply chains. Alternatively, other companies may be hesitant to enter into long-term relationships because such relationships might be perceived as limiting their operational flexibility.

Reluctance to Share, or Use, Relevant Information

One tenet of SCM is that well-run supply chains are characterized by information sharing among their participants. Nevertheless, some organizations are reluctant to share information, particularly information that might be considered proprietary in nature. However, this reluctance can contribute to supply chain problems because members may be making decisions based on erroneous data or assumptions. For example, one cause of the bullwhip effect is asymmetrical information among supply chain participants.

Furthermore, advances in computer hardware and software now permit copious amounts of information to be processed and analyzed relatively quickly. To this end, **supply chain analytics** combines technology with manual employee effort to identify trends, perform comparisons, and

---

[30] Stanley E. Fawcett, Jeffrey A. Ogden, Gregory M. Magnan, and M. Bixby Cooper, "Organizational Commitment and Governance for Supply Chain Success," *International Journal of Physical Distribution & Logistics Management* 36, no. 1 (2006): 22–35.

highlight opportunities in supply chain processes, even when large amounts of data are involved. Supported by technology, supply chain analytics help decision makers in areas such as sourcing, inventory management, manufacturing, quality, sales, and logistics. Supply chain analytics leverage enterprise applications, the Internet, data warehouses, and information obtained from external sources to locate data patterns. For example, frequent shopper cards, such as those offered by grocery chains, offer the opportunity to develop highly detailed profiles of individual customers. Some companies, however, are reluctant to fully utilize the information that comes from these data; they believe that the highly detailed data that can be provided by the cards—what was purchased, when it was purchased, where it was purchased, how it was purchased—potentially violate the customer's right to privacy.

Incompatible Information Systems

Twenty years ago, a major barrier to interorganizational collaboration was incompatible computer hardware; today, by contrast, software compatibility is likely the more pressing issue. A key software question involves the decision between a single integrator approach and a best-of-breed approach. Organizations pursuing a single integrator approach rely on a single vendor to provide all relevant software applications (e.g., inventory management, transportation management, warehouse management). One advantage to the single integrator approach is that there should be coordination across the various applications.[31]

Alternatively, a best-of-breed approach chooses the best application for a particular function, so that an organization could have transportation management software from one company and warehouse management software from another company.[32] However, best-of-breed solutions often require additional software packages to coordinate these different applications—and these integrations don't always proceed smoothly. One well-known example of a not-so-smooth integration involved Hershey Foods' effort to integrate several specialized supply chain software packages. The growing pains of this integration included unfilled candy orders for Halloween and Christmas, longer delivery times, increased inventory levels, and upset customers.[33]

Incompatible Corporate Cultures

Because SCM emphasizes a long-term orientation and partnerships between various participants, it is important that the participants be comfortable with the companies they will be working with. In a broad sense, corporate culture refers to "how we do things around here" and reflects an organization's vision, values, and strategic plans. It's important to recognize that compatible corporate cultures don't require all organizations to be the same. Rather, organizations should identify potential differences that could negatively affect supply chain effectiveness and efficiency. For example, an organization with a participative management style might not mesh very well with an organization that has an autocratic management style.[34]

All manifestations of corporate culture may provide important clues about the ability of companies to work together. For instance, one notable supply chain failure involved the dissolution of the relationship between Office Max and Ryder Integrated Logistics. Although a number of reasons explain why this relationship didn't succeed, the two companies had quite different dress codes. Indeed, a Ryder manager told one of the authors that it was clear from the first face-to-face meeting that the companies were going to have difficulty working together—in large part because of their vastly different dress codes!

---

[31] Joel D. Wisner, G. Keong Leong, and Keah-Choon Tan, *Principles of Supply Chain Management: A Balanced Approach* (Mason, OH: South-Western Publishing, 2005), Chapter 7.
[32] Ibid.
[33] Craig Stedman, "Failed ERP Gamble Haunts Hershey," *Computerworld,* November 1, 1999, 1–2.
[34] Douglas M. Lambert and A. Michael Knemeyer, "We're in This Together," *Harvard Business Review* 82, no. 12 (2004): 114–122.

Globalization

Although much of the discussion so far has focused on domestic supply chains, one should recognize that supply chains are becoming increasingly global in nature. Reasons for the increased globalization of supply chains include lower-priced materials and labor, the global perspective of companies in a supply chain, and the development of global competition, among others.[35] Supply chain integration can be challenging in a domestic setting, but integration challenges are even greater in global supply chains due to cultural, economic, technological, political, spatial, and logistical differences.

Global supply chains translate into both longer and more unpredictable lead times (time from when an order is placed until it is received) for shipments, which increases the chance that customer demand might not be fulfilled, due to a potential out-of-stock situation. In addition, research indicates that glitches are routine occurrences in global supply chains; causes include, but are not limited to, documentation errors, packaging errors, routing errors, incomplete shipments, and failure to follow order guidelines. These and other global supply chain glitches drive up supply chain costs and potentially jeopardize customer satisfaction.[36]

SUPPLY CHAIN INTEGRATION

An individual firm can be involved in multiple supply chains at the same time, and it's important to recognize that expectations and required knowledge can vary across supply chains. For example, food manufacturers may sell to grocery chains, institutional buyers, specialty firms (which might position the food items as gifts), and industrial users (which might use the product as an ingredient in another product that they manufacture). It seems reasonable to assume that the packaging expectations of specialty firms might be more demanding than those of industrial users.

Supply chains are integrated by having various parties enter into and carry out long-term mutually beneficial agreements. These agreements are known by several names, to include *partnerships*, *strategic alliances*, *third-party arrangements*, and *contract logistics*. Whatever they are called, these agreements should be designed to reward all participants when collaborative ventures are successful, and they should also provide incentives for all parties to work toward success. In a similar fashion, the participants should share the consequences when cooperative ventures are less successful than desired.

When an organization enters into a long-term agreement with a source or customer, the organization must keep in mind how this arrangement could affect the rest of the supply chain. Ideally, all participants in the supply chain will meet at one time and work out whatever agreements are necessary to ensure that the entire supply chain functions in the most desirable manner.

To integrate a particular supply chain, the various organizations must recognize the shortcomings of the present system and examine channel arrangements as they currently exist and as they might be. All this is done within the framework of the organization's overall strategy, as well as any logistics strategies necessary to support the goals and objectives of the firm's top management.

Broadly speaking, organizations can pursue three primary methods when attempting to integrate their supply chains. One method is through *vertical integration*, where one organization owns multiple participants in the supply chain; indeed, the Ford Motor Company of the 1920s

---

[35] Pedro Reyes, Mahesh S. Raisinghani, and Manoj Singh, "Global Supply Chain Management in the Telecommunications Industry: The Role of Information Technology in Integration of Supply Chain Entities," *Journal of Global Information Technology Management* 5, no. 2 (2002): 48–67.

[36] Beth Enslow, "Best Practices in Global Trade Management Stress Speed and Flexibility," *World Trade*, January 2006, 36–40.

owned forests and steel mills and exercised tight control over its dealers. The most common examples of vertical integration today are some lines of paint and automotive tires. It's important to recognize that regulations (often in the form of state laws) may limit the degree of vertical integration that will be permitted in particular industries.

A second possible method of supply chain coordination involves the use of *formal contracts* among various participants. One of the more popular uses of contracts is franchising, which attempts to combine the benefits of tight integration of some functions along with the ability to be very flexible while performing other functions. From a supply chain perspective, a franchiser may exert contractual influence over what products are purchased by a franchisee, acceptable vendors (suppliers) of these products, and the distribution of the product to the franchisee. For example, distribution for some McDonald's franchisees in the United States (e.g., food, beverage, and store supplies) is provided by the Martin-Brower Company.

A third method of supply chain coordination involves *informal agreements* among the various organizations to pursue common goals and objectives, with control being exerted by the largest organization in the supply chain. Although this method offers supply chain participants flexibility in the sense that organizations can exit unprofitable or unproductive arrangements quickly and with relative ease, organizations should be aware of potential shortcomings. For one, the controlling organization may be so powerful that the supply chain becomes more like a dictatorship than a partnership. Moreover, the same flexibility that allows for exiting unprofitable or unproductive arrangements also allows parties the ability to switch supply chains when presented with what appears to be a better deal.

Summary

This chapter focused on the supply chain concept and began by defining supply chain and SCM. Supply chains consist of a number of different parties and include the end customer; SCM requires companies to adopt an enterprise-to-enterprise point of view.

The chapter also discussed some of the most prominent models of SCM. Key attributes of SCM, such as customer power, a long-term orientation, and leveraging technology, were identified and described. Various barriers to SCM, such as lack of top management commitment and reluctance to share, or use, relevant data, were also presented. The chapter concluded with a look at issues around integration in SCM.

Questions for Discussion and Review

1. Discuss the differences between a supply chain and supply chain management.
2. Discuss the SCOR, GSCF, and PCF models of supply chain management.
3. Do you agree or disagree that there is value in having standardized supply chain processes? Why?
4. What are four key attributes of supply chain management?
5. What is the difference between a lean supply chain and an agile supply chain? Under what circumstances is each an appropriate supply chain approach to pursue?
6. What is the difference between relational and transactional exchanges? Which is more relevant for supply chain management? Why?
7. This chapter suggests that technology has been at the center of changes taking place that affect the supply chain. Do you agree or disagree? Why?
8. Discuss the impact of the Internet on supply chain management.
9. Discuss some of the ways that inventory can be reduced in the supply chain.
10. Do you agree or disagree that supply chain collaboration can be classified as transactional, tactical information sharing, or strategic in nature? Why?
11. How might regulatory and political conditions act as barriers to supply chain management?
12. Why is top management commitment necessary for successful supply chain management?
13. Some companies are hesitant to use frequent shopper cards because the data provided could violate the customer's privacy. Do you agree or disagree? Why?
14. Discuss the best of breed and single integrator approaches.
15. Do you think corporate cultures are relevant for supply chain management? Why or why not?

16. Why is supply chain integration so difficult in global supply chains?
17. Discuss the factors that distinguish contemporary third-party logistics from earlier types of third-party logistics.
18. What are some reasons for using third-party logistics services? What are some reasons that third-party logistics arrangements aren't always successful?
19. Do you agree or disagree with the sentiment that fourth-party logistics companies (lead logistics providers) merely add unnecessary cost and few service improvements to supply chains? Why?
20. Discuss the three primary methods that organizations can use to integrate their supply chains.

Suggested Readings

Bagchi, Prabir K., and Tage Skjoett-Larsen. "Supply Chain Integration: A European Survey." *International Journal of Logistics Management* 16, no. 2 (2005): 275–290.

Carter, Joseph R., Philip L. Carter, and Robert M. Monczka. "Supply Management Strategies for Turbulent Times." *Supply Chain Management Review* 13, no. 7 (2009): 42–49.

Fawcett, Stanley E., Gregory M. Magnan, and Matthew W. McCarter. "Benefits, Barriers, and Bridges to Effective Supply Chain Management." *Supply Chain Management: An International Journal* 13, no. 1 (2008): 35–48.

Fawcett, Stanley E., Lisa M. Ellram, and Jeffrey A. Ogden. *Supply Chain Management: From Vision to Implementation* (Upper Saddle River, NJ: Prentice Hall, 2007).

Gibson, Brian J., John T. Mentzer, and Robert L. Cook. "Supply Chain Management: The Pursuit of a Consensus Definition." *Journal of Business Logistics* 26, no. 2 (2005): 17–25.

Jacoby, David. *Guide to Supply Chain Management* (Canada: The Economist Newspaper Ltd., 2009).

Lambert, Douglas M., and A. Michael Knemeyer. *Building High Performance Business Relationships* (Sarasota, FL: Supply Chain Management Institute, 2009).

Larson, Paul D., Peter Carr, and Kewal S. Dhariwal. "SCM Involving Small Versus Large Suppliers: Relational Exchange and Electronic Communication Media." *Journal of Supply Chain Management: A Global Review of Purchasing & Supply* 41, no. 1 (2005): 18–29.

Li, Xun, Chen Chung, Thomas J. Goldsby, and Clyde W. Holsapple. "A Unified Model of Supply Chain Agility: The Work-Design Perspective." *International Journal of Logistics Management* 19, no. 3 (2008): 408–435.

Mello, John E., Theodore P. Stank, and Terry L. Esper. "A Model of Logistics Outsourcing Strategy." *Transportation Journal* 47, no. 4 (2008): 5–25.

Reeve, James M., and Mandyam M. Srinivasan. "Which Supply Chain Design Is Right for You?" *Supply Chain Management Review* 9, no. 4 (2005): 50–57.

Sweeney, E., C. M. Wagner, and B. Huber. "Supply Chain Management Diffusion among Firms in the Republic of Ireland." *International Journal of Logistics: Research & Applications* 11, no. 5 (2008): 347–358.

Simatupang, Togar M., and Ramaswami Sridharan. "The Collaboration Index: A Measure for Supply Chain Collaboration." *International Journal of Physical Distribution & Logistics Management* 35, no. 1 (2005): 44–62.

Wisner, Joel D., G. Keong Leong, and Keah-Choon Tan. *Principles of Supply Chain Management: A Balanced Approach.* 2nd ed. (Mason, OH: South-Western Cengage Learning, 2008).

CASE

CASE 5-1   Johnson Toy Company

Located in Biloxi, Mississippi, the Johnson Toy Company is celebrating its 75th year of business. Amy Johnson, who is president, and Lori Johnson, who is vice president, are sisters and are the third generation of their family to be involved in the toy business. The firm manufactures and sells toys throughout the United States. The toy business is very seasonal, with the majority of sales occurring before Christmas. A smaller peak occurs in the late spring–early summer period, when sales of outdoor items are good.

The firm relies on several basic designs of toys—which have low profit margins but are steady sellers—and on new designs of unconventional toys, whose introduction is always risky but promises high profits if the item becomes popular. The firm advertises regularly on Saturday morning television shows for children.

Late last year, just before Christmas, the Johnson Toy Company introduced Jungle Jim the Jogger doll, modeled after a popular television show. Sales skyrocketed, and every retailer's stock of Jungle Jim the Jogger dolls was sold out in mid-December; the Johnson Company could have sold several million more units if they had been available before Christmas. Based on the sales success of this doll, Amy and Lori made commitments to manufacture 10 million Jungle Jim the Jogger dolls this year and to introduce a wide line of accessory items, which they hoped every doll owner would also want to have. Production was well underway, and many retailers were happy to accept dolls in January and February because they were still a fast-selling item, even though the toy business itself was sluggish during these months.

Unfortunately, in the aftermath of a Valentine's Day party in Hollywood, the television actor who portrayed Jungle Jim the Jogger became involved in a widely publicized sexual misadventure, the details of which shocked and disgusted many readers and TV viewers, and we would be embarrassed to describe them. Ratings of the television series plummeted, and within a month it had been dropped from the air. On March 1, the Johnson Company had canceled further production of the Jungle Jim the Jogger dolls, although it had to pay penalties to some of its suppliers because of the cancellation. The company had little choice because it was obvious that sales had stopped.

On April 1, a gloomy group assembled in the Johnson Company conference room. Besides Amy and Lori, those present included Carolyn Coggins, the firm's sales manager; Cheryl Guridi, the logistics manager; Greg Sullivan, the controller; and Kevin Vidal, the plant engineer. Coggins had just reported that she believed there were between 1.5 million and 2 million Jungle Jim the Jogger dolls in retail stores, and Sullivan had indicated there were 2,567,112 complete units in various public warehouses in Biloxi. Vidal said that he was still trying to count all the unassembled component parts, adding that one problem was that they were still being received from suppliers, despite the cancellation.

Amy said, "Let's wait a few weeks to get a complete count of all the dolls and all the unassembled component parts. Lori, I'm naming you to work with Carolyn and Kevin to develop recommendations as to how we can recycle the Jungle Jim item into something we can sell. Given the numbers involved, I'm willing to turn out some innocuous doll and sell it for a little more than the cost of recycling because we can't take a complete loss on all these damned Jungle Jim dolls! Greg says we have nearly 2.6 million of them to play with, so let's think of something."

"Your 2.6-million figure may be low," said Coggins. "Don't forget that there may be nearly 2 million in the hands of the dealers and that they will return them."

"Return them?" questioned Amy. "They're not defective. That's the only reason we accept returns. The retailers made a poor choice. It's the same as if they ordered sleds

and then had a winter with no snow. We are no more responsible for Jungle Jim's sex life than they are!"

Cheryl Guridi spoke up: "You may be underestimating the problem, Amy. One of our policies is to accept the dealer's word as to what is defective, and right now there are a lot of dealers out there claiming defects in the Jungle Jim dolls. One reason that Kevin can't get an accurate count is that returned dolls are showing up on our receiving dock and getting mixed up with our in-stock inventory."

"How can that happen?" asked Amy, angrily. "We're not paying the freight, also, are we?"

"So far, no," responded Guridi. "The retailers are paying the freight just to get rid of them."

"We've received several bills in which the retailer has deducted the costs of the Jungle Jim dolls and of the freight for shipping them back from what he owes us," said Sullivan. "That was one item I wanted to raise while we were together."

"We can't allow that!" exclaimed Amy.

"Don't be so sure," responded Sullivan. "The account in question has paid every bill he's owed us on time for 40 years. Do you want *me* to tell him we won't reimburse him?"

"This is worse than I imagined," said Amy. "Just what are our return policies, Lori?"

"Well, until today, I thought we had only two," said Lori. "One for our small accounts involves having our salespeople inspect the merchandise when they make a sales call. They can pick it up and give the retailer credit off the next order."

"Sometimes they pick up more than defective merchandise," added Coggins. "Often, they'll take the slow movers out of the retailer's hands. We have to do that as a sales tool."

"That's not quite right," interjected Vidal. "Sometimes, the returned items are just plain shopworn—scratched, dented, and damaged. That makes it hard for us because we have to inspect every item and decide whether it can be put back into stock. When we think a particular salesperson is accepting too many shopworn items, we tell Carolyn, although it's not clear to me that the message reaches the salespeople in the field."

"I wish I had an easy solution," said Coggins. "We used to let our salespeople give credit for defects and then destroy everything out in the field. Unfortunately, some abused the system and resold the toys to discount stores. At least now we can see everything we're buying back. I agree we are stuck with some shopworn items, but our salespeople are out there to sell, and nothing would ruin a big sale quicker than for our salespeople to start arguing with the retailer, on an item-by-item basis, as to whether something being returned happens to be shopworn."

"Is there a limit to what a salesperson is permitted to allow a retailer to return?" asked Amy.

"Well, not until now," responded Coggins. "But with this Jungle Jim snafu we can expect the issue to occur. In fact, I have several phone queries on my desk concerning this. I thought I'd wait until after this meeting to return them."

"Well, I think we'd better establish limits—right now," said Amy.

"Be careful," said Lori. "When I was out with the salespeople last year, I gathered the impression that some were able to write bigger orders by implying that we'd take the unsold merchandise back, if need be. If we assume that risk, the retailer is willing to take more of our merchandise."

"Are there no limits to this policy?" asked Amy.

"Informal ones," was Coggins's response. "It depends on the salesperson and the account. I don't think there is much abuse, although there is some."

"How do the goods get back to us under these circumstances?" asked Amy.

"The salespeople either keep them and shuffle them about to other customers, or—if it's a real loser—they ask us what to do," replied Coggins.

"Greg," said Amy, "do our records reflect these returns and transfers?"

"Oh, fairly well," was his response. "We lose track of individual items and quantities, but if the salesperson is honest—and I think ours are—we can follow the dollar amount of the return to the salesperson's inventory, to another retailer, or back here to us. We do not have good controls on the actual items that are allowed for returns. Kevin and I have difficulty in reconciling the value of returned items that wind up back here. Carolyn's records say they're okay for resale, and Kevin says they're too badly damaged."

"I insist on the reconciliation before we allow the goods back into our working inventory," said Guridi. "That way I know exactly what I have here, ready to ship."

"You know, I'm finding out more information about inventories and returns than I thought existed," said Amy.

"Too many trips to Paris, dearest," said Lori, and the others all suppressed smiles.

Amy decided to ignore Lori's remark, and she looked at Guridi and asked, "Are you satisfied with your control over inventories, Cheryl?"

"I have no problem with the ones here in Biloxi," was Guridi's response, "but I have an awful time with the inventories of return items that salespeople carry about with them, waiting to place them with another retailer. I'm not always certain they're getting us top dollar, and each salesperson knows only his or her own territory. When Carolyn and I are trying to monitor the sales of some new item, we never know whether it's bombing in some areas and riding around in salespeople's cars as they try to sell it again."

"Have you now described our returns policy, such as it is?" asked Amy, looking at everybody in the room.

"No," was the response murmured by all. Sullivan spoke: "For large accounts we deduct a straight 2 percent off wholesale selling price to cover defectives, and then we never want to hear about the defectives from these accounts at all."

"That sounds like a better policy," said Amy. "How well is it working?"

"Up until Jungle Jim jogged where he shouldn't, it worked fine. Now a number of large accounts are pleading 'special circumstances' or threatening to sue if we don't take back the dolls."

"They have no grounds for suit," declared Amy.

"You're right," said Coggins, "but several of their buyers are refusing to see our sales staff until the matter is resolved. I just heard about this yesterday and meant to bring it up in today's meeting. I consider this very serious."

"Damn it!" shouted Amy, pounding the table with her fist. "I hope that damned jogger dies of jungle rot! We're going to lose money this year, and now you're all telling me how the return policy works, or doesn't work, as the case may be! Why can't we just have a policy of all sales being final and telling retailers that if there is an honest defect they should send the goods back here to us in good old Biloxi?"

"Most of the small accounts know nothing about shipping," responded Vidal. "They don't know how to pack, they don't know how to prepare shipping documents, and they can't choose the right carriers. You ought to see the hodgepodge of shipments we receive from them. In more cases than not, they pay more in shipping charges than the products are worth to us. I'd rather see them destroyed in the field."

Sullivan spoke up. "I'd object to that. We would need some pretty tight controls to make certain the goods were actually destroyed. What if they are truly defective, but improperly disposed of, then fall into the hands of children who play with them and the defect causes an injury? Our name may still be on the product, and the child's parents will no doubt claim the item was purchased from one of our retailers. Will we be liable? Why can't we have everything come back here? We have enough volume of some returned items that we could think in terms of recycling parts."

Vidal responded, "Recycling is a theoretical solution to such a problem, but only in rare instances will it pay. In most instances the volume is too small and the cost of taking toys apart is usually very high. However, the Jungle Jim product involves such a large volume that it is prudent and reasonable to think up another product that utilizes many of the parts. It would even pay to modify some machines for disassembling the Jungle Jim doll."

"As I listen to this discussion," said Lori, "one fact becomes obvious: We will never have very good knowledge about volume or patterns of returns until it's too late. That's their very nature."

Guridi asked, "Could we have field representatives who do nothing but deal with this problem? The retailers would be told to hang onto the defectives until our claims reps arrive."

Coggins replied, "That would be expensive, because most retailers have little storage space for anything and would expect our claims rep to be there immediately. Besides, it might undermine our selling efforts if retailers could no longer use returns to negotiate with as they talked about new orders."

"That may be," interjected Amy, "but we cannot continue having each salesperson tailoring a return policy for each retailer. That's why we're in such a mess with the jogger doll. We have to get our return policy established, made more uniform, and enforced. We cannot go through another fiasco like Jungle Jim the Jogger for a long time. We're going to lose money this year, no matter what, and I have already told Kevin that there will be virtually no money available for retooling for next year's new products."

Questions

1. From the standpoint of an individual concerned with accounting controls, discuss and evaluate Johnson Toy Company's present policies for handling returned items.

2. Answer Question 1, but from the standpoint of an individual interested in marketing.

3. Propose a policy for handling returns that should be adopted by the Johnson Toy Company. Be certain to list circumstances under which exceptions would be allowed. Should it apply to the Jungle Jim dolls?

4. Should this policy, if adopted, be printed and distributed to all of the retailers who handle Johnson Toy Company products? Why or why not? If it should not be distributed to them, who should receive copies?

5. Assume that it is decided to prepare a statement on returns to be distributed to all retailers and that it should be less than a single double-spaced page. Prepare such a statement.

6. On the basis of the policy in your answer to Question 3, develop instructions for the Johnson Toy Company distribution and accounting departments with respect to their roles and procedures in the handling of returns.

7. Assume that you are Cheryl Guridi, the firm's logistics manager. Do you think that the returns policy favored by the logistics manager would differ from what would be best for the firm? Why or why not?

8. Until the policy you recommend in your answer to Question 3 takes effect, how would you handle the immediate problem of retailers wanting to return unsold Jungle Jim the Jogger dolls?

6 | PROCUREMENT

Key Terms

- Bribes
- Excess (surplus) materials
- Global procurement (sourcing)
- Investment recovery
- ISO 9000
- Kickbacks
- Lean Six Sigma
- Malcolm Baldrige National Quality Award
- Multiple sourcing
- Obsolete materials
- Procurement (purchasing)
- Procurement cards (p-cards)
- Quality
- Scrap materials
- Single sourcing
- Six Sigma
- Socially responsible procurement
- Supplier development (reverse marketing)
- Supply management
- Waste materials

Learning Objectives

- To understand the distinction between procurement, purchasing, and supply management
- To examine procurement objectives
- To learn about supplier selection and evaluation
- To understand quality issues in procurement
- To examine global procurement
- To learn about investment recovery
- To examine socially responsible procurement

Procurement, which refers to the raw materials, component parts, and supplies bought from outside organizations to support a company's operations, is an important activity and closely related to logistics because acquired goods and services must be entered into the supply chain in the exact quantities and at the precise time they are needed. Procurement is also important because its costs often range between 60 and 80 percent of an organization's revenues.

The magnitude of procurement expenditures meant that procurement's historical focus in many organizations was to achieve the lowest possible cost from potential suppliers; oftentimes these suppliers were pitted against each other in "cutthroat" competition involving three- or six-month arm's-length contracts awarded to the lowest bidder. Once this lowest bidder was chosen, the bidding cycle would almost immediately start again, and another low bidder would get the contract for the next several months. Today, by contrast, procurement has a much more strategic orientation in many organizations, and a contemporary procurement manager might have responsibility for reducing cycle times, playing an integral role in product development, or generating additional revenues by collaborating with the marketing department.[1]

---

[1] Carlos Niezen and Wulf Weller, "Procurement as Strategy," *Harvard Business Review* 84, no. 9 (2006): 22–24.

Historically, procurement, **purchasing**, and **supply management** were terms that could be used almost interchangeably, but this is no longer the case. Although procurement and purchasing are sometimes viewed as synonymous terms, supply management is now viewed as a relational exchange approach involving a limited number of suppliers. You might recall from Chapter 5 that relational exchanges adopt a long-term orientation that can be characterized by attributes such as trust, commitment, dependence, and shared benefits.

Electronic commerce continues to bring many changes to the procurement discipline, such as *electronic procurement* and *reverse auctions*, which were discussed in Chapter 2. Moreover, utilization of **procurement cards** (also referred to as **p-cards**) has also grown dramatically with the evolution of electronic commerce. P-cards are similar to charge cards such as Visa and MasterCard that emphasize personal use, with p-cards being used for an organization's buying needs. Organizations generally restrict the number of employees authorized to use procurement cards, and each month, an organization receives a detailed statement listing employees, details of their purchases, and purchase prices. Unlike personal credit cards, with p-cards an organization will make one payment for the total amount of purchases during one month, as opposed to making individual payments for each p-card holder.

P-cards can benefit organizations in several ways, one of which is a reduction in the number of invoices. In addition, these cards allow employees to make purchases in a matter of minutes, as opposed to days, and procurement cards generally allow suppliers to be paid in a more timely fashion. Having said this, p-cards may require control processes that measure usage and identify procurement trends, limit spending during the appropriate procurement cycle, and block unauthorized expenditures at gaming casinos or massage parlors.[2]

In addition, while the benefits of using p-cards increase exponentially as more people within an organization use them, expanding use beyond the domestic market can be a challenge. Issues associated with an expansion of p-cards overseas include currency differences, availability of technology, difference in card acceptance, and cultural issues with the program. For example, in some Asian markets, employee turnover is so high that card security is a major concern.[3]

Because entire textbooks are devoted to procurement, it's really not possible for us to cover all aspects of this topic in just one chapter. We'll begin our discussion with a brief overview of possible objectives for procurement, and this will be followed by a discussion of supplier selection and evaluation. We'll also look at quality issues in procurement, global procurement, investment recovery, and socially responsible purchasing.

PROCUREMENT OBJECTIVES[4]

Because procurement has become more strategic in nature, its primary objective is no longer to only achieve the lowest possible cost of supply. Potential procurement objectives include, but are not limited to, (1) supporting organizational goals and objectives, (2) managing the purchasing process effectively and efficiently, (3) managing the supply base, (4) developing strong relationships with other functional groups, and (5) supporting operational requirements. Each objective will be briefly discussed in the following paragraphs.

First and foremost, procurement's objectives must *support organizational goals and objectives*. If, for example, minimal inventory is an organizational objective, then procurement probably should not be attempting to minimize total procurement costs. With respect to *managing the purchase process effectively and efficiently*, effectively is concerned with how well procurement keeps its promises, whereas efficiently refers to how well (or poorly) procurement uses company

---

[2] Bob Martinson, "The Power of the P-Card," *Strategic Finance*, February 2002, 30–35.
[3] David Hannon, "P-card Program Expansion Is a Global Challenge," *Purchasing* 138, no. 12 (2009): 53–55.
[4] The material in this section is drawn from Robert Monczka, Robert Trent, and Robert Handfield, *Purchasing and Supply Chain Management*, 3rd ed. (Mason, OH: Thomson/South-Western, 2005).

resources in keeping its promises. A third procurement objective, *managing the supply base*, refers to the selection, development, and maintenance of supply sources.

Developing strong relationships with other functional groups recognizes that the interfunctional consequences of procurement decisions require more cooperation and coordination than has traditionally existed between procurement and areas such as logistics, manufacturing, and marketing. *Supporting operational requirements* means that procurement's focus is on satisfying internal customers and can be summarized by buying the right products, at the right price, from the right source, at the right specifications, in the right quantity, for delivery at the right time to the right internal customer.

SUPPLIER SELECTION AND EVALUATION

One of procurement's most important responsibilities involves supplier (vendor) selection and evaluation. The selection and evaluation of suppliers is a process that involves stating an organization's needs and then determining how well various potential suppliers can fulfill these needs (see Figure 6-1). The first step in this process, *identify need for supply*, can arise from a number of considerations, such as the end of an existing supply agreement or the development of a new product. *Situation analysis*, the second step, looks at both the internal and external environment within which the supply decision is to be made. Internal considerations include identification of the relevant stakeholders, where the supply is needed, and the appropriate quantity and quality of the supply, as well as applicable supply policies (e.g., minority supplier initiatives). The external environment includes economic considerations, the legal and

FIGURE 6-1 Supplier Selection Framework

regulatory frameworks controlling the purchase, and the marketplace within which potential suppliers operate.

Identify and evaluate possible suppliers is the third step. A myriad of sources can be used to *identify possible suppliers*, such as salespeople, trade shows, trade publications, and the Internet. It's important to recognize and understand the potential advantages and disadvantages to each source. For example, although trade shows might highlight offerings from several different supply sources (which could facilitate supplier comparisons), the costs to attend or exhibit at trade shows have skyrocketed in recent years; moreover, trade shows are often held only once a year.

Evaluating suppliers can be facilitated if an organization (1) delineates relevant selection criteria and (2) assigns weights to these criteria. With respect to the latter, if an organization uses four relevant selection criteria, should all four be assigned equal weight (i.e., 25 percent per criteria), or should certain criteria be weighted more heavily than others (e.g., two criteria weighted at 30 percent apiece and two others weighted at 20 percent each)? This weighting technique serves as a foundation for generating a rating (score) for each possible supplier, and these ratings are instrumental in the fourth step of the supplier selection process, *select supplier(s)*, which is where an organization chooses one or more companies to supply the relevant product.

Selecting the most appropriate number of suppliers a firm should use has been the subject of continuing debate. Internal considerations, which were mentioned in step 2, could influence the actual decision to use a single-source or a multiple source approach. While the goal of both approaches is to provide the buying organization with the best value of a supplied part, each offers distinct advantages. **Multiple sourcing** proponents argue that by having more than one supplier increased amounts of competition, greater supply risk mitigation and improved market intelligence can arise. **Single sourcing**, on the other hand, consolidates purchase volume with a single supplier with the hopes of enjoying lower costs per unit and increased cooperation and communication in the supply relationship.

The final step of the supplier selection process, *evaluate decision*, involves a comparison of expected supplier outcomes to actual supplier outcomes. There are two primary approaches for evaluating suppliers: process based and performance based. A process-based evaluation is an assessment of the supplier's service and/or production process (typically involving an audit). The performance-based evaluation is focused on the supplier's actual performance on a variety of criteria, such as cost and quality. This evaluation can be facilitated if an organization has explicitly defined selection criteria, as mentioned in step 4.

The preceding paragraphs have presented supplier selection and evaluation as a seemingly straightforward and easy-to-follow process, but supplier selection and evaluation can actually be quite complex. First off, supplier selection and evaluation generally involve multiple criteria, and these criteria can vary both in number and importance, depending on the particular situation. As an example, a study involving the procurement of electronic components[5] looked at 10 possible selection criteria, whereas 16 selection criteria were investigated in a study of overseas vendors by Canadian apparel buyers.[6]

Second, because some vendor selection criteria may be contradictory, it is important to understand potential trade-offs between them. For instance, it may be difficult for a supplier to achieve both competitive pricing and high-quality supply. Third, the evolution of business practices and philosophies, such as just-in-time, green purchasing, and supply chain management, may require new selection criteria or the reprioritization of existing criteria. As an example, whereas EDI capabilities might have been an important supplier selection criteria in the early

---

[5] Neeraj Bharadway, "Investigating the Decision Criteria Used in Electronic Components Procurement," *Industrial Marketing Management* 33, no. 4 (2004): 317–323.
[6] Ismat Thaver and Anne Wilcock, "Identification of Overseas Vendor Selection Criteria Used by Canadian Apparel Buyers," *Journal of Fashion Marketing and Management* 10, no. 1 (2006): 56–70.

1990s, in the contemporary environment Internet-related capabilities (e.g., tracking and pricing) have assumed increased relevance and importance.[7]

Supplier Development (Reverse Marketing)

Our discussion of supplier selection and evaluation has taken a "traditional" approach in the sense that there has been underlying assumptions that (1) suppliers initiate marketing efforts toward purchasers and (2) potential suppliers are available and willing to serve prospective purchasers. However, because it has become increasingly common for potential suppliers to not be available and willing to serve prospective purchasers, some purchasers are taking a more proactive role in the procurement process. To this end, **supplier development (reverse marketing)** refers to "a degree of aggressive procurement involvement not normally encountered in supplier selection" and can include a purchaser initiating contact with a supplier or a purchaser establishing prices, terms, and conditions, among other behaviors.

There are several key reasons for why purchasers are adopting a more proactive and aggressive role in the procurement process. One is the myriad inefficiencies associated with suppliers initiating marketing efforts toward purchasers, such as suppliers possessing inadequate, insufficient, or untimely information. A second reason for more proactive and aggressive procurement is that the purchaser may be aware of important benefits, such as reduced inventory and improved forecasting accuracy, which are unknown to the supplier. Yet another reason is that achieving competitive advantage in the supply chain is predicated on purchasers adopting a more aggressive approach so as to compel suppliers to meet the necessary requirements.[8]

QUALITY ISSUES IN PROCUREMENT

It's important that we operationalize "quality" before beginning our discussion of quality issues in procurement. Consider that the American Society of Quality, which bills itself as the world's leading membership organization focused on quality, defines quality as "a subjective term for which each person has his or her own definition."[9] Although there are somewhat stringent definitions of quality, such as a product that is free from defects, deficiencies, or errors, we will take a more flexible approach and define **quality** as conformance to mutually agreed-upon requirements.

The issue of quality in procurement often represents a delicate balancing act for the involved organizations. That is, if an organization buys an input of inferior quality, it runs the risk of lowering the quality of the final product. If an organization buys an input of higher quality than one's final product, it may be paying for something that is not needed. In short, in the buy–sell relationship, both parties must understand issues of quality and strive to match the quality levels of buyers and sellers in the supply chain.

Today, vendors are expected to have quality programs, and many have worked for years to achieve a good reputation for quality. One way for vendors to convince potential buyers that they are committed to quality is through a program known as ISO (International Standards Organization) 9000 certification. **ISO 9000** is a set of generic standards used to document, implement, and demonstrate quality management and assurance systems. Applicable to manufacturing and service industries, these standards are intended to help companies build quality into every core process in each department. Firms demonstrating a commitment to quality through training, reviews, and continuous improvement can receive ISO 9000 certification.

---

[7] Birsen Karpak, Rammohan R. Kasuganti, and Erdooan Kumcu, "Are You Using Costly Outmoded Techniques to Purchase Materials?" *Business Forum* 27, no. 1 (2005): 14–19.
[8] Michiel Leenders, P. Fraser Johnson, Anna Flynn, and Harold E. Fearon, *Purchasing and Supply Management*, 13th ed. (New York: McGraw-Hill/Irwin, 2006), Chapter 11.
[9] *www.asq.org.*

After achieving ISO 9000 certification, organizations are audited each year and can be recertified every three years. Although ISO 9000 certification continues to become more commonplace throughout the world, it can still be a source of competitive advantage for certain companies. For example, the Web site for Bil-Jax, a North American manufacturer of scaffolds and other construction-related equipment, emphasizes that it is the only full-service manufacturer of scaffolds to have achieved both ISO 9000 certification and ISO 9000 recertification.

Another quality-related concept or practice is known as **Six Sigma**, which emphasizes the virtual elimination of business errors. Those who remember the normal distribution (curve) from their statistics class will recall that Sigmas are related to standard deviations from the mean. The higher the number of deviations included, the more area under the normal curve that is covered. In the case of Six Sigma, or six standard deviations, the area covered is 99.99966 percent, leaving a tiny area, .00034, uncovered. More specifically, the Six Sigma approach suggests that there will be 3.4 defects, deficiencies, or errors per one million opportunities—obviously a very high standard.

From a North American perspective, Six Sigma is a relatively new approach in the sense that it really didn't begin to achieve widespread acceptance—and adoption—until the mid-1990s. Indeed, a recent worldwide Six Sigma study indicated that only about 10 percent of the responding organizations had established a structured performance improvement program prior to 1995. This same study also found that the most significant benefits from Six Sigma have been reduced costs, reduced errors and waste, and reduced cycle time, whereas the key drawbacks have involved overcoming business cultural barriers, investing the required resources (both human and money), and gaining top management commitment.[10]

While traditionally seen as rival initiatives, the integration of Six Sigma with Lean approach, so-called **Lean Six Sigma**, is an area of emerging focus within many companies. Lean Six Sigma integrates the goals and methods of these two approaches in pursuit of quality. What sets Lean Six Sigma apart from its individual components is the recognition that organizations cannot focus only on quality or speed. An organizational focus on improving quality is needed as it relates to responsiveness. Halliburton, an oilfield services provider, has implemented Lean Six Sigma concepts both internally as well as pushing the concept out to their suppliers in an effort to better align their supply base with Halliburton's increasing demand and supply expectations.[11]

Another quality-related initiative is the **Malcolm Baldrige National Quality Award**, which was established in the late 1980s to recognize U.S. organizations for their achievements in quality and performance. Initially only manufacturers, services, and small businesses were eligible for this award, but eligibility was expanded to include health care and educational institutions in the late 1990s.

The Baldrige Quality Awards, which are restricted to organizations headquartered in the United States, require interested parties to submit a formal application that is evaluated by a committee largely made up of private-sector experts in business and quality. Applications are evaluated for achievement and improvement across seven categories: business results; customer and market focus; human resource focus; leadership; measurement, analysis, and knowledge management; process management; and strategic planning.[12] Importantly, organizations that choose not to apply for a Baldrige Award can use these seven categories as a template for evaluating the quality of current and prospective suppliers.

There are substantive differences between ISO 9000 and the Baldrige Award; ISO 9000 essentially allows an organization to determine if it complies with its specific quality system. In contrast, the Baldrige Award is more heavily focused on the actual results from a quality system as well as on continuous improvement.[13] The Baldrige Award also tends to be more externally focused in the sense that organizations benchmark themselves against organizations from outside their particular industry.

---

[10] "Exclusive Worldwide Six Sigma Survey Reveals . . ." *Business Credit*, October 2005, 48–51.
[11] William Atkinson, "Halliburton Pushes Lean Six Sigma to Its Supply Base," *Purchasing* 138, no. 3 (2009): 18–20.
[12] *www.quality.NIST.gov*.
[13] Ibid.

GLOBAL PROCUREMENT (SOURCING)[14]

Chapter 1 pointed out that world trade is expected to experience continued growth in the early part of the twenty-first century, and this increased globalization means that many organizations, rather than relying on local and domestic suppliers, will cast out a much wider net in search of supply sources. Indeed, a survey of approximately 300 senior-level business executives found that the percentage of supply sources outside one's domestic market is projected to increase from 22 to 38 percent in a six-year time span.[15] Similarly, a recent procurement study projected that in 2010 half of all firms will have a global spend of over 40 percent.[16]

Global procurement (sourcing), which refers to buying components and inputs anywhere in the world, is driven by two primary reasons, namely, the factor-input strategy and the market-access strategy. With the factor-input strategy, an organization is seeking low-cost or high-quality sources of supply, whereas the market-access strategy involves sourcing in markets where an organization plans to do significant business.

A global sourcing development model would include the following components: planning, specification, evaluation, relationship management, transportation and holding costs, implementation, and monitoring and improving. Each of these will be briefly discussed next. *Planning* is the first step in global procurement and involves an honest assessment of global sourcing opportunities and challenges. The outcome of this stage should be a set of global procurement policies and procedures that are consistent with an organization's overall objectives. *Specification* involves quantifying and qualifying current sources across a variety of dimensions such as quality, costs, reliability, and standardization, among others.

An earlier section in this chapter discussed supplier selection and evaluation, and although the *evaluation* process associated with global procurement has similarities, there are potential differences as well. For example, should an organization use the same standards to evaluate international sources as are used to evaluate domestic sources? Another component in a global sourcing development framework, *relationship management*, has been discussed in previous chapters. Relationship management in global procurement is exacerbated by potential difficulties in cross-cultural communication such as language and time considerations.

Because global sourcing increases the distance that components and inputs must be moved, managers must consider trade-offs between *transportation and holding costs.* The choice of a faster transportation alternative (e.g., air) will likely create higher transportation costs and lower inventory holding costs; alternatively, a slower transportation alternative (e.g., water) will create lower transportation costs and higher inventory holding costs. *Implementation*, or carrying out, is often a major shortcoming to many global procurement plans; indeed, some organizations fail to specify an implementation plan. Moreover, the greater uncertainty associated with global sourcing means that implementation plans must be flexible and provide guidance for decision making when confronted with the unexpected.

Finally, *monitoring and improving* means that performance measures must be established for global procurement systems and that these measures should be reviewed on a regular basis. Comparisons can be made between actual and expected performance, and the results of these comparisons can be used to improve the global sourcing process. Commonly used performance measures for monitoring global sourcing systems include the percentage of shipments that arrive early or late, completeness of orders, and percentage of orders accepted or rejected on delivery.

Establishing a successful global sourcing strategy can be one of the most difficult assignments for the procurement function. As organizations continue to expand their supply bases,

---

[14] This material in this section is drawn from Donald F. Wood, Anthony Barone, Paul R. Murphy, and Daniel L. Wardlow, *International Logistics*, 2nd ed. (New York: Amacom, 2002), Chapter 14.
[15] Patrick Byrne, "Supply Chain Trends Span the Globe," *Logistics Management*, March 2006, 26–27.
[16] William Atkinson, "The Big Trends in Sourcing and Procurement," *Supply Chain Management Review*, May/June 2008, S48–S50.

many are realizing that hidden cost factors are affecting the level of benefits that were projected to be achieved through this approach. Some of these hidden costs include increased costs of dealing with suppliers outside the domestic market, duty and tariff changes that occur over the life of a supply agreement, increased inventory-related costs associated with global supply chains, and rising levels of logistics cost volatility (e.g., ocean freight rates) that can occur unexpectedly.[17] Thus, when assessing the costs of global sourcing, it is important to examine all cost implications of this strategy.

INVESTMENT RECOVERY[18]

Investment recovery, which identifies opportunities to recover revenues or reduce costs associated with scrap, surplus, obsolete, and waste materials, is often the responsibility of the procurement manager. Investment recovery can provide an organization with the opportunity to simultaneously do well and do good in the sense that investment recovery increases a seller's revenues (reduces a seller's costs) while addressing selected environmental considerations. For example, although aluminum recycling can provide revenues to an organization, the recycling conserves raw materials, uses less energy, and reduces various types of pollution. Figure 6-2 shows an example of how aluminum cans might be recycled.

Because even the best-managed organizations will generate excess, obsolete, scrap, and waste materials, it's important to distinguish among these different categories of material. **Excess (surplus) materials** refer to stock that exceeds the reasonable requirements of an organization, perhaps because of an overly optimistic demand forecast. If an organization has several production facilities, excess materials might be transferred to the other facilities. Unlike excess materials,

FIGURE 6-2 The Recycling of Aluminum Cans
Source: Courtesy of Aluminum Company of America.

---

[17] David Hannon, "The 9 Hidden Costs of Global Sourcing," *Purchasing*, March 12, 2009, 38–41.
[18] Much of the material in this section is drawn from Leenders et al., *Purchasing and Supply Management*.

obsolete materials are not likely to ever be used by the organization that purchased it. Having said this, materials that are obsolete to one organization might not be obsolete to other users; as such, it might be possible to sell obsolete materials to other organizations.

Scrap materials refer to materials that are no longer serviceable, have been discarded, or are a by-product of the production process (e.g., scrap steel when producing an automobile or washing machine). Certain scrap materials, such as copper and nickel, have such economic value that procurement contracts sometimes include a price at which the scrap will be repurchased by the supplier. **Waste materials** refer to those that have been spoiled, broken, or otherwise rendered unfit for further use or reclamation. Unlike scrap materials, waste materials have no economic value.

The ways that organizations manage the investment recovery of excess, obsolete, scrap, and waste materials should be influenced by the materials' classification. Waste materials have limited investment recovery options because they are unfit for further use and have no economic value. As a result, it wouldn't be realistic to search for ways to reuse waste materials elsewhere in an organization or to find prospective buyers for the waste products. On the other hand, there are more expansive investment recovery options for excess materials, to include using them elsewhere within an organization, selling to another organization, returning to the supplier, and selling through a surplus dealer.

SOCIALLY RESPONSIBLE PROCUREMENT

As previously mentioned in Chapter 4, the social responsibility concept suggests that an organization's responsibilities transcend economic considerations, such as the maximization of shareholder's wealth, and should incorporate societal objectives and values. There are social responsibility concerns at the corporate level (e.g., what are the behaviors of a socially responsible organization?), as well as social responsibility issues associated with organizational functions such as procurement. For purposes of this discussion, **socially responsible procurement** refers to "procurement activities that meet the ethical and discretionary responsibilities expected by society."[19]

Research suggests that socially responsible procurement consists of five dimensions, namely, *diversity, the environment, human rights, philanthropy,* and *safety.* Diversity is concerned with procurement activities associated with minority or women-owned organizations, whereas the environment includes considerations such as waste reduction and the design of products for reuse or recycling. Human rights issues include child labor laws as well as sweatshop labor. Philanthropy focuses on employee volunteer efforts and philanthropic contributions, and safety is concerned with the safe transportation of purchased products, as well as the safe operation of relevant facilities.[20]

Many believe that ethical considerations (i.e., standards of conduct and moral principles) are also a part of socially responsible procurement. Indeed, research on procurement ethics dates back to the mid-1960s, and the competitiveness of the contemporary business environment creates—for some companies—a "win at all costs" philosophy that can exacerbate unethical behavior. Areas of ethical concern in procurement include gift giving and gift receiving; **bribes** (money paid before an exchange) and **kickbacks** (money paid after an exchange); misuse of information; improper methods of knowledge acquisition; lying or misrepresentation of the truth; product quality (lack thereof); misuse of company assets, to include abuse of expense accounts; and conflicts of interest, or activity that creates a potential conflict between one's personal interests and the employer's interests.

---

[19] Craig R. Carter and Marianne M. Jennings, "The Role of Purchasing in Corporate Social Responsibility: A Structural Equation Analysis," *Journal of Business Logistics* 25, no. 1 (2004): 145–186.
[20] Ibid.

The topic of socially responsible procurement is much broader than the space devoted to it here indicates. Moreover, it's important to understand that the relevance, importance, and challenges associated with socially responsible procurement are likely to increase in the coming years. As an example, BMW is now requiring potential vendors to answer 29 questions on their social and environmental standards, and the results are an integral part of BMW's vendor selection process.[21]

Summary

Procurement is closely related to logistics because nearly anything purchased must be moved to wherever it is needed—in the right quantity and at the precise time. Logistics services may also be an important focus of procurement activities within an organization. Procurement, an important activity because its costs often range between 60 and 80 percent of an organization's revenues, has assumed greater strategic orientation in many contemporary firms.

The chapter began with a discussion of procurement objectives and the importance for these objectives to be aligned with, and supportive of, those of the organization. One of procurement's most important responsibilities is supplier selection and evaluation, and this can be quite challenging, in part because of the multiple, and sometime conflicting, selection and evaluation criteria. Supplier development (reverse marketing) is becoming a more important part of the procurement process.

Quality issues were discussed, with a particular emphasis on ISO 9000, Six Sigma, Lean Six Sigma, and the Malcolm Baldrige National Quality Award. Global sourcing, which refers to buying components and inputs anywhere in the world, continues to grow in scope. Because of the tremendous distances that can be involved in global sourcing, managers must understand the trade-offs between transportation and holding costs.

The chapter also discussed investment recovery, with a particular emphasis on managing excess, obsolete, scrap, and waste materials. The chapter concluded with a discussion of socially responsible procurement, and we learned that a number of ethical issues are associated with procurement.

Questions for Discussion and Review

1. What is procurement? What is its relevance to logistics?
2. Contrast procurement's historical focus to its more strategic orientation today.
3. Discuss the benefits and potential challenges of using electronic procurement cards.
4. Discuss three potential procurement objectives.
5. Name and describe the steps in the supplier selection and evaluation process.
6. Distinguish between a single sourcing and multiple sourcing approach.
7. What are the two primary approaches for evaluating suppliers? How do they differ?
8. Discuss the factors that make supplier selection and evaluation difficult.
9. Define supplier development, and explain why it is becoming more prominent in some organizations.
10. Why does the issue of quality in procurement represent a delicate balancing act for organizations?
11. What is the role of ISO certification in quality management programs?
12. Describe significant benefits and drawbacks to Six Sigma programs.
13. Discuss the concept of Lean Six Sigma.
14. How do ISO 9000 and the Malcolm Baldrige Quality Award differ?
15. What are the components of the global sourcing development model presented in this chapter? What are some of the challenges of implementing a global sourcing strategy?
16. Pick, and discuss, two components of the global sourcing development model presented in this chapter.
17. Distinguish between excess, obsolete, scrap, and waste materials.
18. Should investment recovery be the responsibility of the procurement manager? If yes, why? If not, which party (parties) should be responsible for investment recovery?
19. Name, and give an example of, the five dimensions of socially responsible purchasing.
20. Discuss some of the ethical issues that are associated with procurement.

---

[21] "BMW Broadens Its Supply Standards," *Supply Management* 14, no. 21 (2009): 11.

Suggested Readings

Cheraghi, S. Hossein, Mohammed Dadashzadeh, and Mutho Subramanian. "Critical Success Factors for Supplier Selection: An Update." *Journal of Applied Business Research* 20, no. 2 (2004): 91–108.

Christensen, John, Christopher Park, Earl Sun, Max Gorainick, and Jayanth Iyengar. "A Practical Guide to Green Sourcing." *Supply Chain Management Review* 12, no. 8 (2008): 14–21.

Handfield, Robert B., and David L. Baumer. "Managing Conflict of Interest Issues in Purchasing." *Journal of Supply Chain Management* 42, no. 3 (2006): 41–50.

Ho, William, Xiaowei Xu, and Prasanta K. Dey. "Multi-Criteria Decision Making Approaches for Supplier Evaluation and Selection: A Literature Review." *European Journal of Operational Research* 202, no. 1 (2010): 16–24.

Johnson, P. Frazier, Michiel R. Leenders, and Harold E. Fearon. "Supply's Growing Status and Influence: A Sixteen-Year Perspective." *Journal of Supply Chain Management* 42, no. 2 (2006): 33–43.

Martinson, Bob. "The Power of the P-Card." *Strategic Finance* 83, no. 8 (2002): 30–36.

Minahan, Tim A. "Strategies for High-Performance Procurement." *Supply Chain Management Review* 9, no. 6 (2005): 46–54.

Sanchez-Rodriguez, Christobal, and Angel R. Martinez-Lorente. "Quality Management Practices in the Purchasing Function: An Empirical Study." *International Journal of Operations & Production Management* 24, no. 7 (2004): 666–687.

Spray, Gregory. "The Art of Procurement Mastery." *Supply Chain Management Review* 13, no. 1 (2009): 36–43.

Teo, Thompson S. H., and Kee-hung Lai. "Usage and Performance Impact of Electronic Procurement." *Journal of Business Logistics* 20, no. 2 (2009): 125–139.

Trent, Robert J., and Robert M. Monczka. "Achieving Excellence in Global Sourcing." *MIT Sloan Management Review* 47, no. 1 (2005): 24–32.

Turner, Martha, and Pat Houston. "Going Green? Start with Sourcing." *Supply Chain Management Review* 13, no. 2 (2009): 14–21.

CASE

CASE 6-1   Tempo Ltd.

Fatih Terim was in his small office in Antalya, a Mediterranean port in southwestern Turkey. He looked at the clock on the wall and realized he had spent the entire afternoon thinking about one thing and one thing only—the most recent meeting with his Romanian business "connection." Terim had just completed a trip to the Balkans and was in his office evaluating his firm's progress in the region. This was necessary because he was thinking of going to Syria for the same reasons that had taken him to the Balkans: finding goods at cheap prices and selling them with handsome markups at home in Turkey or in other neighboring countries.

Terim had established Tempo Ltd. in 1989 in Antalya. Terim, then fresh out of Akdeniz University, quickly became an entrepreneur. The focus of his business was to buy goods from nearby foreign sources and then find buyers for those products in the domestic Turkish market. The first couple of years were easy for Terim because he was working very hard, and the Turkish economy was soaring. With the fall of communism, Terim saw even more opportunities. He started marketing Turkish-made goods to former communist countries around Turkey and in central Asia.

However, the Turkish economy took a major hit in April 1994. The sudden death of the country's president added to the nation's political instability. The value of

Turkish lira (TL) plummeted against the U.S. dollar (USD). In the following years, the Turkish economy took many more hits, including the financial crisis in the Asian markets, the Russian market crash, and most recently, the Argentinean crisis. In 1999, two major earthquakes hit the northwestern part of Turkey, where one-third of the nation's 67 million persons reside and which is the heartland of Turkish industry. Although Turkey recovered quickly from the earthquakes, political instability continued and pushed the entire economy into a slowdown. In 1993, US$1 could buy 7,000 TL. In 2003, that same US$1 could buy 1,567,000 TL. Despite these discouraging events, the Turkish economy still has opportunities for growth. One reason such a major potential still exists is the simple fact that hardworking, sharp-trading people like Fatih Terim never stood still and kept putting together the best deals they could.

Today Terim's company has some connections in almost every European country and is working very hard to maintain these connections by generating steady flows of commerce. Terim's latest trip was to the Balkan nations of Bulgaria, Romania, and Greece. Terim held meetings with key businesspeople in all three nations. In both Bulgaria and Greece, Terim had entered into modest sales agreements that extend into the middle of next year.

In Romania, matters did not move as quickly. Terim's Romanian connection, George Hagi, was not interested in any of the small transactions that Terim was suggesting. Hagi, in an almost mysterious manner, did tell Terim that he looking for a Turkish partner willing to participate in a substantial, although not exactly legitimate, deal. The first aspect was that the customer wanted to buy Turkish chemicals to be used for fertilizers in agriculture. However, the terms of payment from the prospective customers would be in the form of barter rather than cash, and the goods bartered for the chemicals would be *kereste* (lumber). Although *barter* was a term and practice with which Terim was familiar, he had no idea what to do with *kereste*. Over the years, Tempo Ltd. had concentrated its business on small consumer products. However, he wasn't going to let a detail like this get in the way of new markets. He knew he could find a market in Turkey for lumber because little was produced domestically, and both new construction and earthquake reconstruction were underway.

What worried Terim were his new customers. He learned from Hagi that these new customers were either a large state-owned company in North Korea or the North Korean government itself, which is why Terim spent that entire afternoon thinking about just one thing. All day he tried to justify his possible decisions to himself. The problem was that North Korea was a communist regime, and beyond that, North Korea, according to NATO and the United Nations, was a country that provided support to certain terrorist activities all over the world. In early 2002, U.S. President George W. Bush had described Iran, Iraq, and North Korea as an "axis of evil." North Korea and those with whom it traded were under tight scrutiny from both the United Nations and the United States (which still stationed troops in South Korea).

Terim came up with the excuse that if he didn't sell to the North Koreans, someone else would eventually, so why should he give up this money? However, the solution was not that easy. Hagi said in his e-mail to Terim that if the negotiations went well, a party of North Korean bureaucrats would wish to visit Antalya for "inspection" purposes and that Terim would have to cover the costs of entertainment and accommodations. Those accommodations would range from luxurious hotel rooms to young attractive companions, of both sexes, for business-related dinners and receptions. Terim knew exactly what those inspection purposes were. They were pleasure trips for certain bureaucrats in North Korea. Unfortunately, he was also aware that this was the way things worked in Third World governments. Over the years, he had learned the tricks of the trade, and one

thing he knew well was that without the *rusvet* (bribe: the grease money or large amounts of payments specifically for one-time transactions), such risky situations would end up as a "no sale." He wondered whether he should ask the Turkish agricultural chemical manufacturers to help with the entertainment costs. Also, should he and the chemical manufacturers touch base with each other with respect to the *rusvet* that would undoubtedly be expected by the North Koreans? Terim's position regarding *rusvet* was unclear. Indeed, the chemical manufactures should be expected to give him, or Hagi, a kickback for facilitating the sale of chemicals.

"Talk about core competency," Terim mumbled to himself. To get his mind off these sticky issues, he looked into the logistics costs to move the bartered lumber from North Korea. He would need to know those costs before proceeding. He had a couple of options.

The first option would be to ship the lumber by sea from Wonsan, North Korea, through the Sea of Japan, across the Indian Ocean, through the Suez Canal, and into the liman (port) of Antalya, Turkey. (see Exhibits 6-A and 6-B.) This would be the perfect solution, except, he suddenly realized, he would not be able to bring the lumber into Turkey legally because of trade sanctions against North Korea. Hence, this option was dropped.

His second option would be to send the lumber to a country where its entry would be legal. The country to which the kereste could be shipped legally was none other than Romania, one of Turkey's neighbors on the Black Sea. The reason was hidden in history. Since their communist years, Romania and North Korea had had strong ties that remained nearly intact after the fall of communism in Romania. So lumber could be loaded on to a *gemi* (ship) and could be shipped to Romania via the Dardanelles and the Bosphorus (the two straits that make up the gateway to the Black Sea) and finally to the port of Constanta, Romania, in the Black Sea. Once there, the lumber could be covered by new documents, and eventually the origin of the goods could be stated as "Romania," not "North Korea." The lumber could then move by *tir* (truck) to Turkey. This sounded like a feasible solution, but how much would such an operation cost? Terim recalled that Hagi had said that redoing documents in situations like this cost about 16,000,000,000 TL, including *rusvets*.

Terim's mind then shifted to a third option. From Wonsan, the lumber could be shipped to a port in Syria, in this case Latakia. From there, *tirs* could haul the lumber to Iskenderun at the southeastern border of Turkey. Because the border at Iskenderun is the most laxly guarded border in Turkey, small *rusvets* to low-ranking officers at the gates would allow the *kereste* to

EXHIBIT 6-A   **Korean Peninsula**

enter Turkey without any problems. The *rusvets* would be about 10 percent of the kereste shipment's value.

The same could be done at the Liman of Antalya. However, the chances of getting caught were much higher. If Tempo Ltd. were caught red-handed, it would be fined a sum of double the total value of goods entering the country. Thus, this was a fourth, but discarded, option.

Only two options were feasible, and each came with certain risks. One was to ship the *kereste* to Romania, have new documents drawn, falsify the shipment's origin, and then send it to Turkey by *tir*. The other was to send the *kereste* by ship to Syria, truck it to Turkey, and bribe customs inspectors at the Turkish border. Terim was initially concerned with the logistics costs of getting the *kereste* inside the Turkish border. The *kereste* would be of various dimensions, bound together by metal straps into bundles measuring 1 meter by 1 meter by 5 meters, and the North Koreans would deliver and load the *kereste* aboard a break-bulk vessel in a North Korean port.

If Terim could get the *kereste* inside Turkey, it should sell for 783,500,000,000 TL. The Turkish chemical

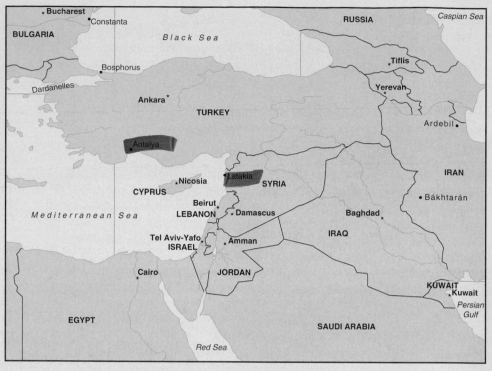

EXHIBIT 6-B Mediterranean Sea

manufacturers expect to be paid 60 days after the chemicals leave the Turkish port, which will be same date as the *kereste* leaves North Korea.

Terim gazed at his notes, which were full of numbers and currency exchange rates.

Ocean transportation costs for Gemi (Shipping lines require payment in U.S. dollars):

Wonsan to Constanta	US$42,000
Wonsan to Latakia	US$33,000
Suez Canal charges	US$3,100
Tir:	
Constanta into Turkey	US$15,000
Latakia into Turkey	US$12,000
Handling fees at the Liman (Syria or Romania)	1.25 percent of the total value of goods
Generating false Romania—origin Documents	16,000,000,000 TL
Projected amount *rusvet* at Syrian–Turkish border	10 percent of shipment's value
Currency exchange rates	US$1 = 1,567,000 TL
Option 1: Wonsan/ Constanta/Turkey would take 43 days	Option 2: Wonsan/ Latakia/Turkey would take 22 days

Questions

1. Should Terim let somebody else complete the transaction because he knows that if he doesn't sell to the North Koreans, someone else will?
2. What are the total costs given in the case for the option of moving via Romania?
3. What are the total costs given in the case for the option of moving via Syria?
4. Which option should Terim recommend? Why?
5. What other costs and risks are involved in these proposed transactions, including some not mentioned in the case?
6. Regarding the supply chain, how—if at all—should bribes be included? What functions do they serve?
7. If Terim puts together this transaction, is he acting ethically? Discuss.
8. What do you suggest should be done to bring moral values into the situation so that the developing countries are somewhat in accordance with Western standards? Keep in mind that the risks involved in such environments are much higher than the risks of conducting business in Western markets. Also note that some cultures see bribery as a way to better distribute the wealth among their citizens.

PART
III

ELEMENTS OF LOGISTICS SYSTEMS

Part III presents a detailed examination of some of the more prominent elements of logistics systems. Chapter 7 looks at demand management, order management, and customer service. Demand management involves managing customer demand through the supply chain, whereas order management deals with incoming orders, and customer service deals with keeping existing customers happy. Chapter 8 discusses inventory management, where you will learn about inventory classifications as well as inventory-related costs. This chapter also examines how much inventory to order, when to order inventory, and special concerns with inventory.

The topic of Chapter 9 is "Distribution Center, Warehouse, and Plant Location." Facility location has moved from a tactical to a strategic consideration in many companies, and Chapter 9 discusses general and specific factors in facility location. Chapter 10 focuses on warehousing management, and you will learn about the various types of warehousing, warehousing's role in a logistics system, and design considerations in warehousing. The effectiveness and efficiency of warehousing operations can be greatly influenced by packaging and materials handling considerations, and Chapter 11 looks at these two topics.

Two chapters are devoted to transportation because it often represents the highest cost logistics activity in a company. Chapter 12 provides an overview of transportation modes and intermediaries, and Chapter 13 covers the management of transportation activities.

Chapter 14, the last chapter in this section, deals with international logistics, although certain other aspects of this topic are touched on in other chapters. International logistics is a rapidly growing and constantly changing field.

7

DEMAND MANAGEMENT, ORDER MANAGEMENT, AND CUSTOMER SERVICE

Key Terms

- Activity-based costing
- Benchmarking
- Cause-and-effect (associative) forecasting
- Collaborative planning, forecasting, and replenishment (CPFR)
- Customer profitability analysis (CPA)
- Customer service
- Demand management
- Judgmental forecasting
- Make-to-order
- Make-to-stock
- Multichannel marketing systems
- Order cycle
- Order delivery
- Order fill rate
- Order management
- Order picking and assembly
- Order processing
- Order to cash cycle
- Order transmittal
- Order triage
- Pick-to-light technology
- Service recovery
- Time series forecasting
- Voice-based order picking

Learning Objectives

- To understand the linkages between demand management, order management, and customer service
- To learn about demand forecasting models
- To examine the order cycle and its four components
- To understand the four dimensions of customer service as they pertain to logistics
- To familiarize you with select managerial issues associated with customer service

This chapter discusses two key issues: (1) how an organization determines what the customer wants and (2) how an organization facilitates the customer getting what is wanted. We will analyze these issues in terms of demand management (how an organization determines what the customer wants) along with order management and customer service (how an organization facilitates the customer getting what is wanted). Demand management is important because effective and efficient supply chains have learned to match both supply and demand; failure to do so can result in oversupply (more supply than demand) or undersupply (less supply than demand) of products. Oversupply likely means higher than desired inventory costs, whereas undersupply can mean a dissatisfied—or even lost—customer.

Order management and customer service begin where demand management ends. The ability to determine that the customer wants, say, a black shovel, is nice, but is the customer able to communicate this desire to an organization? Once the customer's desire for a black shovel is communicated to an organization, is the organization able to fulfill this desire? Although these might seem like basic, commonsense questions, reality may be quite different. Indeed, one lesson learned in the early years of online retailing was that many companies were quite good at understanding and stimulating customer demand as well as receiving orders associated with the demand. Unfortunately, some of these companies were far less adept at processing these orders; orders arrived late (if they arrived at all), incomplete, and with incorrect product(s). Not surprisingly, these fulfillment shortcomings caused a great deal of customer dissatisfaction, which explains why some early online retailers (e.g., etoys.com) are no longer in business.

DEMAND MANAGEMENT

Demand management can be defined as "the creation across the supply chain and its markets of a coordinated flow of demand."[1] A key component in demand management is demand (sales) forecasting, which refers to an effort to project future demand. Without question, demand forecasting is helpful in **make-to-stock** situations (when finished goods are produced prior to receiving a customer order). However, demand forecasting can also be helpful in **make-to-order** situations (when finished goods are produced after receiving a customer order). Make-to-order situations generally involve some combination of standard and custom components, and forecasting could be quite helpful in projecting the standard components needed. For example, although Dell Corporation might not be able to forecast the exact configuration of each order for computers that it receives, Dell might be able to forecast the percentage of orders for desktop and laptop computers (i.e., standard components).

Entire books are devoted to demand forecasting, and space limitations prevent a comprehensive discussion of the topic in this text. Rather, we will offer an overview of demand forecasting so the reader can understand forecasting's role in determining what the customer wants.

Demand Forecasting Models[2]

The three basic types of forecasting models are (1) judgmental, (2) time series, and (3) cause and effect. **Judgmental forecasting** involves using judgment or intuition and is preferred in situations where there are limited or no historical data, such as with a new product introduction. Judgment forecasting techniques include surveys and the analog technique, among others. With survey forecasting, questionnaires (surveys) are used to learn about customer preferences and intentions. A strong understanding of survey design and population sampling methodologies is necessary in survey forecasting, and you should recognize that customer intentions don't always translate into actual behavior. Analog forecasting involves determining an analog (similar item) to the item being forecast and then using the analog's demand history as a basis for the relevant forecast. A key challenge is selecting the appropriate analog to use.

An underlying assumption of **time series forecasting** is that future demand is solely dependent on past demand. For example, if this year's sales were 7 percent higher than last year's sales, a time series forecast for next year's sales would be this year's sales plus 7 percent. Time series forecasting techniques include, but are not limited to, simple moving averages and weighted moving averages. The simple moving average is calculated by summing the demand across different time periods and then dividing by the number of time periods. Because each time period is assigned the same importance (weight), the simple moving average may not adequately reflect recent upturns or downturns in demand. To address this shortcoming, the weighted moving average technique assigns greater importance (weight) to the more recent data. The differences in forecasted demand between the simple and weighted moving averages can be seen in the example in Table 7-1.

---

[1] John T. Mentzer, "A Telling Fortune," *Industrial Engineer*, April 2006, 42–47.
[2] The discussion of demand forecasting models is drawn from Chaman L. Jain, "Benchmarking Forecasting Models," *Journal of Business Forecasting* 24, no. 4 (2005/2006): 9–10, 12 as well as Joel D. Wisner, G. Keong Leong, and Keah-Choon Tan, *Principles of Supply Chain Management: A Balanced Approach* (Mason, OH: South-Western Publishing, 2005), Chapter 5.

TABLE 7-1	Forecast Example Using the Simple and Weighted Moving Average Techniques

Time Period (1)	Demand (2)	Simple Moving Average Weighting Factor (3)	Projected Demand (4; = 2 × 3)	Weighted Moving Average Weighting Factor (5)	Projected Demand (6; = 2 × 5)
Last month	250	.25	62.5	.40	100
Two months ago	230	.25	57.5	.30	69
Three months ago	200	.25	50	.20	40
Four months ago	180	.25	45	.10	18
Forecast			**215**		**227**

Cause-and-effect (also referred to as associative) forecasting assumes that one or more factors are related to demand and that the relationship between cause and effect can be used to estimate future demand. In many countries, for example, there tends to be an inverse relationship between the level of interest rates and the consumers' ability to buy a house (e.g., as interest rates increase, housing sales tend to decrease). Examples of cause-and-effect forecasting include simple and multiple regression; in simple regression, demand is dependent on only one variable, whereas in multiple regression, demand is dependent on two or more variables.

Demand Forecasting Issues

It's important to recognize that the selection of a forecasting technique (or techniques) depends on a variety of factors, such as the situation at hand, forecasting costs in terms of time and money, and the accuracy of various forecasting techniques. With respect to the situation at hand, as pointed out earlier, judgmental forecasting is appropriate where there are little or no historical data available. For instance, Apple Corporation's initial sales estimates for the iPod (a portable digital audio player), which was introduced in 2001, were based on judgment and intuition—the iPod was not only a new product but a somewhat revolutionary product as well. Managers should also understand time and monetary costs associated with each particular forecasting technique. Survey research, for example, can require quite a bit of both money and time, depending on the media (i.e., mail, telephone, electronic, in-person) used to collect and analyze the data.

Forecasting accuracy refers to the relationship between actual and forecasted demand, and accuracy can be affected by various considerations. One of the challenges with the analog technique is selecting the appropriate analog, because an inappropriate selection will reduce forecast accuracy. For instance, when a movie studio releases a sequel to a previously successful motion picture, a forecasting analog based on the initial release will likely generate a different estimate than a forecasting analog based on the performance patterns of sequels to other movies—and one analog will be more accurate than the other.

Forecast accuracy can have important logistical implications, as illustrated at Lighthouse Foods, where improved forecasting resulted in substantial reductions in the amount of finished goods inventory. More specifically, Lighthouse used to carry nearly twice as much inventory as actually needed for certain stock-keeping units (SKUs) because of inaccurate demand forecasts for those items.[3]

Up to this point, we have treated demand forecasting as a discrete entity in the sense that each supply chain member generates its own demand forecasts. You may recall that Chapter 1 briefly mentioned the **collaborative planning, forecasting, and replenishment (CPFR)** concept,

---

[3] Carol Casper, "Demand Planning Comes of Age," *Food Logistics*, January/February 2008, 19–24.

where supply chain partners share planning and forecasting data to better match up supply and demand. Conceptually, CPFR suggests that supply chain partners will be working from a collectively agreed-to single forecast number as opposed to each member working off its own forecast projection. Successful CPFR implementations have yielded smoother ordering patterns, increased sales revenues, decreased safety stock, higher order fill rates, and improved forecasting accuracy.[4] Despite these potential benefits, you should recognize that (1) not all CPFR initiatives have been successful and (2) there can be significant challenges associated with getting supply chain partners to share the relevant data needed to develop the forecast(s).

We'll conclude our discussion of demand forecasting with a brief look at forecasting that is done via computer software. Computer software forecasting dates back over 30 years, and there has been tremendous advancement in its breadth and computational power—forecasts that might have taken hours or days on a mainframe computer can now be generated in a matter of minutes or hours on a personal computer. And although it would seem as if this advancement would contribute to improved forecasts, software-based forecasting continues to be plagued by some of the issues (e.g., inappropriate technique for the situation at hand, costs, and forecast error) discussed earlier in this section. For example, Microsoft's Excel spreadsheet is heavily used for business forecasting, in part because it is relatively easy to learn and its low cost. However, because Excel's statistical procedures are considered to be unreliable and relatively unsophisticated, its forecasts can contain a great deal of error. Alternatively, multimillion-dollar software packages that are solely devoted to demand forecasting have also been problematic on occasion because of difficulty in understanding how to use them.[5] It's important to keep in mind that no software package—regardless of its sophistication and cost—is capable of totally eliminating forecast errors.

ORDER MANAGEMENT

Order management refers to management of the various activities associated with the **order cycle**; the order cycle (which can also be referred to as replenishment cycle or lead time) refers to the time from when a customer places an order to when the goods are received. In recent years some organizations have expanded the order management concept to include the length of time it takes an organization to receive payment for an order, or what is called the **order to cash cycle**.

There is a key link between order management and demand forecasting, in that a firm does not simply wait for orders to arrive to learn what's happening with respect to demand. Forecasts are made of sales and of the inventories that must be stocked so that the firm can fill orders in a satisfactory manner. There is also a key link between order management and customer service because many organizations analyze customer service in terms of order cycle performance.

Before proceeding to a discussion of the four order cycle stages, several points should be made. First, the order cycle should be analyzed not only in terms of total cycle time but in cycle time variability (reliability) as well. Just as longer order cycles necessitate increased levels of inventory, so, too, does greater cycle time variability require additional levels of inventory (regardless of cycle time length). Consider the U.S. railroad that analyzed transit times on one of its origin–destination pairs located approximately 400 miles apart. The railroad discovered an average transit time of 8 days, with a minimum of 3 days and a maximum of 28 days, and the railroad's customers coped with the erratic transit times by holding additional inventory to avoid out-of-stock situations.[6]

[4] Jerry Andrews, "CPFR: Considering the Options, Advantages, and Pitfalls," *Supply and Demand Chain Executive*, April/May 2008, 8–12.

[5] Michael Gilliland and Michael Leonard, "Forecasting Software—The Past and Future," *The Journal of Business Forecasting* 25, no. 1 (2006): 33–36.

[6] Judy A. Perry, "Who's Watching the Numbers That Count?" *Railway Age*, May 2005, 10.

A second point is that order management has been profoundly affected by advances in information systems. For example, one of this book's authors worked in the U.S. trucking industry in the early 1980s, and if a customer telephoned to learn about a shipment's status, a very manual—and, unfortunately, a time-consuming (at a minimum, the phone call had to be answered) and not always successful—shipment tracking process was initiated. Today, by contrast, that same customer doesn't have to place a phone call; in many cases, he/she can simply log on to a particular carrier's Web site to learn about a shipment's status.

You should also recognize that the various activities associated with an order cycle are not uniformly agreed upon. For example, the Supply-Chain Council lists approximately 15 distinct activities as part of the order cycle.[7] By contrast, we view the order cycle as consisting of four components or stages: order transmittal, order processing, order picking and assembly, and order delivery. Each of the four components will be discussed below.

Order Transmittal

Order transmittal refers to the time from when the customer places an order until the seller receives the order. In general, there are five possible ways to transmit orders: in person, by mail, by telephone, by facsimile (fax) machine, and electronically. Each method of order transmittal has advantages and disadvantages, and each performs differently with respect to the cost of ordering, the time to order, the potential for order errors, and ordering convenience. For example, in-person orders greatly reduce the potential for order errors, if for no other reason that the order can be physically inspected prior to being accepted. However, in-person ordering isn't always convenient (or practical) in situations where the supplier is geographically distant.

Although ordering by mail might be more convenient than in-person ordering, mail is considered to be a relatively slow form of order transmittal, and there are occasions when the order never reaches the intended destination (lost in the mail). Ordering by telephone can be fast and convenient, but order errors generally aren't detected until the order is delivered. Many of us have placed a telephone order for home delivery of a large, one-topping pizza—only to be delivered a small, one-topping pizza with the incorrect topping!

Both facsimile and electronic ordering are techniques that have emerged over the past 25 years, and both have had immense impacts on the order transmittal process. The fax can be fast, convenient, and, unlike the telephone, provides hard copy documentation of an order. However, the seller's fax machine can be cluttered with junk (unwanted) faxes, and the quality of the fax transmission can result in hard-to-read orders—which increases the chances of order errors in the form of incorrect product or incorrect quantity. Electronic ordering, which includes electronic data interchange (EDI) and the Internet, can be fast, convenient, and accurate, particularly those orders involving scanners and bar codes. A major concern with ordering via the Internet is the security of the data being transmitted; indeed, there are estimates that the costs associated with the theft of data from Internet transactions now exceed \$350,000 *per incident!*[8]

Order Processing

Order processing refers to the time from when the seller receives an order until an appropriate location (such as a warehouse) is authorized to fill the order. Advances in technology have allowed most firms to computerize many aspects of their order processing systems. For instance, order forms, whether printed or in computer format, are designed so that the use of computers by both the customer and the vendor is facilitated. Similarly, the billing of customers is increasingly done through computerized and electronic networks.

Figure 7-1, which presents an order processing flowchart, highlights that there are many distinct order processing activities. Typical order processing activities include checking an order for

---

[7] http://archive.supply-chain.org/galleries/public-gallery/SCOR%209.0%20Reference%20Guide.pdf.

[8] Scott Roberston, "Hacker Heaven," *American Metal Market*, May 1, 2006, 4–5.

FIGURE 7-1 Flowchart of Order Handling (Order Processing) System

completeness and accuracy, checking the buyer's ability to purchase, entering the order into the system, crediting a salesperson with a sale, recording the transaction, determining inventory location, and arranging for outbound transportation. Although some of the activities must be performed sequentially (e.g., an order can't be transported until a company knows from which location(s) it will be filled), some might be performed simultaneously (e.g., crediting a salesperson with a sale and recording the transaction). Note that one way to reduce order cycle time is to identify activities that can be performed simultaneously and then perform the relevant activities simultaneously, rather than sequentially.

An understanding of the various order processing activities is only a first step, however. Companies differ in their approaches to managing order processing and its activities, and these different approaches can have important implications on order cycle effectiveness and efficiency as well as on customer satisfaction. We'll highlight different managerial approaches by discussing three order processing activities, order receipt, order triage, and the location(s) used to fill an order, in the following paragraphs.

With respect to order receipt, Figure 7-1 indicates that incoming orders can be divided into categories, one for EDI orders that are allowed to bypass checking for completeness and accuracy and one category for all other orders. It could be argued that all orders, regardless of transmission method, should be checked for completeness and accuracy; incomplete or inaccurate orders can negatively affect customer satisfaction and increase costs in the sense of addressing order irregularities. However, checking all orders for completeness and accuracy adds costs and time to the order cycle. Alternatively, companies might structure the order receipt function to reflect historical trends on order completeness and accuracy. Under this scenario, order transmission methods that consistently exhibit superior completeness and accuracy would bypass the order check activity.

Figure 7-1 also contains an order triage activity. The triage concept is often associated with the medical field and refers to classifying patients in terms of the severity of their illness or malady, and the classification allows doctors to prioritize which patients should be attended to before others. Similarly, **order triage** refers to classifying orders according to preestablished guidelines so that a company can prioritize how orders should be filled. However, not all companies prioritize orders, and those that do must decide the attribute(s) used to prioritize (e.g., first in, first served; customer longevity; customer sales). Although there is no one right attribute to use for order prioritization, you should recognize that the chosen attribute(s) are likely to delight some customers (those that exhibit the chosen attribute) and disappoint other customers.

Another key order processing decision (see Figure 7-1) involves determining the location(s) from which an order is to be filled. As was the case with order triage, companies should have clear, consistently applied rules to help in making this decision, but there are companies that decide which facility to use on an order-by-order basis—which can lead to inconsistent order cycle time and cost. A commonsense approach would be to fill an order from the facility location that is closest to the customer, with the idea that this should generate lower transportation costs as well as a shorter order cycle time. Alternatively, an order could be filled from the facility location that currently has the largest amount of requested product; this likely would increase both order cycle time and transportation cost, but could help the seller by reducing excess inventory at a particular location.

Order Picking and Assembly

Order picking and assembly is the next stage of the order management process, and it includes all activities from when an appropriate location (such as a warehouse) is authorized to fill the order until goods are loaded aboard an outbound carrier. Although order picking and assembly is sometimes overlooked because neither activity is very glamorous, order picking and assembly often represents the best opportunity to improve the effectiveness and efficiency of an order cycle; order picking and assembly can account for up to two-thirds of a facility's operating cost and time.[9]

Importantly, the effectiveness and efficiency of order picking and assembly can often be improved without large expenditures. For example, one suggestion involves "shadowing" existing order pickers to learn about their routines and the challenges they face, such as items that aren't where they should be, aisle congestion, or talkative coworkers. Another suggestion is to analyze order pickers' travel time, in part because travel time accounts for between 60 and 80 percent of total pick time. Moreover, travel time can be reduced through better slotting (placement) of products in the relevant facility.[10] For example, a company might place its most heavily demanded items in a fairly central and easily accessible location as opposed to a more remote and less-accessible location.

Order picking and assembly has been greatly affected by advances in technology such as handheld scanners, radio-frequency identification (RFID), and voice-based order picking. **Voice-based order picking** refers to the use of speech to guide order-picking activities. Early voice-based picking systems were characterized by high adoption costs, poor voice quality, and systems that were easily disrupted by other noises. Contemporary voice-based systems, by contrast, are less costly, are more powerful, have better voice quality, and are less cumbersome for workers to use. Companies that have adopted newer-generation voice-based technology have reported increased productivity and higher pick accuracy. The implementation of voice-based order picking at one company resulted in 99.66 percent pick accuracy, which also saved the company nearly $100,000 through the elimination of four order checkers' positions.[11]

Another order-picking technique that has grown in popularity in recent years is **pick-to-light technology**, in which orders to be picked are identified by lights placed on shelves or racks. One advantage to pick-to-light technology is that the worker simply follows the lights from pick to pick, as opposed to the worker having to figure out an optimal picking path. Advantages to pick-to-light technology include higher pick rates (measured by lines picked per hour) as well as fewer picking errors in part because pickers are able to focus on picking rather than on written instructions.[12]

Order Delivery

The final phase of the order cycle is **order delivery**, which refers to the time from when a transportation carrier picks up the shipment until it is received by the customer. Not surprisingly, there have been many changes to the order delivery process in recent years; several of these changes will be highlighted in the following paragraphs. An underlying theme of these changes involves delivery options that represent the customer's increasing power in business transactions.

For example, carriers historically provided a limited number of options in terms of transit time alternatives, and shippers thus had to incorporate the rather inflexible transit times into calculations of the length of an order cycle. However, as pointed out in Chapter 1, some transportation service providers now offer prospective shippers a diverse menu of transit time options. For example, suppose you wanted to use FedEx Express to ship a 20 pound package from Chagrin Falls, Ohio, to New Smyrna Beach, Florida. You could choose from four transit time options—same-day delivery, next delivery by 12 noon, next-day delivery by 4:30, and second-day delivery.[13]

Another key change is that more and more shippers are emphasizing both the elapsed transit time and transit time reliability (variability); recall that increases in order cycle variability

---

[9] Susan Lacefield, "Ten Tips for Faster Picking," *Logistics Management*, July 2005, 71–76.

[10] Ibid.

[11] Joe Ryan, "Speech is Right for the Warehouse," *Speech Technology Magazine*, March 2008, 36–37.

[12] Corrine Kator, "Which Picking Methods Work?" *Modern Materials Handling*, March 2007, 11–13.

[13] *http://www.fedex.com/ratefinder/standalone?method=goToResultSummaryPage.*

translate into higher inventory levels. To this end, more buyers are utilizing delivery appointments that contain delivery windows, or the time span within which an order must arrive. Although some delivery windows are 1 hour in length, others are as narrow as 15 minutes. So, if a carrier has a 9:00 A.M. appointment with a 15-minute delivery window, it must arrive no later than 9:15 A.M. Oftentimes, failure to meet the relevant delivery window means that the carrier must wait for the next open delivery time—which might not be until the end of the day.

A third important change associated with order delivery involves transportation carriers revamping their operations to provide faster transit times to customers. For example, 500 miles traditionally served as the maximum range for overnight service in the trucking industry. In recent years, by contrast, the maximum range for overnight service by truck has been pushed to between 600 and 700 miles. This expanded coverage is important because many shippers are hesitant to pay for premium transportation service such as that provided by expedited carriers and airlines.[14]

CUSTOMER SERVICE

Customers are important to organizations, and organizations that view customers as a "nuisance" may not last very long in today's highly competitive business environment. Consider several metrics associated with unhappy customers; a frequently cited metric is that it costs approximately five times as much to develop a new customer as it does to retain an existing one. In addition, approximately 95 percent of unhappy customers do not communicate their unhappiness to the responsible organization and won't return as customers—but will tell nine people about their unhappiness.[15] Quite simply, it's easier for an organization to keep an existing customer than it is to acquire new customers. To this end, customer service strives to keep customers happy and creates in the customer's mind the perception of an organization that is easy to do business with.

Customer service can be an excellent competitive weapon and is more difficult for competitors to imitate than other marketing mix variables such as price and promotion. Nordstrom's (a high-end retailer) has a long-standing reputation for excellent customer service, and this customer focus often leads Nordstrom's to do things that competitors cannot or will not match. For example, one of the authors was shopping at a Nordstrom's and found a belt that he liked, but the store didn't have the correct size in stock. Several days later, the author received a call from a Nordstrom's salesperson indicating that the desired belt was available for purchase at the local store. The salesperson had located the belt at another Nordstrom's and had the belt expedited—via *airfreight*—to the local store. With a retail value of approximately $45, it's likely that the particular Nordstrom's lost money on this purchase. It's a reasonable assumption, however, that few other retailers would copy Nordstrom's behavior in servicing the customer.

Macroenvironmental changes, such as globalization and advances in technology, are causing organizations and individuals to demand higher levels of customer service. As was pointed out in an earlier chapter, customer expectations continue to increase over time; if the associated performance (service) levels fail to keep up, then customer dissatisfaction is a likely outcome. In addition, as emphasized in this chapter, reliable service enables a firm to maintain a lower level of inventory, especially of safety stocks, which produces lower inventory holding costs. Third, in an increasingly automated and computerized world, the relationships between customers and vendors can become dehumanized. This situation is both frustrating and inefficient from the customer's viewpoint. The firm that can offer a high level of customer service, especially on a personal basis, will find that it has a powerful sales advantage in the marketplace.

---

[14] John D. Boyd, "Getting Grounded," *Traffic World*, April 3, 2006, 18–21.
[15] Jessica Tremayne, "The Science of Service," *Smart Business Cleveland*, March 2009, 61–66.

Furthermore, the increased use of vendor quality-control programs necessitates higher levels of customer service. In recent years, many firms, especially retailers and wholesalers, have become more inventory conscious. This emphasis has resulted in computer-assisted analysis to identify vendors that consistently give either good or bad levels of service. In the past, with manual systems, repeated and serious customer service errors occurred before a vendor's activities were singled out for corrective action. Today, these factors are automatically programmed into computers, and companies are able to closely monitor the quality of service they receive from each vendor.

We've talked at some length about customer service, but we've yet to offer a formal definition of it. Keeping in mind that there are myriad customer service definitions, for our purposes **customer service** will be defined as "the ability of logistics management to satisfy users in terms of time, dependability, communication, and convenience."[16] Let's take a closer look at each of these four dimensions of customer service.

Time

Time refers to the period between successive events, and, clearly, the order cycle is an excellent example of the time dimension of customer service. At the risk of sounding redundant, many businesses today are looking to reduce order cycle times—longer cycle times translate into higher inventory requirements.

Dependability

Dependability refers to the reliability of the service encounter and consists of three elements, namely, consistent order cycles, safe delivery, and complete delivery.[17] Our earlier discussion of the order cycle highlighted the importance of consistency (reliability/dependability)—inconsistent order cycles necessitate higher inventory requirements. And although order cycle time is important, an increasing number of companies are trading off order cycle speed for order cycle consistency. More specifically, these companies are willing to accept a slower order cycle so long as it exhibits a high level of consistency.

Safe delivery brings loss and damage considerations into play. Product can be lost or damaged for a multitude of reasons, but the reasons are rather immaterial to a customer—a lost or damaged product can cause a variety of negative ramifications for a customer, such as out-of-stock situations. **Order fill rate**, or the percentage of orders that can be completely and immediately filled from existing stock, is one way of measuring the completeness of delivery. As is the case with loss and damage, incomplete deliveries result in negative customer ramifications, such as out-of-stock situations.

It is unlikely that loss and damage can ever be totally eliminated; because orders are picked and assembled, they are handled—and every time a product is handled, there are opportunities for loss or damage. However, the seller may be able to minimize the number of times an order is handled, perhaps by redesigning the order pick process. And, even if an organization has highly accurate demand forecasting, it's also unlikely that it will be able to achieve a 100 percent fill rate (i.e., all incoming orders are filled completely). Consider the situation of the McDonald's restaurant where two people walked in and *placed a take-out order for 142 Egg McMuffins*! Although the restaurant was successfully able to fill this order (but not before ensuring that the two customers could pay for it), the inventory needed to fill it meant that a lot of other orders for Egg McMuffins went unfilled, at least until the next scheduled delivery of foodstuffs.

---

[16] Roger A. Kerin, Steven W. Hartley, and William Rudelius, *Marketing*, 9th ed. (Boston, MA: McGraw-Hill/Irwin, 2009), Chapter 16.
[17] Ibid.

Communication

Effective communication should be a two-way exchange between seller and customer, with the goal of keeping both parties informed. Moreover, effective communication requires that the correct parties be involved in the process; if a customer has a logistics-related question, then the customer should be communicating with someone with logistics expertise. Moreover, customer service can be enhanced if *complete information* is exchanged between the participants; a delivery address can be helpful, but detailed characteristics of the delivery address would be even more helpful, as illustrated by the case of the transportation company that was responsible for delivering a $750,000 shipment of computer racks. What the transportation company didn't find out—until it actually made the delivery—was that the customer was located on the 17th floor of an office building in the central business district of a major city. Because neither the transportation company nor the office building had the appropriate equipment to facilitate the shipment's handling, the delivery had to be delayed until the proper equipment could be located and brought to the building.[18]

Two-way communication between seller and customer has certainly benefited from technological advances such as cell phones, smart phones, and the Internet. These technological advances allow for less costly and more frequent contacts between the two parties. However, technology such as text messaging and the Internet can depersonalize the communication process, which is why periodic telephone interaction and even face-to-face contact between seller and customer are recommended.[19] You should recognize that personal communication is an essential part of conducting business in many cultures.

Convenience

The convenience component of customer service focuses on the ease of doing business with a seller. Having said this, different customers may have different perceptions of the "ease of doing business" concept. For example, for a college student the ease of doing business with a bank might mean access to automatic teller machines, whereas for a small business owner it might mean bank tellers who specifically focus on commercial deposits and withdrawals. As such, sellers should have an understanding of their customer segments and how each segment views the ease of doing business.

Moreover, from the seller's perspective, certain costs may be associated with convenience; for example, there may be a charge for pizza that's delivered to your residence or workplace (or "free delivery areas" might be very small in geographic coverage). As a result, sellers must assess the extent to which their customers are willing to pay for convenience. In recent years, many airlines have discovered that allowing customers to arrange their own travel via the Internet is quite cost effective for the airlines in that the costs of processing an electronic ticket are approximately $1 compared to $10 for processing a paper ticket. As a result, customers who arrange their travel by telephoning an airline's customer service agent are often charged a fee for talking to the service agent (a service that for many years was "free" to the customer).

The convenience dimension also plays a key role in a consumer's purchasing decision. Today's consumer likes to have multiple purchasing options at his/her disposal, and organizations have responded by developing **multichannel marketing systems**, that is, separate marketing channels to serve customers. A retailer, for example, can facilitate customer purchasing with brick-and-mortar stores (one channel) as well with a Web site (another channel). The convenience dimension in multichannel marketing systems is increasingly manifested through customer orders in one channel (e.g., online) and customer delivery in another channel (e.g., in store).[20]

---

[18] John Paul Quinn, "How to Avoid Communication Breakdowns," *Logistics Management*, April 2006, 37–41.
[19] Ibid.
[20] Paul Brooks, "The Multichannel Challenge," *Logistics Manager*, October 2008, 50.

MANAGING CUSTOMER SERVICE

In addition to understanding what customer service is, the logistician faces multiple managerial considerations with customer service. The remainder of this chapter will discuss four specific considerations: customer profitability analysis, establishing customer service objectives, measuring customer service, and service failure and recovery.

Customer Profitability Analysis

Customer profitability analysis (CPA) refers to the allocation of revenues and costs to customer segments or individual customers to calculate the profitability of the segments or customers. CPA suggests that different customers (segments) consume differing amounts and types of resources; for example, some customers might require telephone-based communication with an organization, whereas other customers are able to communicate electronically with an organization. CPA is also facilitated by the sophistication of contemporary information management systems that allow both revenue and cost activities to be directly assigned to specific customers or segments.[21]

CPA explicitly recognizes that all customers are not the same, and some customers are more valuable than others to an organization. CPA can be used to identify different groups of customers from a profitability perspective, and such a grouping can better help in allocating an organization's resources. One suggested classification, for example, divides customers into three groups (A, B, and C), and "A" customers represent those that make a positive contribution to the bottom line. Although "B" customers might not be profitable, they allow for volume purchasing; "C" customers are highly unprofitable and might be candidates for elimination.[22] From a resource allocation perspective, an organization should pursue different logistical approaches for different customer groups. With respect to product availability, for example, organizations might attempt to minimize or avoid stockout situations for A customers, while limiting product availability for C customers.

CPA has been facilitated by the acceptance of activity-based costing in the sense that activity-based costing suggests that different products are characterized by differences in the amount and types of resources consumed. (Appendix 7-A provides a closer look at activity-based costing.) As an example, one specialty distributor of fluid-related products established activity-based costing as the foundation of a CPA program. The distributor, which served approximately 2,000 customers prior to initiating CPA, learned that 150 customers accounted for 90 percent of company profits. In addition, the CPA identified over 1,000 unprofitable customers; the distributor no longer does business with them.[23]

Establishing Customer Service Objectives

Because customer service standards can significantly affect a firm's overall sales success, establishing goals and objectives is an important management decision. Goals tend to be broad, generalized statements regarding the overall results that the firm is attempting to achieve. Unfortunately, some firms' statements of customer service goals are couched in platitudes and lack the specifics of how the goals are to be achieved. This is a serious problem because if the customer service objectives or standards are not stated in specific terms, they may be ignored or be too vague to provide any real guidance to operating personnel.

Objectives, the means by which goals are to be achieved, state certain minimum requirements and are more specific than goals. Objectives should be *specific, measurable,*

---

[21] Erik M. van Raaij, Maarten J. A. Vernooij, and Sander van Triest, "The Implementation of Customer Profitability Analysis: A Case Study," *Industrial Marketing Management* 32, no. 7 (2003): 573–583.

[22] Jason Bader, "How to Grade Customer Profitability," *Electrical Wholesaling*, October 2006, 36–39.

[23] Victoria F. Kickham, "Staying Focused on Hose," *Industrial Distribution*, October 2008, 22–25.

achievable, and *cost-effective*; the latter two are extremely important because relatively small increases in the overall level of customer service objectives can substantially increase the costs of maintaining the increased level of customer service. In other words, although it might be possible to achieve a particular objective, to do so might be cost prohibitive. Consider, for example, an objective to reduce order-picking errors from 5 to 2 percent within a 12-month time period; let's assume that this objective is *specific* and *measurable*. Although 12 months might be a *reasonable* time period in which to achieve the 3 percent reduction in order pick errors, what will it *cost* to achieve this reduction? Will the company be forced to hire additional personnel to check the picked orders? Will the current order-picking process need to be restructured, perhaps through the addition of new technology? Can the company afford new people or new technology? If so, is the improvement in customer service (i.e., from 5 percent order-picking errors to 2 percent order-picking errors) worth the additional costs?

A central element in establishing customer service goals and objectives is determining the customer's viewpoint, and this means asking customers for their insights about customer service. For example, what services would the customer like to receive that presently aren't available from the seller? What services do customers view as the most important? How well does the seller currently provide what the customer wants? What could be improved?

Because customer service is a competitive tool, it's also important to learn how the customer evaluates the service levels of competing sellers. Many companies evaluate their service performance through **benchmarking**, which refers to a process that continuously identifies, understands, and adapts outstanding processes found inside and outside an organization. Well-run organizations benchmark not only against competitors (where possible) but against best-in-class organizations as well.

For maximum results, organizations should engage in *performance benchmarking*, which compares quantitative performance (e.g., fill rate performance), as well as *process benchmarking*, which is qualitative in nature and compares specific processes (e.g., how organizations achieve their fill rates). From a managerial perspective, performance benchmarking identifies gaps in a desired result, while process benchmarking provides information as to why the gaps exist.

The nature of the product also affects the level of the customer service that should be offered. Substitutability, which refers to the number of products from which a firm's customers can choose to meet their needs, is one aspect. If a firm has a near monopoly on an important product (i.e., few substitutes are available), a high level of customer service is not required because a customer who needs the product will buy it under any reasonable customer service standard. However, if many products can perform the same task, then customer service standards become important from a competitive marketing point of view.

Another product-related consideration when establishing customer service goals and objectives is where the product is in its product life cycle. A product just being introduced needs a different kind of service support than one that is in a mature or declining market stage. When introducing a new product, companies want to make sure that there is sufficient supply of it to meet potential customer demand, and so companies might use expedited transportation to protect against out-of-stock situations. It is far less likely that the same company would use expedited transportation to guard against an out-of-stock situation with a product in the decline phase of the product life cycle.

Establishing minimum acceptable order sizes is an ever-present customer service problem because many customers want to order smaller quantities at more frequent intervals. Orders of decreasing size make diminishing (and eventually negative) contributions to profits. In any particular marketing situation, detailed analysis is needed regarding both why small orders are placed and the possible reactions of existing customers to a new policy that requires either a larger minimum order size or a surcharge on small orders to offset losses. A number of retail stores, for example, require a specified level of spending before customers are allowed to pay with credit cards.

Measuring Customer Service

Grandiose statements and platitudes regarding a firm's level of customer service represent little more than rhetoric unless the customer service standards to support them are actually implemented. To accomplish this, a systematic program of measurement and control is required, because *you can't manage what you can't measure*. Control is the process of taking corrective action when measurements indicate that the goals and objectives of customer service are not being achieved. Measurement by itself is merely wasted time and effort if no action is taken based on the feedback received. The actions taken after deficiencies have been identified can lead to an effective and efficient customer service program.

Several key issues are associated with measuring customer service, one of which involves determining the data sources to be used. Ideally, an organization might want to collect measurement data from both internal and external sources. With respect to internal sources, an organization might audit credit memos, which are the documents that must be issued to correct errors in shipping and billing. Comparing them with the volume of error-free activity gives a measure of relative activity accuracy in performance. External measurement data can be collected from actual customers, as illustrated in Figures 7-2 and 7-3. Figure 7-2 shows a relatively short form used by a company located in Northern Spain to learn the data and time of product delivery. The form in Figure 7-3 is a bit more detailed and asks customers about mistakes in quantities received as well as whether the correct product was shipped, along with other issues.

FIGURE 7-2 Form Used By a Spanish Firm for Surveying the Time Element of Delivery Service
The customer is asked to provide the invoice number, note the date that the order was received, and fax it (toll free) to the shipper. *Source:* SFT Group.

CALIDAD DEL SERVICIO DE ALMACÉN

Estimado cliente,

*Con objeto de seguir mejorando nuestro servicio, le rogamos conteste a este breve cuestionario y nos lo envíe a nuestro **fax GRATUITO 900 121 875**, o por correo, a la atención de la Srta. Rosa Pereda, si desea asegurar la confidencialidad (en algunos envíos por fax consta el nombre de la empresa).*

- ¿ Hay equivocaciones en las cantidades de los materlales que les suministramos ?

Muchas veces .... ☐
A menudo .... ☐
Algunas veces .... ☐
Casi nunca .... ☐
Nunca lo tuvimos .... ☐

OBSERVACIONES Y CONSEJOS:

_____
_____
_____

- ¿ Hay equivocaciones en las referencias de los materiales (servir un tipo por otro)?

Muchas veces .... ☐
A menudo .... ☐
Algunas veces .... ☐
Casi nunca .... ☐
Nunca lo tuvimos .... ☐

OBSERVACIONES Y CONSEJOS:

_____
_____
_____

- El embalaje, ¿ es el correcto y los mate- riales llegan bien o no es correcto y los productos llegan dañados ?

Mal muchas veces .... ☐
Mal a veces .... ☐
Normal .... ☐
Bueno (mejor que la media) .... ☐
Muy bueno .... ☐

OBSERVACIONES Y CONSEJOS:

_____
_____
_____

- El paquete exteriormente y el albarán interior, ¿ recogen toda la información que Vd. necesita ?

Información mala .... ☐
Información normal .... ☐
Información buena .... ☐

OBSERVACIONES Y CONSEJOS:

_____
_____
_____

FIGURE 7-3   Form Used By a Firm Located in Northern Spain to Query Customers About Several Service Elements

Question 1 asks about mistakes in quantities shipped. Question 2 asks whether correct goods were shipped. Question 3 asks about the adequacy of packaging, and Question 4 is about labeling. The completed form can be returned by toll-free fax.

A second key issue associated with customer service measurement is determining what factors to measure. Some firms choose those aspects of customer service that are the easiest to measure, which isn't necessarily a good idea because aspects that are difficult to measure may provide better insights into customer likes and dislikes. Some firms choose those aspects of

TABLE 7-2	Select Customer Service Measures
Customer Service Dimension	**Measure**
Time	Order cycle time
	Inquiry response time
Dependability	Perfect order
	On-time delivery
Communication	Customer complaints
	Order status information
Convenience	Returns process
	Response to emergency situations

customer service that they believe are most important, which isn't necessarily a good idea either because these aspects might be relatively unimportant from the customer's perspective.

Because so many potential customer service measurements exist, it's not possible to provide a simple list that would be applicable across the board. At a minimum, the measures should be consistent with the four dimensions of customer service—time, dependability, communication, and convenience—discussed earlier in this chapter. Table 7-2 provides representative customer service measures for each of these four dimensions.

In addition, the metrics that are chosen should be relevant and important from the customer's perspective. While this might seem like the proverbial "no brainer," consider the call center that measured customer service in terms of the length of customer calls, with shorter call lengths preferred to longer call lengths. As such, the call center singled out a particular employee for "improvement" because her call times were much longer than those of other call center employees. Additional research indicated that this "laggard" employee was actually *the most effective employee* when measured in terms of the number of customer problems solved per day. In short, the call center's primary customer service metric—the time length of customer calls—was different than the customer's primary customer service metric—solving the problem at hand.[24]

Although customer service must be measured if it is to be managed, organizations should resist the tendency to "measure everything that moves." Excessive measurement can strain an organization because it requires the collection of tremendous amounts of data, and once collected, the data must be analyzed. This can result in "analysis paralysis," or the idea that so much time is required for analysis that there's little if any time left to make decisions based on the data. Rather, organizations should utilize a limited number of meaningful and relevant metrics and it's possible for organizations to use only *one* customer service metric as illustrated in the previous paragraph's call center anecdote.

Service Failure and Service Recovery

Regardless of how well an organization is run, some situations will occur where its actual performance does not meet the customer's expected performance (i.e., a service failure). Service failure has emerged as a prominent business issue in recent years, in part because organizations have learned that customers can easily become disaffected. For example, some sources suggest that nearly two-thirds of customers who experience a problem with *purchases of less than $5* won't do business with that company again.[25] Service failure is particularly relevant to the order cycle; examples of order-related service failures include lost delivery, late delivery, early delivery, damaged delivery, incorrect delivery quantity, among others.

---

[24] No author, "Mistaken Metrics," *T&D*, February 2009, 88.
[25] John Tschohl, "Turning Service into Opportunities," *TWICE: This Week in Consumer Electronics*, March 27, 2006, 78.

Given that service failures are inevitable, organizations will be faced with service recovery decisions. For our purposes, **service recovery** will refer to a process for returning a customer to a state of satisfaction after a service or product has failed to live up to expectations. Although service recovery often generates significant out-of-pocket costs, good (or excellent) service recovery may actually result in *increased* customer loyalty. Moreover, satisfactory service recovery can increase a customer's willingness to recommend the offending organization; unsatisfactory service recovery magnifies the initial failure.[26]

There is no set formula for service recovery, in part because each service failure is unique in its impact on a particular customer. Having said this, there are general guidelines for dealing with service recovery, and it's important to recognize that these guidelines may not only assuage the customer but also result in an organization improving its operations.[27] For example, one recovery guideline is fair treatment for customers. In the logistics discipline, one example of fair treatment involves service guarantees by transportation companies; if a shipment misses various delivery parameters (e.g., on time, undamaged), then customers can receive a full refund (or aren't billed for the transportation). Besides reducing customer risk, many transportation companies that have implemented service guarantees have improved relevant aspects of their performance such as on-time delivery, which has meant a decrease in the amount of payouts for deficient service.

Summary

Demand management deals with determining what customers want, and a key component involves demand forecasting. The chapter discussed basic demand forecasting models along with select forecasting issues such as cost and accuracy.

The chapter also looked at order management and the order cycle, which refers to the period of time from when the order is placed until it is received. Four components of an order cycle—order transmittal, order processing, order picking and assembly, and order delivery—were identified and discussed in some detail.

Customer service was the third major topic addressed in this chapter, and its four dimensions—time, dependability, communication, and convenience—were discussed. The chapter also looked at managing customer service, with a specific focus on CPA, establishing customer service objectives, measuring customer service, and service failure and service recovery.

Questions for Discussion and Review

1. What is the relationship between demand management, order management, and customer service?
2. Discuss the three basic demand forecasting models.
3. Discuss several demand forecasting issues.
4. Define and describe the order cycle. Why is it considered an important aspect of customer service?
5. What are some causes of order cycle variability? What are the consequences of order cycle variability?
6. List the various methods of order transmittal, and discuss relevant characteristics of each.
7. What are some advantages and disadvantages to checking all orders for completeness and accuracy?
8. Define order triage, and explain how it can affect order processing.
9. Discuss how the effectiveness and efficiency of order processing can be improved without large expenditures.
10. What is pick-to-light technology, and how can it improve order picking?
11. Discuss the order delivery stage of the order cycle.
12. How can customer service act as a competitive weapon?
13. How are macroenvironmental factors causing organizations and individuals to demand higher levels of customer service?
14. List and discuss the three elements of the dependability dimension of customer service.
15. What are some advantages and disadvantages to technological advances designed to facilitate buyer–seller communications?
16. What is customer profitability analysis, and how might it be used in logistics?
17. Define and explain how organizations might engage in benchmarking.
18. How do characteristics such as substitutability and product life cycle stage influence the development of customer service goals and objectives?
19. Describe some of the key issues associated with measuring customer service.
20. What is meant by service recovery? How is it relevant to logistics?

---

[26] Leonard L. Berry and Jonathan A. Leighton, "Restoring Customer Confidence," *MHS* 24, no. 1 (2004): 15–19.
[27] Gail Scott, "Service Recovery," *Healthcare Executive*, January/February 2009, 44–47.

Suggested Readings

Cederlund, Jerold P., Rajiv Kohli, Susan A. Sherer, and Yao Yuliang. "How Motorola Put CPFR into Action." *Supply Chain Management Review* 11, no. 7 (2007): 28–35.

Forslund, Helena. "Performance Gaps in the Dyadic Order Fulfillment Process." *International Journal of Physical Distribution & Logistics Management* 36, no. 8 (2006): 580–595.

Francis, Joe. "Benchmarking: Get the Gain without the Pain." *Supply Chain Management Review* 12, no. 3 (2008): 22–29.

Gardner, Chris, Cheryl Harrity, and Kate Vitasek. "A Better Way to Benchmark." *Supply Chain Management Review* 9, no. 3 (2005): 20–28.

Guerreiro, Reinaldo, Sergio Rodrigues Bio, Elvira Vazquez, and Villamor Merschmann. "Cost-to-Serve Measurement and Customer Profitability Analysis." *International Journal of Logistics Management* 19, no. 3 (2008): 389–407.

Gustavsson, Mattias and Patrik Jonsson. "Perceived Quality Deficiencies of Demand Information and Their Consequences." *International Journal of Logistics: Research & Applications* 11, no. 4 (2008): 295–312.

Hofman, Debra. "Getting to World-Class Supply Chain Measurement." *Supply Chain Management Review* 10, no. 7 (2006): 18–24.

Johnson, Carol J., Curtis M. Grimm, and Valdis Blome. "Customer Service in the Baltic Region: An Exploratory Study." *International Journal of Logistics Management* 18, no. 2 (2007): 157–173.

Maltz, Arnold, Eliot Rabinovich, and Rajiv Sinha. "Order Management for Profit on the Internet." *Business Horizons* 48, no. 2 (2005): 113–123.

Mentzer, John T., and Mark A. Moon. "Understanding Demand." *Supply Chain Management Review* 8, no. 4 (2004): 38–45.

Syntetos, A. A., M. Keyes, and M. Z. Babai. "Demand Categorisation in a European Spare Parts Logistics Network." *International Journal of Operations & Production Management* 29, no. 3 (2009): 292–316.

Thomas, Rodney. "Exploring Relational Aspects of Time-Based Competition." *International Journal of Physical Distribution & Logistics Management* 38, no. 7 (2008): 540–550.

CASE

CASE 7-1   Handy Andy, Inc.

Handy Andy, Inc., produced garbage/trash compactors at a factory in St. Louis, Missouri, and sold them throughout the United States. Nearly all sales were in large urban areas where trash collection costs were high.

The basic unit was about 3 feet high, 2 feet deep, and 1 1/2 feet wide. A deluxe model had the same dimensions but contained more features. Because most of the sales represented units to be placed in existing kitchens, a wide variety of colors and trims were manufactured, providing an exterior that would match almost any kitchen decor. The standard model came in five colors with three different trims for a total of 15 different combinations. The deluxe model came in 8 colors and 4 different trims for a total of 32 different combinations. Retail prices were set by the dealer, with prices for the standard model ranging between $310 and $350 and for the deluxe model between $390 and $450. Sales in an area were usually slow until trash collectors, faced with rising landfill costs, raised their rates per can of refuse picked up.

Because of the sporadic sales patterns and the wide number of colors and trims available, retailers usually stocked only a display unit or two. They had available an expensively printed brochure that included paint chips so buyers could select the color and finish they wanted. When the retailer completed the sale, he or she would take the order and promise delivery and installation within a given number of days. In each major city, there was one major Handy Andy dealer (factory distributor). Each dealer maintained a complete stock of all styles and trims of the Handy Andy compactors. (Handy Andy, Inc., insisted that these factory distributors stock at least five units each of the 47 different styles available.) The general agreement between the factory distributors and Handy Andy was that the factory distributor would deliver and install the compactor within five days after the distributor who had made the sale informed the factory distributor. For the delivery and installation, the factory distributor received 9 percent of the unit's wholesale price, half paid by distributor who had made the sale and half paid by Handy Andy as a credit against future orders.

José Ortega worked in Handy Andy's distribution department in the St. Louis headquarters. He currently was working on a project to determine whether the compactor's warranty should be extended from one year to two years. The units were well built, and there had been almost no warranty work requested in the first year of each model's life. Because Handy Andy would have no records of work performed after the one-year period had expired, Ortega was randomly contacting buyers, using long-distance phones. Their names and phone numbers came from postcards they had mailed in to register the warranty at time of purchase (see Exhibit 7-A). The phrase at the bottom of the

---

MAIL WITHIN FIVE DAYS OF INSTALLATION!

Serial Number _____
(8-digit number under the switch)
Purchased from:
Dealer's name_____

City_____

Date of purchase_____/_____/200_____
                        MONTH   DAY
Your
name_____

Address_____

City_____State_____ZIP_____

This card requires no postage. Just fill out and drop in any mail-box. Your warranty is good for one year from the date of pur-chase, as determined by our records. Contact your dealer first if you have questions.

HANDY ANDY, INC.
St. Louis, MO 63129

EXHIBIT 7-A   Return Postcard

---

card referring to Handy Andy's records was to keep the buyer from waiting for a problem to occur and then mailing in the card. Whether this statement was necessary was unknown because so few defects had been reported. Ortega was in the process of contacting 500 purchasers who had owned the compactors for between one year and four years (when they had first been introduced) to determine whether the compactors had required repairs and, if so, the extent and cost of the repairs. In talking to purchasers, Ortega was impressed by the fact that there were remarkably few complaints involving the durability of the compactors.

Another type of complaint did arise, however, one that Ortega had difficulty understanding until he heard many buyers, usually from the same few cities,

tell an almost identical story. It appeared that in these cities the factory distributor would contact individuals who had purchased Handy Andy compactors from other, smaller dealers and would attempt to have them cancel the original order. The factory distributor told the buyer that the model originally requested was out of stock but that a better model could be supplied for the same price. The factory distributors also indicated that the buyers would receive better service if they bought from them because, they claimed, they provided service for all Handy Andy models sold in their area. In addition, the factory distributors in these few cities indicated that they, not Handy Andy, Inc., stood behind the one-year warranty.

Ortega realized that he was uncovering a larger problem than he had been assigned to explore. He chatted briefly with his supervisor, who told him to revise the format of his interview to include a few more questions concerning the installation. She also told him to begin calling individuals who had owned compactors for less than a year. Ortega did this, and the only new information he uncovered was that the factory distributors in almost all cities did a better job of installing compactors that they had sold than they did those sold by smaller dealers. The delivery was faster (in terms of elapsed time since sale), more time was spent explaining to the customer how the compactor worked, and phone calls were made to the customer 3 and 10 days after installation to make certain that the customer had no additional questions concerning the compactor's operation. When a compactor that had been sold by a smaller dealer was delivered, it was frequently left in the middle of the kitchen with scarcely a word exchanged between the customer and the installation personnel.

Ortega had another meeting scheduled with his supervisor. As he entered her office, he was surprised to see Handy Andy's vice president of marketing also sitting in the office. Ortega's supervisor asked him to tell the vice president the results of his interviews.

The marketing vice president asked Ortega, "Do you think this pattern exists in all markets?"

"No," was Ortega's reply. "I'd say it was a problem in Jacksonville, Baltimore, Cleveland, Louisville, Denver, and San Diego. It may be a problem in Dallas and New Orleans. My sample wasn't very well structured in a metropolitan market sense; you will recall that it was a nationwide sample that was trying to look at repairs."

Questions

1. Is this a customer service problem? Why or why not?
2. Marketing channels are the arrangement of intermediaries (wholesalers, retailers, and the like) that the firm uses to achieve its marketing objectives. Is the problem discussed in Handy Andy's marketing channels? Why or why not?
3. Logistics channels handle the physical flow of goods or services. Is the problem discussed in Handy Andy's logistics channel? Why or why not?
4. It appears that the factory distributors are exploiting the smaller dealers. Yet from what we can tell, Handy Andy in St. Louis has heard no complaints from the smaller dealers. Why wouldn't they complain?
5. What should Handy Andy's marketing vice president do? Why?
6. Redesign the warranty postcard, staying within the same dimensions, and include questions or statements that will make it easier for Handy Andy headquarters to detect whether installation practices of the type discussed in this case occur.
7. In the case is the statement, "The factory distributors in these few cities indicated that they, not Handy Andy, Inc., stood behind the one-year warranty." Is this a problem for Handy Andy? Why or why not?
8. Assume that the situation described in question 7 is a problem. How should the firm deal with it?

APPENDIX 7-A

Activity-based costing is focused on better understanding the cost of a product by identifying what activities drive particular costs. Unlike traditional accounting techniques, activity-based costing attempts to trace an expense category to a particular cost object. With activity-based costing, cost objects consume activities, and activities consume resources.[28]

Activity-based costing consists of five steps:

- Identify activities
- Determine cost for each activity
- Determine cost drivers
- Collect activity data
- Calculate product cost[29]

This five-step activity-based costing process will be illustrated by the following hypothetical example. Suppose that a company is interested in applying the activity-based costing process to its order cycle process for two products that it sells. So, we've identified the relevant activities (step 1); next comes a determination of cost for each activity, as shown in Table 7A-1.

---

[28] "Calculating Activity Based Costing," *Bloomsbury Business Library—Actionlists & Checklists*, 2007, 21.
[29] Ibid.

TABLE 7A-1	Cost for Each Activity
Activity	**Cost**
Order transmittal	$1,000
Order processing	$3,000
Order picking and assembly	$12,000
Order delivery	$6,000

TABLE 7A-2	Activity Data and Product Cost Calculation				
Activity	**Cost**	**Product 1 Data**	**Product 1 Cost**	**Product 2 Data**	**Product 2 Cost**
Order transmittal	$1,000	3 orders	$300	7 orders	$700
Order processing	$3,000	4 activities	$1,200	6 activities	$1,800
Order picking and assembly	$12,000	110 boxes	$6,600	90 boxes	$5,400
Order delivery	$6,000	30 locations	$4,500	10 locations	$1,500
Total	**$22,000**		**$12,600**		**$9,400**

Step 3 requires us to determine cost drivers, and in this example, they are order transmittal → number of orders; order processing → number of processing activities; order picking and assembly → number of boxes; order delivery → number of delivery locations.

The two remaining steps, activity data and product cost calculation, appear in Table 7A-2. With respect to order transmittal, three orders were received for Product 1 and seven orders for Product 2, for a total of 10 orders. Because Product 1 accounts for 30 percent of the total orders (3/10), the relevant transmittal cost is $300, which represents 30 percent of the $1,000 total order transmittal cost. Likewise, because Product 2 accounts for 70 percent of the total orders (7/10), its relevant transmittal costs are $700. The product costs for the three other activities are calculated in a similar fashion. Note that the data in Table 7A-2 indicate that the total order cycle cost is $22,000; according to the activity-based costing process, Product 1 is responsible for $12,600 in costs, and Product 2 is responsible for $9,400.

Before concluding this brief discussion of activity-based costing, it's important to recognize that the cost drivers can vary from organization to organization and should be driven by company-specific considerations such as organizational structure, operational structure, and products.[30] For example, in our hypothetical example, the number of delivery locations was the cost driver associated with order delivery. Another potential cost driver for order delivery could be the number of customers receiving deliveries.

---

[30] John Karolefski, "Time Is Money," *Food Logistics*, June 2004, 18–22.

8 | INVENTORY MANAGEMENT

Learning Objectives

- To learn about the ways that inventory can be classified
- To discuss inventory costs and the trade-offs that exist among them
- To identify when to order and how much to order, with a particular emphasis on the economic order quantity
- To differentiate the various inventory flow patterns
- To discuss special concerns with inventory management
- To identify several contemporary approaches to managing inventory

Inventory refers to stocks of goods and materials that are maintained for many purposes, the most common being to satisfy normal demand patterns. In production and selling processes, inventories serve as cushions to accommodate the fact that items arrive in one pattern and are used in another pattern. For example, if you eat one egg a day and buy eggs by the dozen, every 12 days you would buy a new container of eggs, and the inventory of eggs remaining in your refrigerator would decline at the rate of one egg per day.

Inventory management is a key component in logistics and supply chain management, in part because inventory decisions are often a starting point, or driver, for other business activities, such as warehousing, transportation, and materials handling. Moreover, different organizational functions can have different inventory management objectives. Marketing, for example, tends to want to ensure that sufficient inventory is available for customer demand to avoid potential stockout situations—which translate into higher inventory levels. Alternatively, the finance group generally seeks to minimize the costs associated with holding inventory, which translates into lower inventory levels. As if managing these seemingly conflicting objectives within one organization isn't challenging enough, supply chains are made up of multiple organizations—each of which may have its own distinct inventory management philosophy. Indeed, each link in the supply chain may prefer having other links maintain the inventory.

Organizations strive for the proper balance (i.e., right amount) of inventory, but achieving the proper balance can be quite difficult because of the trade-offs between inventory carrying cost and stockout cost, both of which will be discussed in greater detail later in this chapter. More specifically, holding high levels of inventory (overstock) result in high inventory carrying costs and low (or no) stockout costs. Alternatively, holding low levels of inventory result in low inventory carrying costs and some (high) stockout costs.

It is important to note here that inventory carries its greatest cost after value has been added through manufacturing and processing. Finished goods inventories are, therefore, much more expensive to hold than raw materials or work in progress. Carrying costs for inventories can be significant, and the return on investment to a firm for the funds it has tied up in inventory should be as high as the return it can obtain from other, equally risky uses of the same funds.

This chapter begins with a brief look at various classifications of inventory, followed by a discussion of inventory costs. Next is an examination of when to order inventory and how much inventory to order. This chapter also looks at inventory flows and special concerns with inventory and concludes by discussing several contemporary approaches to managing inventory.

INVENTORY CLASSIFICATIONS

It's important to understand the various classifications of inventory because the classification can influence the way that inventory is managed. Inventory generally exists to satisfy demand and can be classified as cycle (base) stock, safety (buffer) stock, pipeline (in-transit) stock, or speculative stock. Each type is explained in the following paragraphs.

Cycle, *or base*, **stock** refers to inventory that is needed to satisfy normal demand during the course of an order cycle. With respect to the egg example at the beginning of this chapter, one dozen (12) eggs represent the cycle stock—we use one egg per day, and we buy eggs every 12 days. Recall that Chapter 7 indicated that order cycle times continue to decrease in length, meaning that the associated levels of cycle stock continue to decrease as well.

Safety, *or buffer*, **stock** refers to inventory that is held in addition to cycle stock to guard against uncertainty in demand or lead time. For example, uncertainty in demand could come from the fact that you occasionally decide to make a three-egg omelet as opposed to eating one egg per day. As an example of lead-time uncertainty, you may sometimes buy eggs every 14 days, rather than every 12 days. In both cases, a few extra eggs would ensure that you won't run out of eggs. As pointed out in Chapter 7, higher levels of uncertainty lead to higher levels of safety stock (SS).

Pipeline, *or in-transit*, **stock** is inventory that is en route between various fixed facilities in a logistics system such as a plant, warehouse, or store. Pipeline inventory is represented here by eggs that are in transit between a chicken farm and, say, a food wholesaler's distribution center or between the retail store and your kitchen.

Speculative stock refers to inventory that is held for several reasons, including seasonal demand, projected price increases, and potential shortages of product. For example, the fact that eggs are associated with Easter (e.g., Easter egg rolls and colored eggs) tends to cause an increase in demand for them prior to the Easter holiday.

Although inventory generally exists to satisfy demand, in some situations inventory is carried to stimulate demand, also known as **psychic stock**. This type of inventory is associated with retail stores, and the general idea is that customer purchases are stimulated by inventory that they can see.[1] This concept helps to explain, in part, why some retailers stock huge amounts of certain merchandise.

---

[1] Paul D. Larson and Robert A. DeMaris, "Psychic Stock: An Independent Variable Category of Inventory," *International Journal of Physical Distribution & Logistics Management* 20, no. 7 (1990): 27–37.

INVENTORY COSTS

You might remember the basic accounting equation that assets are equal to liabilities plus stock-holder's equity. The managerial significance of the accounting equation is that assets must be paid for in some manner; quite simply, *assets cost money*, which means that inventory costs money. Not only does inventory appear as an asset on company balance sheets, but it tends to be one of the largest assets (in terms of dollar value) on the balance sheets. As such, it's important for logisticians to have an understanding of inventory costs.

The data in Table 8-1 offer insights about the absolute and relative magnitude of inventory costs in the United States between 2000 and 2008. From an absolute perspective, Table 8-1 indicates that the value of business inventory has been in the neighborhood of $2 trillion in recent years. In relative terms, inventory costs in the twenty-first century represent approximately one-third of total logistics costs.

We will take a closer look at three inventory costs—carrying cost, ordering cost, and stockout cost—that should factor into an organization's inventory management policy. The logistics manager must understand both the nature of each of these costs and the trade-offs among them.

Inventory Carrying Costs

A prominent concern involves the costs associated with holding inventory, which are referred to as **inventory carrying (holding) costs**. In general, inventory carrying costs are expressed in percentage terms, and this percentage is multiplied by the inventory's value. The resulting number represents the dollar value associated with holding the particular inventory. As an example, referring to Table 8-1, when the value of business inventory in 2000, $1,478 billion, is multiplied by the carrying cost in 2000, 25.3 percent, the relevant carrying costs are $374 billion.

Not surprisingly, an increase or decrease in the carrying cost percentage will affect the relevant inventory expense. Generally speaking, companies prefer to carry lower inventory as the carrying cost percentage increases, in part because there is greater risk (e.g., obsolescence) to hold-ing the inventory. As a result, the determination of a carrying cost percentage should be quite important for many companies. However, the reality is that a recent study showed that slightly more than 50 percent of the surveyed companies had an established inventory carrying cost. Moreover, approximately 20 percent of the study respondents either did not know, or did not have access to,

TABLE 8-1 Magnitude of Inventory Costs

Year	Value of Business Inventory ($ billion)	Inventory Carrying Cost (%)	Inventory Carrying Cost ($ billion)	Total Logistics Cost ($ billion)	Inventory as a Percentage of Total Logistics Cost
2000	1,478	25.3	374	1,007	37.1
2001	1,403	22.8	320	966	32.2
2002	1,451	20.7	300	917	32.7
2003	1,508	20.1	304	947	32.4
2004	1,650	20.4	337	1,028	32.8
2005	1,773	22.3	395	1,180	33.5
2006	1,863	24.0	447	1,306	34.2
2007	2,026	24.1	487	1,397	34.9
2008	1,965	21.4	420	1,344	31.3

Sources: 19th Annual State of Logistics Report (June 18, 2008) and 20th Annual State of Logistics Report (June 19, 2009) both prepared by Rosalyn Wilson for the Council of Supply Chain Management Professionals (*www.cscmp.org*).

TABLE 8-2	Components of Inventory Carrying Cost
Obsolescence costs	
Inventory shrinkage	
Storage costs	
Handling costs	
Insurance costs	
Taxes	
Interest costs	

their organization's inventory carrying cost.[2] The lack of knowledge about inventory carrying costs is reflected by the fact that a commonly used estimate today for inventory carrying costs is 25 percent—a figure that dates from the mid-1950s.[3] Table 8-1 suggests that the range of inventory carrying costs in the twenty-first century has been between 20 and 25 percent.

Inventory carrying costs consist of a number of different components (see Table 8-2), and the importance of these factors can vary from product to product. For example, perishable items such as dairy products, meat, and poultry are often sold with expiration dates, causing them to have little or no value after a certain date. By contrast, a box of lead pencils loses its value much more slowly through time. These two examples illustrate the *obsolescence* category of inventory carrying costs and refer to the fact that products lose value through time. Note that some products (e.g., perishables) lose their value much more quickly than others (e.g., pencils).

Inventory shrinkage is another component of inventory carrying cost and refers to the fact that more items are recorded entering than leaving warehousing facilities. Shrinkage is generally caused by damage, loss, or theft, and although shrinkage costs can be reduced, such efforts often generate other costs. For example, although better packaging may reduce damage, loss, or theft costs, better packaging likely translates into increased packaging costs.

Another component of inventory carrying costs, *storage* costs, refers to those costs associated with occupying space in a plant, storeroom, or warehousing facility. Some products have very specialized storage requirements; ice cream, for example, must be stored at a temperature below –20 degrees Fahrenheit. You should recognize that specialized storage requirements, such as refrigeration, result in higher storage costs. *Handling* costs, another component of inventory carrying costs, involve the costs of employing staff to receive, store, retrieve, and move inventory. Note that specialized storage requirements may also increase handling costs; a refrigerated warehouse requires workers to wear gloves, head coverings, and coats to protect them from the cold temperatures.

Insurance costs, which insure inventory against fire, flood, theft, and other perils, are another component of inventory carrying costs. Insurance costs are not uniform across products; diamonds, for example, are more costly to insure than shampoo. *Taxes* represent yet another component of inventory carrying costs, and they are calculated on the basis of the inventory on hand on a particular date; considerable effort is made to have that day's inventory be as low as possible. Finally, *interest costs* take into account the money that is required to maintain the investment in inventory. In the United States, the prime rate of interest has traditionally provided a convenient starting point when estimating the interest charges associated with maintaining inventory.

Some inventory items have other types of carrying costs because of their specialized nature. Pets and livestock, for example, must be watered and fed. Tropical fish must be fed and have oxygen added to the water in which they are kept. Another cost, although it is generally excluded from carrying cost, is opportunity cost—the cost of taking a position in the wrong materials. This can be an issue for those companies that engage in speculative inventory. Opportunity costs are also incurred by firms that hold too much inventory in reserve for customer demand.

---

[2] "What's Your Inventory Carrying Cost, and Why Don't You Know It?" *Ioma's Inventory Management Report*, January 2005, 2–4.

[3] See L. P. Alford and John R. Bangs, eds., *Production Handbook* (New York: Ronald, 1955).

Ordering Costs

Ordering costs refer to those costs associated with ordering inventory, such as order costs and setup costs. Order costs include, but are not limited to, the costs of receiving an order (e.g., the wages of a person who takes orders by telephone), conducting a credit check, verifying inventory availability, entering orders into the system, preparing invoices, and receiving payment. Note that a number of the ordering costs involve the order transmittal and order processing components of the order cycle. Setup costs are those necessary to modify production processes to make the products necessary to satisfy particular orders.

Trade-Off between Carrying and Ordering Costs

The trade-off that exists between carrying and ordering costs is that they respond in opposite ways to the number of orders or size of orders. That is, an increase in the number of orders leads to higher order costs and lower carrying costs. We'll illustrate this trade-off with a mathematical example; but before doing so, it's necessary to understand how to calculate ordering costs and carrying costs.

Ordering cost can be calculated by multiplying the number of orders per year times the ordering cost per order. Because of the assumption of even outward flow of goods, inventory carrying costs are applied to one-half of the order size, a figure that represents the average inventory. Average inventory is multiplied by the carrying costs of the inventory (expressed as a percentage of the dollar value).

Suppose weekly demand is 100 units, order cost per order is $80, the value of an item is $50, and carrying cost is 20 percent of the value of an item. If we place one order per year for the product,

Ordering cost = number of orders per year (1) × ordering cost per order ($80),

or

Ordering cost = 1 × $80 = $80

Carrying cost = average inventory [(100 × 52)/2] × carrying costs [value of the product ($50) × carrying cost (.20)],

or

Carrying cost = 2,600 × $10 = $26,000

Alternatively, look what happens to ordering and carrying costs if we place one order per week:

Ordering cost = 52 orders × $80 per order, or $4,160

Carrying cost = average inventory (50) × carrying cost ($10), or $500.

Stockout Costs

If avoiding oversupply were the only problem associated with inventories, the solution would be relatively simple: Store fewer items. However, not having enough items can be as bad as, and sometimes worse than, having too many items. Indeed, costs (e.g., lost revenue) can accrue during stockouts, when customers demand items that aren't immediately available.

Although calculation of stockout costs can be difficult and inexact, it is important for organizations to do so because such knowledge can be beneficial when determining how much inventory to hold, keeping in mind that a trade-off must be balanced between inventory carrying costs and stockout costs. **Stockout costs,** or estimating the costs or penalties for a stockout, involve an understanding of a customer's reaction to a company being out of stock when a customer wants to buy an item.

Consider the following customer responses to a particular stockout situation. How should they be evaluated?

1. The customer says, "I'll be back," and this proves to be so.
2. The customer says, "Call me when it's in."
3. The customer buys a substitute product that yields a higher profit for the seller.
4. The customer buys a substitute product that yields a lower profit for the seller.
5. The customer places an order for the item that is out of stock (a **back order**) and asks to have the item delivered when it arrives.
6. The customer goes to a competitor only for this purchase.
7. The customer goes to a competitor for this and all future purchases.

Clearly, each of these situations has a different cost to the company experiencing a stockout. For example, the loss in situation 1 is negligible because the sale is only slightly delayed. The outcome from situation 2 is more problematic in that the company doesn't know whether the customer will, in fact, return. Situation 7 is clearly the most damaging, because the customer has been lost for good, and it's necessary to know the cost of developing a new customer to replace the lost customer. As pointed out in Chapter 7, a commonly used guideline is that it costs five times as much to acquire a new customer as it does to retain an existing one.

To illustrate the calculation of stockout costs, assume for simplicity's sake that customer responses to a stockout can be placed into three categories: delayed sale (brand loyalty), lost sale (switches and comes back), and lost customer. Assume further that, over time, of 300 customers who experienced a stockout, 10 percent delayed the sale, 25 percent switched and came back, but the remaining 65 percent were lost for good (see Table 8-3).

The probability of each event taking place can be used to determine the average cost of a stockout. More specifically, as illustrated in Table 8-3, each probability is multiplied by the respective loss to yield an average cost per event. These average costs are then summed, and the result is the average cost per stockout. A delayed sale is virtually costless because the customer is brand loyal and will purchase the product when it becomes available. The lost sale alternative results in a loss of the profit that would have been made on the customer's purchase. In the lost customer situation, the customer buys a competitor's product and decides to make all future purchases from that competitor; the relevant cost involved is that of developing a new customer.

Having an understanding of how to calculate stockout costs highlights several key managerial issues. As a general rule, the higher the average cost of a stockout, the better it is for the company to hold some amount of inventory (SS) to protect against stockouts. In addition, the higher the probability of a delayed sale, the lower the average stockout costs—and the lower the inventory that needs to be held by a company. For example, if we switch the probabilities in Table 8-3 for brand loyalty and lost customer (i.e., brand loyal probability is .65, lost customer probability is .10), then the average cost of a stockout becomes $129.25 (as opposed to Table 8-3's $789.25).

TABLE 8-3	Determination of the Average Cost of a Stockout		
Alternative	**Loss**	**Probability**	**Average Cost**
1. Brand-loyal customer	$00.00	.10	$00.00
2. Switches and comes back	37.00	.25	9.25
3. Lost customer	1,200.00	.65	780.00
Average cost of a stockout		1.00	$789.25

Note: These are hypothetical figures for illustration.

Trade-Off between Carrying and Stockout Costs

The trade-off between carrying and stockout costs is that both move in opposite directions—higher inventory levels (hence higher inventory carrying costs) result in lower chances of a stockout (hence lower stockout costs). One way to illustrate this relationship is to look at the trade-offs between levels of SS and the number of stockouts prevented, as illustrated in Table 8-4. In this example, we assume that inventory can only be ordered in multiples of 10 and that each unit of inventory is valued at $480 with carrying costs of 25 percent. As a result, the incremental carrying costs of moving from 0 units of SS to 10 units of SS are as follows: $(10 \times \$480) \times .25 = \$1,200$. Likewise, the incremental carrying costs of moving from 10 to 20 units of SS are $1,200.

This example also assumes that the various levels of SS prevent a certain number of stockouts. For example, holding 10 units of SS for an entire year allows the firm to prevent 20 stockouts; moving from 10 to 20 units of SS allows 16 additional orders to be filled. Using an average cost per stockout of $400, an SS of 10 units allows the firm to prevent 20 stockouts, which saves the firm $8,000 ($400 × 20). The savings of $8,000 is much greater than the additional carrying costs of $1,200, so the firm wants to hold at least 10 units of SS. Twenty units of SS result in $1,200 of additional carrying costs, whereas the additional stockout costs avoided are $6,400 (16 × $400). According to the data in Table 8-4, the optimum quantity of SS is 70 units. At this point, the cost of 10 additional units of inventory is $1,200, and $1,200 is saved in stockout costs.

WHEN TO ORDER

A key issue with respect to inventory management involves when product should be ordered; one could order a fixed amount of inventory (**fixed order quantity system**), or orders can be placed at fixed time intervals (**fixed order interval system**). In a fixed order quantity system, the time interval may fluctuate while the order size stays constant; for example, a store might always order 200 cases of soft drinks. Its first order might be placed on January 3, a second order on January 6 (three-day interval), with a third order on January 11 (five-day interval). By contrast, in a fixed order interval system, the time interval is constant, but the order size may fluctuate. For example, a man goes grocery shopping with his wife every Sunday. Although the time interval for shopping is constant at seven days, the shopping list (inventory requirements) differs from week to week.

There needs to be a **reorder (trigger) point** (i.e., the level of inventory at which a replenishment order is placed) for there to be an efficient fixed order quantity system. Reorder points (ROPs) are relatively easy to calculate, particularly under conditions of certainty; an ROP is equal to the average daily demand (DD) in units times the length of the replenishment cycle (RC):

$$ROP = DD \times RC$$

TABLE 8-4	Determination of Safety Stock Level				
Number of Units of Safety Stock	Additional Safety Stock ($480 per Unit)	25% Annual Carrying Cost	Total Value of Incremental Safety Stock	Additional Orders Filled	Stockout Costs Avoided
10	$4,800	$1,200	$1,200	20	$8,000.00
20	9,600	2,400	1,200	16	6,400.00
30	14,400	3,600	1,200	12	4,800.00
40	19,200	4,800	1,200	8	3,200.00
50	24,000	6,000	1,200	6	2,400.00
60	28,800	7,200	1,200	4	1,600.00
70	33,600	8,400	1,200	3	1,200.00

Suppose, for example, that average DD is 40 units, and the RC is 4 days. The ROP in this example is 40 × 4, or 160 units; in other words, when the inventory level reaches 160 units, a reorder is placed.

The ROP under conditions of uncertainty can be calculated in a similar manner; the only modification involves including an SS factor:

$$ROP = (DD \times RC) + SS$$

Continuing with the previous example, suppose that the company decides to hold 40 units of SS. The ROP becomes (40 × 4) + 40, or 200 units.

The fact that a fixed order quantity system works best when there is a predetermined ROP indicates that this system requires relatively frequent, if not constant, monitoring of inventory levels. Under a fixed order quantity system, if sales start to increase, the ROP will be reached more quickly, and a new order will automatically be placed. In most fixed order interval systems, by contrast, inventory levels are monitored much less frequently—often just before the scheduled order time. The infrequency of inventory monitoring makes the fixed interval system much more susceptible to stockout situations, and one is more likely to see higher levels of SS in a fixed interval system. It's entirely possible that a company could have some of its inventory under a fixed order quantity system, whereas other inventory uses a fixed order interval system.

HOW MUCH TO ORDER

Economic Order Quantity

A long-standing issue in inventory management concerns how much inventory should be ordered at a particular time. The typical inventory order size problem, referred to as the **economic order quantity (EOQ)**, deals with calculating the proper order size with respect to two costs: the costs of carrying the inventory and the costs of ordering the inventory. The EOQ determines the point at which the sum of carrying costs and ordering costs is minimized, or the point at which carrying costs equal ordering costs. Assuming that carrying costs and ordering costs are accurate, the EOQ "is absolutely the most cost-effective quantity to order based on current operational costs."[4] The nature of carrying costs and ordering costs are presented in Figure 8-1.

The basic EOQ model is grounded in the following assumptions:

1. A continuous, constant, and known rate of demand
2. A constant and known replenishment or lead time
3. A constant purchase price that is independent of the order quantity
4. All demand is satisfied (no stockouts are allowed)
5. No inventory in transit
6. Only one item in inventory or no interaction between inventory items
7. An infinite planning horizon
8. Unlimited capital availability.

Mathematically, the EOQ can be calculated in two ways; one presents the answer in dollars, the other in units. In terms of dollars, suppose that $1,000 of a particular item is used each year, the order costs are $25 per order submitted, and inventory carrying costs are 20 percent. The EOQ can be calculated using this formula:

$$EOQ = \sqrt{2AB/C}$$

---

[4] Dave Piasecki, "Optimizing Economic Order Quantity," *IIE Solutions* 33, no. 1 (2002): 30–33, 39.

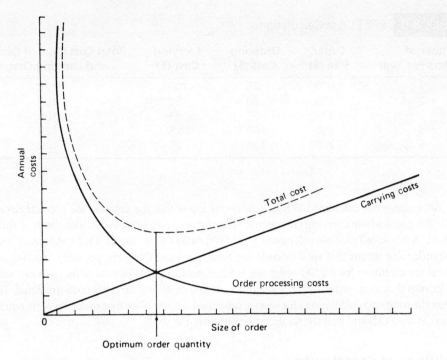

FIGURE 8-1 Determining EOQ by Use of a Graph

where

EOQ = the most economic order size, in dollars

A = annual usage, in dollars

B = administrative costs per order of placing the order

C = carrying costs of the inventory (expressed as an annual percentage of the inventory's dollar value)

Thus:

$$EOQ = \sqrt{2 \times 1{,}000 \times 25/.20} = \sqrt{250{,}000} = \$500 \text{ order size}$$

Alternatively, the EOQ can be calculated in terms of the number of units that should be ordered. Using the same information as in the previous example and assuming that the product has a cost of $5 per unit, the relevant formula is:

$$EOQ = \sqrt{2DB/IC}$$

where

EOQ = the most economic order size, in units

D = annual demand, in units (200 units; $1,000 value of inventory/$5 value per unit)

B = administrative costs per order of placing the order

C = carrying costs of the inventory (expressed as an annual percentage of the inventory's dollar value)

I = dollar value of the inventory, per unit

Thus:

$$EOQ = \sqrt{2 \times 200 \times 25/.20 \times 5} = \sqrt{10{,}000/1} = 100 \text{ units}$$

TABLE 8-5	EOQ Cost Calculations			
Number of Orders Per Year	Order Size ($)	Ordering Cost ($)	Carrying Cost ($)	Total Cost (Sum of Ordering and Carrying Cost) ($)
1	1,000	25	100	125
2	500	50	50	100
3	333	75	33	108
4	250	100	25	125
5	200	125	20	145

Although we've calculated EOQs, how do we know that the answers are correct? Because the EOQ is the point where carrying costs equal ordering costs, we need to calculate both of these costs (see Table 8-5). Recall that we calculated $500 (100 units) to be the EOQ. As shown in Table 8-5, a $500 order size means that we'll be ordering twice per year; the corresponding ordering costs are $50. Average inventory for a $500 order size is $250, meaning that our carrying costs are $50. Thus, we've proven that at an order size of $500, our ordering costs and carrying costs are equal. Table 8-5 presents the total cost calculations for several other order sizes. Note that ordering costs equal carrying costs at the EOQ and that the total cost is minimized as well.

Conditions of Uncertainty

You should recognize that organizations rarely, if ever, are lucky enough to manage inventories in an environment characterized by certainty for all eight of the EOQ assumptions presented above. Consider, for example, how an unexpected event might impact the continuous, constant, and known rate of demand assumption. An excellent illustration involves the death of entertainer Michael Jackson in mid-2009, which caused a tremendous surge in the sales of his recorded music.

Since the contemporary business world is characterized by a great deal of uncertainty, the basic EOQ model can be modified to account for one or more conditions of uncertainty. For instance, an EOQ can be calculated under conditions of demand uncertainty, lead time uncertainty, or demand *and* lead time uncertainty. These and other modifications increase the mathematical complexity in calculating an EOQ and several supply chain management textbooks contain detailed examples of the EOQ modified for various conditions of uncertainty.

INVENTORY FLOWS

The figures from the fixed order quantity (e.g., EOQ) and the SS calculations can be used to develop an inventory flow diagram, which graphically depicts the demand for, and replenishment of, inventory. Figure 8-2 presents an illustration of inventory flow, based on the following assumptions: an EOQ of 120 units, SS of 60 units, average demand of 30 units per day, and a replenishment or order cycle of two days. Further, the beginning inventory is equal to the SS plus the EOQ (60 + 120 = 180). Recall from earlier in this chapter that the ROP can be calculated as $(DD \times RC) + (SS)$, or $(30 \times 2) + (60) = 120$ units.

As shown in Figure 8-2, 180 units of inventory are available for sale at the beginning of day 1 (point A). The DD of 30 means that 150 units are available for sale at the beginning of day 2, and 120 units are available at the beginning of day 3. Because 120 units represent the ROP (point B), an order is placed at the beginning of day 3. Because SS is not to be used under normal circumstances, reordering at 120 units means that 60 units (SS) will be on hand two days later when the EOQ arrives. The EOQ of 120 units arrives at point C, and then total inventory increases to 180 units at point D.

The rate of sales doubles to 60 beginning on day 5, the ROP is hit at 120 units at the beginning of day 6 (point E), and another order is placed. Demand continues at 60 units on day 6, meaning

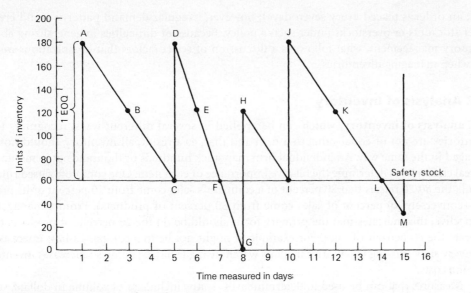

FIGURE 8-2   Inventory Flow Diagram

that the regular inventory is exhausted, and at point F the SS is starting to be used. Demand is also 60 on day 7, leaving us with no inventory (point G) at the end of day 7. The EOQ arrives before opening on day 8, boosting the inventory to 120 units (point H), which is also the ROP. Beginning on day 8, the demand settles back to 30 units per day.

Continuing with Figure 8-2, from point H, inventory is depleted 30 units on day 8 and 30 more on day 9, leaving the inventory at 60 (point I). The inventory ordered on day 8 arrives prior to opening on day 10, meaning that we have 180 units in stock at the beginning of day 10 (point J). Thirty units are demanded on days 10 and 11; inventory is thus 120 units (point K), and another reorder is placed at the beginning of day 12. Demand is 30 units on days 12 and 13, and inventory has reached 60 units (point L). However, because of a transportation delay, the RC is three days instead of two, and instead of arriving at the beginning of day 14, it arrives at the beginning of day 15. Day 14's demand of 30 units will be satisfied from SS (point M), and the EOQ arrives shortly thereafter.

The inventory flow example presented in Figure 8-2 illustrates that SS can prevent against two problem areas: an increased rate of demand and a longer-than-normal replenishment. This example also illustrates that when a fixed order quantity system such as an EOQ is used, the time between orders may vary. As long as demand was normal at 30 units and the RC took two days, the time between orders was four days. However, when sales doubled to 60 units per day, the time between orders fell to two days.

As noted earlier in this chapter, one requirement for the utilization of a fixed order quantity system is that the level of inventory must constantly be monitored; when the ROP is hit, the fixed order quantity is ordered. With continuing advances in computer hardware and software, many firms have the capability to constantly monitor their inventory and hence have the option of using a fixed order quantity system such as the EOQ. An ROP for each item can be established electronically so it can indicate when the stock has been depleted to the point where a new order should be placed. Increasingly, these orders can be transmitted electronically.

INVENTORY MANAGEMENT: SPECIAL CONCERNS

The discussion up to this point illustrates that generalizations concerning inventory management are often hard to make. For example, it might seem like a good idea for a company to strive for minimizing stockouts, except that to actually accomplish this might require inordinately large SSs. Alternatively, a fixed order interval policy might be attractive because of its simplicity (e.g., an order is placed every seven days); however, irregular demand patterns could create either stockouts or overstocks under such a policy. Because of difficulties in generalizing about inventory management, what follows is a discussion of select factors that organizations might face when managing inventories.

ABC Analysis of Inventory

ABC analysis of inventory, which can be applied in several different ways, recognizes that inventories are not of equal value to a firm and that, as a result, all inventory should not be managed in the same way. An individual firm may stock hundreds or thousands of items, and it is a real challenge to determine the relative importance of each item. One commonly used rule of thumb, the *80/20 rule*, is that 80 percent of a company's sales come from 20 percent of its products (conversely, 20 percent of sales come from 80 percent of products). From a managerial perspective, this indicates that the primary focus should be on the 20 percent of products that generate the 80 percent of sales. For example, it might not be in a company's best interests to store very slow-moving inventories in all its warehousing facilities; doing so increases inventory carrying costs.

Measures that can be used to determine ABC status include sales volume in dollars, sales volume in units, the fastest-selling items, item profitability, or item importance. For instance, with respect to item importance, a firm supplying medicine to hospitals might need to stock certain items because they are critically important. Thus, in terms of item importance, ABC might be operationalized as follows: A items could be the ones with the highest criticality, B items could be those with moderate criticality, and C items could have low criticality. Similar approaches could be applied to other measures of ABC status such as sales volume in dollars and item profitability.

One issue with ABC analysis involves a determination of what percentage of items should be classified as A, B, and C, respectively. Although no right or wrong answers characterize this issue, it's important to recognize that either too high or too low a percentage of A items may reduce the potential efficiencies to be gained from the classification technique.

A second issue with ABC analysis involves how it can be used by managers. One use, as suggested earlier, is that ABC analysis can determine stocking patterns in warehousing facilities. For example, one company achieved a 25 percent space reduction in its logistics network by locating SS at only one warehousing facility.[5] In addition, ABC analysis could be used to determine how frequently inventory gets monitored; A items might be checked daily (or, increasingly, hourly), B items weekly, and C items monthly.

Dead Inventory

Some companies have added a fourth category, D, to ABC analysis. D stands for either "dogs" or **dead inventory** (**dead stock**), which refers to product for which there is no sales during a 12-month period. Dead inventory increases inventory carrying costs and takes up space in warehousing facilities, and a structured process should be in place for managing it. For example, because dead inventory has often been associated with overproduction of items that customers don't want (or need), one suggestion would be to make items to order, as opposed to make items to stock. However, an increasing source of dead inventory involves special, highly customized orders that never end up with the customer, perhaps because the customer no longer wants or needs the product. Suggestions for dealing with this situation include partial (or full) prepayment by the customer as well as a no-return policy.[6]

---

[5] Mary Aichlmayr, "The Quick, the Dead, and the Slow Movers," *Transportation & Distribution*, February 2002, 38–42.
[6] Scott Stratman, "Special Orders," *Electrical Wholesaling*, May 2006, 52–53.

FIGURE 8-3 **Advertisement from a Service That Helps Firms Donate Excess Inventories to Charitable Causes**
Source: Courtesy of Educational Assistance, Ltd., Glen Ellyn, IL 60137.

Companies might also market their dead stock more aggressively, perhaps through drastic price reductions or bunching it with more attractive merchandise. Companies might also attempt to sell their dead inventory to companies that specialize in selling such items; Internet sites are available that specialize in selling off dead stock (e.g., deadstockbroker.com). Some dead items can be donated to charitable causes, usually resulting in a partial tax write-off; Figure 8-3 is an ad from a service that helps firms find recipients for inventory donations.

Organizations occasionally resort to seemingly desperate measures to manage their dead inventory. Consider the organization with a storage facility located next to a river that flooded on a seasonal basis. During one particularly rainy year, the organization placed all of its dead stock on a deck attached to the storage facility—and discovered one day that the dead stock had been carried away by rising floodwater from the river.[7] Companies can also throw away dead inventory, if for no other reason than to free up space in a warehousing facility. A well-known example of this behavior involved Atari, a video game maker, which in 1983 *dumped between 10 and 20 trailerloads of video games at a New Mexico landfill!* However, such behavior should only be a last resort, because in so doing a company is, in effect, throwing away money.

Inventory Turnover

Inventory turnover refers to the number of times that inventory is sold in a one-year period. Inventory turnover can be calculated by dividing the cost of goods sold by the average inventory, where average inventory is the sum of beginning and ending inventory divided by 2. For example,

---

[7] Jason Bader, "Distributor Power Tools: The Inventory Obituary," *Doors and Hardware*, March 2007, 61.

suppose the cost of goods sold is $675,000, beginning inventory is $200,000 and ending inventory is $250,000. The inventory turnover for this data is as follows:

Cost of goods sold ($675,000) ÷ Average inventory [($200,000 + $250,000) ÷ 2],

or

$675,000 ÷ $225,000, which equals 3.

Although there is no optimal inventory turnover ratio, inventory turnover figures can provide important insights about an organization's competitiveness and efficiency. Thus, a particular organization can compare its turnover figures to those of direct competitors or other organizations with "desirable" turnover ratios. With respect to efficiency, low turnover indicates that a company is taking longer to sell its inventory, perhaps because of product obsolescence or pricing problems.[8]

By contrast, high turnover may signal a low level of inventories, which can increase the chance of product stockouts. Despite this, most organizations today strive to increase their inventory turnover, and one way to do this is by reducing average inventory. Although reducing average inventory is easier said than done, you should recognize that an understanding of two concepts discussed earlier in this section, ABC analysis and dead inventory, can help to reduce average inventory. For example, eliminating some or all of a company's dead inventory automatically reduces both beginning and ending inventory—hence average inventory is also reduced.

Complementary and Substitute Products

This book takes a rather narrow view of **complementary products** and defines them as inventories that can be used or distributed together, such as razor blades and razors. These products may only intensify the pressures on retailers or wholesalers concerned with inventory maintenance. For example, consider the following dilemma: "So many complementary items exist for cooking meat and fish that you'll never be able to display them in the same section (of the store)." Possible complementary products for the meat and fish section include cheeses, seasonings, skewers, skillets, and wines, among others.[9]

Another issue associated with complementary products involves the amount of inventory to be carried. Purchasing a canister vacuum cleaner, for example, generally means that a customer will periodically need to buy replacement bags for the canister. As such, the canister bags might be slow sellers, and some might argue that the bags should be dropped in favor of faster-moving products. Others, however, would point out that the sale and display of these bags is necessary to support the sale of canister vacuums.

Substitute products refer to products that can fill the same need or want as another product. The substitutability can occur at a specific product level (e.g., one brand of cola is viewed as a substitute for another brand of cola), or it can occur across product classes (e.g., potatoes may be viewed as a substitute for rice). As pointed out previously in this chapter, knowledge of substitutability has important implications with respect to stockout costs and the sizes of SSs to be maintained. Thus, if a consumer has little hesitation in making substitutions, there would appear to be minimal penalties for a stockout. However, a point may be reached where customers become sufficiently annoyed at having to make substitutions that they decide to take their business elsewhere. Because of the many possibilities for substitutability, many grocery chains target in-stock rates of 95 percent for individual stores so that sufficient substitutes exist for a customer to purchase a substitute item rather than go to a competing store.

[8] " 'Turns' for the Better—Inventory Turns Impact Profits and Stock Prices," *Dow Theory Forecasts* 58, no. 4 (2002), 1, 4.
[9] James Mellgren, "Category Complements: Increasing Specialty Food Sales," *Gourmet Retailer*, June 2006, 38–44.

Moreover, some substitute product decisions are much more challenging than others. Consider, for example, some of the issues that hospitals confront with respect to substitute products:

- What safety risks does a substitute product pose for patients and hospital staff?
- Is the substitute product compatible with current equipment?
- How will information about the substitute product be communicated to hospital staff?
- How do a patient's insurance requirements impact the ability to use a substitute product?[10]

It's also important that companies have a thorough understanding of substitution patterns. For example, in many cases, substitutions are two-way, meaning that if brand A is substitutable for brand B, then brand B is substitutable for brand A. In some situations, however, one-way relationships exist; a bolt 7/16 inch in diameter could be used in place of a bolt that is 1/2 inch in diameter, but the reverse may not hold.

CONTEMPORARY APPROACHES TO MANAGING INVENTORY

Much of what has been discussed to this point represents traditional thinking about inventory management. Although traditional thinking about inventory continues to be relevant, additional approaches have evolved, and this chapter concludes with a look at three such approaches—lean manufacturing, service parts logistics, and vendor-managed inventory.

Lean Manufacturing (Lean)

Broadly speaking, **lean manufacturing** (also referred to as **lean**) focuses on the elimination of waste and the increase of speed and flow. The lean manufacturing approach identifies seven major sources of waste, one of which is inventory. Just-in-time (JIT) is one of the best-known lean inventory practices; we'll take a closer look at JIT in the paragraphs that follow.

From an inventory perspective, the **JIT approach** seeks to minimize inventory by reducing (if not eliminating) SS, as well as by having the required amount of materials arrive at the production location at the exact time that they are needed. Although the JIT approach is generally associated with inventory management because of its focus on minimizing inventory, the consequences of JIT actually go far beyond inventory management. The JIT approach has a number of important implications for logistical efficiency, one of which is that suppliers must deliver high-quality materials to the production line; because of JIT's emphasis on low (no) SS, defective materials result in a production line shutdown. Improved product quality from suppliers can be facilitated by looking at suppliers as partners, as opposed to adversaries, in the production process.

JIT emphasizes minimal inventory levels, and as a result customers tend to place smaller, more frequent orders. As such, it is imperative that suppliers' order systems be capable of handling an increased number of orders in an error-free fashion. In addition, because the transit-time reliability tends to decrease with distance, suppliers need to be located relatively close to their customers.

The combination of smaller, more frequent shipments and close supplier location means that trucking is an important mode of transportation in the JIT approach. As such, production and distribution facilities should be designed to support truck shipments—that is, there should be truck docks to facilitate product loading and unloading. Although this may appear to be the proverbial "no-brainer," consider the case of a U.S. manufacturer that designed a state-of-the-art distribution facility to be served by rail, only to switch to a JIT approach, thus making the new facility totally worthless. In fact, some companies involved in JIT have designed their production facilities so that trucks can drive inside them, thus bringing the product that much closer to the

---

[10] Colleen Cusick, "Successful Substitutions Are a Product of Good Communication," *Material Management in Health Care*, March 2008, 28–31.

FIGURE 8-4 Trailer That Opens on the Side and Is Used for Rapid Discharge of Parts
It was designed for use by carriers serving manufacturers with just-in-time inventory management systems. *Source:* Photo courtesy Fruehauf Corporation.

actual production point. Figure 8-4 shows a truck trailer that opens on its side for rapid discharge of parts for JIT inventory management.

Other examples of lean inventory include Efficient Consumer Response (ECR), which is associated with the grocery and beverage industries, and Quick Response (QR), which is associated with the apparel industry. Where JIT tends to encompass movement of materials and component parts from supplier to producer, ECR and QR tend to focus on product movement from manufacturer to retailer.

Although lean is an important concept in contemporary logistics, a confluence of events suggests that organizations should carefully consider the potential trade-offs before adopting a lean philosophy. More specifically, the lean philosophy was conceived and nurtured in an environment—low fuel prices, minimal transportation congestion, local or regional sourcing, and limited terrorism—far different than today's environment. Today's emphasis on global sourcing translates into longer and more erratic transit times—and longer and more erratic transit times don't align very well with lean's emphasis on shipments that arrive exactly when needed. In a similar fashion, today's high fuel prices (by historical standards) cause transportation companies to focus on lower costs through moving larger freight volumes—a practice that doesn't align very well with lean's emphasis on smaller shipments.

Service Parts Logistics

Service parts logistics involves designing a network of facilities to stock service parts, deciding upon inventory ordering policies, stocking the required parts, and transporting parts from stocking facilities to customers.[11] Long viewed as an afterthought or—even worse—as a nuisance, service parts logistics has gained greater attention and appreciation in recent years. One reason for this is that the customer expectations associated with service parts logistics continue to increase, particularly in the automotive industry where the *maximum* customer wait time for repair or replacement parts is one day.[12] Another reason for increased emphasis on service parts logistics is that the worldwide economic slowdown of 2008 and 2009 caused many organizations to repair, rather than replace, aging or defective equipment.

Service parts logistics creates a variety of potential challenges for logisticians; one challenge is it can be extremely difficult to forecast the demand for the necessary parts. For example, although companies might have some knowledge about the repair parts needed for routine or preventive maintenance of products, it is virtually impossible to forecast when the product might break down or fail. The difficulties in forecasting demand lead to challenges with respect to which parts to carry, the appropriate stocking levels for the parts that are carried, and higher inventory levels, among others.[13]

Another challenge involves the number of warehousing facilities that should be used in service parts logistics. One possibility is to locate the parts at numerous warehousing facilities in that this allows the parts to be fairly close to potential customers, and in emergency situations, where time is of the essence, this can be critical to customer satisfaction. Alternatively, the parts could be located at one centralized facility; although this would require use of premium transportation for some shipments, this cost can be offset by the inventory cost savings that result from inventory being held in only one facility.

These and other challenges have led some organizations to outsource their service parts logistics to companies that specialize in this area (see Figure 8-5). For example, Choice Logistics has developed expertise in managing service parts logistics for technology and telecommunications companies. Choice Logistics offers prospective customers approximately 400 stocking facilities, ranging in size from 100 to 10,000 square feet, in over 90 countries. Importantly, superior inventory control is cited as the most prominent reason for using service parts logistics specialists such as Choice Logistics.[14]

This discussion of service parts logistics offers an opportunity to point out the importance of informal considerations when managing inventories and making logistics-related decisions. Several years ago, the owner of an automotive parts distributor became concerned with the amount of inventory his company was holding. A visit to the distributor's storage facility revealed that it was literally overrun with oil filters from one particular manufacturer; this one brand of oil filters accounted for approximately 20 percent of the facility's total inventory, a figure far higher than its actual demand.

At first glance, the solution seemed clear: Reduce the inventory of oil filters to a level more in line with demand. However, there was a reason for the high inventory of oil filters: The oil filter manufacturer sponsored annual contests that offered all-expenses–paid trips for two to attractive vacation locations such as Hawaii, and the trips were awarded based on the amount of oil filters purchased in a particular time frame. Because the distributor's spouse had become quite fond of these annual trips, each year the owner placed very large orders for the particular brand of oil filters, despite that fact that they weren't needed. As a result, the "obvious" solution to the problem— reducing the inventory of oil filters—wasn't feasible because the owner wanted to please his spouse. In this situation, personal considerations were more important than professional ones, and you should recognize that personal considerations often play a very important role when making decisions in family-run businesses.

---

[11] Mehmet Ferhat Candas and Erhat Kutanoglu, "Benefits of Considering Inventory in Service Parts Logistics Network Design Problems with Time-Based Service Constraints," *IIE Transactions* 39, no. 2 (2007): 159–176.
[12] Anthony Coia, "The Replacement Fillers," *Automotive Logistics*, September–October 2008, 28–32.
[13] Lisa Harrington, "Getting Service Parts Logistics Up to Speed," *Inbound Logistics*, November 2006, 72–79.
[14] William Hoffman, "A Bigger Part," *Traffic World*, January 19, 2009, 17.

FIGURE 8-5 Advertisement from a Parts Bank Service
Source: Courtesy of Associated Distribution Logistics (ADL).

Vendor-Managed Inventory (VMI)

In traditional inventory management, the size and timing of replenishment orders are the responsibility of the party using the inventory, such as a distributor or a retailer. Under **vendor-managed inventory (VMI)**, by contrast, the size and timing of replenishment orders are the responsibility of the manufacturer. Operationally, VMI allows manufacturers to have access to a distributor's or retailer's sales and inventory data, and this access is accomplished electronically by electronic data interchange (EDI) or the Internet. Although VMI is often associated with consumer products, it also has been applied to industrial products such as airplanes, construction equipment, fasteners (e.g., bolts and screws), and heating and cooling systems, among others.

VMI represents a huge philosophical shift for some organizations in the sense that they are allowing another party to have control over their inventories. This is a situation that necessitates tremendous trust on the part of distributors and retailers because of the potential for unscrupulous manufacturers to abuse the system by pushing unneeded inventories onto downstream parties.

VMI's benefits for distributors include reduced inventories, fewer stockouts, and improved service by having the right product available at the right time. Manufacturers can benefit from VMI in terms of improved forecasts that are based on actual point-of-sale data as well as from a reduction in ordering errors by distributors. Alternatively, one drawback to VMI is inadequate data sharing between the relevant parties, in part because of trust and control concerns. Another VMI drawback is that some manufacturer or distributor employees may resist the change to a new and different system. In addition, organizations that adopt VMI must recognize that the process will not produce immediate benefits.[15]

Summary

Inventory is a key component in logistics because inventory decisions are often a starting point for other business activities. The chapter began with a look at the various classifications of inventory, and this was followed by a discussion of inventory costs. When deciding what levels of inventories to maintain, companies try to minimize the costs associated with both too much and too little inventory. Too much inventory leads to high inventory carrying costs; too little inventory can lead to stockouts and the associated stockout costs. The worst outcome of a stockout is to lose both a sale and all future business from the customer.

The chapter also addressed when to order inventory, as well as how much inventory to order, and we learned that ROPs signify stock levels at which a new order should be placed. With respect to how much to order, the EOQ minimizes ordering costs and inventory carrying costs.

The chapter looked at special concerns associated with inventory management, including ABC analysis and inventory turnover, and we learned that an understanding of ABC analysis can help organizations increase their inventory turnover. The chapter concluded with a discussion of several contemporary approaches to managing inventory.

Questions for Discussion and Review

1. How might different organizational functions have different inventory management objectives?
2. What makes it difficult for managers to achieve the proper balance of inventory?
3. Distinguish among cycle, safety, pipeline, and speculative stock.
4. Define what is meant by inventory carrying costs, and list its primary components.
5. What are ordering costs, and what is the trade-off between inventory carrying costs and ordering costs?
6. Discuss the concept of stockout costs. How can stockout costs be calculated?

---

[15] *http://www.vendormanagedinventory.com/about.php.*

7. Distinguish between a fixed order quantity and fixed order interval system. Which one generally requires more safety stock? Why?
8. Explain the logic of the EOQ model.
9. What assumptions are associated with the EOQ model?
10. How can inventory flow diagrams be useful to a logistics manager?
11. Discuss what is meant by ABC analysis of inventory. What are several measures that can determine ABC status?
12. Define what is meant by dead inventory. What are several ways to manage it?
13. In what ways can inventory turnover provide important insights about an organization's competitiveness and efficiency?
14. Discuss some of the managerial challenges that complementary products present.
15. What are substitute items, and how might they affect safety stock policies?
16. How might a hospital's decisions with respect to substitute products differ from a supermarket's decisions with substitute products?
17. How do the consequences of JIT go far beyond inventory management?
18. Why should organizations carefully consider potential trade-offs before adopting a lean philosophy?
19. Discuss some challenges that service parts logistics creates for logistics managers.
20. How does vendor-managed inventory differ from traditional inventory management?

Suggested Readings

Davis, Don, Jim Buckler, Adam Mussomeli, and Dan Kinzler. "Inventory Transformation Revlon Style." *Supply Chain Management Review* 9, no. 5 (2005): 53–59.

Hadley, Scott W. "A Modern View of Inventory." *Strategic Finance* 86, no. 1 (2004): 31–35.

Herrin, Richard. "How to Calculate Safety Stocks for Highly Seasonal Products." *Journal of Business Forecasting* 24, no. 2 (2004): 6–10.

Lee, Hau L., and Seungjin Whang. "The Whose, Where, and How of Inventory Control Design." *Supply Chain Management Review* 12, no. 8 (2008): 22–29.

Matson, Jack E., and Jessica O. Matson. "Just-in-Time Implementation Issues among Automotive Suppliers in the Southern USA." *Supply Chain Management: An International Journal* 12, no. 6 (2007): 432–443.

Metersky, Jeff, and J. Michael Kilgore. "How to Improve Your Inventory Deployment." *Supply Chain Management Review* 8, no. 7 (2004): 26–32.

Rungtusanatham, Manus, Elliot Rabinovich, Bryan Ashenbaum, and Cynthia Wallin. "Vendor-Owned Inventory Management Arrangements in Retail: An Agency Theory Perspective." *Journal of Business Logistics* 28, no. 1 (2007): 111–135.

Taylor, John C., Stanley E. Fawcett, and George C. Jackson. "Catalog Retailer In-Stock Performance: An Assessment of Customer Service Levels." *Journal of Business Logistics* 25, no. 2 (2004): 119–137.

Williams, Brent D., and Travis Tokar. "A Review of Inventory Management Research in Major Logistics Journals." *International Journal of Logistics Management* 19, no. 2 (2008): 212–232.

Woensel, Tom van, Karel van Donselaar, Rob Broekmeulen, and Jan Fransoo. "Consumer Responses to Shelf Out-of-Stocks of Perishable Products." *International Journal of Physical Distribution & Logistics Management* 37, no. 9 (2007): 704–718.

CASE

CASE 8-1   Low Nail Company

After making some wise short-term investments at a racetrack, Chris Low had some additional cash to invest in a business. The most promising opportunity at the time was in building supplies, so Low bought a business that specialized in sales of one size of nail. The annual volume of nails was 2,000 kegs, and they were sold to retail customers in an even flow. Low was uncertain how many nails to order at any time. Initially, only two costs concerned him: order-processing costs, which were $60 per order without regard to size, and warehousing costs, which were $1 per year per keg space. This meant that Low had to rent a constant amount of warehouse space for the year, and it had to be large enough to accommodate an entire order when it arrived. Low was not worried about maintaining safety stocks, mainly because the outward flow of goods was so even. Low bought his nails on a delivered basis.

Questions

1. Using the EOQ methods outlined in Chapter 8, how many kegs of nails should Low order at one time?

2. Assume all conditions in Question 1 hold, except that Low's supplier now offers a quantity discount in the form of absorbing all or part of Low's order-processing costs. For orders of 750 or more kegs of nails, the supplier will absorb all the order-processing costs; for orders between 249 and 749 kegs, the supplier will absorb half. What is Low's new EOQ? (It might be useful to lay out all costs in tabular form for this and later questions.)

3. Temporarily, ignore your work on Question 2. Assume that Low's warehouse offers to rent Low space on the basis of the *average* number of kegs Low will have in stock, rather than on the maximum number of kegs Low would need room for whenever a new shipment arrived. The storage charge per keg remains the same. Does this change the answer to Question 1? If so, what is the new answer?

4. Take into account the answer to Question 1 *and* the supplier's new policy outlined in Question 2 *and* the warehouse's new policy in Question 3. Then determine Low's new EOQ.

5. Temporarily, ignore your work on Questions 2–4. Low's luck at the racetrack is over; he now must borrow money to finance his inventory of nails. Looking at the situation outlined in Question 1, assume that the wholesale cost of nails is $40 per keg and that Low must pay interest at the rate of 1.5 percent per month on unsold inventory. What is his new EOQ?

6. Taking into account all the factors listed in Questions 1, 2, 3, and 5, calculate Low's EOQ for kegs of nails.

9

DISTRIBUTION CENTER, WAREHOUSE, AND PLANT LOCATION

Key Terms

- Agglomeration (industry cluster)
- Brownfields
- Center-of-gravity approach
- Expatriate workers
- Facility closing
- Facility location
- Facility relocation
- Free trade zone
- Grid systems
- Intermodal competition
- Intramodal competition
- Inventory tax
- Locavore strategy
- Maquiladora
- Pure materials
- Quality-of-life considerations
- Right-to-work laws
- Supplier parks
- Sweatshops
- Weight-gaining products
- Weight-losing products

Learning Objectives

- To examine the strategic importance of facility location
- To explain the general process of determining the optimum number of facilities
- To describe the major factors that influence facility location
- To examine a site's specialized location characteristics
- To explain location decisions using simple grid systems
- To learn about facility relocation and facility closing

Facility location is a logistics/supply chain activity that has evolved from a tactical decision to one of tremendous strategic importance in numerous organizations. In particular, this chapter discusses **facility location**, which refers to choosing the locations for distribution centers, warehouses, and production facilities to facilitate logistical effectiveness and efficiency. The chapter begins with an overview of the location process, followed by a discussion of the strategic importance of facility location. Next is a discussion of how to determine the optimum number of facilities, which is followed by a look at general and specific influences on facility location. The chapter next describes several basic techniques for choosing general locations and concludes with a discussion of facility relocation and facility closing.

The location decision process involves several layers of screening or focus, with each step becoming a more detailed analysis of a smaller number of areas or sites. The initial focus is on the region, the delineation of which can vary depending on whether a company has a multinational or domestic focus. Thus, a multinational company might initially focus on a region of the world, such as Western Europe, the Pacific Rim, or North America. By

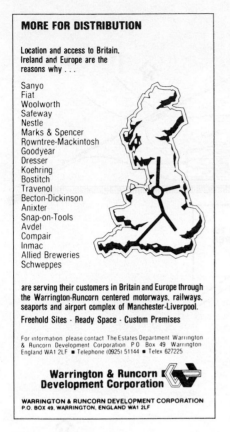

FIGURE 9-1 Advertisement Showing a Site's
Location as an Advantage in Reaching British
and Continental European Markets
Source: Warrington and Runcorn Development
Corporation, England.

contrast, a domestic focus might target a state (province/territory) or group of states
(provinces/territories).

The next focus is more precise; it usually involves a selection of the area(s) in which the
facility will be located, as illustrated in Figure 9-1, from a brochure describing a site in the
Manchester–Liverpool area of England. Once this has been determined, a detailed examination of various locations within the selected area is appropriate. Figure 9-2 shows a map of
a specific site along the Little Calumet River, between Chicago, Illinois, and Hammond,
Indiana.

This detailed examination should include a physical inspection of the location as well as a
thorough analysis of relevant zoning and regulatory considerations. Failure to do so can result in
costly—and potentially embarrassing—mistakes, as illustrated by the unfortunate experience of
a major supermarket chain. The company picked a site for a new grocery store, received the
appropriate construction permits, built the store, hired relevant personnel, and stocked the store
with products. Several days before the store's grand opening, the parent company was threatened
with legal action by a competing supermarket that had a store located across the street from the
new store. The legal action referred to the relevant zoning laws—which had not been checked
prior to beginning construction—that prohibited any new grocery store from being built within
a one-mile radius of the existing grocery store! As a result, the supermarket chain had to cancel its
grand opening, close the brand-new store, transfer the products to other stores, and lay off many
of the newly hired personnel.[1]

---

[1] Example drawn from one author's personal experience.

FIGURE 9-2 Location Map and Site Plan for an Available Industrial Site on the Little Calumet River
Source: Courtesy of Donald F. Schroud of Hiffman Shaffer Anderson, Inc.

THE STRATEGIC IMPORTANCE OF FACILITY LOCATION[2]

Logistics managers face a marketplace that is dynamic and ever-changing, and this dynamism and change are two reasons why facility location has evolved from a tactical to a strategic consideration. Facilities such as manufacturing plants and warehousing represent fixed points where goods are produced, processed, assembled, or stored. Because these facilities can be very expensive to lease or build, companies are often hesitant to close them. However, poorly located facilities can negatively impact logistical effectiveness (e.g., due to longer and less reliable delivery

---

[2] The discussion in this section is based on factors identified in John J. Coyle, C. John Langley, Brian J. Gibson, Robert A. Novack, and Edward J. Bardi, *Supply Chain Management: A Logistics Perspective*, 8th ed. (Mason, OH: South-Western Cengage Learning, 2009), Chapter 12.

times) and efficiency (e.g., due to increased delivery costs). This section discusses several over-arching factors that can influence facility location decisions.

Cost Considerations

Cost considerations are hardly new to logistics managers; recall from Chapter 1 that the systems approach to logistics is predicated on the total costs of various logistics activities. Today's cost considerations arise because many consumers are sensitized to buy products only when prices are low, as illustrated by the following quote: "Price cuts are like management heroin. They're addictive. Customers develop a craving for big discounts and an aversion to full prices."[3] If retailers offer consistently low prices, then their costs must also be consistently low in order for organizations to be profitable.

   This low-price/low-cost framework has caused many companies to manufacture in countries characterized by plentiful and low-cost labor. Manufacturing in countries with low labor costs worked reasonably well, until the tremendous surge in oil prices in 2008 forced many companies to reconsider their manufacturing locations because of soaring transportation costs. More specifically, record high transportation costs during 2008 offset the manufacturing cost savings from low-wage countries. Although at the time of publication oil costs are about 55 percent of their 2008 peak, a number of organizations have reconfigured their logistics networks to bring some production facilities closer to key consumer markets.

Customer Service Expectations

One point that has been repeatedly emphasized in this text is that customer service expectations continue to increase over time. We know, for example, that today's customers are looking for faster and more reliable order cycles, but how are faster and more reliable order cycles operationalized from a facility location perspective? Should an organization rely on one or two facilities to serve its customers, or should it rely on multiple facilities to serve them? The former alternative leads to fewer facilities and lower inventory costs, but higher transportation costs; the latter leads to more facilities and higher inventory costs, but lower transportation costs.

Location of Customer or Supply Markets

Improvements in transportation and technology (e.g., air conditioning) allow consumers to migrate relatively easily from one region or country to another. An example of such migration can be seen in Table 9-1, which lists the five most populous states in the United States in 1960, 1980, and 2005. Note that in 1960, four of the five most populated states were located in the Northeast and Midwest, whereas in 2005, the three most populous states were located in

TABLE 9-1	Five Most Populous States in the United States—1960, 1980, 2005		
Rank	**1960**	**1980**	**2005**
1	New York	California	California
2	California	New York	Texas
3	Pennsylvania	Texas	New York
4	Illinois	Pennsylvania	Florida
5	Ohio	Illinois	Illinois

Sources: Derived from data at *www.census.gov*.

---

[3] Cecile Rohwedder, "U.K. Grocers Wage Price War, Yet Most Can Declare Victory," *The Wall Street Journal*, August 10, 2009, A1, A8.

the West, Southwest, and Southeast. This population shift necessitates different production and distribution facility locations than in the 1960s, and cities like Atlanta, Dallas, and Memphis are today important distribution hubs in the United States.

Economic growth is another variable that influences the location of customer markets in the sense that organizations sometimes expand their geographic scope to serve new customers. From purely a population perspective, China and India have been potentially attractive markets because the two countries account for approximately one-third of the world's population. What makes China and India even more attractive today is that both are experiencing tremendous growth in the number of middle-class families—families that often prefer name-brand Western goods and services.

By the end of 2012, for example, McDonald's is projected to have approximately 1,500 restaurant locations in China, up from 1,000 at the end of 2008. In addition to selecting the new store locations, the new stores will need to be supplied with foodstuffs and the like, which will likely necessitate additional distribution facilities to be located in China. This expansion also highlights supply location issues, such as will McDonald's use current, or new, suppliers for the new restaurants? The use of current suppliers might lead to lengthy supply lines—and possibly longer and more erratic transit times—but would allow McDonald's to work with familiar companies. Alternatively, new suppliers might be located in closer proximity to the new restaurants and distribution facilities, but McDonald's will need to learn how to work with the new suppliers.

The sustainability concept is another strategic consideration that can potentially impact the location of supply markets. You might recall from Chapter 1 that sustainability refers to products that meet present needs without compromising the ability of future generations to meet their needs. A key sustainability issue involves the sourcing of products, and an emerging trend involves food companies that pursue a **locavore strategy**, that is, purchasing locally grown or produced foods. Locavore foods are desirable from a sustainability perspective because they reduce carbon footprints related to production and transportation.[4]

DETERMINING THE NUMBER OF FACILITIES

An early, albeit overlooked, step in the facility location decision should involve determining the total number of facilities that a firm should operate. That is, rather than asking the question, "Where should we locate a new facility?" organizations should be thinking about the optimal number of facilities in their system. Although an additional facility may indeed be required, the general trend in recent years has been for companies to reduce the number of facilities in their distribution networks.

Few firms start business on one day and have a need for large-scale production and distribution the next day. Rather, distribution and production facilities tend to be added one at a time, as needed. The need for additional distribution and production facilities often arises when an organization's service performance from existing facilities drops below "acceptable" levels. Retailers, for example, might add a distribution center when some of its stores can no longer consistently be supplied within two days by existing facilities.

Most analytical procedures for determining the number of facilities are computerized because of the vast number of permutations involved, as well as the complementary relationships between current facilities in a distribution network. Analyzing, for example, whether an organization with 250 stores and five distribution centers should add or remove one distribution center is challenging enough in and of itself. Factoring in that each distribution center is designed to serve a specific number of retail locations—and serve as a backup to one or more of the other distribution centers—makes the decision even more complex. Furthermore, conducting sensitivity analysis on varying levels of customer service could result in an entirely different series of ideal facility locations, depending on the level of customer service that is expected.

---

[4] Kate Leahy, "The Era of Sustainability," *Restaurants and Institutions*, October 2008, 38–46.

Fortunately, a number of software packages exist to help organizations determine both the number and location of facilities in their logistics networks. Chicago Consulting, for example, annually develops a list entitled, "The 10 Best Warehouse Networks," which lists those available for serving the U.S. population; in 2006, Chicago Consulting debuted a list of "The 10 Best Chinese Warehouse Networks" for serving mainland China (see Figure 9-3). Although these lists are limited in the sense that they only look at one component in location (how long it takes to get

THE 10 BEST CHINESE WAREHOUSE NETWORKS
Networks with the Lowest Possible "Time-to-the-Chinese Population"

Number of Warehouses	Average Distance to the Chinese Population (Miles)	Average Transit Lead-Time to the Chinese Population (Days)	Best Warehouse Locations		
ONE	504	3.38	XINYANG		
TWO	377	2.55	LIANYUAN	FEICHENG	
THREE	309	2.15	PINGXIANG	JINAN	ZIYANG
FOUR	265	1.87	PINGXIANG CHANGCHUN	JINING	ZIYANG
FIVE	228	1.65	SHAOGUAN CHANGCHUN	HANDAN NANJING	ZIYANG
SIX	207	1.53	SHAOGUAN CHANGCHUN	HANDAN NANJING	NEIJIANG URUMQI
SEVEN	184	1.42	GUANGZHOU CHANGCHUN HONGHU	HANDAN JINGJIANG	NEIJIANG URUMQI
EIGHT	168	1.31	GUANGZHOU CHANGCHUN HONGHU	LIAOCHENG YIXING BAOJI	YIBIN URUMQI
NINE	154	1.24	BEILIU CHANGCHUN YUEYANG	LIAOCHENG LIYANG BAOJI	YIBIN URUMQI ZHANGZHOU
TEN	141	1.20	BEILIU CHANGCHUN YUEYANG TIANJIN	KAIFENG YIXING BAOJI	YIBIN URUMQI ZHANGZHOU

The 10 Best Chinese Warehouse Networks have been developed based on the lowest possible transit lead-times to "customers" represented by the Chinese population. For example, Xinyang provides the lowest possible lead-time for one warehouse. Any other place will increase transit lead-time to the Chinese population. Similarly putting any three warehouses in any locations other than Pingxiang, Jinan or Ziyang will cause the transit lead-time to be higher than 2.15 days.

© Chicago Consulting
8 South Michigan Avenue, Chicago, IL 60603
(312) 346-5080, www.chicago-consulting.com

Chicago Consulting ❮❯

FIGURE 9-3 Chicago Consulting's 10 Best Chinese Warehouse Networks

Source: Courtesy of Terry Harris, Managing Partner of Chicago Consulting.

from a particular city—or cities—to the majority of the country's population), the network is valuable in showing how altering the number of facilities affects transit time to the particular population. With respect to China, for example, going from two to five warehouses allows a company to save nearly one day of lead time to the Chinese population. By contrast, moving from five to ten warehouses saves a bit less than one-half day in lead time.[5]

GENERAL FACTORS INFLUENCING FACILITY LOCATION

Tangible products are the combination of raw materials, component parts, and labor—with the mixture varying from product to product—made for sale in various markets. Thus, raw materials, component parts, labor, and markets all influence where to locate a manufacturing, processing, or assembly facility. Warehouses, distribution centers, and cross-docking facilities exist to facilitate the distribution of products. Their locations are in turn influenced by the locations of plants whose products they handle and the markets they serve.

The discussion that follows covers the location of manufacturing, processing, assembly, and distribution facilities along the supply chain. The relative importance of each factor varies with the type of facility, the product being handled, its volume, and the geographic locations being considered. Although much of the discussion deals with single facilities, the decision process often involves a combination of facilities, in which case one must take into account the relationships among them.

Natural Resources

The materials used to make a product must be extracted directly from the ground or sea (as in the case of mining or fishing) or indirectly (as in the case of farm products). In some instances, these resources may be located great distances from the point where the materials or their products will be consumed. For materials that lose no weight in processing, known as **pure materials**, the processing point can be anywhere near the raw material source and the market.

However, if the materials must be processed at some point between where they are gathered and where they are needed, their weight-losing or weight-gaining characteristics become important for facility location. If the materials lose considerable weight in processing, known as **weight-losing products**, then the processing point should be near the point where they are mined or harvested, largely to avoid the payment of unnecessary transportation charges. If the raw materials gain weight in processing, known as **weight-gaining products**, then the processing point should be close to the market. Sugar derived from sugar beets provides an example of a weight-losing product (a yield of roughly 1 pound of sugar from 6 pounds of sugar beets), whereas bottled soft drinks are an example of a weight-gaining product.

In addition to its use for bottling, water (of one type or another) is a requirement for the location of many facilities. For some industrial processes, water is used for cooling, and in some climates, it is possible to use naturally flowing water for air conditioning during warm months. Some processing operations require water both for cleaning purposes and as a medium for carrying away waste. Water is also necessary for fire protection, and the fire insurance premiums charged depend on the availability of some type of water supply.

Historically, the relationship between natural resources and facility location revolved around how the natural resources would be incorporated into products making their way toward consumers. Over the past quarter century, however, discussion of natural resources and facility location has increasingly factored in environmental and sustainability considerations. One set of considerations involves the various types of pollution, namely, air, noise, and water, while another environmental consideration involves the conservation of natural resources.

---

[5] *www.chicago-consulting.com.*

Moreover, developing nations often face an interesting dilemma with respect to facility location—especially manufacturing plants—and environmental considerations. By limiting the number and scope of environmental regulations associated with manufacturing facilities, developing countries can speed their economic growth and thus help raise their standard of living. Doing so, however, greatly increases the likelihood of damaging, perhaps irreversibly, a country's natural resources, not to mention creating potential health-related problems for its citizens.

Regarding real estate, distribution and production facilities may require large parcels of land to facilitate effective and efficient operations. An example of land requirements for a particular type of facility is a 250,000–square foot distribution center that could require at least 50 acres of land. In general, real estate tends to be more plentiful and less costly in more rural locations—locations that might not have adequate transportation or labor resources. Some companies, particularly those needing large-capacity facilities, view the availability and costs of real estate to be as important a locational determinant as transportation and labor considerations.[6]

Population Characteristics—Market for Goods

Population can be viewed as both a market for goods and a potential source of labor. Customer considerations, particularly as they affect customer service, play a key role in where consumer goods companies tend to locate their distribution facilities. In fact, the popular press is replete with stories involving distribution facilities being located in a particular area so that companies can better serve their current and potential customers.

Planners for consumer products pay extremely close attention to various attributes of current and potential consumers. Not only are changes in population size of interest to planners, but so are changes in the characteristics of the population—particularly as those characteristics influence purchasing habits. With respect to population characteristics, longer life spans can increase the demand for health-related products such as prescription medications.

In an effort to learn more about population size and characteristics, many countries conduct a detailed study, or census, typically once every 10 years or so. Although census methodologies and the type of information collected often vary across countries, the resulting data can provide valuable insights for distribution planners in terms of where populations are growing and at what rates. For instance, although a 2005 update to the 2000 U.S. Census projected a 10 percent increase in total population between 2000 and 2010, the population growth is unlikely to be uniform across the various states. Population in the Northeast, for example, is expected to grow at approximately 4 percent, compared to a 14 percent projected growth in the West.[7]

Population Characteristics—Labor

Labor is a primary concern in selecting a site for manufacturing, processing, assembly, and distribution. Organizations can be concerned with a number of labor-related characteristics: the size, the unemployment rate, the age profile, and skills and education of the available workforce, its prevailing wage rates, and the extent to which it is, or might be, unionized. These and other labor characteristics should be viewed as interrelated rather than as distinct attributes. For example, there may be a positive relationship between the age of the workforce and the prevailing wage rates (i.e., higher wage rates may be associated with an older workforce). Alternatively, there may be an inverse relationship between unemployment and wages (i.e., higher unemployment rates may be associated with lower relative wage rates).

Labor wage rates are a key locational determinant as supply chains become more global in nature. For example, hourly compensation data (including benefits) among manufacturing firms

---

[6] William Atkinson, "DC Siting—What Makes the Most Sense?" *Logistics Management & Distribution Report*, May 2002, S63–S66.
[7] "Interim State Population Projections, 2005," *www.census.gov*.

in 2007 indicate average compensation of $24.59 in the United States, $19.75 in Japan, and $37.06 in Germany. By contrast, hourly compensation rates were $6.58 in Taiwan and $2.92 in Mexico.[8]

Thus, in relative terms, a company could have approximately similar compensation costs by hiring either eight Mexican workers or one U.S. worker. This wage differential at least partly explains the popularity of the **maquiladora** assembly plants located just south of the U.S.–Mexican border. These plants, which began in the mid-1960s, provided much needed jobs to Mexican workers and allowed for low-cost, duty-free production so long as all the goods were exported from Mexico. In the first few years of the twenty-first century, many maquiladoras went out of business, in part because companies established production plants in even lower-wage countries such as China and Guatemala. Since 2004, however, there has been a resurgence of maquiladoras in part by focusing on high-value goods that depend on fast time to market, such as high-tech products. Other reasons for the maquiladora resurgence include the worldwide economic slowdown that began in 2007 as well as higher fuel prices.[9]

Companies interested in locating in countries with low-cost labor should recognize that there are sometimes limits to the number of supervisory personnel that can be brought in from other countries. The host-country's government may also insist that its own nationals be trained for and employed in many supervisory posts. In addition, countries with low-cost labor often have a multitude of **sweatshops**, which can be viewed as organizations that exploit workers and that do not comply with fiscal and legal obligations toward employees. Although many companies recognize that they have social responsibilities, which would include fair labor practices, to date only slightly more than 10 percent have formal requirements that address sweatshop labor.[10]

A workforce's union status is also a key locational determinant for some organizations. From management's perspective, unions tend to result in increased labor costs, due to higher wages, and less flexibility in terms of job assignments, which often forces companies to hire additional workers. As a result, some organizations prefer geographic areas in which unions are not strong; in the United States, for example, some states have **right-to-work laws**, which mean that an individual cannot be compelled to join a union as a condition of employment. Indeed, since 2000 non–U.S. automakers have chosen to locate new production plants in right-to-work states such as Alabama (Hyundai), Georgia (Kia), Mississippi (Nissan), and Texas (Toyota).

However, the mere presence of a union doesn't necessarily mean that the union is a strong advocate for workers. Consider that the all-China Federation of Trade Unions (ACFTU), which represents over 130 million Chinese workers, is controlled by the Chinese government. As such, the ACFTU sometimes faces conflicting objectives in the sense of deciding what's good for the government versus what's good for the workers—and the workers' concerns aren't always the top priority.

Racial, ethnic, and cultural considerations may also be important population characteristics. Many organizations, particularly those with a national or international presence, have workforces comprised of different races, ethnicities, and cultures. There may be a hesitancy to establish facilities in areas that are not racially, ethnically, or culturally diverse because it may be difficult to transfer workers to such locations. Moreover, an emerging issue involves managing so-called **expatriate workers**, or those employees who are sent to other countries for extended periods of time. Expatriate assignments can be costly, ranging up to $1 million per assignment, and turnover rates currently run between 20 and 40 percent. What makes the expatriate situation relevant to the current discussion is that the turnover tends to be caused by socialization, rather than technical (i.e., employee knowledge and skills), factors. Indeed, a leading cause of expatriate turnover involves family-related issues.[11]

---

[8] *http://www.bls.gov/news.release/ichcc.t02.htm.*

[9] Bill Dibenedetto, "Maqs Are Back," *The Journal of Commerce*, October 13, 2008, 22.

[10] Garrett Brown, "Why Sweatshops Won't Go Away," *Industrial Safety and Hygiene News* 40, no. 6 (2006): 70–71.

[11] No author, "Expatriates Are Twice as Likely to Leave Jobs," *HRFocus*, August 2006, 9.

Taxes and Incentives

Although labor considerations are important for location decisions, taxes can also be important, particularly with respect to warehousing facilities. Warehousing facilities, and the inventories they contain, are often viewed as a prime source of tax revenues by the relevant taxing organizations. From a community's standpoint, warehousing facilities are desirable operations to attract because they add to the tax base while requiring relatively little in the way of municipal services. No list of taxes is complete; a partial list includes sales taxes, real estate taxes, corporate income taxes, corporate franchising taxes, fuel taxes, unemployment compensation taxes, social security taxes, and severance taxes (for the removal of natural resources).

Of particular interest to logisticians and supply chain managers is the **inventory tax**, analogous to personal property taxes paid by individuals. As a general rule, the inventory tax is based on the value of inventory that is held on the assessment date(s). Not surprisingly, many logistics managers attempt to have their inventories as low as possible on the assessment date(s), and businesses may offer sales to reduce their inventory prior to the assessment date.

Although between 10 and 15 U.S. states currently assess inventory taxes, they have become increasingly difficult to collect, in part because of a lack of agreement on what is meant by inventory. Some states, for example, classify intellectual property as inventory.[12] In addition, although a state may offer various exemptions from inventory taxes, not all counties within that state will take advantage of the exemptions. Other inventory exemptions deal more explicitly with distribution activities or functions. Some states exempt goods that are stored in public warehouses; some states exempt goods passing through the state on a storage-in-transit bill of lading.

As if business taxes are not difficult enough to understand, they represent only one side of the coin; the other side is to know the value of services being received in exchange for the taxes. A general rule of thumb is that the services received represent only about 50 percent of the taxes paid, and this imbalance may cause businesses to invest more money to receive the required level of service. For example, inadequate police services might cause a warehousing facility to hire its own security force.

To further complicate matters, governments may offer incentive packages as an inducement for firms to locate facilities in a particular area. To give you an example of the potential magnitude of incentive packages, the state of North Carolina provided Google approximately $210 million in incentives—including over $180 in tax benefits—over a 30-year period in return for locating a series of computer warehouses in Lenoir, North Carolina. In addition to tax credits, North Carolina also provided Google with job development grants, road widening, and railroad rerouting, among other benefits.[13]

Transportation Considerations

Transportation considerations in the form of transportation *availability* and *costs* are a key aspect of facility location decisions because transportation often represents such a large portion of total logistics costs. Moreover, it has been suggested that all things (such as space cost and labor availability) being equal, "the best locations are generally those where the best transportation services are located."[14]

Transportation availability refers to the number of transportation modes (**intermodal competition**) as well as the number of carriers within each mode (**intramodal competition**) that could serve a proposed facility. The evaluation of transportation availability is likely to depend on the type of facility that is being looked at. For instance, a manufacturing plant might need both rail service (to bring in raw materials) and truck service (to carry the finished goods), whereas a distribution center might need just truck service.

---

[12] Kathleen Hickey, "Taxing Logistics," *Traffic World*, May 10, 2004, 15–16.

[13] Nanette Byrnes and Coleman Cowen, "The High Cost of Wooing Google," *Business Week*, July 23, 2007, 50–56.

[14] William Atkinson, "Finding the Right Space in the Right Place," *Logistics Management*, May 2004, S76–S79.

As a general rule, the existence of competition, whether intermodal, intramodal, or both, tends to have both cost and service benefits for potential users. Limited competition generally leads to higher transportation costs and means that users have to accept whatever service they receive. Thus, a poor location can significantly increase transportation costs as well as negatively affect customer service.

Geographically central facility locations are often the result of transportation costs and service considerations. With respect to transportation costs, centralized facilities tend to minimize the total transit distances, which likely results in minimum transportation costs. Centralized facilities can also maximize a facility's service area, as shown in Figure 9-4, which illustrates truck distances from the state of Oklahoma. Note how many states are located within 1,000 miles (generally considered two-day service by truck) of Oklahoma.

Proximity to Industry Clusters

When looking at facility location considerations, early business logistics textbooks discussed the **agglomeration** concept, which "refers to the net advantages which can be gained by a sharing of common locations by various enterprises."[15] Although agglomeration continues to be a key factor in facility location, it is better known today as the **industry cluster** concept. Silicon Valley, a collection of high-technology firms located in the southern part of San Francisco, California, is a well-known industry cluster.

Industry clusters come in a number of different sizes and shapes; one type of cluster offers organizations *proximity to key suppliers*. For example, Honda's most recent U.S. assembly plant, which opened in 2008, is located in Greensburg, Indiana, in large part because many of Honda's existing automotive suppliers are located within one-half day's transit time from the new facility. Proximity to key suppliers has been the catalyst in the development of **supplier parks**, a concept that developed around automakers and their suppliers in Europe and has spread to other continents, including North America. With supplier parks, key suppliers locate on, or adjacent to, automobile assembly plants, which helps to reduce shipping costs and inventory carrying costs. As an example, a supplier park will be developed approximately 1,000 feet from Volkswagen's automotive production facility in Tennessee and is scheduled to open in 2011. When fully operational, the supplier park will provide engines, transmissions, and various parts for automotive production.[16]

Industry clusters can provide potential advantages to prospective participants in terms of facility and transportation considerations. With respect to facilities, the relative proximity of manufacturers in a particular cluster could allow for capacity pooling in the sense that a manufacturer with excess capacity could produce goods for a manufacturer with an excess of orders. From a transportation perspective, industry clusters could allow for faster and more consistent delivery, particularly with supplier parks where many suppliers are located a short distance from their customer(s). Inbound and outbound transportation costs could also be lower in industrial clusters; lower inbound transportation costs result from volume purchases of inbound goods, whereas lower outbound transportation costs result from volume shipments of finished goods.[17]

Trade Patterns

As pointed out earlier in the chapter, firms producing consumer goods follow changes in population to better orient their distribution systems, and there are shifts in the markets for industrial

---

[15] James L. Heskett, Nicholas A. Glaskowsky, Jr., and Robert M. Ivie, *Business Logistics*, 2nd ed. (New York: Ronald Press, 1973), Chapter 12.

[16] No author, "VW to Build Supplier Park in Tennessee," *Automotive Logistics*, January–March 2009, 6–7.

[17] Lifang Wu, Xiaohan Yue, and Thaddeus Sim, "Supply Clusters: A Key to China's Success," *Supply Chain Management Review* 10, no. 2 (2006): 46–51.

FIGURE 9-4 Truck Distances from Oklahoma

Source: Oklahoma Department of Commerce.

goods as well. General sources of data regarding *commodity flows* can be studied, much like population figures, to determine changes occurring in the movement of raw materials and semi-processed goods. The availability and quality of such data often vary from country to country, and it may be difficult to compare data across countries because of different methodologies used to collect the data.

With respect to commodity flows, logisticians are especially interested in (1) how much is being produced and (2) where it is being shipped. If a firm is concerned with a distribution system for its industrial products, this information would tell how the market is functioning and, in many instances, how to identify both the manufacturers and their major customers. At this point, the researcher would understand the existing situation and would try to find a lower-cost production–distribution arrangement.

The development and implementation of multicountry trade agreements have generated profound impacts on trade patterns. For example, the United States, Canada, and Mexico are part of the North American Free Trade Agreement (NAFTA). Although Canada has long been the largest trading partner of the United States, since NAFTA's passage, Mexico has become the United States' third-largest trading partner. From a logistics perspective, this has increased the north–south movement of product, and the Interstate 35 corridor (which runs north–south between Mexico and Canada) has become a hotbed for distribution activity. Oklahoma City, Oklahoma, and Dallas, Texas, are two locations along Interstate 35 that have seen a dramatic increase in the construction of distribution facilities in recent years.

Trade patterns have also been influenced among those countries that are members of the European Union (EU). When the EU consisted of 15 countries, the central location and strong transportation infrastructures of the so-called "Benelux" countries (Belgium, the Netherlands, and Luxembourg) were a favored location for distribution facilities to serve EU countries, and many companies operated only one distribution facility to serve their EU customers. However, the EU's expansion into Central and Eastern European countries has substantially increased its geographic footprint. The vast geographic territory of the expanded EU has caused many companies to operate one major distribution facility and several regional facilities to serve their EU customer base. In addition, as EU expansion has pushed eastward, Poland and the Czech Republic have become favorite distribution sites because of their relatively central geographic location.[18]

Quality-of-Life Considerations

An increasingly important locational factor is what can broadly be called **quality-of-life considerations**. Although it may be difficult to develop a standardized list of quality-of-life factors, their intent is to incorporate nonbusiness factors into the business decision of where to locate a plant or distribution facility. Examples of quality-of-life factors include cost of living, educational opportunities, crime rates, employment opportunities, the weather, and cultural amenities, among others.

There are a number of reasons for including quality-of-life considerations as a factor in facility location. For one, employees who are able to live a reasonable lifestyle tend to be happier and more loyal; happy and loyal employees are less likely to leave their jobs and less likely to offend prospective customers. Second, because many organizations now compete nationally and internationally for talent, less-than-desirable geographic locations might hinder the recruiting process. Third, the increasing emphasis on business relationships means that suppliers and customers may be visiting an organization's facilities. Attractive locations serve as a greater incentive for such visits than do unattractive locations.[19]

---

[18] John W. McCurry, "Heading East," *Site Selection*, September–October 2008, 708–719.
[19] Bill King, "Four Reasons Why Quality of Life Is a Site Selection Consideration," *Expansion Management*, May 2004, 80.

Locating in Other Countries

Quality-of-life considerations can be especially important when companies are thinking of facility locations in nondomestic countries. For example, Bahrain promotes itself as a business-friendly location in the Persian Gulf region due to low taxes and operating costs. From a quality-of-life perspective, Bahrain has a number of excellent hotels, a world-class airport, plentiful and affordable housing, low taxes and crime rates, shopping malls, and outstanding schools.[20]

Besides quality-of-life considerations, many other factors are to be considered if a firm is looking for a plant, office, or distribution site outside its home country. Many of these considerations are governmental in nature and deal with the relevant legal system, political stability, bureaucratic red tape, corruption, protectionism, nationalism, privatization, and expropriation (confiscation), as well as treaties and trade agreements.

On an international scale, some workforces are considered mobile (migrants) and will move from one nation to another in search of work. Because of poor economic conditions in their home countries, migrant workers often exhibit a willingness to work at jobs that home country workers find unappealing. As an example, approximately 10 percent of employers in the United Kingdom continue to hire migrant workers despite a falling demand for labor that began in 2008 as well as record high levels of unemployment among UK workers.[21]

SPECIALIZED LOCATION CHARACTERISTICS

The preceding discussion focused on some of the more common general considerations in selecting the site of a manufacturing, distributing, or assembling facility. This section deals with more specialized, or site-specific, considerations that should be taken into account in the facility location decision. Most of these considerations are invisible boundaries that can be of great significance in the location decision.

Land may be zoned, which means that there are limits on how the land can be used. For example, a warehouse might be allowed only in areas set aside for wholesale or other specified commercial operations. Restrictions on manufacturing sites may be even more severe, especially if the operation might be viewed as an undesirable neighbor because of the fumes, noise, dust, smoke, or congestion it may create. Distribution facilities are often considered to be more desirable because the primary complaints tend to involve only traffic volume and congestion caused by the trucks that serve the facilities. If a community is attempting to encourage, or discourage, business activity, zoning classifications can be changed, although the process may be time consuming.

Union locals have areas of jurisdiction, and a firm's labor relations manager may have distinct preferences regarding which locals he or she is willing to deal. Even though an individual union may ratify national labor agreements, local supplemental agreements often reflect the unique characteristics of a particular area. The different supplemental agreements provide companies with differing levels of managerial flexibility (or inflexibility).

Once a precise site is under consideration, many other issues should be dealt with before beginning construction or operations. For example, a title search may be needed to make sure that a particular parcel of land can be sold and that there are no liens against it. Engineers should examine the site to ensure that it has proper drainage and to ascertain the load-bearing characteristics of the soil.

Environmental regulations may require that due diligence be carried out with respect to who previously owned a prospective site and how it was used. One key environmental issue in some economically developed countries involves the use of **brownfields,** or locations that contain chemicals or other types of industrial waste. Brownfields are an important locational issue

---

[20] *http://www.bahrain.com/moving_to_bahrain.aspx.*
[21] *www.propertymanagement.co.uk.*

because many are found in urban areas that are often desirable from a locational point of view. Brownfield developments in the United States, which now number over 50,000 sites, continue to grow in popularity because of the emergence of environmental insurance as well as legislation that makes it easier and less costly to develop brownfield sites.[22]

Another specialized characteristic involves the weather, and location decisions can be influenced by the potential for tornadoes, floods, and hurricanes, among others. Indeed, an increase in both the number and intensity of hurricanes affecting the United States since 2003 has led one company to reject any facility locations that are within 200 miles of the Gulf Coast, in part because just the *threat of a hurricane* resulted in increased employee absenteeism.[23]

Free Trade Zones

A highly specialized site in which to locate is a free trade zone, also known as *foreign trade zones*, *export processing zones*, or *special economic zones*. In a **free trade zone**, nondomestic merchandise may be stored, exhibited, processed, or used in manufacturing operations without being subjected to duties and quotas until the goods or their products enter the customs territory of the zone country. Free trade zones have become extremely popular in recent years; as an example, India has approved over 250 new special economic zones since 2005.[24] Free trade zones are often located at, or near, water ports, although they can also be located at, or near, airports.

Free trade subzones refer to specific locations at an existing free trade zone—such as an individual company—where goods can be stored, exhibited, processed, or manufactured on a duty-free basis. There are approximately 500 free trade subzones in the United States, and they are particularly popular among automotive manufacturers. For example, 17 of the 20 subzones in Detroit, Michigan, involve automobile manufacturers.[25]

FINDING THE LOWEST-COST LOCATION

Many products are a combination of several material inputs and labor. Traditional site location theory can be used to show that one or several locations will minimize transportation costs. Figure 9-5 shows a laboratory-like piece of equipment that could be used to find the lowest-cost location, in terms of transportation, for assembling a product consisting of inputs from two sources and a market in a third area.

Although most solutions to locational problems currently involve computer analysis, such analysis may not be needed if the relevant parameters are not too complex. Thus, grid systems can be used to determine an optimal location (defined as the lowest cost) for one additional facility.

GRID SYSTEMS

Grid systems are important to locational analysis because they allow one to analyze spatial relationships with relatively simple mathematical tools. **Grid systems** are checkerboard patterns that are placed on a map, as in Figure 9-6, and the grid is numbered in two directions: horizontal and vertical. Recall from geometry that the length of the hypotenuse of a right triangle is the square root of the sum of the squared values of the right triangle's two legs. Grid systems are placed so that they coincide with north–south and east–west lines on a map (although minor distortion is caused by the fact that east–west lines are parallel, whereas north–south lines converge at both poles).

---

[22] Kristin Gunderson Hunt, "Urban Squeeze Builds Fresh Interest in Developing Contaminated Land," *Business Insurance*, December 3, 2007, 23–24.

[23] Peter Cleaveland, "Set Your Sites on Incentives," *Food Engineering*, June 2006, 64–70.

[24] *http://www.sezindia.nic.in/HTMLS/about.htm*.

[25] See *www.foreign-trade-zone.com*.

This is a simplified demonstration showing the various "pulls" which exist to determine the industrial location which minimizes the total ton miles of transportation used to transport both inputs and output. This method can be used for situations where there are "pulls" in three directions—either two sources of supply and one market, or one source of supply and two separate markets.

Assume we have two inputs, one produced in Long Beach and one produced in Seattle. The two inputs are combined to make a product which is sold in New York City. Assume further that to produce ten tons of the product consumed in New York, we must combine seven tons of the product which comes from Long Beach with five tons of the product which comes from Seattle. Assume finally that a transportation system is available anywhere and that the transport costs per ton mile are the same for either input or for the final product.

We take a circular table, placing a map of the U.S. on it and pairs of pegs on the table edge in the vicinity of Long Beach, Seattle, and New York as they are on the tabletop map. The pairs of pegs are so that a piece of string can pass between them.

We knot together three pieces of string, with all of them ending in one knot. To one of the pieces of string, which we pass through the pegs near Seattle on our map, we attach five identical metal washers (each one repre-senting one ton). We attach seven washers to a second piece of string and pass it through the pegs in the vicinity of Long Beach on our tabletop map. To the third piece of string we attach ten washers and place it through the pegs in the vicinity of New York.

Then we take the knot and gently lift it to a point above the center of the table, with the washers on all three strings pulling down. We then drop the knot and it comes to rest at the spot on the map which represents the point in the U.S. where the manufacturing operation (for combining these two inputs into the single product) should locate. No other point will require less transportation effort—measured in ton-miles of freight moved.

(If transportation costs, or rates, differ on a per ton mile for each of the commodities or products involved, this can be taken into account by having the number of washers "weighted" to take into account the varying rates as well as the differences in weight being shippped. If for example in the situation described above carriers charged twice as much per ton mile to carry the finished product as they charged for carrying inputs, one would attach 20 washers (2 × 10) on the string reaching toward New York.)

Adapted from: Alfred Weber, *Theory of the Location of Industries*, translated by Carl J. Friedrich (Chicago: Univ. of Chicago Press, 1929).

FIGURE 9-5   Example of Transportation Forces Dictating Plant Location

A **center-of-gravity approach** can be used for locating a single facility so that the distance to existing facilities is minimized. Figure 9-6 shows a grid system placed over a map of five existing retail stores. At issue is where a warehousing facility to serve these stores should be located. Assuming that each store receives the same volume and that straight-line distances are used, the best (lowest-cost) location for a warehousing facility to serve the five stores is determined by taking the average north–south coordinates and the average east–west coordinates of the retail stores.

FIGURE 9-6 Center-of-Gravity Location for a Warehouse Serving Five Retail Stores

In Figure 9-6, the grid system has its lower left (southwest) corner labeled as point zero, zero (0,0). The vertical (north–south) axis shows distances north of point 0,0. The horizontal (east–west) axis shows distances to the east. In this example, the average distance north is (3 + 1 + 3 + 2 + 3) or 12. This figure is divided by the number of stores (5), resulting in a north location of 12/5 or 2.4 miles. The average distance east is (1 + 2 + 3 + 4 + 6) or 16; 16 divided by 5 equals 3.2 miles. Thus, the best (lowest-cost) location is one with coordinates 2.4 miles north and 3.2 miles east of point zero.

Because it's not likely that each store will place equal demands on a prospective warehousing facility, the center-of-gravity approach can be easily modified to take volume into account—the *weighted center-of-gravity approach*. The idea behind the weighted center-of-gravity approach is that a prospective warehousing facility will be located closer to the existing sites with the greatest current demand.

To illustrate the weighted center-of-gravity approach, consider the preceding five-store example, but modify the assumption that each store receives the same volume. Assume that store 1 receives 3 tons of shipments per month, store 2 receives 5 tons, store 3 receives 4 tons, store 4 receives 2 tons, and store 5 receives 6 tons. To calculate the north weighted center-of-gravity location, each north coordinate is multiplied by the corresponding volume, and these values are summed; this total is then divided by the sum of the monthly volume. This procedure is repeated to calculate the east weighted center-of-gravity location.

The new data (see Table 9-2) indicate that the monthly volume for the five locations is 20 tons (3 + 5 + 4 + 2 + 6) and that the weighted center-of-gravity location is 2.6 miles north and 3.7 miles east. Thus, the weighted approach locates a warehousing facility slightly more north and more east than what was determined in the basic center-of-gravity approach (2.4 miles north; 3.2 miles east).

The two approaches just described are relatively simple and straightforward, and the calculations can be done relatively quickly to provide approximate locations of centralized facilities, at least in a transportation sense. Because neither the center-of-gravity nor the weighted center-of-gravity approach is very sophisticated, adjustments may have to be made to take into account real-world considerations such as taxes, wage rates in particular locations, volume discounts, the cost and quality of transport services, and the fact that transport rates taper with increased distances. These considerations increase the complexity, as well as the time, to do the necessary calculations and partially explain why some companies have turned to specialized software packages to help them with facility location decisions.

TABLE 9-2	Weighted Center-of-Gravity Example				
Store	North Location	East Location	Monthly Volume (tons)	North × Volume	East × Volume
1	3	1	3	(3 × 3) = 9	(1 × 3) = 3
2	3	3	5	(3 × 5) = 15	(3 × 5) = 15
3	2	4	4	(2 × 4) = 8	(4 × 4) = 16
4	1	2	2	(1 × 2) = 2	(2 × 2) = 4
5	3	6	6	(3 × 6) = 18	(6 × 6) = 36
Total			20	52	74
Weighted average				2.6	3.7

FACILITY RELOCATION AND FACILITY CLOSING

Two specialized situations conclude this discussion of location choice, one involving facility relocation (associated with business growth) and the other involving facility closing (associated with business contraction). More specifically, **facility relocation** occurs when a firm decides that it can no longer continue operations in its present facility and must move operations to another facility to better serve suppliers or customers. **Facility closing**, by contrast, occurs when a company decides to discontinue operations at a current site because the operations may no longer be needed or can be absorbed by other facilities.

A common reason for facility relocation involves a lack of room for expansion at a current site, often because of a substantial increase in business. In the United States, this has involved the relocation of industrial plants and warehousing facilities from aging and congested central cities to more attractive sites in suburban locations. Land costs and congestion in the central cities often make expansion difficult (or impossible), and transportation companies generally prefer the suburban sites because there is less traffic congestion to disrupt pickups and deliveries.

In theory, the relocation decision involves a comparison of the advantages and disadvantages of a new site to the advantages and disadvantages of an existing location. Although this inevitably involves quantitative comparisons, companies should also consider the potential consequences of relocation on their human resources—consequences that may not be easily quantified.

For example, plant relocations inevitably result in a plethora of employee-related questions, including: How many current employees will be offered positions at the new facility? Will the company use years of service, employee productivity, or other factors to decide who gets offered positions at the new facility? What happens to employee seniority? What percentage, if any, of relocation expenses will be paid by the employer? Will older employees be offered incentives to retire rather than relocate? Will employees who decide not to relocate be offered severance benefits?

Employers should keep current employees informed of planned relocations and how such relocations might affect them. Relocation information from other sources could lead to confusion, anger, and lower morale and could easily affect the productivity of the existing facility at a time when hiring replacements is likely to be very difficult. It's also important for employers to be cognizant of relevant legislation at the federal and state levels. For example, U.S. federal legislation in the form of the Worker Adjustment and Retraining Notification (WARN) Act mandates that employers give 60 days' notice about plant closings and mass layoffs. Many individual states have additional requirements concerning large-scale employee layoffs.

Companies should also recognize that, no matter how well planned beforehand, a relocation from one facility to another is rarely trouble free; at a minimum, relocation glitches can add to logistics costs and detract from customer service. For example, transferring equipment, furniture, and supplies from an old facility to a new one may take longer than expected. Also, a newly constructed plant or warehousing facility is likely to have flaws or shortcomings that are only discovered after occupancy.

Facility closings can occur for various reasons, such as eliminating redundant capacity in mergers and acquisitions, improving supply chain efficiency, poor planning, or an insufficient volume of business. Whatever the reason(s), it is imperative for an organization to clearly specify why a plant is being closed. As an example, Michelin closed a tire manufacturing plant in Kitchener, Ontario (Canada), in mid-2006 and shifted production to other tire plants in the United States. Michelin cited several reasons for the plant closing, including that the Kitchener facility had the lowest capacity among the company's North American tire plants.[26]

Although facility closings are largely a business-oriented decision, other considerations may come into play. Union contracts, for example, may prohibit (or limit) certain facilities from being closed. The human impact of facility closings should be considered as well; individuals are not only losing their jobs and pay, but some individuals may suffer a loss of self-esteem as well. Unpleasant as it may be, employees should be kept informed by their employers throughout the closing process. Poorly handled facility closings can result in tremendous amounts of unwanted negative publicity for a company, which does little more than exacerbate an already unpleasant situation. The bankruptcy of LTV Steel in the early twenty-first century provides one such example; unfortunately, many LTV workers first learned about key pieces of bankruptcy information from various media, including television and the Internet, before being notified by the company.[27]

Summary

This chapter discussed several issues associated with the location of warehousing, manufacturing, and assembly facilities. Facility location has moved from a tactical to a strategic consideration at many organizations, and the chapter looked at the strategic importance of facility location. General factors in facility location were looked at, including population characteristics and trade patterns. Population characteristics are a double-edged sword in facility location in the sense that a population serves both as a market for goods as well as a source of labor. Changing trade patterns, spurred in part by multicountry trade alliances, have had a profound influence with respect to the location of distribution facilities.

This chapter also discussed specialized location characteristics and presented several examples of how grid systems can be useful for determining the lowest-cost location for a facility. The chapter concluded with a look at facility relocation and facility closing; companies should be cognizant of the human dimension associated with both relocation and closing.

Questions for Discussion and Review

1. Explain how the location decision process involves several layers of screening or focus.
2. How have cost considerations influenced facility location decisions?
3. In what way is the location of customer markets a strategic consideration in facility location?
4. Discuss the factors that influence the number of facilities that a firm chooses to operate.
5. How does a raw material's status as pure, weight losing, or weight gaining influence the facility location decision?
6. Discuss how population can be viewed as both a market for goods and a source of labor.

---

[26] Brad Dawson, "Michelin Won't Budge on Canadian Plant Closing," *Rubber and Plastic News*, March 2006, 1, 22.
[27] Jennifer Scott Cimperman and Sandra Livingston, "Stumbling LTV Losing Support, Critics Say; Poor Handling of Crisis Has Angered Public, Union and Politicians," *The Plain Dealer*, April 15, 2001, 1A+.

7. What are maquiladoras? Why has there been a resurgence in maquiladoras in recent years?
8. Discuss the advantages and disadvantages to locating manufacturing, assembly, or distribution facilities in countries with relatively low wages.
9. What are right-to-work laws? How do they influence locational decisions?
10. What are expatriate workers? What challenges do they face?
11. Why have inventory taxes become increasingly difficult to collect?
12. How do transportation considerations influence facility location decisions?
13. What are industry clusters, and what are some of their potential advantages?
14. Discuss how multicountry trade agreements have influenced the location of production or distribution facilities.
15. Explain why quality-of-life issues should be considered in the facility location decision.
16. Beyond the general factors discussed in this chapter, what additional considerations are important when a firm is thinking of locating a facility (facilities) in other countries?
17. Briefly describe specialized, or site-specific, considerations that should be taken into account in the facility location decision.
18. What is a free trade zone? What functions might be performed in it?
19. Discuss advantages and disadvantages to grid systems, such as the center-of-gravity and weighted center-of-gravity approaches.
20. Distinguish between facility relocation and facility closing. How should companies deal with their human resources (workers) in both situations?

Suggested Readings

Banker, Steve. "The Tax Efficient Supply Chain." *Supply Chain Management Review* 13, no. 2 (2009): 44–49.

Haytko, Diana L., John L. Kent, and Angela Hausman. "Mexican Maquiladoras: Helping or Hurting the US/Mexico Cross-Border Supply Chain?" *International Journal of Logistics Management* 18, no. 3 (2007): 347–363.

Kenny, Michael. "New Jersey WARN Act Creates New Obligations for Private Employers Contemplating Plant Closings or Mass Layoffs." *Employee Relations Law Journal* 34, no. 1 (2008): 41–46.

Knemeyer, A. Michael, Walter Zinn, and Cuneyt Ergolu. "Proactive Planning for Catastrophic Events in Supply Chains." *Journal of Operations Management* 27, no. 2 (2009): 141–154.

Melo, M. Teresa, Stefan Nickel, and F. Saldanha-da-Gama. "Facility Location and Supply Chain Management: A Review." *European Journal of Operational Research* 196, no. 2 (2009): 401–412.

Mentzer, John T. "7 Keys to Facility Location." *Supply Chain Management Review* 12, no. 4 (2008): 25–31.

Morphy, Erika. "Sweatshops in the Supply Chain." *Export Today's Global Business* 16, no. 10 (2000): 22–29.

Mueller, Glenn R. "Brownfields Capital—Unlocking Value in Environmental Redevelopment." *Journal of Real Estate Portfolio Management* 11, no. 1 (2005): 81–92.

Pfohl, Hans-Christian, and Karin Gareis. "Supplier Parks in the German Automotive Industry: A Critical Comparison with Similar Concepts." *International Journal of Physical Distribution & Logistics Management* 35, no. 5 (2005): 302–317.

van der Heijden, Johannes A. V., and Marloes L. van Engen. "Expatriate Career Support: Predicting Expatriate Turnover and Performance." *International Journal of Human Resource Management* 20, no. 4 (2009): 831–845.

Wu, Lifang, Xiaohang Yue, and Thaddeus Sim. "Supply Clusters: A Key to China's Success." *Supply Chain Management Review* 10, no. 2 (2006): 46–51.

CASE

CASE 9-1   Aero Marine Logistics

Aero Marine Logistics (AML) was incorporated as a private limited company in South Delhi in the year 1996. The promoters of AML are two professionals who had gathered 15 years of experience working for Tata Steel (one of the biggest and oldest companies in India) in the field of shipping, customs clearance, forwarding, and transportation. Over the last five years, AML has been successful in building an infrastructure and pool of experienced personnel to handle the entire gamut of logistics. In fact, it was one of the first companies to offer door-to-door delivery. It considers itself the specialist in customized solutions and services—a concept that is still unheard of in the transportation industry in the rural belts of northern India. AML handles the entire package of logistics for all its customers. Some of the services they offer include the following:

- *Import consolidation.* AML has a well-spread network of offices and trade connections in the United States, Europe, the Far East, and the Middle

East to render import consolidation by both air and sea to any part of India. It promises a personalized prompt service with value for cost.

- *Door-to-door services.* AML is fully equipped to deliver door to door, which includes cargo pickup from the supplier's warehouse, warehousing prior to customs clearance, complete customs clearance of exports from overseas, and freight booking with airlines/shipping lines to receive cargo in India. It also undertakes local customs clearance and transportation to deliver to the door of the customer.
- *Exports.* AML has expertise in handling exports of various kinds of cargo by ocean and by airfreight. It ensures the timely movement of cargo at the most competitive rates. It takes care of both the complete export documentation formalities and the physical movement of cargo.
- *Consultancy on customs and logistics.* AML is well equipped with professionals to guide customers regarding various modes of transportation and to help customers to optimize utilization of space and save on freight. It acts as liaison with different authorities like the RBI (Reserve Bank of India), Port Authority of India, India Civil Aviation Regulatory Body, TEXPROCIL (The Cotton Textiles Export Promotion Council of India), DGFT (Directorate General of Foreign Trade), and so forth, on behalf of clients for various permissions and quotas related to import and export of cargo. This could perhaps be classified as its most valuable service, which it hopes will build up its brand image. The red tape, bureaucracy, lack of work ethic, and corruption preclude anyone lacking either clout or established relationship channels (with *babus*, or permanent government employees, notorious for their apathy toward fulfilling job duties and with a penchant for bribe taking) to do business in India.

To enable it to offer these services, AML has partnered with various associates all over the globe to render forwarding services to all its customers. It has a covered warehouse space of 1,000 square meters and has the ability to arrange for additional space. It has its own two 407 Tata trucks for pickup and delivery of small consignments. It has dedicated a fleet of five low-bed trailers for pickup and delivery of containers. All the field personnel have been provided with two-wheelers for faster conveyance between various points of work.

AML has grown rapidly and recently established an online presence whereby clients can place orders online and check the status of their cargo. So far the increase in sales from the online presence has not been much. Most of AML's clients are spread out in rural areas, and except for customers in Delhi, most do not have access to the Internet.

Today AML is handling an average of 200-plus TEUs (20-foot container equivalents) of imports and exports every month between Delhi and Mumbai (Bombay), which is the nearest big port (a distance of 1,407 kilometers). (See Exhibit 9-A.) Luckily, most containers are used for traffic in both directions; moving empties is unproductive. Main items for export are bathroom fittings and spares, machine spares and agricultural equipment, machine spares and chemicals, scientific equipment, medical equipment spares and chemicals, food processing machinery, furniture and kitchen equipment, and interiors. Main items for import are automobile engines and spares, cotton yarn, food products, electronics, televisions and components, rice, stone for stone crafting, and so on.

Recently, one of the AML partners, Mr. S. Singh, was approached by the chairman of Freshfoods, Mr. R. Maan, with a promise of a huge potential volume (150,000 kilograms per month) for importing frozen mushrooms from Europe if AML would build up its Indian infrastructure to handle such volumes. Freshfoods is the biggest regional exporter/importer of food products in North India. It was founded 20 years ago by a collective of farmers wanting to find markets for their surplus produce of exotic and non-native foods (like avocados and strawberries) that did not have much local demand except for five-star hotels catering to mostly foreign tourists. The shift in eating habits in recent years had prompted Mr. Maan to promote mushrooms as a daily food item in a major way. To keep the price of imported mushrooms comparable with locally grown food items, huge quantities would have to be transacted to make use of economies of scale.

Mr. Singh realized that the first order from Mr. Maan was an experiment and that further orders would depend on whether the product caught on or not. AML needed to bet on a huge surge in demand for frozen mushrooms in the region if it wanted to be part of this new trend from the very beginning. Singh's partner— Mr. Kumar—is wary of investing heavily on the basis of this one order. After some bargaining, Mr. Mann agreed that Freshfoods would ship approximately

EXHIBIT 9-A   Map of India

150,000 kilograms of mushrooms per month for 12 months and will pay US$.20 per kilogram of mushrooms.

If AML decided to handle this product, it would need to add some equipment to its flatbed trailers to provide power to the refrigeration units on the containers. This is a one-time cost of Rs 9 lakhs (Rs 1 lakh = US$2,222). With temperatures soaring to 50 degrees Celsius (and the hot wind called *loo*—notorious for deaths associated with heat waves) for most of the long, hot summer, the energy costs of meeting special conditions could be prohibitive. AML expects them to total about Rs 3 lakhs on an annual basis.

Mr. Singh then made inquiries to his rail carrier about the costs of leasing refrigerated containers. He was disappointed to learn that leasing was almost impossible. The container-leasing companies wanted exorbitant rates because there was no backhaul traffic requiring refrigerated equipment and because some areas in North India were too isolated if they needed to send a worker to service malfunctioning equipment. The container-leasing company did, however, offer to sell used refrigerated 20-foot containers for Rs 7 lakhs apiece and would agree to service them for one year at an additional cost of Rs 1 lakh per container. The used containers could be expected to last another five years. In a meeting involving Mr. Singh, Mr. Maan, and Mr. Veejay, a carrier representative, it was decided that ten 20-foot containers would be sufficient to handle the projected volume of mushrooms. Each container would make one round-trip each month. The cost of ocean freight expense from Amsterdam to Mumbai is US$1,700 for a single 20-foot container. The cost of land transportation per single 20-foot container from Mumbai to Delhi is US$300. Return costs for empty containers from Delhi to Mumbai to Amsterdam are half as much, although about 10 percent of the time another cargo can be found that will cover the costs of return transport.

As the meeting broke up, Mr. Veejay said that the mushrooms were not a very dense cargo and that Mr. Singh could be using 40-foot refrigerated containers, which held twice as much as a 20-foot container, though handling costs were less than twice as much. The cost of ocean freight from Amsterdam to Mumbai is US$2,600 for a single 40-foot container. The cost of transportation per single 40-foot container from Mumbai to Delhi is US$500. Return costs from Delhi to Mumbai to Amsterdam are half as much, although about 10 percent of the time another cargo can be found that will cover the costs of return transport. Mr. Veejay felt that the 40-foot containers would need to be purchased. Five would be needed, with each making one round-trip per month. Containers were only

available new, and the cost would be Rs 15 lakhs apiece. Maintenance anywhere was guaranteed for the first year, and the containers had an estimated life of 10 years.

Questions

1. What would the first-year costs be to AML if it purchased the 10 used 20-foot containers? How long would it take to recoup the investment, assuming that the mushroom traffic continued?
2. What would the first-year costs be to AML if it purchased five new 40-foot containers? How long would it take to recoup the investment, assuming that the mushroom traffic continued?
3. Is one of the alternatives in Questions 1 and 2 riskier? Why?
4. Mr. Singh has read about the supply-chain concept that attempts to identify and link all the participants from suppliers' suppliers to customers' customers. Who are all the participants in the supply chain, a part of which has been discussed in the case?
5. Logistics partnerships involve sharing costs and risks. What are *all* the costs and risks that this venture entails? How might they be shared?
6. With some help from your instructor, divide into groups representing most or all of the supply-chain members identified in Question 4 and negotiate an agreement or agreements that share the costs, risks, and possible profits and losses from the venture being considered.

10

WAREHOUSING MANAGEMENT

Key Terms

- Accumulating (bulk making)
- Allocating (bulk breaking)
- Assorting
- Contract (third-party) warehousing
- Cross-docking
- Distribution center
- Dunnage

- Fixed slot location
- Hazardous material(s)
- Multiclient warehousing
- Occupational Safety and Health Administration (OSHA)
- Paperless warehousing
- Private warehousing

- Public warehousing
- Regrouping function
- Sorting out
- Throughput
- Variable slot location
- Warehouse
- Warehousing

Learning Objectives

- To understand the role of warehousing in a logistics system
- To learn about public, private, contract, and multiclient warehousing

- To expose you to select considerations when designing warehousing facilities
- To examine some prominent operational issues in warehousing

A recurring theme in previous chapters has been the changing nature of the logistics discipline and the individual functions that comprise it. In the systems approach of logistics, changes to one function affect other functions as well. Indeed, many of the changes described in previous chapters—such as electronic ordering, facility consolidation, and lean inventories—have especially affected warehousing management.

Although some experts have speculated that these changes would diminish warehousing's relevance in logistics systems, warehousing has adapted by expanding its offerings of value-added services, which refer to additional processing of an order beyond the storage and picking of it. Popular value-adding services include custom labeling, promotional packs, grouping and sorting of products, kitting for production, display building and packaging, and price marking.[1]

This chapter begins with an overview that defines what is meant by warehousing and discusses the role of warehousing in a logistics system. This is followed by analysis of public, private, contract, and multiclient warehousing. Next comes a section devoted to design considerations in warehousing, with particular attention to trade-offs in design considerations. The chapter concludes with an examination of some key operational issues in warehousing, such as productivity, safety, and security.

Warehousing, which refers to "that part of a firm's logistics system that stores products (raw materials, parts, goods-in-process, finished goods) at and between points of origin and

---

[1] Maida Napolitano, "Value Turns Warehouses into DCs," *Modern Materials Handling*, December 2007, 55–61.

FIGURE 10-1 **Adding a Warehousing Facility: Shorter-Haul Transportation**

point of consumption,"[2] and transportation are substitutes for each other, with warehousing having been referred to as "transportation at zero miles per hour." Figure 10-1, which presents an example of the trade-off between warehousing and transportation, indicates that placing a warehousing facility between the producer and customers adds a new layer of costs (those associated with warehousing) into the system. Moreover, the warehousing facility generates shorter-haul transportation routes (from the producer to the facility; from the facility to the customers); as a general rule, short-haul transportation tends to be more costly per mile than long-haul transportation. However, the increased costs of short-haul transportation may be offset by lower transportation costs per unit of weight associated with volume shipments.

If the introduction of warehousing into a supply chain simply shifts business costs across various logistics activities, then why is warehousing desirable? A key reason for warehousing is because patterns of production and consumption do not coincide, and warehousing serves to match different rates or volumes of flow. Canned fruits and vegetables are examples of one extreme in which production occurs during a relatively short period, but sales are spread throughout the year. Because of changes in logistics thinking in recent years, the other extreme—sales concentrated in a relatively short time period, steady production rates throughout the year—is more likely to be addressed by having the production occur closer to the demand period.

Sometimes, larger quantities of goods are purchased than can be consumed in a short period of time, and warehousing space is needed to store the surplus product. This can occur for several reasons, such as guarding against anticipated scarcity or to benefit from a seller's advantageously priced deal.

Much of the preceding discussion could be viewed as a market-oriented approach to warehousing. However, warehousing management can also be relevant to production and raw materials considerations. For example, an automobile manufacturer might purchase extra amounts of steel in response to anticipated steel shortages.

Moreover, warehousing facilitates the **regrouping function** in a supply chain. This function involves rearranging the quantities and assortment of products as they move through the supply chain and can take four forms—accumulating, allocating, assorting, and sorting out. Accumulating and allocating refer to adjustments associated with the *quantity of product,* whereas assorting and sorting out refer to adjustments associated with *product assortment.*

---

[2] Douglas M. Lambert, James R. Stock, and Lisa M. Ellram, *Fundamentals of Logistics Management* (New York: Irwin McGraw-Hill, 1998), Chapter 8.

Thus, **accumulating** (also referred to as **bulk making**) involves bringing together similar stocks from different sources, as might be done by a department store that buys large quantities of men's suits from several different producers. **Allocating** (also referred to as **bulk breaking**), by contrast, involves breaking larger quantities into smaller quantities; continuing with our suit example, whereas the department store might buy 5,000 suits in size 42 short, an individual store might only carry 15 or 20 suits in this size.

Assorting refers to building up a variety of different products for resale to particular customers; our department store example might want to supply individual stores with a number of different suit sizes (e.g., size 36, size 38, and size 40) and styles (e.g., two-button suits and three-button suits). **Sorting out** refers to "separating products into grades and qualities desired by different target markets."[3] For example, a department store chain may sell $1,000 men's suits only in stores located in high-income areas, whereas $600 men's suits might the highest-priced suit sold in less-affluent areas.

Warehousing can be provided by warehouses, distribution centers, or cross-docking facilities. **Warehouses** emphasize the storage of products, and their primary purpose is to maximize the usage of available storage space. **Distribution centers** emphasize the rapid movement of products through a facility, and thus they attempt to maximize **throughput** (the amount of product entering and leaving a facility in a given time period).

The increased emphasis on time reduction in supply chains has led to the growth of **cross-docking**, which can be defined as "the process of receiving product and shipping it out the same day or overnight without putting it into storage."[4] According to a recent study of cross-docking trends, the most important benefits to cross-docking include improved customer service, reduced transportation costs, and reduced warehousing space.[5]

The experiences of Saks Inc., an upscale retail department store, illustrate some of the potential benefits from cross-docking. For example, it takes just *seven minutes* to move a carton from the inbound dock to an outbound trailer at the Saks cross-dock facility. Moreover, on a daily basis the Saks cross-dock can handle four times as much product, with one-half the labor, of its predecessor facility; in other words, the cross-dock facility is approximately *eight times* as productive as its predecessor![6]

Because cross-docking is predicated on time reduction, the design of cross-dock facilities is an important consideration. Figure 10-2 shows a traditional "I-shaped" cross-dock design—rectangular, long, and as narrow as possible.[7] Other possible cross-dock designs include "H," "L," "T," and "U" configurations, and their applicability depends on the amount and nature of cross-docking.[8]

PUBLIC, PRIVATE, CONTRACT, AND MULTICLIENT WAREHOUSING

In addition to understanding the distinctions among warehouses, distribution centers, and cross-dock facilities, organizations must decide the proper mix in terms of owning (private warehousing) or renting (public, contract, multiclient warehousing) warehousing space. Because companies have different strategies, goals, and objectives, there is no correct mix of owning or renting. Thus, one organization might use only public warehousing, another organization might use only private warehousing, and a third organization might use a mix of public, private, contract, and multiclient warehousing. Each has distinct characteristics that might be either attractive or unattractive to potential users, and these characteristics are discussed in the following sections.

---

[3] William D. Perreault, Jr., Joseph P. Cannon, and E. Jerome McCarthy, *Basic Marketing,* 16th ed. (New York: McGraw-Hill Irwin, 2008), Chapter 11.

[4] No author, "2008 Cross-Docking Trends Report," Saddle Creek Corporation, 2008.

[5] Ibid.

[6] Connie Robbins Gentry, "Distribution Utopia," *Chain Store Age,* November 2005, 70–72.

[7] Maida Napolitano, *Making the Move to Cross-Docking* (Oak Brook, IL: Warehousing Education and Research Council, 2000).

[8] Carroll McCormick, "Crossdock Design: Not as Simple as Imagined," *Canadian Transportation & Logistics,* March 2007, 30.

RECEIVING
DOORS

Facility should
be as narrow as
possible

SHIPPING
DOORS

FIGURE 10-2   Ideal Facility for Pure Supplier Consolidation (Full Pallet Movement)
Source: Reprinted by permission of the Warehousing Education and Research Council.

Public Warehousing

Public warehousing serves (is supposed to serve) all legitimate users and has certain responsibilities to those users. Public warehousing requires no capital investment on the user's part, which can certainly be an important consideration when the cost of borrowing money (interest rates) is high. With public warehousing, the user rents space as needed, thus avoiding the costs of unneeded space. A related advantage is that users should have a fairly exact determination of their warehousing costs since public warehousing space tends to be rented on a month-to-month basis.

Public warehousing can also be attractive to prospective users because other parties have responsibilities for personnel decisions and regulatory issues. As pointed out in Chapter 4, warehousing is one of two major sources of labor in logistics (the other is transportation), and warehousing employees are often unionized, thus adding to the managerial challenges. At a minimum, when using public warehousing the recruitment, selection, compensation, motivation, and evaluation of warehousing employees are the responsibility of the warehousing company and not the customer (user).

With respect to regulatory issues, warehousing labor safety practices in the United States are monitored by the **Occupational Safety and Health Administration (OSHA)**. From a managerial perspective, because OSHA standards are complex and lengthy, it can be quite costly and challenging to comply with OSHA regulations. As was the case with personnel decisions, when using public warehousing, regulatory issues are the responsibility of the warehousing provider and not the warehousing customer.

Public warehousing offers more locational flexibility than do company-owned facilities, and this can be important when a company is entering new markets. For example, an organization may want to start off slowly in new markets or may be uncertain how well its products will be received in these markets, and public warehousing can provide storage services in these markets without an overwhelming capital commitment.

Public warehousing may provide a number of specialized services that aren't available from other sources. For example, public warehousing is heavily involved in such value-added services as repackaging larger shipments into retail-size quantities and then shrink-wrapping them, assisting in product recalls, and doing price marking, product assembly, and product testing.

Perhaps the biggest drawback to public warehousing is the potential lack of control by the user. For example, sometimes public warehousing doesn't have the space availability required by a particular user. And even if space is available, users may have little say in where their goods are stored—they may be placed wherever space is available, which may result in part of a user's inventory being stored in one area and the remainder in another. Moreover, some public warehousing is not open 24 hours a day, meaning that prospective users may not be able to access their products as needed or that users may need to tailor their operations to fit those of the public warehouse.

Private Warehousing

Private warehousing, which is owned by the firm storing goods in the facility, generates high fixed costs and thus should only be considered by companies dealing with large volumes of inventory. In so doing, the high fixed costs can be spread out over more units of inventory, thus reducing the cost per unit of storage. The largest users of private warehousing are retail chain stores; they handle large volumes of merchandise on a regular basis.

In addition to large volumes, private warehousing also tends to be feasible when demand patterns are relatively stable. Fluctuating demand patterns could at times lead to insufficient storage space for product, in which case the company might need to use public warehousing as a supplement, thus increasing total warehousing costs. At other times, by contrast, there could be too much space (excess capacity), which costs money as well.

Assuming both sufficient demand volume and stability of demand, private warehousing offers potential users a great deal of control over their storage needs. For example, the storage facility can be constructed to the user's specifications, which is a particularly attractive feature when a company has unique storage or handling requirements, as is the case with steel beams and gasoline. Moreover, in private warehousing, companies can control product placement with a facility; some products, for instance, should not be stored on the floor. Another aspect of control is that private warehousing offers access to products when an organization needs (or wants) them, as opposed to an organization having to tailor its activities to match a public facility's operating hours.

Private warehousing is also characterized by several important drawbacks, including the high fixed cost of private storage and the necessity of having high and steady demand volumes. In addition, a high–fixed cost alternative such as private warehousing becomes less attractive in times of high interest rates because it is more costly to secure the necessary financing to build or lease the facility (to be fair, interest rates in some nations, such as the United States, have been relatively low in recent years).

Private warehousing may also reduce an organization's flexibility in responding to changes in the external environment. For example, companies that utilize private warehousing are susceptible to changing demand patterns, such as those experienced with the passage of multicountry trade alliances. Likewise, organizational flexibility can be affected by mergers with, or acquisitions of, other companies, as illustrated by the case of a multibillion-dollar company that acquired a competitor's production and private warehousing facilities. Although the production facilities added much-needed manufacturing capacity, the warehousing facilities were largely redundant in nature. Yet the acquiring company had little choice but to continue operating them because of substantial penalties (e.g., labor compensation) that would have been incurred if the facilities were closed.

Contract Warehousing

Organizations historically had two choices with respect to renting or owning warehousing facilities—public (renting) and private (owning). In the early 1990s, contract warehousing emerged as a second option for renting warehousing space. Although **contract warehousing** (also referred to as **third-party warehousing**) has been defined in a number of different ways, in this text it refers to "a long term, mutually beneficial arrangement which provides unique and specially tailored warehousing and logistics services exclusively to one client, where the vendor and client share the risks associated with the operation."[9]

Contract warehousing expenditures in the United States are more than $25 billion annually and are expected to grow between 5 and 10 percent annually over the next few years, with this growth coming largely at the expense of public warehousing. More specifically, contract warehousing has embraced value-adding activities such as customization, reverse logistics, and repair and refurbishment to a greater degree than has public warehousing.[10] From a cost perspective, contract warehousing tends to be less costly than private warehousing but more costly than public warehousing.

Contract warehousing is a preferred alternative for many organizations because it simultaneously mitigates the negative aspects and accentuates the positive aspects of public and private warehousing. More specifically, contract warehousing allows a company to focus on its core competencies (what it does best), with warehousing management provided by experts—experts who solely focus on the client's needs and wants.[11] In addition, contract warehousing potentially offers the same degree of control as private warehousing because key specifications can be included in the contract. For example, if a certain product should not be stored on the floor, then this can be explicitly reflected in the particular contract.

With respect to changes in the external environment, contract warehousing is viewed as more flexible than private warehousing but less so than public warehousing. This flexibility depends in part on the length of the contract; as the contract length increases, the flexibility to respond to change decreases. Three- to five-year contracts appear to allow sufficient time for the warehousing provider to learn the client's business while allowing clients some flexibility in case the agreement fails to produce acceptable results.

Multiclient Warehousing

Another warehousing alternative, multiclient warehousing, has become popular in the first part of the twenty-first century. In essence, **multiclient warehousing** mixes attributes of contract and public warehousing. For example, where contract warehousing is generally dedicated to just one customer and public warehousing may be used by any number of customers, a limited number of customers (at least two, but no more than one dozen) utilize a multiclient facility. In a similar fashion, the services in a multiclient facility are more differentiated than those in a public facility, but less customized than would be found in contract warehousing.

Furthermore, where public warehousing services are purchased on a month-to-month basis, multiclient warehousing services are purchased through contracts that cover at least one year. Multiclient facilities are particularly attractive to smaller organizations that don't have sufficient volumes to (1) build their own storage facilities or (2) use traditional one client contract warehousing services.[12]

---

[9] Warehousing Education and Research Council, *Contract Warehousing: How It Works and How to Make It Work Effectively* (Oak Brook, IL: Author, 1993).
[10] William Hoffman, "Contract Warehousing Evolves," *Traffic World*, January 31, 2005, 16.
[11] John R. Johnson, "Bigger and Better," *Warehousing Management*, October 2000, 22–25.
[12] William Hoffman, "Dividing the Box," *Journal of Commerce*, February 25, 2008, 23.

DESIGN CONSIDERATIONS IN WAREHOUSING

General Considerations

One of the best pieces of advice with respect to the design of warehousing facilities is to use common sense, as illustrated by the businessperson who was convinced that warehouses were bland, boring, and visually unappealing. He decided to build a more aesthetically pleasing facility and designed a warehouse with black floors, reasoning that black floors would stand out compared to other warehouses.

Although the black floor was certainly eye-catching, it was an unmitigated disaster in part because the floor showed more dirt than comparable facilities. Moreover, the black floor was extremely slippery—meaning that forklifts had a harder time stopping (some actually crashed into the walls!), and warehouse workers were more prone to falling. This anecdote provides an excellent example of form triumphing over function or style triumphing over substance. From a commonsense perspective, the primary design consideration should be the facility's function—be it long-term storage or product movement—in the relevant logistics system, with aesthetics a secondary consideration.

One commonsense piece of advice is that prior to designing a warehousing facility, the quantity and character of goods to be handled must be known. Indeed, one of the early challenges of online commerce for bricks-and-mortar organizations was that many of them attempted to fulfill online orders through warehousing facilities largely designed to supply retail store locations. Online orders tend to be much smaller than those going to retail stores; as a consequence, picking and assembling one or two items is much different from picking and assembling a pallet load of items.[13]

A second commonsense piece of design advice is that it's important for an organization to know the purpose to be served by a particular facility because the relative emphasis placed on the storage and distribution functions affects space layout. For example, a storage facility with low rates of product turnover should be laid out in a manner that maximizes utilization of the cubic capacity of the storage facility. Alternatively, because a distribution-oriented facility attempts to maximize throughput rather than storage, the facility should be configured to facilitate the flow of product into and out of it.

Trade-Offs

Trade-offs must be made among space, labor, and mechanization with respect to warehousing design. Spaciousness may not always be advantageous because the distances that an individual or machine must travel in the storing and retrieving functions are increased. Moreover, unused space is excess capacity, and we know that excess capacity costs money. Alternatively, cramped conditions can lead to such inefficiencies as the product damage that can be caused by forklift puncture and movement bottlenecks caused by insufficient aisle width, to name but two.

Before layout plans are made, each item that will be handled should be studied in terms of its specific physical-handling properties, the volume and regularity of movement, the frequency with which it is picked, and whether it is fast or slow moving compared to other items. This so-called product profiling might suggest, for example, that fast-moving items "be placed close to where order selectors go to pick them, in an effort to reduce walking time."[14]

Many trade-offs are inevitable when designing the structure as well as the arrangement of the relevant storage and handling equipment. Several of these trade-offs are discussed in this section, and these trade-offs are often more complex than they appear because individual trade-offs are not independent from one another. Although there may not to be "right" or "wrong" answers with respect to warehousing design, an understanding of the various trade-offs might help managers make more efficient, as opposed to less efficient, decisions.

---

[13] James A. Cooke, "The Physical Challenges of the Virtual Sale," *Logistics Management & Distribution,* October 2000, 67–73.

[14] Ibid.

The experiences of PDI Logistics, a pharmaceutical distributor and third-party logistics provider, provide an excellent example of trade-offs among various warehousing design factors. PDI was experiencing dramatic annual growth in its business—so much growth that it quickly approached the capacity of its existing storage facility. Rather than build a new facility, PDI redesigned its existing facility with very narrow aisles (less than 5 feet wide), thus permitting better storage density. PDI saved money by not having to build a new facility, but because the very narrow aisles required highly specialized lift trucks, its equipment costs increased. However, because of this new equipment, PDI uses approximately one-third the number of employees as in the past, thus decreasing its labor costs.[15]

Fixed versus Variable Slot Locations for Merchandise

You might remember from Chapter 7 that order picking and assembly represents the best opportunity to improve the effectiveness and efficiency of the order cycle. One possible way to improve the effectiveness and efficiency of order picking and assembly involves figuring out where to store product in a warehouse or distribution center. To this end, organizations need to understand the attributes of fixed and variable slot locations for merchandise.

With a **fixed slot location,** each stock-keeping unit (SKU) has one or more permanent slots assigned to it (think of a parking garage that assigns particular parking spaces to certain individuals). This can provide stability in order picking in the sense that the company should always know where a specific SKU is located. However, this may result in low space utilization, particularly with seasonal products.

Alternatively, a **variable slot location** involves empty storage slots being assigned to incoming products based on space availability. One example of variable slot location is the closest available storage position, with "closest" defined as the shortest travel time to an entrance or exit point. Although variable slot location generally results in more-efficient space utilization, from an order-picking perspective it requires a near-perfect information system because there must be flawless knowledge of each product's location.

Build Out (Horizontal) versus Build Up (Vertical)

A general rule of thumb is that it's cheaper to build up than build out; building out requires more land, which can be quite expensive, particularly in certain geographic locations. Alternatively, although building costs decline on a cubic-foot basis as one builds higher, warehousing equipment costs tends to increase. Moreover, the build-up versus build-out issue illustrates the importance of understanding interfunctional trade-offs when thinking about warehousing design. For example, the Midlands section of Britain, located between London and Birmingham, is a popular site for distribution centers—there is available land for development, and the land is reasonably priced. Having said this, Midlands' locational popularity is dependent on a highway system offering speedy, reliable, and cost-efficient transportation service.[16]

Order-Picking versus Stock-Replenishing Functions

Organizations must decide whether workers who pick outgoing orders and those who are restocking storage facilities should work at the same time or in the same area. Although the latter scenario may result in fewer managerial personnel being needed, it may also lead to congestion within the facility due to the number of workers. One suggestion to reduce congestion is for order pickers and stock replenishers to use different aisles for their respective activities—again, this requires a very good information system to identify where a given employee is at any time.

---

[15] Mary Aichlmayr, "Before Building, Cube Out with Narrow Aisles," *Transportation & Distribution*, June 2002, 42–43.
[16] Stan Luxenberg, "Warehouses for Warsaw," *NREI*, October 2004, 28–30.

Two-Dock versus Single-Dock Layout

A two-dock layout has receiving docks on one side of a facility and shipping docks on the other side, with goods moving between them. In a one-dock system, each and every dock can be used for both shipping and receiving, typically receiving product at one time of the day and shipping it at another time. Viewed from overhead, the goods move in a U-shaped rather than a straight configuration. This alternative reduces the space needed for storage docks, but it requires carriers to pick up and deliver at specific times. In addition, this alternative may also result in an occasional mix-up in that received product is sometimes reloaded into the vehicle that delivered it.

Conventional, Narrow, or Very Narrow Aisles

Aisle width might seem like an arcane issue until you realize that as aisle space increases, the storage capacity of a facility decreases. For example, narrow aisles (defined as between 9.5 and 12 feet wide) can store 20–25 percent more product than conventional aisles (more than 12 feet wide), while very narrow aisles (defined as less than 8 feet) can store 40–50 percent more product than conventional aisles.[17] However, it is easier to operate mechanical equipment in wider aisles, and wider aisles reduce the chances of accidents and product damage.

Moreover, narrower aisles require specialized storage and handling equipment, such as narrow aisle (very narrow aisle) forklifts, that are capable of simultaneously moving both vertically and horizontally. These specialized forklifts are more expensive to buy or lease than are conventional forklifts and they require enhanced operator skills, such as sharper eye, hand, and foot coordination, relative to conventional forklifts.[18]

Paperless Warehousing versus Traditional Paper-Oriented Warehousing Operations

A **paperless warehousing** facility generates and uses few or no paper documents and instead relies on some type of technology, such as bar codes or radio-frequency identification (RFID), to accomplish many of the relevant tasks. Because paperless warehousing requires more sophisticated technology than paper-intensive systems, paperless systems are not inexpensive. It's possible, however, for paperless systems to have payback periods of approximately 18 months. Several important benefits are seen with paperless warehousing, such as reduced clerical work, improved order-picking efficiency, and a decrease in picking and shipping errors. For example, most paper-based systems require picked orders to be manually entered into a computer system. This information is often verified at the order staging area, a process that can delay shipping and add to order processing costs but doesn't catch all errors.[19]

Other Space Needs

Although many would assume that the primary role of warehousing involves the storage of product, recent estimates suggest that only approximately *10 percent* of a facility's cubic capacity is actually occupied by product.[20] Because every warehousing facility sets aside areas for nonstorage activities, it's important to know about them. These nonstorage activities include, but are not limited to, the following:

1. An area where transport drivers and operators can wait while their equipment is loaded or unloaded
2. Staging, or temporary storage, areas for both incoming and outgoing merchandise

---

[17] Mary Aichlmayr, "Narrow-Aisle: Form Follows Lift-Truck Function," *Material Handling Management*, June 2009, 18–20.
[18] Tom Andel, "Narrow Aisle Forklifts," *Modern Materials Handling*, May 2008, 21.
[19] Mickey Jaffe, "Winning the War Against Paper," *Aftermarket Business*, October 2005, 64–65.
[20] "Warehouses Must Balance Space and Time," *Modern Materials Handling*, June 2006, 21.

3. Employee washrooms, lunchrooms, and the like
4. Pallet storage and repair facilities (Facilities that receive unpalletized materials but ship on pallets may require a pallet-assembly operation.)
5. Office space, including an area for the necessary computer systems
6. An area designed to store damaged merchandise that is awaiting inspection by claim representatives
7. An area to salvage or repair damaged merchandise
8. An area for repacking, labeling, price marking, and so on
9. An area for accumulating and baling waste and scrap
10. An area for equipment storage and maintenance (e.g., battery-powered lift trucks need to be recharged on a regular basis)
11. Specialized storage for hazardous items, high-value items, warehousing supplies, or items needing other specialized handling (such as a freezer or refrigerated space)
12. A returned or recycled goods processing area

When designing warehousing facilities, it's also important to keep in mind external space-related needs, which unfortunately are sometimes overlooked. These include areas for vehicles waiting to be loaded and unloaded, space for vehicle maneuvering (e.g., turning, backing up), and employee parking.

WAREHOUSING OPERATIONS

Because operating a warehousing facility has many facets, efficient and effective warehousing management can be an exacting task. Workforce motivation can be difficult because of the somewhat repetitive nature of the work. It can also be strenuous and physically demanding, and on occasion warehousing facilities can be dangerous places. Some of the more prominent operational issues are discussed in the following sections.

Warehousing Productivity Analysis

Recall from Chapter 4 that productivity is a measure of output divided by input, and although a number of different productivity metrics can be used to assess warehousing productivity, not all are relevant to all kinds of facilities. Representative measures of warehousing productivity include cases shipped per person, product lines shipped per person, pallets shipped per person, average warehouse capacity used, and forklift capacity used, among others. These and other productivity metrics can be utilized to provide comparisons within an organization through time.

In addition, external data may be available that can be used for benchmarking purposes depending on the relevant metrics being analyzed. Suppose, for example, that the cases shipped per hour at a particular warehouse increased from 72 to 84 over a two-year period. Although this represents a 16.7 percent ([84–72]/72) productivity improvement over the two years, the 84 cases per hour might be viewed much differently when compared to 2009 warehousing industry data that show a median of 129 cases shipped per hour and a best practice metric of more than 250 cases per hour.[21]

It's important to recognize that increases in warehousing productivity do not always require significant investment in technology or mechanized or automated equipment. For example, one suggestion for improving warehousing productivity involves a review of existing procedures and practices to identify the tasks that are creating the largest inefficiencies and then developing methods to reduce or eliminate the inefficiencies without adding to or upgrading present technology or equipment. Organizations can also examine their facility layouts; long horizontal runs and frequent backtracking could be symptoms of layout problems. Something as basic as adding cross

---

[21] Karl B. Manrodt and Kate L. Vitasek, "DC Measures 2009," *WERC Watch*, Spring 2009.

aisles could reduce the length of horizontal runs as well as the length of backtracking. Furthermore, although research suggests that worker incentives such as monetary awards can improve warehousing productivity, some worker incentive programs have been counterproductive because they ended up costing more than they were saving.[22]

Safety Considerations

Warehouses, distribution centers, and cross-docking facilities can be dangerous places to work and Figure 10-3 provides a listing of workplace safety issues; many of these safety issues are associated with warehousing facilities. You should recognize that many suggestions for dealing with

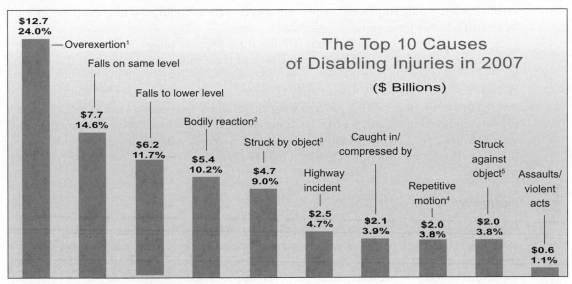

The Top 10 Causes of Disabling Injuries in 2007 ($ Billions)

$12.7 / 24.0% — Overexertion[1]
$7.7 / 14.6% — Falls on same level
$6.2 / 11.7% — Falls to lower level
$5.4 / 10.2% — Bodily reaction[2]
$4.7 / 9.0% — Struck by object[3]
$2.5 / 4.7% — Highway incident
$2.1 / 3.9% — Caught in/compressed by
$2.0 / 3.8% — Repetitive motion[4]
$2.0 / 3.8% — Struck against object[5]
$0.6 / 1.1% — Assaults/violent acts

[1]Overexertion – Injuries caused from excessive lifting, pushing, pulling, holding, carrying, or throwing
[2]Bodily reaction – Injuries caused from slipping or tripping without falling
[3]Struck by object – Such as a tool falling on a worker from above
[4]Repetitive motion – Injuries due to repeated stress or strain
[5]Struck against object – Such as a worker walking into a door

	Percent
Fall on same level	36.7%
Fall to lower level	33.5%
Bodily reaction	17.7%
Struck by object	13.6%
Caught in/compressed by	5.6%
Assault/violent acts	4.4%
Highway incident	−2.8%
Overexertion	−5.7%
Struck against object	−9.3%
Repetitive motion	−34.6%

Real Growth Trends Last Ten Years
(Percent change by category)

Year	$ Billions
1998	37.1
1999	41.1
2000	44.2
2001	47.4
2002	51.7
2003	50.7
2004	48.6
2005	48.3
2006	48.6
2007	53.0

Liberty Mutual Workplace Safety Index 1998–2007

FIGURE 10-3   Workplace Safety Issues

Source: Reprinted with permission of Liberty Mutual Research Institute of Safety.

---

[22] Maida Napolitano, "Low Cost Ways to Boost Warehouse Efficiency," *Logistics Management*, August 2003, 59–64.

warehousing safety are common sense—and low cost—in nature. Consider, for example, some of the OSHA suggestions to improve warehouse safety: "prohibit 'dock jumping' (jumping from dock plate to dock plate) by employees"; "prohibit stunt driving (of forklifts) and horseplay"; and "keep floors clean and free of slip and trip hazards."[23] Moreover, an organization that is truly committed to warehousing safety would explicitly measure it and incorporate safety metrics as part of each employee's performance review.[24]

Warehousing safety can be influenced by governmental regulations; in the United States, safety standards have been set for warehousing equipment and operations, and OSHA inspectors make frequent visits to industrial workplaces to ensure regulatory compliance. Forklift operations and equipment have received particular attention from OSHA in part because of the number of death and injuries associated with forklift operations. For example, only trained and certified warehousing employees are permitted to operate a forklift, and forklift operators must be recertified every three years.

Warehouse safety considerations fall into three primary categories—employee, property, and motor vehicles[25]—and we'll discuss each of these in the paragraphs that follow. With respect to *employee safety*, consider one warehousing professional's advice: "It costs more to recruit, train, and replace a worker than to provide a safe environment."[26] Workers can be injured due to improper lifting procedures, trying to carry too heavy a load, failing to observe proper hand clearances, and the like. Back and shoulder injuries are the most frequent among warehousing personnel; back support belts and braces are becoming more widely used, but they are only of value if workers also receive adequate training in how to safely lift various loads.

PROPERTY

Warehousing facilities generate large volumes of waste materials, such as empty cartons, steel strapping, and broken pallets, as well as wood and nails used for crating and **dunnage** (material that is used to block and brace products inside carrier equipment to prevent the shipment from shifting in transit and becoming damaged). The various waste materials must be properly handled because they pose threats to employee safety and may also be fire hazards.

Moreover, even with the best of practices, some goods that are received, stored, and shipped will be damaged. Special procedures must be established for handling broken or damaged items, if only from the standpoint of employee safety. A broken bottle of household ammonia, for example, results in three hazards: noxious fumes, broken glass, and a slippery floor. Aerosol cans pose hazards that are affected by the product in the cans. For example, cans of shaving cream cause little problem in fires because if they explode, the shaving cream serves to extinguish the fire; that is not the case with aerosol cans containing paints or lacquers, and such cans are often kept in special cages because in a fire they might become burning projectiles.

Indeed, fires are a constant threat in warehousing, in part because many materials used for packaging are highly flammable. In addition, although plastic pallets last longer, are cleaner, and are less likely to splinter than wooden pallets, they tend to be a greater fire risk. High-rise facilities are more susceptible to fires because the vertical spaces between stored materials serve as flues and help fires burn. You should recognize that warehouse fires may result in substantial property damage as well as injury or death, as illustrated by a 2008 warehouse fire in South Korea that injured 17 and killed 40 people.

[23] *www.osha.gov/Publications/3220_Warehouse.pdf.*
[24] Susan Lacefield, "12 Steps to Better Warehouse Safety," *Logistics Management,* May 2004, 59–63.
[25] Joe Nowlan, "Safety Doesn't Have to Hurt Your Budget," *Industrial Distribution,* January 2008, 25–27.
[26] Ed Engel, "Getting a Lift from Safety," *Warehousing Management,* January–February 2001, 54–57.

A 2009 report by the National Fire Protection Association indicated that U.S. warehousing fires decreased by approximately 70 percent between 1980 and 2006, averaging 1,350 fires per year between 2003 and 2006. The report also indicated that the most common causes of warehousing fires between 2003 and 2006 were (1) electrical distribution or lighting equipment; (2) intentionally set fires; and (3) heating equipment. Moreover, approximately 20 percent of all warehousing fires between 2003 and 2006 began with trash or waste materials.[27] Many warehousing fires can be prevented by common sense; flammable products, for example, should not be stored near heat sources (such as space heaters).

MOTOR VEHICLES

We mentioned earlier that forklift operations and equipment have been a particular focus of governmental safety regulations. Indeed, according to OSHA, approximately 100 employees are killed and 95,000 injured every year while operating forklifts in warehousing facilities.[28] These deaths and injuries are caused by reckless operation of the equipment as well as poor communication. It is not unheard of, for example, for a forklift operator to be *inside a truck trailer* as it pulls away from a loading/unloading dock. This often results in a forklift accident, with the forklift falling from the trailer floor to the parking area.

There are other truck-related safety considerations in warehousing in addition to the forklift-inside-a-truck issue. For example, tractor-trailer drivers who are backing into loading/unloading docks should utilize a lookout person to alert the driver about employees who might be walking behind the vehicle. Moreover, wheel chocks—hard-rubber wedges that are inserted under truck tires—can guard against intentional or unintentional trailer movements.[29]

Hazardous Materials

Hazardous materials (hazmat) often receive special attention from logistics managers because of the injuries, death, and property damage they can cause. According to the Institute of Hazardous Materials Management, a **hazardous material** "is any item or agent (biological, chemical, physical) which has the potential to cause harm to humans, animals, or the environment, either by itself or through interaction with other factors."[30] Examples of hazardous materials include explosives, flammable liquids, and flammable solids.

Government regulations often require that shipping documents indicate the hazardous nature of the materials being transported. Warehouse employees should note these warnings when receiving materials and similarly should include such warnings on outbound shipping documents when materials leave warehouses. Government regulations also require organizations to create a materials safety data sheet (MSDS) for each hazardous product to be stored in a facility. The MSDS should contain explicit storage and handling information as well as what to do in case of an emergency.[31]

Hazmat experts generally agree that the applicable regulations should only provide a starting point for proper storage of hazardous materials, in part because for some situations no regulations exist. These experts further suggest that hazmat storage can be managed effectively by answering four questions: *What* material is being stored? *Why* is it being stored? *Where* is it being stored? *How* is it being stored?[32]

A number of design elements must also be considered with the storage of hazardous materials. Buildings that store hazmat often have specially constructed areas so that materials can be

[27] http://www.nfpa.org/assets/files//PDF/Warehouseexecsum.pdf.
[28] http://www.osha.gov/Publications/3220_Warehouse.pdf.
[29] Nowlan, "Safety Doesn't Have to Hurt Your Budget."
[30] http://www.ihmm.org/dspWhatIsHazMat.cfm.
[31] David Maloney, "Hazmat: Handle with Care," *Modern Materials Handling*, March 2004, 61–65.
[32] Todd Nighswonger, "Are You Storing Hazardous Materials Safely?" *Occupational Hazards*, June 2000, 45–47.

contained in the case of an accident. Likewise, these facilities may have walls and doors that can withstand several hours of intense fire. It's also important for a hazmat storage facility to have proper sprinkling systems as well as excellent ventilation.

Warehousing Security

Warehousing security focuses on two primary issues, namely, protecting products and preventing their theft. Key threats to warehousing security include theft, pilferage, heat and humidity, vandalism, fire, and loss of electricity, among others.[33] It is estimated that these threats to warehousing security cause losses in the range of four to five times the products' value. Moreover, these threats can result in lost sales opportunities (both in the present and in the future), customer dissatisfaction, additional costs to enhance warehousing security, and the administrative time and costs associated with filing claims, and more.[34] Figure 10-4 shows some of the security measures

STRESS SECURITY IN LAYOUT
This layout shows good use of fences and walls for security and for access control at doors and gates. Opportunities for collusion and theft are cut by separation of receiving dock, shipping dock, storage area, and driver waiting room. Such a layout permits close direction of trucks by one guard, at a central station, with a clear view of yard and truck-enclosure areas at docks. Tightened security is provided by combined systems: guard services, access controls, loudspeakers and intercom, and closed-circuit TV, all centered at the control station.

FIGURE 10-4 How to Plan a Thief-Resistant Warehouse
Source: Courtesy of Modern Materials Handling.

---

[33] Linda Pohle, "What to Do with a Warehouse," *SDM: Security Distribution and Management*, September 2008, 64–70.
[34] Roger Morton, "Keep Product from Wandering Off," *Transportation & Distribution*, June 1999, 84–87.

that can be built into a warehouse; note that the design presented in Figure 10-4 limits access to parking, offices, warehousing space, and dock space.

In general, warehousing security can be enhanced by focusing on people, facilities, and processes. In terms of people, one area of focus should be the hiring process for warehousing workers; a starting point might be determining whether an individual facility even has a formal hiring process. In terms of a facilities focus, a number of different low-tech (e.g., fences) and high-tech (e.g., closed-circuit video cameras) devices can help to enhance warehousing security; an obvious trade-off is the cost of the various devices. In terms of processes to improve warehousing security, the more times a shipment is handled, the greater the opportunities for loss or damage. Thus, logisticians would do well to reduce the number of times an individual shipment is handled. Table 10-1 highlights some possible shortcomings in warehousing security.

Interest in providing building security for warehouses and other distribution facilities is a primary concern for many organizations because product at rest is particularly susceptible to many of the threats to warehousing security. Electronic devices can be especially helpful in providing various building-related security functions. For example, closed-circuit television cameras can be used to view different areas of a particular facility. In areas where there should be no movements, it is possible to have monitoring devices store the image that contains no movement in digital memory and, when a change in the image occurs—such as would be caused by intruders in a freight storage area—initiate an alarm. Unfortunately, organizations sometimes fail to activate or monitor their closed-circuit cameras, which defeats their purpose. Moreover, security experts suggest that closed-circuit television and alarms are relatively ineffective in controlling pilferage.[35]

A second type of electronic device is used to control access to particular facilities. An example is a magnetically encoded tag that each employee must insert into a sensing device that records the event and determines whether the door or gate should be unlocked. A third category of electronic devices is invisible photoelectric beams and many types of listening devices that can record unauthorized movements. Within a warehouse, heavier security may be placed around

TABLE 10-1	Possible Shortcomings in Warehousing Security
Shortcoming	**Comment**
Making it too easy for dock personnel to work in collusion with truck drivers	Fewer than 5 percent who commit crimes are prosecuted
Relying on safeguards that simply don't work	Security cameras aren't always turned on
Approach to theft is too reactive	Don't wait until theft reaches an "unacceptable" level
Not weeding out on-the-job substance abusers or dealers	Approximately 90 percent of drug users either steal or deal to support their habit
Not checking your checkers on a frequent basis	They may become complacent
Not making it easy to report theft and substance abuse	Outsourcing the reporting may be more effective
Hiring high-risk employees	An ounce of prevention is worth a pound of cure

Source: Julia Kuzeljevich, "The Seven Deadly Sins in Warehouse Security," *Canadian Transportation & Logistics*, April 2006, 44.

---

[35] Julia Kuzeljevich, "The SEVEN DEADLY SINS in Warehouse Security," *Canadian Transportation & Logistics*, April 2006, 44.

areas where higher-value material is kept. There is virtually no limit to the sophistication or cost of the security devices that can be employed. Having said this, the more sophisticated security devices also tend to be more expensive, and organizations are faced with the trade-off of whether the additional protection is worth the additional cost.

Before concluding our look at warehousing security, you should recognize the worldwide impact of the terrorist attacks of September 11, 2001, on warehousing security. Cold-storage facilities, for instance, enacted more stringent security procedures because these facilities often contain large quantities of ammonia, a key ingredient for making a bomb.[36] In addition, food distributors continue to experience a dramatic increase in theft because, in an age of terrorism, food theft is not a high priority for local, state, or federal law enforcement.[37]

Cleanliness and Sanitation Issues

At first glance, cleanliness and sanitation might seem like issues that are more relevant to, say, restaurants and hospitals than to warehousing operations. However, warehousing cleanliness and sanitation are of paramount importance in many industries, such as the food service industry where clean and sanitary warehouses reduce the likelihood of food-borne illnesses. Moreover, clean and sanitary warehousing facilities have a positive impact on employee safety, morale, and productivity while also reducing employee turnover.[38]

Fortunately, warehouse cleanliness and sanitation are not predicated on complex theories or costly technology, but rather on common sense and diligence. For example, one prominent warehousing consultant suggests that cleanliness and sanitation can be facilitated by putting the "junk and old stuff" at the back of a facility where it is out of the way (and often out of sight). Another suggestion is to purchase a powered sweeper and use it at least once a day.[39]

Summary

This chapter focused on warehousing, the sites where inventories are stored for varying periods of time, and began with a discussion of why warehousing exists in a logistics system. A key reason for warehousing is that production and consumption may not coincide, and warehousing can help smooth out imbalances between them. The chapter discussed the differences among warehouses, distribution centers, and cross-docking facilities.

This chapter also discussed public, private, contract, and multiclient warehousing. Public warehousing has a number of established duties regarding the care of goods, and customers pay only for the space that is actually used to store their products. Private warehousing is owned by the firm using such facilities, and it is best used when an organization has large and steady demand patterns. Contract warehousing involves specially tailored warehousing services that are provided to one client on a long-term basis.

Multiclient warehousing, a relatively new alternative, is a mixture of public and contract warehousing.

Various design considerations are relevant to warehousing, with trade-offs among them. For example, a decision to build up or out can affect a facility's utilization of labor, mechanization, and automation. Similarly, organizations that prefer a fixed slot location for merchandise may have to build larger facilities to have a sufficient number of storage slots.

The chapter concluded with an examination of some of the more prominent issues in warehousing operations. The material in this section emphasized that commonsense, low-cost approaches can facilitate effective and efficient management of warehousing operations. For example, warehousing safety could be enhanced if employees refrain from jumping from one dock plate to another.

---

[36] Kristi Labetti, "Designing for Security," *Frozen Food Age*, June 2002, 38–39.

[37] "Controlling Workplace Security," *Refrigerated Transporter*, January 2004, 18–20.

[38] Ned Bauhof, "Keeping It Clean," *Beverage World*, July 2007, 77.

[39] Jim Apple, "Have You Done Your Housekeeping Chores?" *Modern Materials Handling*, April 2004, 64.

Questions for Discussion and Review

1. Why does warehousing exist in a supply chain?
2. Explain the four ways that warehousing facilitates the regrouping function.
3. Distinguish among warehouses, distribution centers, and cross-docking facilities.
4. Discuss the disadvantages to public warehousing.
5. What are the advantages and disadvantages of private warehousing?
6. Discuss why contract warehousing is a preferred alternative for many organizations.
7. How does multiclient warehousing mix attributes of public and contract warehousing?
8. Explain how common sense can be helpful in terms of warehousing design.
9. In terms of warehousing design, give examples of trade-offs involving space, labor, and mechanization.
10. Distinguish between fixed and variable slot locations. How might they affect warehousing design?
11. Discuss the trade-offs associated with order-picking versus stock-replenishing functions.
12. Explain the relevance of aisle width in warehouse design.
13. What are some potential nonstorage space needs that might impact warehousing design?
14. How can warehousing productivity be improved without significant investment in technology or equipment?
15. What is OSHA's role in warehousing safety?
16. Discuss how fires are a constant threat in warehousing.
17. What is a hazardous material? What design elements should be considered when storing hazardous materials?
18. Discuss how warehousing security can be enhanced by focusing on people, facilities, and processes.
19. How can electronic devices be helpful in providing warehouse security?
20. How are cleanliness and sanitation issues relevant to warehousing operations?

Suggested Readings

Armstrong, Richard D. "An Overview of Warehousing in North America." *Journal of Transportation Law, Logistics & Policy* 73, no. 1 (2006): 48–53.

Baker, Peter, and Marco Canessa. "Warehouse Design: A Structured Approach." *European Journal of Operational Research* 193, no. 2 (2009): 425–436.

Baker, Peter, and Zaheed Halim. "An Exploration of Warehouse Automation Implementations: Cost, Service and Flexibility Issues." *Supply Chain Management: An International Journal* 12, no. 2 (2007): 129–138.

Bowen, John T. "Moving Places: The Geography of Warehousing in the U.S." *Journal of Transport Geography* 16, no. 6 (2008): 379–387.

Cook, Robert L., Brian Gibson, and Douglas MacCurdy. "A Lean Approach to Cross Docking." *Supply Chain Management Review* 9, no. 2 (2005): 54–59.

de Koster, M. B. M., and P. M. J. Warffemius. "American, Asian, and Third-Party International Warehouse Operations in Europe." *International Journal of Operations and Production Management* 25, no. 8 (2005): 762–780.

Hales, H. Lee. "Put Your Warehouse in Order." *Industrial Engineer*, February 2006, 34–38.

Lu, Chin-Shan, and Ching-Chao Yang. "Evaluating Key Logistics Capabilities for International Distribution Center Operators in Taiwan." *Transportation Journal* 45, no. 4 (2006): 9–27.

Ludwig, Timothy D., and David T. Goomas. "Real-Time Performance Monitoring, Goal-Setting, and Feedback for Forklift Drivers in a Distribution Centre." *Journal of Occupational and Organizational Psychology* 82, no. 2 (2009): 391–403.

Min, Hokey. "The Applications of Warehouse Management Systems: An Exploratory Study." *International Journal of Logistics: Research & Applications* 9, no. 2 (2006): 111–126.

CASE

CASE 10-1   Minnetonka Warehouse

Wayne Schuller managed a warehouse in Minnetonka, Minnesota. His major concern was the number of workers to assign to his single unloading dock. After he began contracting with motor carriers for deliveries, he found that they were assessing him stiff penalties if their trucks had to wait to be unloaded. Wayne started adding larger crews at the unloading dock, but often they seemed idle because there were no trucks to unload. Wayne recalled from college that queueing theory might be applicable to such a problem.

The theory of queueing is an analysis of the probabilities associated with waiting in line, assuming that orders, customers, and so on arrive in some pattern (often a random pattern) to stand in line. A common situation is that on the average a facility may have excess capacity, but often it is more than full, with a backlog of work to be done. Often, this backlog has costs associated with it, including penalties to be paid or customers who walk away rather than wait. If a firm expands its capacity to reduce waiting times, then its costs go up and must be paid even when the facility is idle. Queueing theory is used to find the best level of capacity, the one that minimizes the costs of providing a service and the costs of those waiting to use the service.

After some further research specific to his firm, Wayne determined the following facts:

1. Trucks arrive randomly at the average rate of four per hour, with a deviation of plus or minus one.
2. A team of two warehouse workers can unload trucks at the rate of five per hour, or one every 12 minutes.
3. A team of three warehouse workers can unload trucks at the rate of eight per hour, or one every 7.5 minutes.
4. A team of four warehouse workers can unload trucks at the rate of 10 per hour, or one every 6 minutes.
5. A team of five warehouse workers can unload trucks at the rate of 11 per hour, or one every 4.45 minutes.
6. The unloading times given in the preceding items (1–5) are average figures.
7. Each warehouse worker receives $14 per hour, must be paid for an entire shift, and—because of union work rules—cannot be assigned to other tasks within the warehouse.
8. Because of its contract with the carriers, the Minnetonka warehouse must pay the motor carriers that own idle trucks at the rate of $60 per hour while the trucks stand idle, waiting to be unloaded.

Use a software package that enables you to perform queueing operations. Note that the variable defined as number of servers (# servers) denotes number of teams of workers and accompanying equipment working as a complete server. In the situation described, the number of teams or servers is always 1, although the number varies in terms of costs and output.

Questions

1. For each of the four work team sizes, calculate the expected number of trucks waiting in the queue to be unloaded.
2. For each of the four work team sizes, calculate the expected time in the queue—that is, the expected time a truck has to wait in line to be unloaded.
3. For each of the four work team sizes, what is the probability that a truck cannot be unloaded immediately?
4. Which of the four work team sizes results in the lowest cost to Wayne?
5. Wayne is also considering rental of a forklift to use in truck unloading. A team of only two would be needed, but the hourly cost would be $38 per hour ($28 for the workers and $10 for the forklift). The two workers could unload a truck in 5 minutes. Should Wayne rent the forklift?
6. Disregard your answer to Question 5. Labor negotiations are coming up, and Wayne thinks he can get the union to give way on the work rule that prohibits warehouse workers on the unloading dock from being given other assignments when they are not unloading trucks. How much would Schuller save in unloading dock costs if he could reassign warehouse workers to other tasks when they are not unloading trucks, assuming that he has picked a good team of workers and each worker works eight hours a day?

11

PACKAGING AND MATERIALS HANDLING

Key Terms

- Building-blocks concept
- Closed-loop systems
- Cubes out
- Ergonomics
- Globally Harmonized System of Classification and Labeling of Chemicals (GHS)
- Materials handling (material handling)
- Packaging
- Pallet (skid)
- Part-to-picker systems
- Picker-to-part systems
- Shrink-wrap
- Slip sheet
- Unit load (Unitization)
- Weighing out

Learning Objectives

- To know how product features and characteristics affect packaging and materials handling
- To familiarize you with packaging fundamentals such as packaging functions and labeling
- To appreciate select issues that affect packaging such as environmental protection and packaging inefficiencies
- To learn about unit loads and the unit load platform
- To identify materials handling principles and materials handling equipment

This chapter deals with the physical handling of products and provides you with an example of the interconnectedness of logistics activities, with a particular emphasis on packaging and materials handling. You should keep in mind that packaging and materials handling decisions should not be made in isolation; rather, Chapter 10's discussion pointed out that certain warehousing decisions have distinct materials handling implications. For example, a decision to reduce aisle width to improve space utilization likely necessitates materials handling equipment capable of functioning in narrower aisles.

Each product has unique physical properties that, along with the normally accepted volumes or quantities in which it is traded or moved, determine how and when the product is packaged. A product may move in bulk from the manufacturer to a wholesaler, where the product may be placed into some type of container (e.g., barrel, box, or crate) prior to further distribution.

In turn, packaging attributes strongly influence materials handling concerns; nonpackaged products necessitate different handling than do packaged products. For example, bulk items (i.e., free flowing or loose) can be handled by pumps, shovels, or conveyor devices. Nonbulk materials can be placed in various types of containers and can be handled by such conveyances as carts, cranes, dollies, and forklifts.

This chapter begins with a discussion of product characteristics and how they might affect packaging and materials handling. Next, the chapter looks at several fundamentals of packaging, such as its promotional and protective functions as well as labeling considerations. This is followed by a discussion of select packaging issues that includes environmental protection and packaging inefficiencies. The chapter next examines unit loads and unit load platforms such as pallets and slip sheets. The chapter concludes with an examination of materials handling, with a particular emphasis on 10 materials handling principles and types of materials handling equipment.

PRODUCT CHARACTERISTICS

Various product characteristics can influence packaging and materials handling considerations. One is the product's physical characteristics; substances exist in three forms—solid, liquid, and gas—and each form has specific packaging requirements. For instance, metal cylinders are one method for the packaging of gases, whereas metal pails can be used for the packaging of liquids. Another physical characteristic is the product's ability to withstand the elements; coal piles can be exposed to rain, whereas salt piles cannot. In a similar vein, some products can be exposed to freezing conditions, but others cannot. Product density (weight per volume) is yet another physical characteristic that can affect packaging considerations.

The physical characteristics of some goods change while they are moving in the logistics channel. Fresh fruits and vegetables are the best-known examples. Even after they are picked, they continue to give off gases and moisture and to generate heat—a process known as respiration. Fruits and vegetables are harvested before they are ripe so they will reach the retail stores as they ripen. Ripening processes can be delayed through the use of lower temperatures or application of gases.

Products such as fresh produce, meats, fish, and baker's yeast are referred to as perishables. They require special packaging, loading, storage, and monitoring as they are moved from source to customer. The growth in popularity of washed, cut lettuce sold in plastic bags is an example of how packaging can benefit several members of the supply chain. The lettuce grower benefits because smaller, misshaped heads can be used, not merely the eye-pleasing, "perfect" heads. Both the retailer and the customer benefit because the shelf life is much longer for bagged lettuce than for head lettuce (bagged lettuce also carries a higher markup than does head lettuce).

Tropical fish are carried in plastic bags with enough water to cover them, but no more than necessary, to keep weight down. The area in the bag above the water is filled with oxygen. Sometimes tranquilizers are added to water to keep fish calm. The bag is sealed and placed in a plastic foam cooler, similar to a picnic cooler, which is then placed inside a cardboard box. Fish must be transported within 36 hours, although the time can be extended if oxygen is added to the bags.

In addition to physical characteristics, products also possess chemical characteristics that affect the manner in which they should be handled. Certain pairs of products are incompatible. For example, commodities that are sensitive to ethylene, such as broccoli, lettuce, and watermelon should never be held for more than a few hours in the same area as products that emit ethylene, such as apples, pears, and tomatoes. Prolonged exposure to ethylene can cause ethylene-sensitive products to yellow, soften, and decay.

The various properties of goods must also be made known to consumers to help them make the correct buying decision and care for the product properly. For example, Figure 11-1 is a portion of a fabric-care label that goes on Levi's jeans sold in Japan. Figure 11-2 is used for marking lumber and indicates that the (a) position is for the trademark of the accrediting agent, such as the National Hardwood Lumber Association or the Pacific Lumber Inspection Bureau; (b) identifies the specific mill; (c) indicates whether lumber is heat-treated; and (d) is for the country of origin, which is necessary if the lumber is exported. In recent years, interest has grown in having an additional symbol that indicates the wood used for packing was free of insects. Nations in various parts of the world are concerned that untreated wood and wood materials used in packing carries a wide variety of unwanted insects.

品 質 表 示

綿　100%

リーバイ・ストラウス ジャパンK.K.

米 国 製

FIGURE 11-1　Portion of Fabric-Care Label for Levi's Jeans Sold in Japan
From left to right the pictures say, wash at 40 degrees centigrade, use no chlorine bleach, iron at the medium temperature setting; the jeans can be dry cleaned. The text below the label gives the fabric content, the nation of origin, and the name *Levi Strauss.　Source:* Courtesy of Levi Strauss Japan K.K.

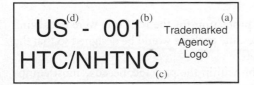

FIGURE 11-2　Lumber Markings
Source: American Lumber Standard Committee, Inc.

PACKAGING FUNDAMENTALS

Packaging can be thought of in terms of the **building-blocks concept**, where a very small unit is placed into a slightly larger unit, which then might be placed into a larger unit, and so on. Consider the various bags, cans, cartons, jars, and so on that the customer sees on the shelves of a grocery store. These units were likely unpacked from some larger container, such as a crate or box, and these crates or boxes might have been delivered to the store on a unit load (which will be discussed later in the chapter).

The building-blocks hierarchy is important to remember because each of the different building blocks is inside another, and their total effect should be to protect the product. They function in a complementary sense. When the consumer-size package is very solid, the larger packaging elements require less-sturdy packaging materials because the smaller packages are themselves sturdy. Alternatively, when the smallest package isn't very solid (e.g., the retail packaging for lightbulbs), the larger packaging elements will require very sturdy packaging materials and/or careful arrangement of the smallest product to minimize damage.

Packaging, which refers to materials used for the containment, protection, handling, delivery, and presentation of goods, serves three general functions: to promote, to protect, and to identify (label) the relevant product. It's important to understand that these functions can sometimes come into conflict. For example, although from a retailing standpoint it may be desirable to have an attractive promotional message on the outside of each box, when these boxes are in a warehouse, the same message might make it easier for a thief to determine quickly which boxes contain the most valuable items. Using an alternative identification scheme, such as code numbers on the outside of the box, will likely reduce opportunities for theft (the would-be thief will have to open boxes to see what is inside them).

Promotional and Protective Functions of Packaging

Although packaging is thought to be primarily protective, it may also contain features with a sales (promotional) orientation. With the growth of mass merchandising and a corresponding reduction in the number of salespeople, for many products customers can examine only the printing and pictures on closed cartons before making their choices. Some merchants build displays using box or case lots of goods to create the impression that they have made an extra-large purchase of a certain item, presumably at a lower price per unit that is then being passed on to the consumer. In this instance, it would be appropriate to display some advertising on the outside of the box.

A protective package should perform the following functions:

1. Enclose the materials, both to protect them and protect other items from them.
2. Restrain them from undesired movements within the container when the container is in transit.
3. Separate the contents to prevent undesired contact, such as through the use of corrugated fiberboard partitions used in the shipment of glassware.
4. Cushion the contents from outside vibrations and shocks.
5. Support the weight of identical containers that will be stacked above it as part of the building-blocks concept.
6. Position the contents to provide maximum protection for them. If one were packaging combined sets of wastebaskets and lamp shades, the package would be designed so that the lamp shades were protected by the wastebaskets.
7. Provide for fairly uniform weight distribution within the package, because most equipment for the automatic handling of packages is designed for packages whose weight is evenly distributed. Also, individuals handling packages manually assume that the weight inside is evenly distributed.
8. Provide enough exterior surface area so that identification and shipping labels can be applied, along with specific instructions such as "This Side Up" or "Keep Refrigerated." Today, this would also mean providing a uniform location for the application of bar codes. Handling symbols, such as a picture of an umbrella meaning "Keep Dry," might also be used.
9. Be tamperproof to the extent that evidence of tampering can be noticed (mainly at the retail level of packaging for some foods and drugs).
10. Be safe in the sense that the package itself (both in conjunction with the product carried and after it has been unpacked) presents no hazards to consumers or to others.

Figure 11-3 shows a checklist indicating the range of considerations that go into package choice. Firms that sell packaging material are helpful sources of information to potential users and they often provide technical advice as well.

---

[1] Logistics Dictionary, *www.tntfreight.com*.

checklist for box users

The corrugated box contains and protects your product, but it can also serve many functions which aid in packing, storage, distribution, marketing and sales. This checklist is a guide to the information you'll want to supply to your box maker. He can then offer suggestions and recommendations to utilize every value-added advantage that corrugated can offer.

YOUR PRODUCT

	yes	no
1. Have you given your box maker a description of your product and its use, the exact dimensions, weight and physical characteristics?	☐	☐
2. Is the product likely to settle or shift?	☐	☐
3. Is it perishable, fragile, or hazardous in any way?	☐	☐
4. Will it need extra protection against vibration, impact, moisture, air, heat or cold?	☐	☐
5. Will it be shipped fully assembled?	☐	☐
6. Will more than one unit be packed in a box?	☐	☐
7. Will accessories, parts or literature be included with the product?	☐	☐
8. Have you provided your box maker with a complete sample of your product as it will be packed?	☐	☐

YOUR PACKING OPERATION

	yes	no
1. Is your box inventory adequately geared to re-order lead time?	☐	☐
2. Is your box inventory arranged to efficiently feed your packing lines?	☐	☐
3. Is your inventory of boxes properly stored?		
4. Will you be setting up the boxes on automatic equipment? (If so, what type? Size? Method of closure?)	☐	☐
5. Will your product be packed automatically? (If so, with what type of equipment?)	☐	☐
6. If more than one unit or part goes into each box, have you determined the sequence?	☐	☐
7. Will inner packing—shells, liners, pads, partitions—be inserted by hand?	☐	☐
8. Is your closure system—tape, stiches, glue—compatible with the box, packing line speed, customer needs and recycling considerations?	☐	☐
9. Will the box be imprinted or labeled?	☐	☐
10. Will a master pack be used for a multiple of boxes to maintain cleanliness or appearance?	☐	☐
	☐	☐

YOUR STORAGE

	yes	no
1. Have you determined the gross weight of the filled box?	☐	☐
2. Does the product itself help support weight in stacking?	☐	☐
3. Will the bottom box have to support the full weight in warehouse stacking?	☐	☐
4. Will boxes be handled by lift trucks which use clamps, finger lifts or special attachments?	☐	☐
5. Will filled boxes be palletized? (The size of pallet and pallet pattern may justify a change in box design or dimensions, if only to reduce or eliminate overhang.)	☐	☐
6. Would a change in box style or size make more efficient use of warehouse space?	☐	☐
7. Will filled boxes be subject to unusual conditions during storage—high humidity, extreme temperatures, etc.?	☐	☐
8. Is the product likely to be stored outdoors at any time during its distribution?	☐	☐
9. Would color coding simplify identification of various packed products?	☐	☐

YOUR SHIPPING

	yes	no
1. Have you reviewed the appropriate rules of the transportation service you intend to use (rail, truck, air, parcel post, etc.)?	☐	☐
2. Is your container authorized for shipment of your product?	☐	☐
3. If the package is not authorized, have you requested appropriate test shipment authorization from the carrier?	☐	☐
4. Does your product require any special caution or warning label or legend for shipment?	☐	☐
5. Have you determined the actual inside dimensions of the transportation vehicle so that you can establish how your filled boxes will be stacked or braced?	☐	☐

YOUR CUSTOMER

	yes	no
1. Does your customer have any special receiving, storage or handling requirements that will affect box design?	☐	☐
2. Will the box be used as part of a mass display?	☐	☐
3. Is the box intended as a display-shipper?	☐	☐
4. Will it contain a separate product display?	☐	☐
5. Will it be used as a carry-home package, requiring a carrying device?	☐	☐
6. Does it need an easy-opening feature?	☐	☐
7. Can surface design, symbols or colors relate to promotional materials or to other products of the same corporate family?	☐	☐
8. Should instructions or opening precautions be printed on the box?	☐	☐
9. Can the box be made to better sell your product?	☐	☐

FIGURE 11-3   Checklist for Box Users

Source: Copyright permission granted from the Fibre Box Association.

Package Testing and Monitoring

To properly design a protective packaging system requires three important kinds of information: the severity of the distribution environment, the fragility of the product to be protected, and the performance characteristics of various cushion materials. When new products or new packaging techniques are about to be introduced, it is sometimes advisable to have the packages pretested.

Various packaging material manufacturers and trade organizations provide free package testing, and independent testing laboratories can also be used. The packages are subject to tests that attempt to duplicate all the expected various shipping hazards: vibrations, dropping, horizontal impacts, compression (having too much weight loaded on top), overexposure to extreme temperatures or moisture, and rough handling.

In addition to the testing of new products or new packages, shippers should keep detailed records on all loss and damage claims. Statistical tests can be applied to the data to determine whether the damage pattern is randomly distributed. If it is not, efforts are made toward providing additional protection for areas in the package that are overly vulnerable. Carriers also have provisions that allow shippers to follow special rules while testing new packaging materials. For instance, United Parcel Service (UPS) customers ship sample parcels to various UPS district offices, and UPS employees at those sites then report back with comments about how well the packaging withstood the UPS trip.

Related to package testing is actual monitoring of the environment the package must pass through. This is done by enclosing recording devices within cartons of the product that are shipped. The measuring devices may be very simple, such as hospital-like thermometers that record only temperature extremes and springs that are set to snap only if a specified number of g's (a measure of force) are exceeded. Kaiser Aluminum, which was troubled with problems of water-stain damage, devised the small sticker with the happy face shown in Figure 11-4. Above the happy face's smile are two eyes, but one of the eyes is printed in a special ink that dissolves when it comes into contact with moisture. If the receiver of the shipment notices that the eye is distorted, he or she can assume that the shipment has been exposed to moisture and should be inspected for damage. More sophisticated devices record a series of variables over time, such as temperature, humidity, and acceleration force and duration (in several directions). Acceleration force and duration are usually recorded along three different axes, making it possible to calculate the precise direction from which the force originated.

Sophisticated monitors are expensive, but they may be necessary to solve a problem of recurrent in-transit damage. Less-complicated devices are used to record temperatures and may or may not be used as the basis for a damage claim against a carrier. They may be used aboard a shipper's own equipment to ensure quality control. A frozen-food distributor wants to be certain that its product has not thawed and been refrozen in transit. Large shipments of apples are accompanied by a mechanical temperature recorder, which provides the receiver with a greater workable knowledge of each load, such as information on temperature variation that may affect the speed at which the receiver should handle and merchandise the apples.

FIGURE 11-4   Kaiser Aluminum's Moisture-Alert Label

When the product is shipped, both eyes are normal; that is, they look like the eye on the left. The figure shows how the label looks after the product is exposed to moisture. The receiver is to record the conditions of the label in the shipping document.

Labeling

Packaging is usually done at the end of the assembly line, so package labeling also occurs there, because using this location avoids accumulating an inventory of preprinted packages. This is also a key point for control because this is where there is an exact measure of what comes off the assembly line. As the packaged goods are moved from the end of the assembly line, they become stocks of finished goods and become the responsibility of the firm's outbound logistics system. Near the point where product packaging occurs, it is necessary to maintain a complete inventory of all the packages, packing materials, and labels that will be used.

Mouse Pads

Once the material being packaged is placed into the box and the cover is closed, the contents are hidden. At this point, it becomes necessary to label the box. Whether words or code numbers are used depends on the nature of the product and its vulnerability to pilferage. Retroflective labels that can be read by optical scanners may also be applied. Batch numbers are frequently assigned to food and drug products, so they may be more easily traced in case of a product recall. Figure 11-5 shows a small sampling of labels that can be purchased for individual placement on cartons or pallets.

FIGURE 11-5 Examples of Shipping Labels

Source: Uline.

Many regulations govern the labeling of packaging, including the labeling of weight, specific contents, and instructions for use. Today, much of this information must also be placed outside the larger cartons as well, because some retail outlets sell in carton lots, and the buyer does not see the consumer package until he or she reaches home. In an increasingly global economy, it is important to recognize that labeling regulations differ from country to country. As a general rule, labeling requirements and enforcement tend to be more stringent in economically developed countries than in economically developing ones.

Moreover, labeling requirements within a particular country can differ from state to state (or province to province). In the United States, the liquor (alcoholic beverage) industry is heavily regulated, and states have liquor control boards that are responsible for regulating liquor-related activities, including labeling, within state borders. For example, the Pennsylvania Liquor Control Board (PLCB) mandates that the following information be on all cases of products received in any of its warehouses:

- The PLCB/state item number
- A brief description of the product (including name, size, and vintage or proof)
- The Shipping Container Code (SCC) (barcode and readable—must appear on two adjacent sides, see "Label Placement" for details)[2]

The PLCB's labeling guidelines further spell out case code requirements and specifications (e.g., the size of identification numbers), SCC label requirements and specifications (e.g., only 14-digit SCCs are currently acceptable), label placement [e.g., the SCC label must be placed 1 1/4 inches (plus or minus 1/8 inch) from the container's bottom], packaging information (e.g., the ability to withstand transport, handling, and stacking), and shipping instructions (e.g., loads should be placed on slip sheets whenever possible). Note the specificity of these guidelines, and consider how easy it might be to make an error. Failure to comply with these labeling guidelines subjects the offending organization to surcharges, administrative fees, or penalty charges.[3]

HAZARDOUS MATERIALS

It's also important to realize the special labeling requirements associated with hazardous materials. Although hazardous materials were defined and discussed in Chapter 10, almost any material can possess hazardous qualities under certain conditions; for example, flour dust can explode and grain in elevators can self-ignite and burn. Special care is needed to handle these and many other substances.

Governmental regulations address labeling of hazardous materials, and while the specific requirements differ for each hazardous commodity, all of the requirements involve labeling, packaging and repackaging, placing warnings on shipping documents, and notifying transportation carriers in advance. For example, a common requirement on transferring flammable materials is that the vehicle and the receiving or discharging device both be electrically grounded. Care must be taken to properly clean tanks, pumps, hoses, and cleaning apparatus to avoid contamination of the next cargo that is handled. Shipping documents must also indicate whether the cargo is of hazardous nature, and sometimes additional documentation is required. Packages, containers, trailers, and railcars carrying hazardous materials must carry distinct signs, or placards, identifying the hazard.

Because hazardous materials are increasingly being stored and transported across country borders, the United Nations (UN) has played an active role in developing a global system to classify and label hazardous materials. One of the UN's more recent efforts in this area involved its Globally Harmonized System of Classification and Labeling of Chemicals (GHS), which was first adopted

[2] http://www.lcb.state.pa.us/plcb/cwp/view.asp?a=1338&Q=554711&PM=1.
[3] Ibid.

in 2002. The GHS has been revised twice, most recently in 2009, and it provides three key pieces of classification and labeling information: (1) a symbol, (2) a signal word (e.g., "danger"), and (3) a hazard statement (e.g., "explosion; severe projection hazard").[4] Unfortunately, to date fewer than 70 countries have implemented the GHS.

ISSUES IN PACKAGING

Environmental Protection

Public concern for environmental protection has profoundly impacted the packaging industry on a worldwide basis. Indeed, a recent study indicated that over 80 percent of consumers view packaging as a major environmental issue.[5] Many materials used in packaging are increasingly being recycled; disposable packing materials are often viewed as wasteful, and their disposal is becoming increasingly expensive as costs increase for dumping in landfill sites.

In recent years, plastic packaging has become a frequent target for environmental critics. Although the use of plastic for packaging has grown dramatically over the past quarter century— plastic tends to be cheaper, more versatile, and more consumer friendly than paper—plastic leaves a great deal to be desired from an environmental perspective. One of plastic's most frequently cited shortcomings is the length of time it takes to biodegrade, which can be up to *several hundred years*. Importantly, biodegradable plastics (sometimes referred to as bioplastics), which are derived from plant material, have found their greatest usage to date in packaging applications, despite costing approximately twice as much as conventional plastics.[6]

Another shortcoming to plastic is that its manufacture is often dependent on petroleum, which is a diminishing natural resource (and an extremely costly resource in recent years). A third environmental concern with plastic packaging involves litter, and sometimes this litter has unintended ecological consequences. For example, plastic litter in the Pacific Ocean off the California coast is estimated to kill 100,000 marine animals a year either from ingestion or strangulation.[7]

A key problem facing those trying to choose packaging materials is that each nation's (and, for that matter, each state's or province's) regulations can differ in terms of acceptable packaging. One reason that regulations differ is that different entities view environmental problems differently and enact regulations that address the issues of current concern to them. For instance, the California example cited in the previous paragraph prompted legislation aimed at reducing plastic packaging due to litter-related as well as ecological considerations. Other plastic-related legislation, by contrast, is aimed at reducing the amount of packaging material that ends up in landfills.

Firms can adopt one or more of the following environmentally friendly packaging strategies. One is to reduce the amount of packing materials used, but this is tempered by the fact that, as pointed out earlier, transportation carriers may have a great deal of influence on packaging specifications for goods they are transporting. Possible suggestions to reduce the amount of packing materials include the use of just one material, which should improve recyclability, as well as changing a product or format to minimize packaging waste.[8] One of the most noteworthy examples of packaging reduction is Germany's Packaging Ordinance that was enacted in the early 1990s. This legislation attempted to address Germany's solid waste problem by requiring manufacturers to take back and either reuse or recycle postconsumer packaging. Similar legislation was adopted by the European Union in the mid-1990s.

A second packaging strategy is to use environmentally friendly packaging materials. For example, Aveda is a cosmetics company that takes pride in its environmental consciousness,

---

[4] http://www.unece.org/trans/danger/publi/ghs/ghs_rev02/English/06e_annex2.pdf.
[5] Rosie Baker, "When Less Is Moreish," *In-Store*, January 2009, 25–26.
[6] Lou Reade, "A Growing Biodegradable Plastics Industry," *Chemicals & Industry*, July 27, 2009, 14–16.
[7] Steve Toloken, "California Cracking Down on Plastic Litter," *Plastic News*, September 26, 2005, 9.
[8] Trish Lorenz, "No More Pass the Parcel," *Design Week*, April 14, 2005, 9.

particularly with respect to product packaging. Between 2000 and 2004, Aveda was able to raise the use of postconsumer recycled content in its shampoo bottles from 45 to 80 percent, with some product lines reporting 100 percent postconsumer recycled content.[9] And, even though plastic tends to be an environmentally unfriendly product, some plastics are less environmentally friendly than others. Polyvinyl chloride (PVC), commonly referred to as vinyl, is an extremely unfriendly plastic because it produces dioxin, a highly carcinogenic (cancer-causing) chemical.

A third strategy is to use reusable containers, such as refillable glass beverage bottles. This cannot be done for all products, because problems arise when goods in reused containers are contaminated by traces of whatever product had been carried earlier. As an example, dressed poultry (i.e., the removal of blood and feathers after slaughter) often carries salmonella organisms (which are killed in cooking), and the organisms survive in the wooden crates used by the poultry processor and then may spread to vegetables if they are transported later in the same crate. As a result, the U.S. Food and Drug Administration (FDA) issued an order restricting the reuse of such containers to avoid food contamination.

An increasing number of companies currently utilize returnable containers of some type in their operations. For example, Do it Best, a hardware and lumber retailer, utilizes plastic containers to ship items such as light bulbs, batteries, and tools from its distribution centers to its retail stores. In addition to being reusable over long periods of time, the plastic containers can be stacked up to six layers high and provide better overall protection than traditional corrugated packaging.[10]

The fourth environmentally friendly packaging strategy is to retain or support services that collect used packaging and recycle it. This strategy is well suited for companies that receive large quantities of packaged products; if sufficient units of waste material can be collected, it is easier to process for reuse. Recycling companies can specialize in plastic bottles, wooden pallets, cardboard cartons, aluminum cans, and glass bottles, among others.

Note that both the third and fourth strategies add a returned packaging loop to the supply chain and are examples of **closed-loop systems**, or those that consider the return flow of products, their reuse, and the marketing and distribution of recovered products.

Before concluding our look at packaging and environmental protection, you should recognize that dust and vapors produced during bulk-cargo transfer operations are also being scrutinized more closely by public agencies. Coal dust can be blown for several miles from a large coal pile. In port areas, bulk materials that were once stored outside are now in enclosed structures. For products still left outside, elaborate vacuum systems are used to capture the dust created by handling, and ditches around the facility capture rainwater runoff so that it can be run through filters. Some states require handlers of petroleum products, including retail gasoline stations, to install vapor recovery systems. For liquids with vapor-escape problems, the transfer processes are redesigned so that tanks and other receptacles are loaded from the bottom rather than the top.

Metric System

The United States, along with Liberia and Myanmar (formerly Burma), are the only three countries in the world that do not currently use the metric system of measurement. Although this lack of uniformity might have been a relatively minor nuisance 30 years ago, economic globalization has led to increasing pressure on U.S. exporters to market their products overseas in metric units. Indeed, some importing nations levy fines against products that are not sold in metric measurements. More and more products are being packaged and sold in metric units, with the nonmetric equivalents printed in smaller type. For example, residents of the United States used to be able to

[9] Danielle Sacks, "It's Easy Being Green," *Fast Company,* August 2004, 50–51.
[10] Sara Pearson Spector, "Do It Best Relies on Reusables," *Modern Materials Handling,* April 2009, 32.

purchase soft drinks in 16-ounce containers. Today, by contrast, the 16-ounce beverage container has been replaced by the 0.5-liter (approximately 16.9 ounces) beverage container.

One U.S. industry that has prominently embraced the metric system is the liquor-producing industry. This industry's conversion to the metric system, which began in the 1970s, illustrates several of the potential challenges that might stand in the way of the United States formally adopting the metric system. As pointed out earlier in the chapter, the liquor industry is heavily regulated in the United States, and one example of this regulation is the high taxes that are applied to alcoholic beverages. These taxes became an issue in converting to the metric system because they were drawn up to be applicable to half pints, pints, quarts, and other English units of measure, as opposed to half liters and liters. Moreover, the liquor industry's adoption of the metric system also caused some short-term packaging issues because the cartons that were used for transporting and storing quart bottles were in some cases just a bit too small to hold 1-liter bottles.

Identifying Packaging Inefficiencies

We introduced the building-blocks concept of packaging earlier in this section, and to refresh your memory, this means that a very small unit is placed into a slightly larger unit, which is then placed into a larger unit, and so on. The building-blocks concept is also useful for analyzing packaging inefficiency in the sense that packaging inefficiency tends to be compounded as one moves from a very small unit to a smaller unit, to a small unit, and so on. Packaging inefficiency can have a number of undesirable logistics consequences, to include increased loss, increased damage, slower materials handling, higher storage costs, and higher transportation costs.

The compounding nature of packaging inefficiency is illustrated in the hypothetical example involving desktop tape dispensers that is presented in Table 11-1. According to Table 11-1, less than one-third of the available case cube is occupied by actual product, while approximately three-quarters of available pallet space is occupied by cases. Multiplying the case efficiency (31.6 percent) by the pallet load efficiency (75.4 percent) means that less than 25 percent (23.8 percent) of available pallet space is occupied by actual product. One implication of this level of inefficiency is that an increased number of pallets will be needed, which in turn leads to higher storage and transportation costs.

TABLE 11-1   A Hypothetical Example of Packaging Inefficiency

Product:	One (1) desktop tape dispenser (cube = 30 inches) 12 dispensers per carton
Product cube per carton:	30 cubic inches × 12 dispensers = **360 cubic inches**
Carton dimensions:	1,140 cubic inches
Carton efficiency:	Product cube per carton divided by carton cube **360/1,140 = 31.6%**
60 cartons can be put on a pallet Pallet capacity:	90,720 cubic inches
Carton cube per pallet:	1,140 cubic inches per carton × 60 cartons = **68,400 cubic inches**
Pallet load efficiency:	Carton cube per pallet divided by pallet capacity **68,400/90, 720 = 75.4%**
Carton efficiency times pallet load efficiency = the amount of pallet cube that is actually product	**31.6% × 75.4% = 23.8%**

The identification of packaging inefficiencies is important because these inefficiencies have been described as the "last frontier" of logistics savings opportunities. Moreover, there can be impressive cost savings as well as service improvements from improved packaging efficiency. For example, R. G. Barry, a footwear manufacturer, reduced transportation spending by 25 percent and warehousing costs by 35 percent through improved packaging. Similar to the example presented in Table 11-1, R. G. Barry's savings resulted from optimizing "the box inside the carton, and then the carton on the pallet, and then the pallet in the warehouse." The improved packaging efficiency has also led to a substantial reduction in damaged product for R. G. Barry.[11]

Packaging's Influence on Transportation Considerations

Carriers' tariffs and classifications influence the type of packaging and packing methods that must be used. More specifically, in freight classification documents, the type of packaging can be specified in the following manner: The commodity is listed, followed by a comma and then by a phrase—such as "in machine-pressed bales," "in barrels," "in bales compressed in more than 18 lb. per square foot," "folded flat, in packages," "celluloid covered, in boxes," "SU" (setup), or "KD" (knocked down)—or disassembled and packed so that it occupies two-thirds or less of the volume it would occupy in its setup state).

The carriers established these different classifications for two main reasons. First, packaging specifications determined by product density encourage shippers to tender loads in densities that make the best use of the equipment's weight and volume capabilities. IKEA, the Swedish-based home furnishings chain, designs many of its products so that they can be shipped in a dense form. Such products are often displayed unassembled in retail stores, and customers realize that they can easily take them home in their automotive vehicles.

Second, carrier specifications for protective packaging reduce the likelihood of damage to products while they are being carried; this, in turn, reduces the amount of loss and damage claims placed against the carrier. Figure 11-6 shows the type of label (the "box maker's certificate," or BMC) that motor carriers and railroads require on fiber boxes used for shipping freight. It is the fiber box manufacturer's assurance to the motor carriers and railroads that

FIGURE 11-6 Boxmaker's Guarantee
Source: Courtesy of the American Trucking Association.

---

[11] William Hoffman, "Thinking Inside the Box," *Traffic World*, December 11, 2006, 17.

the boxes will be sturdy enough to meet their handling specifications. Note that a number of measures are used. For example, the size limit shown, 75 inches, means that the material should not be used in a package where the total length, width, and height, when added together, exceed 75 inches.

It is difficult to know exactly how much carrier tariffs and classifications control shippers' packaging. Responsibility for damage in transit is one issue subject to carrier–shipper contract negotiation; if the carrier remains liable, the carrier specifies the level of packaging protection to be used. If the shipper assumes responsibility, the shipper may choose the type of packaging to use. Carrier deregulation has allowed corrugated packaging manufacturers and their customers to innovate with performance outside the traditional carrier packaging rules. As specific contract rates are negotiated between individual carriers and shippers, packaging requirements may, of course, be one element of negotiation.

Airlines, express delivery companies, and the U.S. Postal Service also have packaging requirements, although they are somewhat less detailed than those used by rail and motor common carriers. With respect to international shipments, the International Air Transport Association regulates the packaging of air shipments, and limited packaging requirements apply to ocean shipments. However, exporters nearly always buy additional insurance coverage for their export shipments, and the type of packaging influences the insurance rates.

UNIT LOADS IN MATERIALS HANDLING

As mentioned earlier in this chapter, the packaging of materials is based on the building-blocks concept of putting products in containers that will provide efficient yet manageable units. This section discusses unit loads, an extension of the building-blocks concept to very large quantities. A **unit load (unitization)** refers to consolidation of several units (cartons or cases) into larger units to improve efficiency in handling and to reduce shipping costs.[12] Handling efficiency can be facilitated by mechanical devices such as a pallet jack or forklift as well as by using a **pallet** or **skid** (a small platform made of plastic, steel, or wood on which goods are placed for handling by mechanical means). Figure 11-7 shows a unit load resting on an automatic guided vehicle.

The unit load offers several advantages, one of which is additional protection to the cargo because the cartons are secured to the pallet by straps, shrink-wrapping, or some other bonding device that provides a sturdier building block. A second unit load advantage is that pilferage is discouraged because it can be difficult to remove a single package or its contents. Also, a pallet can be stacked so that the cartons containing the more valuable or more fragile items are on the inside of the unit load. The major advantage of the unit load is that it enables mechanical devices to be substituted for manual labor, and numerous machines have been devised that can quickly build up or tear down a pallet load of materials. Robots can be used when more sophisticated integrated movements are needed for loading or unloading pallets.

The unit load does have its limitations, however. It represents a larger quantity of an item than a single box—often 30–50 times as much. Therefore, it is of limited value to companies that deal in small quantities. And, although one unit load advantage is that mechanical devices can be substituted for manual labor, these mechanical devices cost money to purchase or lease. Manual pallet jacks (trucks) can range in price from $350 to $3,000, whereas conventional forklifts can range in price from $15,000 to $30,000. Moreover, routine maintenance (another expense) should be performed on forklifts to keep them in optimal operating condition.

Yet another drawback to the unit load is the lack of standardization in terms of pallet sizes. Although the International Standards Organization (ISO) has established six international pallet

---

[12] *http://cscmp.org/digital/glossary/glossary.asp.*

FIGURE 11-7 **Automated Guided Vehicle**
Source: Photo courtesy of Dematic Corp, Rapistan Division, Grand Rapids, MI.

size standards (see Table 11-2)—four in metric units, two in English units—literally hundreds of different pallet sizes are used by companies in the United States. As a result, many shipments that are exported from the United States must be repalletized, which means an increase in manual labor, and thus a diminution in potential advantages to the unit load concept.[13]

TABLE 11-2	ISO Pallet Standards
Dimensions millimeters (width × length)	**Dimensions inches (width × length)**
1,219 × 1,016	48.00 × 40.00
1,000 × 1,200	39.37 × 47.24
1,165 × 1,165	44.88 × 44.88
1,067 × 1,067	42.00 × 42.00
1,100 × 1,100	43.30 × 43.30
800 × 1,200	31.50 × 47.24

Source: ISO Standard 6780: Flat Pallets for Intercontinental Materials Handling.

---

[13] "Marshall White on the State of Pallets," *Modern Materials Handling*, March 2006, 53–58.

FIGURE 11-8   A Warehouse Where Unit Loads Are Broken Down into Boxes
Source: Courtesy of the Interlake Corporation.

The discussion in this chapter thus far has emphasized the building of loads from small blocks into large blocks. However, the reverse is also true; that is, the large units or blocks must be broken down into their smaller component blocks, with the very smallest unit being the single item that the retail customer carries home. Figure 11-8 illustrates this by showing a high-rise warehouse four tiers high. At the right, a lift truck places full unit loads into a gravity-flow rack system. As they are used, the pallets move to the left, where order pickers break down the unit loads into single boxes.

The Unit Load Platform

An important issue with respect to unit loading concerns the platform (basic unit) on which to place the unit load. As mentioned before, the pallet is generally viewed as the basic unit in unit loading. In the United States, the wooden pallet has long been the backbone of the unit load in the sense that the vast majority (between 90 and 95 percent) of pallets are made of wood. Pallets can also be constructed from plastic, wood composites (such as fiberboard), paper, and metal. Each pallet material has its advantages and disadvantages, with price being a major drawback to both plastic and steel pallets. For example, a new 48-inch-by-40-inch wood pallet costs around $15, whereas a new 48-inch-by-40-inch plastic pallet costs approximately $100; a new 48-inch-by-42-inch aluminum pallet costs upward of $250.

However, one potential advantage to plastic and metal is their longevity relative to wood; although wood pallets might last only one use, some companies view wood's life span as between two and three years. Plastic pallets, by contrast, last at least five years, and life spans of over 10 years are not uncommon, whereas metal pallets can last for over 20 years. Another shortcoming of wood pallets is that they can break and splinter, which could pose safety dangers to workers and also necessitates pallet repairs (assuming the pallet is salvageable). Neither plastic nor metal pallets are likely to break and splinter, thus improving worker safety and resulting in minimal repair costs. Furthermore, wood and plastic are much more flammable than is metal; you might recall from Chapter 10 that fires are a regular threat in warehousing.

Yet a further disadvantage of wood pallets is their weight relative to plastic and metal, with a typical 48-inch-by-40-inch wood pallet weighing approximately 50 pounds, compared to 30 pounds for a similar-sized plastic pallet and 20 pounds for a 48-inch-by-40-inch aluminum pallet. Fifty pounds is a significant weight in many logistics systems because it represents the approximate weight at which there is a noticeable increase in injuries, particularly back injuries, from manual handling.

Although pallets are a popular unit load platform, one disadvantage (regardless of material) is their height (approximately 6 inches), meaning that pallets may occupy as much space as a layer of cases of canned soft drinks. When goods are loaded aboard pallets into railcars, trailers, or containers, the space occupied by the pallet is unproductive. One alternative to the pallet is a

slip sheet, a flat sheet of either fiberboard material or plastic, which is placed under the unit load. **Shrink-wrap** (plastic wrapping that when heated shrinks in size to form a cover over the product) or banding straps are used to attach the unit load to the slip sheet. Until the early part of the twenty-first century, one major drawback was high product damage rates due to the fragility of the slip sheets. However, advances in technology have created stronger plastics to construct slip sheets as well as improved materials handling equipment for moving slip sheets. As a result, the damage rates for slip sheeted products are much improved.

Beyond the Unit Load

The next step in the building-blocks process is to stow the unit load pallets into a waiting truck trailer, railcar, or container van. Increasingly this stowage is based upon load-planning software, and Figure 11-9 shows a computer printout from this type of software. The load-planning software depicted in Figure 11-9 suggests how to load a container with different sizes of cartons and tells where the loads for several customers should be loaded. The software recognizes, for example, that some cartons cannot be laid on their sides or cannot have other cartons placed on top of them. The software also takes into account the load's center of gravity and the allowable weights on axles. When planning for refrigerated loads, the software will also take into account the need for air spaces.

Slight clearances must be maintained between pallets to allow for the loading and unloading processes. Bracing or inflatable dunnage bags (see Figure 11-10) are used to fill narrow empty spaces, and when inflated, they fill the void space and function as both a cushion and a brace. A problem involved with any bracing or cushioning device is that the load is subjected to forces from all directions. Even when cargoes are properly braced, various forces such as vibration, pitch, and roll can still cause damage. Continued vibrations may loosen screws on machinery or cause the contents of some bags or packages to settle, changing the type of support they give to the materials packed above them. For products that present this problem, special preloading vibrators are used to cause the load to settle immediately.

FIGURE 11-9 Computer-Generated Load Plan
Source: Courtesy of TOPS Engineering Corp.

FIGURE 11-10 Inflated Dunnage Bags Between Pallets
Source: Courtesy of Sea-Land Service Inc.

Some goods are so heavy that they utilize the railcar's, trailer's, or container's weight capacity without filling its cubic capacity (a situation called **weighing out**). These loads, such as heavy machinery, must be carefully braced, and the weight must be distributed as evenly as possible. In highway trailers, for example, it is dangerous to have one side loaded more heavily than the other. In addition, the load should be distributed evenly over the axles.

MATERIALS HANDLING

As a supply chain is linked together, one of the concerns of those involved with logistics is the physical transfer of the product from one party to another: How will product be handled? In what form will it be? In what quantities? What kind of equipment is needed to handle or to store product? Materials handling processes generally receive little public attention, although there are periodic exceptions, such as the new baggage-handling system at Heathrow (London, United Kingdom) Airport's Terminal 5, which opened in March 2008. Within one week of Terminal 5's opening, approximately 30,000 pieces of luggage were "misplaced," due to software and hardware glitches, and this malfunction forced the bags to be sent to airports *outside the United Kingdom* to be sorted and returned to their rightful owners!

For our purposes, **materials handling** (also referred to as **material handling**) will be defined as "short-distance movement that usually takes place within the confines of a building such as a plant or DC and between a building and a transportation service provider."[14] This short-distance movement distinguishes materials handling from transportation (which will be discussed in Chapters 12 and 13).

Nearly all products that are packaged—often in consumer-size boxes, bottles, or cans—are handled by the building-block concept of packaging that has been described previously. The other way that products, especially large quantities of products, are handled is in *bulk*. Bulk materials are in loose rather than in packaged form and are handled by pumps, shovel devices, conveyor belts (see Figure 11-11), or the mere force of gravity. The decision must be made as to where in the supply chain the bulk materials should be placed into smaller containers for further sale or shipment. Sometimes, bagged and bulk quantities of the same material are part of the same shipment; for example, bagged rice is placed on top of bulk rice to provide load stability on ocean vessels.

Bulk cargoes have various handling characteristics, one of which is *density*. Consider three different bulk materials, namely, iron ore, coal, and grain, each of which is characterized by a different density. One particular type of ship uses only two-thirds of its cubic capacity when carrying iron ore, yet the 15,800 tons of ore lower the vessel to its maximum allowable draft of

---

[14] John J. Coyle, C. John Langley, Jr., Brian J. Gibson, Robert A. Novack, and Edward J. Bardi, *Supply Chain Management: A Logistics Perspective*, 8th ed. (Mason, OH: South-Western Cengage Learning, 2009), Appendix 11-A.

FIGURE 11-11   Conveyor Belt

Source: Shutterstock Photo.

24 feet, 8 inches. Alternatively, when loaded with coal, the vessel **cubes out**; that is, the cubic capacity is filled before reaching its weight capacity, and the vessel is lowered to only 20 feet, 6 inches. Grain loads are of lower density than either coal or iron ore; the ship's draft when full of grain is slightly less than 20 feet.[15]

A material's *angle of repose* is the size of angle that would be formed by the side of a conical stack of that material. The greater the angle, the higher the pile of materials that can be placed on a specific land area. Anthracite coal has an angle of repose of approximately 27 degrees, whereas for iron ore the angle is 35 degrees. This means more cubic yards of ore can be stockpiled on a given site and that the ore can be carried on a slightly steeper, narrower conveyor belt.

Bulk liquids also have unique handling characteristics. Resistance to flow is measured as viscosity, which can be lowered by increasing the temperature of a liquid. Molasses, cooking oils, and many petroleum products are heated before an attempt is made to pump them.

Gases have unique handling properties, although most of them are handled within completely enclosed pipeline systems. An exception is liquefied natural gas, or LNG, which is cooled and compressed into liquid form that is 1/630 of its volume in gaseous state. In its liquefied, highly pressurized state, it is transported by oceangoing vessels in special tanks.

The handling process itself may change the characteristics (or quality) of the product. Rice grains cannot fall far without being broken. This influences the design of loading and unloading facilities so that the grains of rice never drop more than a few feet at any one time. When sugar is handled, a dust is formed because of abrasion between sugar crystals. This dust is also sugar, but it is in much finer form and has different sensitivities to moisture. The dust must be separated from the rest of the sugar, or the quality of the final bakery product in which the sugar is used will be affected.

---

[15] Correspondence from the Reiss Steamship Company to the authors.

An ideal equipment configuration for one bulk cargo may not be able to handle another. Another consideration is the size of particle of the cargo in question; costs are involved in pulverizing to a uniform size so it can be handled by pneumatic or slurry devices.

Materials Handling Principles[16]

The Material Handling Institute, a leading nonprofit trade association that represents the materials handling industry, has developed a list of 10 materials handling principles. These principles are particularly important when laying out the design of a warehousing facility or when troubleshooting to learn why a system is not performing well. The Material Handling Institute suggests that these principles, which are listed below, are "the key to greater productivity, customer service, and profitability." We'll list, describe, and provide one key point for each of the 10 material handling principles.

1. The *planning principle*. All material handling should be the result of a deliberate plan where the needs, performance, objectives, and functional specification of the proposed methods are completely defined at the outset. Key point: The plan should reflect an organization's strategic and tactical objectives.

2. The *standardization principle*. Material handling methods, equipment, controls, and software should be standardized within the limits of achieving overall performance objectives and without sacrificing needed flexibility, modularity, and throughput. Key point: Standardization refers to both equipment and operating procedures.

3. The *work principle*. Material handling work should be minimized without sacrificing productivity or the level of service required of the operation. Key point: The shortest distance between two points is a straight line.

4. The *ergonomic principle*. **Ergonomics** refers to the science that seeks to adapt work or working conditions to suit the abilities of the worker. With this principle, human capabilities and limitations must be recognized and respected in the design of material handling tasks and equipment to ensure safe and effective operations. Key point: Ergonomics encompasses both physical and mental tasks.

5. The *unit load principle*. Unit loads shall be appropriately sized and configured in a way that achieves the material flow and inventory objectives at each stage in the supply chain. Key point: Less effort and work is required to collect and move many individual items as a single load.

6. The *space utilization principle*. Effective and efficient use must be made of all available space. Key point: Overhead space should be considered as a storage option.

7. The *system principle*. Material movement and storage activities should be fully integrated to form a coordinated, operational system that spans receiving, inspection, storage, production, assembly, packaging, unitizing, order selection, shipping, transportation, and the handling of returns. Key point: Information and material flow should be integrated and viewed as concurrent activities.

8. The *automation principle*. Material handling operations should be mechanized or automated where feasible to improve operational efficiency, increase responsiveness, and improve consistency and predictability. Key point: Preexisting processes and methods should be simplified and/or reengineered before adopting mechanization or automation.

9. The *environmental principle*. Environmental impact and energy consumption should be considered as a criteria when designing or selecting alternative equipment and material handling systems. Key point: Containers and pallets should be designed for reusability and/or biodegradability.

10. The *life cycle cost principle*. A thorough economic analysis should account for the entire life cycle of all material handling equipment and resulting systems. Key point: Organizations should develop plans for the replacement of obsolete equipment.

---

[16] The material in this section comes from "The Ten Principles of Material Handling," *www.mhia.org*.

Materials Handling Equipment

A comprehensive discussion of materials handling equipment is beyond the scope of this text. Having said this, it's important to recognize that decisions about materials handling equipment can affect the effectiveness, efficiency, and safety of logistics systems. Although forklifts, for example, facilitate the effective and efficient handling of unit loads, forklifts can be dangerous, and tens of thousands of forklift-caused injuries occur annually in the United States.

Moreover, it is important that the materials handling equipment be aligned with an organization's objectives, customers, and products. This seems to be common sense, but the authors are aware of a consumer products company that redesigned one of its storage facilities with the primary purpose to be a state-of-the-art showcase in terms of materials handling equipment. Less than a year later, the storage facility had to be redesigned because the state-of-the-art materials handling equipment was inconsistent with the types of products sold by the company as well as with its customers' ordering requirements.

Materials handling equipment can be divided into two categories—storage equipment and handling equipment. Examples of storage equipment include shelves, racks, and bins, whereas examples of handling equipment include conveyor systems, lift trucks, carts, and cranes. Although storage and handling equipment are very different, the choice of one often influences the choice of the other. For example, the use of storage racks allows for narrow aisles, but narrow aisles require specialized handling equipment capable of moving both vertically and horizontally.

Materials handling equipment can also be categorized in terms of whether they are labor intensive, mechanized, or automated. True automation, such as automatic guided vehicles, refers to an absence of human intervention, whereas mechanization refers to equipment that complements, rather than replaces, human contact (e.g., forklift).[17] A key trade-off among labor, mechanization, and automation involves the relevant volumes; because automation is a very high–fixed cost option, sufficient volume is needed to make it cost-effective. It has been suggested that automation becomes economically viable only when a facility handles at least 50,000 cartons a day.[18]

Decisions as to materials handling equipment can also be influenced by an organization's order picking and assembly system. In **picker-to-part systems**, an order picker goes to where a product is located, such as with a forklift, whereas in **part-to-picker systems**, the pick location is brought to the picker, such as with carousels. These two systems involve trade-offs between travel time; recall that travel time accounts for between 60 and 80 percent of total order-picking time.

Summary

Many considerations, such as a product's physical characteristics, must be taken into account when thinking about packaging and materials handling decisions. Packaging can be thought of in terms of the building-blocks concept where a very small unit is placed into a slightly larger unit, and so on. The chapter looked at a number of packaging issues and began by distinguishing between packaging's protective and promotional functions. We also learned that correct package labeling can impact the effectiveness and efficiency of logistics systems. Packaging has important environmental consequences and four environmentally friendly packaging strategies were identified and discussed.

---

[17] Mary Aichlmayr, "Making a Case for Automation," *Transportation & Distribution*, June 2001, 85–90.
[18] Ibid.

Unit loads (unitization) were also discussed, with a particular emphasis on the characteristics of wood, plastic, and metal pallets. The chapter then turned to an examination of materials handling and identified some of the challenges associated with handling the various types of bulk products.

Ten materials handling principles that can improve the effectiveness and efficiency of logistics systems were identified and described. The chapter concluded with a discussion of materials handling equipment; this equipment should be aligned with an organization's objectives, customers, and products.

Questions for Discussion and Review

1. How do product characteristics influence packaging and materials handling considerations?
2. What is the building-blocks concept? How is it applied to the handling of packaged goods?
3. What are the three general functions of packaging? How might they come into conflict?
4. The chapter describes approximately 10 functions that a protective package should accomplish. Does every package have to accomplish every function? Explain.
5. What information is needed to design a protective package properly?
6. Describe some of the devices that are used to monitor conditions during the journey that a shipment makes.
7. Why is it important to recognize that labeling requirements may differ from country to country?
8. Discuss some of the labeling requirements associated with hazardous materials.
9. What are some environmental disadvantages to plastic packaging?
10. What environmentally friendly packaging strategies might a firm adopt?
11. Discuss some of the potential challenges to adopting the metric system in the United States.
12. How can reducing packaging inefficiencies improve the performance of a logistics system?
13. How do transportation tariffs and classifications influence the type of packaging and packing methods?
14. Discuss the advantages and disadvantages of the unit load.
15. What trade-offs exist between wood, plastic, and metal pallets?
16. What issues does the logistics manager face once unit loads have been placed onto a transportation vehicle?
17. Discuss the various handling characteristics associated with bulk cargoes.
18. Of the 10 materials handling principles discussed in this chapter, which two are most surprising to you? Why?
19. Why is it important that materials handling be aligned with an organization's objectives, customers, and products?
20. How might an organization's order picking and assembly system influence its decisions on materials handling equipment?

Suggested Readings

Dempsey, Patrick G., and Wayne S. Maynard. "Manual Materials Handling." *Professional Safety* 50, no. 5 (2005): 20–25.

Denis, D., M. St.-Vincent, D. Imbeau, and R. Trudeau. "Stock Management Influence on Manual Materials Handling in Two Warehouse Superstores." *International Journal of Industrial Ergonomics* 36, no. 3 (2006): 191–201.

Drickhamer, David. "AGVS: Pick Up and Deliver." *Material Handling Management*, August 2005, 16–18.

Garcia-Arca, Jesus, and Jose Carlos Prado. "Packaging Design Model from a Supply Chain Approach." *Supply Chain Management Review* 13, no. 5 (2008): 375–380.

Jahne, Marianne. "Packages and Physical Distribution: Implications for Integration and Standardization." *International Journal of Physical Distribution & Logistics Management* 34, no. 2 (2004): 123–139.

Jung, Myung-Chul, Joel M. Haight, and Andris Freivalds. "Pushing and Pulling Carts and Two-Wheeled Hand Trucks." *International Journal of Industrial Ergonomics* 35, no. 1 (2005): 79–89.

Klevas, Jenny. "Organization of Packaging Resources at a Product-Developing Company." *International Journal of Physical Distribution & Logistics Management* 35, no. 2 (2005): 116–131.

Ray, Charles D., and Edgar Deomano. "Bark Occurrence in U.S. and Canadian Wooden Pallets." *Forest Products Journal* 57, no. 3 (2007): 84–88.

Roodbergen, Kees Jan, and Iris F. A. Vis. "A Survey of the Literature on Automated Storage and Retrieval Systems." *European Journal of Operational Research* 194, no. 2 (2009): 343–362.

Rokka, Joonas, and Liisa Uusitalo. "Preference for Green Packaging in Consumer Product Choices—Do Consumers Care?" *International Journal of Consumer Studies* 32, no. 5 (2008): 516–525.

Twede, Diana, Diane Mollenkopf, and Christina Guzman-Siller. "A Market-Driven Investigation of Pallet Trends in Grocery Chains." *Journal of Food Distribution Research* 38, no. 1 (2007): 161–169.

CASE

CASE 11-1 Let There Be Light Lamp Shade Company

Started in Madison, Wisconsin, after the student unrest of the 1960s had died down, the Let There Be Light Lamp Shade Company served an upscale local market for many years. It designed and built custom lamp shades and lamp globes. In the mid-1980s, some architects who had once studied under Frank Lloyd Wright in nearby Spring Green were commissioned to design several large public buildings in Asia. A total of 5,400 identical lights were to be installed, and the Let There Be Light Lamp Shade Company wished to bid on the work. Terms of sale would include delivery to the foreign port where the buyer would take possession.

Transportation costs would be a hurdle. In the initial design, the shades were cylinders that were 11 inches high and 11 inches in diameter and were packed into boxes that were 12 by 12 by 12 inches. (We refer to these shades as style A.) The packages cost 60 cents each and weighed 1 pound each. The shades cost $4 each to manufacture. They weighed 9 pounds each and 10 pounds packaged.

They would be shipped to the Port of Oakland. The land rate to Oakland was $1,000 per 40-foot container, without regard to weight, although the weight of the load could not exceed 44,000 pounds per loaded container because of highway weight restrictions. The interior dimensions of the intermodal container were 8 feet wide by 8.5 feet high by 40 feet long.

Ocean rates from Oakland to the overseas port were $22 per ton (2,000 pounds), except that the ocean conference used a measurement ton that indicated that for bulky loads every 40 cubic feet would equal 1 ton for rate-making purposes. (That is, a shipment weighing, say, 130 pounds and occupying 80 cubic feet would cost as though it weighed 4,000 pounds.) Insurance costs were 2 percent of the value of the shipment ready to be loaded aboard ship in Oakland. (This is calculated as all of the company's costs up to this point.)

Because of the large size of the order, Let There Be Light Lamp Shade Company realized that it could custom design a shade that, rather than being a cylinder, would be shaped like a cone. The advantage to that was that the shades could be nested. Some padding would be required between the shades, but the nested shades would also help protect each other. However, cutting out material for conical shapes results in waste, so production costs would be higher. Two alternative cone-shaped designs were proposed (referred to as styles B and C).

Style B cost $5 per shade to manufacture and could be shipped nested in packages of six. The package dimensions were 12 by 12 by 48 inches, and when holding six shades, a package weighed 62 pounds. Each package cost $2, and this included padding between the shades.

Style C cost $6 per shade to make and could be shipped nested in packages of 10. The package dimensions were 12 by 12 by 50 inches, and when holding 10 shades, a package weighed 101 pounds. Each package cost $3, including padding between the individual shades.

Questions

1. How many style A shades can be loaded into an intermodal container?
2. How many style B shades can be loaded into an intermodal container?
3. How many style C shades can be loaded into an intermodal container?
4. What are the total costs of delivering the style A shades to the port of importation?
5. What are the total costs of delivering the style B shades to the port of importation?
6. What are the total costs of delivering the style C shades to the port of importation?
7. Which style would you recommend? Why?

12 | TRANSPORTATION

Key Terms

- Accessorial service
- Barge
- Broker
- Common carrier
- Consignee
- Contract carrier
- Container
- Department of Transportation (DOT)
- Dimensional (dim) weight
- Exempt carrier

- Freight forwarder
- Intermodal transportation
- Land bridge services
- Less-than-truckload (LTL)
- Line-haul
- Lock
- Parcel carriers
- Piggyback transportation
- Private carrier
- Rail gauge

- Shippers' associations
- Slurry systems
- Surface Transportation Board
- TEU
- Terminal
- Ton miles
- Transportation
- Truckload (TL)
- Unit load devices (ULD)

Learning Objectives

- To provide an overview of transportation infrastructures in several countries
- To identify the five modes of transportation and learn about their respective characteristics
- To discuss intermodal transportation

- To familiarize you with several types of transportation specialists
- To learn how different types of regulation impact transportation
- To identify the legal classification of transportation carriers

Transportation, which can be defined as the actual, physical movement of goods and people between two points, is pivotal to the successful operation of any supply chain because it carries the goods, literally, as they move along the chain. Transportation influences, or is influenced by, the logistics activities discussed in previous chapters to include the following:

1. Transportation costs are directly affected by the location of the firm's plants, warehouses, vendors, retail locations, and customers.
2. Inventory requirements are influenced by the mode of transport used. High-speed, high-priced transportation systems require smaller amounts of inventories in a logistics system, whereas slower, less-expensive transportation requires larger amounts of systemwide inventory.
3. The transport mode selected influences the packaging required, and carrier classification rules dictate package choice.

4. The type of carrier used dictates a manufacturing plant's materials handling equipment, such as loading and unloading equipment and the design of the receiving and shipping docks.

5. An order-management philosophy that encourages maximum consolidation of shipments between common points enables a company to give larger shipments to its carriers and take advantage of volume discounts.

6. Customer service goals influence the type and quality of carrier and carrier service selected by the seller.

This chapter begins with a brief look at the transportation infrastructure in various countries throughout the world, and this is followed by a thorough discussion of the five different types, or modes, of transportation: air, motor carrier (truck), pipeline, rail, and water (these are listed in alphabetical order). The chapter also discusses intermodal transportation and transportation specialists and concludes with an examination of transportation regulation and the legal classification of carriers.

In keeping with past practice in this and other basic logistics texts, the discussion of transportation will primarily be presented from the perspective of the United States and will primarily focus on domestic (within the U.S.) transportation. Having said this, readers should recognize that an individual country's topology, economy, infrastructure, and other macroenvironmental factors could result in a different transportation system than that found in the United States. Moreover, the globalization of the world's economy means that an increasing number of shipments are being transported between multiple countries (international transportation), a topic that will be discussed in Chapter 14.

OVERVIEW OF TRANSPORTATION INFRASTRUCTURE

Because readers of this text increasingly reside outside of the United States, we believe it would be helpful to present a brief comparison of the transportation infrastructure that exists in five highly populated countries located on various continents. These infrastructure data, which appear in Table 12-1, indicate wide disparities in the various infrastructures; at a minimum, a lack of infrastructure makes it difficult to use that mode in domestic (within-country) transportation.

The relevant infrastructure statistic for air transportation in Table 12-1 is the number of paved runways over 3,047 meters (approximately 10,000 feet). This length is significant because a

TABLE 12-1	Infrastructure Statistics in Several Countries				
	Brazil	**China**	**Germany**	**Nigeria**	**United States**
Air[a]	7	59	13	6	191
Highway (paved)	96,353 km	1,515,571 km	644,480 km	28,980 km	4,209,835 km
Pipeline (oil)	4,517 km	20,204 km	3,379 km	3,396 km	244,620 km
Broad gauge (1.676 m) rail	5,709 km				
Standard gauge (1.435 m) rail	194 km	77,084 km	41,641 km		226,427 km
Narrow gauge (1.000 m) rail	22,954 km		75 km	3,505 km[b]	
Water (inland)	50,000 km	123,964 km	14,500 km	3,200 km	41,009 km

[a]Number of paved runways over 3,047 m (approximately 10,000 feet).
[b]gauge = 1.067 m.

Source: The World Factbook, www.cia.gov, 2009.

10,000-foot runway has generally been viewed as adequate for accommodating the largest existing wide-body aircraft (although the 10,000-foot benchmark may increase for airports served by the Airbus A-380 jetliner), and wide-body aircraft are essential to long-haul international movements. According to Table 12-1, the United States by far has the most airports with paved runways of at least 10,000 feet, an indication that the United States is well positioned to participate in long-haul international movements. Although China currently reports nearly 60 airports with 10,000 foot runways, this number should increase dramatically because the country plans to construct nearly 100 new commercial airports by 2020.

The infrastructure statistics for highway, pipeline, rail, and water, presented in kilometers (1 kilometer is equivalent to approximately 0.62 miles), provide some interesting findings. For example, although Brazil and China are approximately the same geographic size, China currently has about 16 times more-paved highway kilometers than Brazil. The data also indicate that oil pipelines are much more prevalent in the United States, and that China has much more extensive inland waterways, relative to the four other countries listed in Table 12-1.

The information on **rail gauge** (the distance between the inner sides of two parallel rail tracks) is also enlightening. Both China and the United States use only one size—standard— rail gauge (1.435 meters) in their rail infrastructure. Brazil, by contrast, uses broad gauge (1.676 meters), standard gauge, *and* narrow gauge (1.000 meter) in its rail infrastructure, whereas Nigeria uses only narrow gauge rail—with Nigeria's narrow gauge measured at 1.067 meters rather than 1.000 meter. The data on rail gauge are important because nonuniform rail gauge within a country, or between neighboring countries, means that shipments moving by rail will need to be transferred from one vehicle to another, which adds to both delivery time and costs.

TRANSPORTATION MODES

Each of the five modes of transportation exists because of certain attributes that provide one or more advantages over the other modes of transportation. The attractiveness of a particular mode depends on the following attributes[1]:

- Cost (price that a carrier charges to transport a shipment)
- Speed (elapsed transit time from pickup to delivery)
- Reliability (consistency of delivery)
- Capability (amount of different types of product that can be transported)
- Capacity (volume that can be carried at one time)
- Flexibility (ability to deliver the product to the customer)

It is important to recognize that public policy can affect a mode's performance on these attributes. Railroads, for example, were the dominant mode, as measured by **ton miles** (the number of tons multiplied by the number of miles transported) and revenues, in the United States from the nineteenth century through the middle part of the twentieth century. However, the development of the U.S. Interstate Highway System allowed motor carriers to improve their speed, reliability, and flexibility, and although railroads still have the largest share of ton miles, motor carriers now account for the majority of freight revenues. From a public policy perspective, construction costs of the Interstate Highway System were primarily paid for by the U.S. government (90 percent), with the remaining construction costs paid for by state governments. This funding by both the federal and state governments is significant because U.S. railroads have been responsible for the construction costs of their track systems, whereas rail construction costs

---

[1] Drawn from David J. Bloomberg, Stephen LeMay, and Joe B. Hanna, *Logistics* (Upper Saddle River, NJ: Prentice Hall, 2002), Chapter 7.

in other nations are often covered by the national government. As such, the U.S. railroads have a substantial cost disadvantage relative to motor carriers, and this cost disadvantage must be captured in railroad pricing practices.

We'll take a rather detailed look at each of the five modes in this section, and the discussion will be presented alphabetically by mode, beginning with airfreight.

Airfreight

When one thinks of air transportation, one immediately thinks of speed, particularly on the **line-haul** (terminal-to-terminal movement of freight or passengers); modern jet aircraft are capable of traveling between 500 and 600 miles per hour, a speed that far exceeds any other form of transportation. Indeed, air is generally the fastest mode of transportation for shipments exceeding 600 miles, although some motor carriers now offer overnight service of between 600 and 700 miles.

However, air transportation is a quite expensive form of transportation, and the line-haul cost of airfreight service is regarded as its primary disadvantage; many companies simply cannot afford to have their shipments travel by air. Moreover, because most shippers and **consignees** (receivers of freight) are not located at an airport, this requires transportation from the shipper to the origin airport as well as from the destination airport to the consignee. This **accessorial service** (transportation service that is supplemental to the line-haul) adds to both transportation costs and transit time and also increases the number of times a shipment is handled (thus increasing handling costs and the opportunities for loss and damage).

Unlike other forms of transportation, the great majority of airfreight is carried in the freight compartments of passenger airplanes (so-called belly freight). This belly freight limits the capacity available for air shipments and is particularly problematic with respect to narrow-body (single-aisle) aircraft. A narrow-body Boeing 737-800, for example, can carry approximately 10 tons of belly freight, whereas a wide-body Boeing 777-200 can carry approximately 60 tons of belly freight.[2] However, wide-body aircraft devoted to all-cargo service have impressive carrying capacity; the latest version of an all-cargo Boeing 747 can carry almost 150 tons (see Figure 12-1). Likewise, the freighter version of the world's largest commercial jetliner, the Airbus A-380, has projected cargo capacity of nearly 150 tons.

The cost, speed, and capacity attributes mean that, for the most part, airfreight is best suited to high-value, lower-volume products that are of a perishable nature or otherwise require urgent or time-specific delivery. Airfreight rates discourage bulky cargo and use **dimensional weight** (also called **dim weight**), which considers a shipment's density (the amount of space occupied in relation to actual weight) to determine a shipment's billable weight.[3] Examples of products that move by air include the following:

- Auto parts and accessories
- Cut flowers and nursery stock
- Electronic or electrical equipment, such as cell phones and iPods
- Fruits and vegetables
- Machinery and parts
- Metal products
- Photographic equipment, parts, and film
- Printed matter
- Wearing apparel

The reliability of airfreight is somewhat problematic. On the one hand, air's tremendous speed relative to the other modes offers the potential to "make up lost time" that isn't possible

[2] Data derived from Continental Airlines' cargo division, *www.cocargo.com*.
[3] *http://www.ups.com/content/us/en/resources/ship/packaging/dim_weight.html?srch_pos=1&srch_phr=dim+weight*.

FIGURE 12-1 Airfreight Capabilities

Source: Courtesy of Lufthansa Cargo.

with the other modes. Alternatively, because so much airfreight is belly freight, the increasing congestion and resultant delays associated with air passenger transportation mean congestion and delays for airfreight. Moreover, weather conditions such as fog, snow, and thunderstorms can have an adverse effect on the reliability of airfreight transportation. Indeed, Federal Express located its first (and still primary) hub in Memphis, Tennessee, in part because Memphis rarely experiences foggy conditions.

Motor Carriers

The backbone of the U.S. highway system is the Interstate Highway System (its formal name is the National System of Interstate and Defense Highways), which was approved by federal legislation in 1956. This nearly 47,000-mile, high-speed, limited-access highway system has had a profound impact on economic development in the United States over the past 50 years. From a logistics perspective, many companies began to locate manufacturing, assembly, and distribution facilities in close proximity to interstate highways. Indeed, part of Wal-Mart's success has been attributed to its ability to recognize the logistical opportunities of the interstate system before competitors did. Likewise, close proximity to one or more interstate highways has been a major determinant in the location of manufacturing facilities for non-U.S. automakers such as BMW, Honda, and Toyota.[4]

The most important business user of the highway system is the motor carrier (trucking) industry. One way of classifying motor carriers is according to whether they carry **less-than-truckload (LTL)** or **truckload (TL)** traffic. **LTL** shipments range from about 150 to 10,000 pounds; they are often too big to be handled manually, yet they do not fill an entire truck. Trucks that carry LTL freight have space for and plan to carry shipments of many other customers simultaneously. Unlike TL carriers, LTL carriers operate through a system of **terminals** (a facility where freight is shifted between vehicles), and from each terminal small trucks go out to customers, delivering and picking up shipments. These shipments are then taken to a terminal, where they are loaded aboard line-haul trucks, which are driven to a terminal near the freight's destination. The goods are unloaded from the line-haul carrier, move through the terminal, and are loaded aboard a small truck for local delivery. Prominent LTL carriers include ABF Freight System, FedEx Freight, UPS Freight, and YRC (formerly Yellow Freight and Roadway).

TL carriers focus on shipments of greater than 10,000 pounds, and although the exact weight depends on the product, it is close to the amount that would physically fill a truck trailer. For glassware, this might be 18,000 pounds; for canned goods, it might be 40,000 pounds. Although TL traffic may involve only one customer, it is possible that large shipments (greater than 10,000 pounds) from several customers can be consolidated into a TL shipment. Whereas LTL shipments are routed through terminals, TL shipments tend to move directly from the

---

[4] "Roads to Somewhere," *The Economist*, June 24, 2006, 36–38.

shipper's location to the consignee's location. Prominent TL carriers include J.B. Hunt, Schneider National, Swift Transportation, and Werner Enterprises.

Although LTL companies tend to be limited in the type of freight that they haul—primarily dry freight such as apparel, books, and greeting cards, among others—TL companies can carry a plethora of freight types. These include, but are not limited to, dry freight, foodstuffs, refrigerated products, liquid products, animals and livestock, automobiles, and steel. Overall, although motor carriers have the ability to haul many different kinds of freight, their capacity is limited by highway weight and size (width, length) restrictions. For example, motor carriers using the Interstate Highway System are limited to a maximum gross vehicle weight of 80,000 pounds. With respect to size considerations, truck trailers can be a maximum of 102 inches wide; the maximum length for tractor–trailer combinations varies from state to state. You should recognize that some countries do not have size and weight restrictions for motor carriers.

Although U.S. motor carriers can travel wherever there are roads, their length of haul is mitigated by several factors, such as speed limits and hours-of-service (HOS) rules. HOS rules have been the subject of near-constant legislation in the United States since the beginning of the twenty-first century, and rather than trying to articulate the relevant rules, suffice it to say that—unlike automobile drivers—truck drivers are limited in terms of the number of hours that can be driven in a 24-hour period, as well as the number of hours that can be driven in a one-week period.

Both HOS and highways speed limits have long been justified on the basis of safety concerns, and several states (e.g., Indiana and Washington) mandate a two-tier speed limit policy in which the maximum speed for motor carriers is lower than for noncommercial vehicles. Having said this, several U.S. states have eliminated, or are in the process of eliminating, the lower maximum speed limit for truckers, which could potentially increase motor carriers' length of haul. Readers should recognize that each country may have its own hours of service rules for motor carrier operators as well as its own speed limits.

Without question, the primary advantage for motor carriers is flexibility, or the ability to deliver the product to the customer (or where the customer has relatively easy access to it). For example, if you bought this textbook at your university's bookstore, this book was delivered there by some type of motor carrier, perhaps an LTL carrier. If you bought this textbook from an online site, then it was most likely delivered to your residence by a truck, perhaps a small package truck. Indeed, a longtime slogan of the American Trucking Associations (a trade group that represents motor carrier interests) was, "If you have it, it moved by truck."

As was the case with airfreight, weather considerations also affect the reliability of motor carrier delivery, and relevant weather considerations include ice, fog, snow, flooding, and high winds (which can affect bridge crossings). The reliability of motor carrier service is also affected by highway congestion, which is caused by increased travel demand, weather, roadway incidents (e.g., disabled vehicle or accident), and construction. Highway congestion tends to be most severe in major metropolitan areas and is not likely to be alleviated by additional highway construction. Rather, technology-based approaches, such as intelligent transportation systems and computer routing software that factors in congestion, are being used to deal with road congestion.

Although the cost of motor carrier service is lower than for airfreight, motor carriers tend to be more costly than the remaining modes of transportation. Moreover, there can be significant cost variation depending on the type of motor carrier service that is purchased. Expedited trucking, such as provided by Panther Expedited Services and FedEx Custom Critical, tends to have the highest cost per *hundredweight* (100 pounds), whereas TL transportation tends to have the lowest cost per hundredweight.

These cost variations highlight the importance of understanding the trade-offs between logistical activities that have been discussed throughout the text. For example, suppose an organization manufactures 8,000 pounds of crayons per day. The company could have one 8,000-pound LTL shipment each day, or the company could accumulate five days of crayons into one 40,000-pound TL shipment. This would be done to take advantage of the lower TL rate per hundredweight; however, to receive the lower TL rate, the company will need to hold an inventory of crayons, thus increasing inventory and storage costs.

Pipelines

Pipelines are a unique mode of transportation because it is the only one without vehicles, and this is significant for several reasons. First, there is no need for vehicle operators, an important consideration given that vehicle operators in some modes, such as airplane pilots and ship captains, can achieve annual compensation in excess of $100,000. In addition, vehicle operators sometimes engage in work stoppages (e.g., strikes) and can be the cause of accidents. The lack of vehicles also means that pipeline transportation is one way; other modes have two-way transportation, a fronthaul and a backhaul. The backhaul is often a significant source of excess capacity, or unused available space.

Pipelines' lack of vehicles means that it is the most reliable form of transportation, in part because there aren't vehicle-related disruptions (such as accidents), and pipelines are virtually unaffected by adverse weather conditions. Having said this, pipelines tend to be the slowest form of transportation; the lack of vehicles means that the relevant product needs to be forced through the pipeline, often by pumping stations. The slow speed for pipelines is significant because this increases overall transit times and thus necessitates additional inventory in the logistics system.

From a capability perspective, pipelines are quite limited in the sense that products must be liquid, liquefiable, or gaseous in nature. Indeed, pipelines are probably best known for transporting petroleum products, and petroleum pipelines are characterized as either crude oil or product pipelines. *Gathering lines*, which are 6 inches or smaller in diameter, start at each well and carry crude oil to concentration points. *Trunk lines* carry crude oil from gathering-line concentration points to the oil refineries. Their diameter varies from 3 to 48 inches; 8- to 10-inch pipe is the most common size. Product pipelines carry products such as gasoline or aviation fuel from the refineries to tank farms (storage tanks) located nearer to customers. These products are stored at the tank farms and then delivered to customers by truck or by rail, an indication that pipelines have limited delivery flexibility.

Slurry systems allow bulk commodities to become liquefiable by grinding the solid material to a certain particle size, mixing it with a liquid to form a fluid muddy substance, pumping that substance through a pipeline, and then decanting the liquid and removing it, leaving the solid material. Although water is the most common liquid used in slurry systems, other liquids, such as methanol, can be used. The Black Mesa pipeline, which transports pulverized coal from northern Arizona to an electric-generating station, is probably the best-known slurry pipeline currently in operation; other slurry pipelines in current operation transport phosphate, limestone, copper concentrate, and iron concentrate.

Although pipelines tend to have limited capabilities with respect to the products that can be transported, pipelines are capable of transporting very large product volumes. For example, the 48-inch Trans-Alaska pipeline, which is 789 miles long, has a discharge capacity of 2 million barrels of oil per day. Moreover, pipelines are quite costly to construct and thus have high fixed costs; however, because these fixed costs can be spread over rather large capacities, pipelines offer their users a relatively low cost per unit.

Railroads

Although approximately 560 freight railroads operate in the United States, over 90 percent of the rail industry's revenues and ton-miles are accounted for by the seven Class I (2007 revenues of at least $359.6 million) freight railroads.[5] Moreover, the U.S. railroad industry is dominated by four

---

[5] *www.aar.org.*

freight carriers, the Burlington Northern (BN), CSX, Norfolk Southern (NS), and Union Pacific (UP); the BN and UP dominate rail freight transportation west of the Mississippi River, whereas CSX and NS have a similar position east of the Mississippi River.

This level of market concentration and domination isn't found in the other modes, and from a practical perspective it can create limited service and pricing options for potential customers. One possible manifestation of limited service options might be seen in the railroads' rather uneven reliability in recent years, some of which can be linked to adverse weather conditions. In recent years, major U.S. railroads have dealt with blizzards, tropical storms, and severe flooding that have damaged and destroyed many miles of rail track.

U.S. freight railroads present an intriguing paradox in the sense that they are not either the "best" or "worst" on any of the six attributes (capability, capacity, cost, flexibility, reliability, speed) that we're using as a basis of comparison for the five transport modes. For example, although freight railroads have the potential to transport many different kinds of products (capability), they tend to transport lower-value, high-volume shipments of bulk-type commodities such as coal, chemicals, farm products, and nonmetallic minerals. Having said this, the growth of intermodal transportation (which will be more fully discussed later in the chapter) has given railroads access to manufactured and packaged products, which tend to be of higher value. Overall, railroads are superior to air, motor, and pipeline, but inferior to water, in terms of their ability to transport different kinds of products.

Similarly, rails possess less flexibility (ability to deliver the product to the customer) than motor carriers, unless the customer is located on a rail line or has a rail siding (a track that runs from a main line to a particular facility). However, rails generally have greater flexibility than air, water, and pipeline. In terms of the volume that can be carried at any one time (capacity), rails are superior to air and motor, but not as good as pipeline or water. Boxcars (used to carry general freight), hopper cars (used to carry products like coal and minerals), and tank cars (used for liquid or liquefiable products) have usable carrying capacities of approximately 110 tons. Although this dwarfs the 25-ton capacity of a typical truck trailer, consider that the carrying capacity of one dry bulk **barge** (flatboard boat used to transport heavy products) is about 1,750 tons.[6]

Freight railroads are also right in the middle of the five modes when it comes to cost (price that a carrier charges to transport a shipment) and speed (elapsed transit time from pickup to delivery) considerations. Although railroads are less expensive than air and motor, they are more expensive than pipeline and water. Alternatively, railroads are faster than both pipeline and water, but slower than air and truck.

Water

Freight moves by water on the Great Lakes, using vessels called lake freighters (lakers), as well as on inland waterways, using barges. Waterborne commerce also moves via oceangoing vessels between the mainland states (Lower 48) and Alaska, Hawaii, and Puerto Rico. Our discussion will focus on the inland waterways, primarily rivers, which are dredged to a depth of 9 feet—the minimum depth required for most barges. Although minimum dredging depths might appear to be a rather mundane topic, it is actually quite important in the sense that inland water transportation is somewhat unreliable due to weather-related conditions such as drought and icing.

Drought creates problems because when water levels drop below acceptable levels, barges are forced to reduce their loads, or barge traffic might be halted altogether, situations that require alternate means of transportation. During 2006, for example, drought conditions effectively shut down the Missouri River, and some shipments that normally moved by barge were shifted to trucks or rail, which resulted in higher transportation costs.[7]

---

[6] Center for Ports and Waterways, *A Modal Comparison of Domestic Freight Transportation Effects on the General Public* (College Station, TX: Texas Transportation Institute, 2007).
[7] Thomas Gallagher, "Drought Halts Barge Traffic on Missouri River," *The Journal of Commerce*, July 31, 2006, 36.

Flooding is another weather-related consideration that can affect the reliability of inland water transportation. For example, severe flooding along parts of the Mississippi River during June 2008 caused severe disruptions to barge transportation, with agricultural shipments particularly affected.[8] Icing is a problem in northern states such as Minnesota and Wisconsin; the ice closes the rivers and prevents year-round operation. Because of this, customers can stockpile inventories in the fall to last through winter months or can use alternate methods of transportation.

However, not all of the unreliability associated with U.S. inland water transportation is weather related. More specifically, the waterways' **lock** system (a lock raises or lowers barges so they can meet the river's level as they move upstream or downstream) also contributes to transport unreliability. Many locks on the U.S. inland waterway system are quite old, with some locks dating to the 1930s, and their maintenance needs tend to increase as a function of age. With preventive maintenance of locks currently the exception rather than the rule, when a lock malfunctions, the related repairs can take months to complete—a situation with potentially adverse consequences for shippers and barge operators.[9]

Inland water transportation in the United States is also characterized by slow average speeds of approximately six miles per hour. It should be noted that transit times will be affected by the direction of travel; upstream movements that go against the prevailing current will be slower than downstream movements. In addition, inland waterways can be circuitous in nature, which can add to transit time. And, as previously pointed out, transit times may be extended because of lock-related maintenance considerations.

In terms of positive attributes, inland water transportation is relatively inexpensive to users. At one time, inland water transportation was considered to be the least expensive form of transportation, but fuel taxes that were imposed on inland water transportation in the 1980s permitted pipelines to become the least expensive mode. Nevertheless, inland water transportation is quite inexpensive when compared to rail and motor carrier transportation. As a general guideline, on a ton-mile basis, rail costs are approximately two to three times as high as inland water carriers, whereas truck costs are approximately 20–30 times higher than inland water carriers'.

Although inland water carriers tend to focus on lower-value bulk commodities that can be handled by mechanical means such as pumps, scoops, and conveyors, many different kinds of products can be carried. The predominant commodity moved by barge is petroleum and petroleum-related products, followed by coal. Other products that move extensively in the inland waterway system include food and farm products, industrial chemicals, and minerals and stone. And, as pointed out in the previous section, inland water carriers can carry much greater volumes than can rail and truck.

INTERMODAL TRANSPORTATION

We have discussed each mode as if they act in isolation from the other modes, but in an increasingly global economy, multiple modes are used to transport a shipment from its origin to its destination. For our purposes, **intermodal transportation** refers to transportation when using a container or other equipment that can be transferred from the vehicle of one mode to the vehicle of another mode without the contents being reloaded or disturbed.[10] With intermodal transportation, two or more modes work closely together in an attempt to utilize the advantages of each mode while at the same time minimizing their disadvantages. For example, a company might use **piggyback transportation**, that is, either truck trailer-on-flatcar or container-on-flatcar, to take advantage of rail's low transportation costs on the line-haul along with truck's ability to provide door-to-door

---

[8] Ari Natter, "After the Floods," *Shipping Digest*, July 14, 2008, 90–91.
[9] *www.mvs.usace.army.mil/floodfight/L-D/LD21.pdf*.
[10] This definition comes from Barton Jennings and Mary C. Holcomb, "Beyond Containerization: The Broader Concept of Intermodalism," *Transportation Journal* 35, no. 3 (1995): 5–13.

FIGURE 12-2   RoadRailer Trailer; Note Rail Wheels on Rear, Signifying That It Can Operate on Highway or on Rails

Source: Courtesy of RoadRailer Division, Wabash National Corp.

service. Figure 12-2 shows a drawing of a RoadRailer vehicle, which conceptually facilitates intermodal transportation because the vehicle can operate on both highways and railways.

As evident in our definition, the **container**, which for our purposes is defined as "large reusable steel boxes used for intermodal shipments,"[11] is an important type of equipment in intermodal transportation. Containers are moved by mechanical devices such as container cranes, and companies need only handle a container and not the freight inside it—thus providing a dramatic reduction in freight handling costs. Because the container is interchangeable among rail, truck, and water carriers, containers can be used in intermodal applications and provide the advantages offered by each of several modes. Both ocean carriers and railroads have developed methods of handling two or more containers at one time, thereby reducing the number of individual lifting and storage moves.

Containers are generally 8 feet wide, 8 feet high, and between 10 and 53 feet long. Most containers are dry-cargo boxes, although some are insulated and come with temperature-controlling devices. Specialized intermodal containers are also available that carry tanks for holding liquids or gases as well containers that hold insulated or refrigerated cargo. Figure 12-3 shows several different types of containers.

Airfreight containers, often referred to as **unit load devices** (**ULDs**), are constructed of lightweight metals and come in different sizes. Unlike the containers in Figure 12-3, airfreight

---

[11] *http://en.wikipedia.org/wiki/Shipping_containers.*

FIGURE 12-3 Various Types of Intermodal Surface Containers

Source: Ports of the World, 14th ed., CIGNA Property & Casualty Companies.

ULDs have somewhat irregular shapes, dictated by the contours of the fuselage into which they must fit.

Although intermodal containers can range between 10 and 53 feet in length, a commonly used metric is **TEU**, which stands for 20-foot equivalent unit, and volumes of intermodal traffic are commonly expressed as so many TEUs, meaning they would fill that many 20-foot containers. Water ports, for example, are often ranked in terms of the number of TEUs that are handled in a particular period of time. Likewise, containerships are measured by the number of TEUs that can be carried, and containership capacity continues to increase over time. Consider that in 1990—around the year that many of today's college undergraduates were born—the largest capacity containership was approximately 4,400 TEUs. By contrast, the largest capacity containership today is approximately 15,000 TEUs; a South Korean shipbuilder has announced plans to build a ship capable of carrying *22,000 TEUs*!

Not only did the container revolutionize freight handling, it also spurred cooperation between various modes to develop more effective and efficient transport offerings, such as land bridge services. Rather than all water service between two ports, **land bridge services** involve the use of surface transportation—usually rail transportation—between the origin and destination port. Consider, for example, a shipment of pineapples from Hawaii to Europe. Rather than the shipment going by water from Hawaii through the Panama Canal and then on to Europe, under land bridge service, the pineapples would move by containership from Hawaii to a U.S. West Coast water port. From this port, the containers of pineapple would be placed on railcars and shipped across the United States to an East Coast port, where the containers would be loaded onto a vessel for continuation of the shipment to Europe. Although the land bridge adds to total transportation costs, the primary advantage to land bridge service is the reduction in total transit time from the origin to destination port.

TRANSPORTATION SPECIALISTS

In addition to the five basic modes and intermodal transportation, a number of different transportation specialists can provide value-added services to prospective customers and we'll discuss several transportation specialists in the paragraphs that follow. **Freight forwarders** are not modes, but from the shipper's viewpoint, they are analogous to other carriers. There are two types of domestic freight forwarders—surface and air—and they can best be thought of as consolidators of freight.

Surface carriers give volume discounts to customers shipping large quantities of freight at one time. For example, the LTL rate from city A to city B might be $5 per 100 pounds for shipments less than 20,000 pounds, whereas the TL rate might be $2 per 100 pounds when shipments of 20,000 pounds or more are tendered. TL rates are lower than LTL rates for three reasons: (1) the shipper loads the goods, and the consignee unloads the trailer; (2) the load goes directly from shipper to consignee without passing through terminals; and (3) paperwork, billing, and other administrative costs are little more for a 25,000-pound shipment than they would be for a 250-pound shipment.

The freight forwarder exists by offering a service to shippers that must use LTL rates because they do not generate enough volume to use TL rates. Without the freight forwarder, the shipper has to use the $5 LTL rate. The freight forwarder, however, offers the same transportation service for a rate between the LTL and TL rate—say, $4 per 100 pounds. This is possible because the freight forwarder consolidates enough small shipments to reach a volume of at least 20,000 pounds and thus qualifies for the $2 per 100 pound TL rate. The freight forwarder typically offers pickup and delivery service but does not perform the line-haul service, which is done by motor carriers or railroads (in terms of intermodal service).

The air forwarding industry works with the air carriers, and air forwarders consolidate shipments and tender them in containers that are ready for aircraft loading. This results in significant ground-handling savings for the airlines. Therefore, airlines encourage forwarder traffic because it results in an agreeable division of labor: The forwarders provide the retailing function and deal with each individual shipper and consignee, and the airline concentrates on wholesaling, moving the forwarders' loaded containers among major cities.

Some forwarders specialize in certain cargoes. A common example is in the garment industry, in which many small garment firms send large numbers of a few garments each to retail shops in most large cities. The garment forwarders use special containers in which the garments are on hangers and thus ready for display on arrival. Another specialized forwarder relocates house pets. The firm handles health inspection prior to shipment, arranges for cages and quarantines (if required), books flights, and handles all documentation.

Shippers' associations perform basically the same function as surface and airfreight forwarders, except that they do not operate as profit-making organizations. Shippers' associations are membership cooperatives where membership can be based on different considerations, such as shipping a particular commodity or commodities, belonging to a particular industry, or being located in a particular area. Although shippers' associations tend to be thought of as providing a large number of transportation-related services for their members (full-service associations), some shippers' associations are primarily focused on achieving the lowest rates for their members ("rate negotiator" associations). The main benefit of shippers' associations, whether they are full service or rate negotiators, is transportation cost savings for its members.[12]

Brokers are another type of transportation specialist; they are companies that look to match a shipper's freight with a carrier to transport it. Brokers look to secure the best transportation rate and service package available for shippers, while attempting to ensure that carriers operate as close

---

[12] Information from the Web site of the American Institute for Shippers' Associations, *www.shippers.org*.

as possible to maximum capacity. Brokers can handle both LTL and TL shipments; those handling LTL shipments consolidate them and then turn them over to motor carriers, freight forwarders, or shippers' associations. With respect to TL shipments, brokers will retain a particular carrier and receive a portion of the transportation charges as compensation.

In some cases, third-party logistics companies are involved in arranging transportation services. They try to find clients with complementary transportation needs so that equipment utilization can be increased, which should reduce transportation costs to the respective clients. As an example, Exel Logistics was able to persuade Chrysler and Ford to share space on trucks that were delivering repair parts to both Chrysler and Ford dealerships in a particular geographic area. Exel was able to show both Chrysler and Ford that dedicated equipment (that is, equipment carrying only Chrysler or only Ford parts) led to additional equipment, additional shipments, and excess capacity for each party—thus increasing the costs of distributing the repair parts.

Much of the discussion up to this point has assumed that we are dealing with shipments that weigh at least several hundred pounds. We'll conclude our discussion of transportation specialists by looking at **parcel carriers**, companies that specialize in transporting parcels, which are often referred to as packages that weigh up to 150 pounds. Parcel shippers have a variety of potential options available to them, one of which is Parcel Post, a service of the U.S. Postal Service that was specifically established to send packages through the mail system. Parcel Post has size (130 inches in combined length and girth) and weight limitations (70 pounds), with transportation charges based on weight, distance, and shape.[13] In most cases, a parcel must be transported to the post office by the shipper, but it will be delivered to the receiver's actual mailing address.

Another option for parcel shippers is United Parcel Service (UPS), which financially dwarfs any other transportation company in the United States (2009 revenue from package deliveries of approximately $45.3 billion). UPS was able to attract customers in its early years because it offered certain services, such as automatic daily pickups, multiple delivery attempts, and the return of undeliverable packages, that were not available from competitors such as Parcel Post—and UPS was able to offer this service at rates that were competitive with Parcel Post. Unlike the Parcel Post, UPS rates include both pickup and delivery, and today UPS offers a range of parcel services via several modes of transport, including truck, rail, and air.

Whereas UPS started as a package delivery company that emphasized line-haul movement by truck and in the 1980s expanded into air transportation, Federal Express (now FedEx Express) started as a package delivery company that emphasized service by air transportation and expanded into line-haul movement by truck (FedEx Ground). Both UPS and FedEx now offer package shippers service options that include same-day service involving air transportation, next-day service involving air or truck, and second-day service involving air or truck, among others. The size and weight limitations for packages shipped by UPS and FedEx are similar with both carriers limiting package sizes to a maximum of 108 inches in length and 165 inches in girth. And while the maximum package weight for UPS and FedEx is 150 pounds, both carriers mandate special guidelines and procedures when shipping packages that weigh more than 70 pounds (UPS) or 75 pounds (FedEx).

Package services are also available from Greyhound Lines (called Greyhound Package Express), which is the primary intercity bus company in the United States. As is the case with UPS and FedEx, several service options are available for package delivery, such as same-day service (which generally uses a courier company) and standard service (where the packages travel in special compartments on the bus). Packages that are sent via Greyhound Package Express are limited to a maximum weight of 100 pounds.[14]

---

[13] *http://www.usps.com/send/waystosendmail/senditwithintheus/parcelpost.htm.*
[14] *http://www.shipgreyhound.com/guide/.*

TRANSPORTATION REGULATION

The five modes of transportation have been influenced, and continue to be influenced, by various types of regulation by federal, state, and local governments. You may not be aware, for example, that until late 2007 commercial airline pilots in the United States faced mandatory retirement upon reaching 60 years of age (65 is now the mandatory retirement age for commercial pilots). Likewise, you might not be aware that there are very specific guidelines for the placement of lighting on truck trailers. The existence of these and other regulations have implications not only for transportation companies, but also for users of transportation companies because regulations can affect the effectiveness and efficiency of a user's logistics system. Indeed, regulation costs money—regulations need to be codified, government agencies (regulatory bodies) exist to enforce the regulations.

Our discussion in this section will focus on federal regulation of transportation in the United States, and we will look at environmental, safety, and economic regulation. However, before proceeding with this discussion, readers should recognize that the level and degree of transportation regulation varies from country to country. For example, many of the world's more industrialized economies have instituted fairly stringent regulations with respect to vehicle emissions (air pollution) from transportation equipment. In lesser economically developed countries, emissions regulations are much less stringent—if they exist at all. We're not here to judge the appropriateness or inappropriateness of transportation regulation in individual countries; rather, logisticians need to understand the relevant transportation regulations of the countries in which they conduct business as well as the cost and service implications of these regulations.

Environmental Regulation

The Environmental Protection Agency (EPA), a U.S. federal regulatory agency that was established to protect human health and the environment, influences transportation in a number of different ways. A major transportation-related concern of the EPA involves various types of pollution such as noise and air pollution. With respect to noise, the EPA is responsible for enforcing noise emissions from transportation equipment such as rail locomotives and truck tractors. In terms of air pollution, the EPA has mandated that heavy-duty truck engines must meet stringent emissions standards. The most recent engine standards, which went into effect in 2007, require the use of ultra-low-sulfur diesel fuel, which contains a maximum 15 parts per million sulfur compared to low sulfur diesel's maximum 500 parts per million sulfur content.

The EPA is also quite concerned with resource conservation, and this is particularly germane in that transportation accounts for approximately two-thirds of the petroleum consumption in the United States. As such, improved fuel efficiency and reduced consumption of petroleum have become important issues for many transportation companies. For example, Continental Airlines is today approximately 35 percent more fuel efficient per passenger-mile flown than in 1997, and Continental uses electric (as opposed to fossil fuel) ground handling equipment as often as possible.[15]

Safety Regulation

The **Department of Transportation (DOT)** is the U.S. federal government body with primary responsibility for transportation safety regulation. Although the DOT's safety responsibilities encompass all five modes of transportation, safety regulation of inland water carriers is primarily the responsibility of the U.S. Coast Guard, which is now part of the U.S. Department of Homeland Security. The key federal government safety agency for each mode, along with an example of its roles or responsibilities, will be discussed in the following paragraphs.

---

[15] *http://www.continental.com/web/en-US/content/company/globalcitizenship/environment.aspx.*

The Federal Aviation Administration (FAA) has primary responsibility for air transportation safety and strives to improve the safety and efficiency of aviation. One of the FAA's primary roles involves airspace and air traffic management and to this end the FAA operates airport towers and air traffic control centers.[16] The Federal Motor Carrier Safety Administration (FMCSA), a relatively new government agency, started operations in January 2000 and is focused on reducing crashes, injuries, and fatalities involving large trucks and buses. As such, the FMCSA has primary responsibility for developing, monitoring, and ensuring compliance with the commercial driver's license program for operators of commercial motor vehicles.[17]

The Office of Pipeline Safety (OPS), which is part of the Pipeline and Hazardous Materials Safety Administration, is responsible for safety considerations for natural gas and liquid pipelines. The OPS has responsibility for establishing and enforcing regulations with respect to pipeline design, construction, and operation.[18] Among its myriad responsibilities, the Federal Railroad Administration (FRA) also has primary responsibility for safety in the U.S. railroad industry. The FRA employs over 400 safety inspectors who investigate five distinct disciplines, namely, hazardous materials; motive power and equipment; operating practices, including drug and alcohol issue; track structures; and signal and train control issues.[19] Finally, the U.S. Coast Guard (USCG), has primary responsibility for marine (water) safety considerations. Several prominent USCG safety roles include responsibility for marine licensing and documentation as well as regular inspections of U.S. and foreign vessels.[20]

Economic Regulation

Economic regulation in transportation refers to control over business practices and activities such as entry and exit, pricing, service, accounting and financial issues, and mergers and acquisitions. Federal economic regulation of transportation in the United States, which began in the 1870s, was justified because of transportation's economic and social importance as well as a belief that transportation companies would not act in the public's best interest without government regulation.[21] Economic regulation resulted in the creation of two key economic regulatory bodies: the Interstate Commerce Commission (ICC), with authority over rail, motor, inland water, and oil pipelines, and the Civil Aeronautics Board (CAB), with authority over air transportation.

Although a comprehensive discussion of the economic regulation of transportation is beyond the scope of this book, one of the authors worked for an LTL company while the company was economically regulated, and his experiences offer insight into the challenges presented by economic regulation. For example, under economic regulation, price competition among LTL carriers was limited, and carriers could set their prices through collective ratemaking (i.e., sharing cost and price information with each other) without fear of legal prosecution. This meant that all LTL carriers charged the exact same prices for transporting shipments between any two points, and when companies couldn't compete on price, they were forced to compete on service. As such, one reason that the author's employer chose the name "AAA Trucking Corporation" was because it would be the first listing in a telephone book.

Beginning in the late 1970s, various sectors of the transportation industry experienced a reduction in economic regulation (also referred to as deregulation), and in 1985 the CAB went out of existence. The ICC was legislated out of existence in 1995, and its remaining economic regulatory functions were transferred to a new agency, the **Surface Transportation Board (STB)**,

---

[16] http://www.faa.gov/about/safety_efficiency/.
[17] http://www.fmcsa.dot.gov/about/what-we-do/keyprograms/keyprograms.htm.
[18] http://www.phmsa.dot.gov/pipeline/about.
[19] http://www.fra.dot.gov/us/content/3.
[20] http://www.uscg.mil/hq/cg5/cg54/docs/MSPerformancePlan.pdf.
[21] Donald V. Harper, *Transportation in America*, 2nd ed. (Englewood Cliffs, NJ: Prentice Hall, 1982), Chapter 19.

which is affiliated with the DOT. Although the STB has primary responsibility for resolving rail-road rate and service disputes and reviewing potential rail mergers, it continues to have some jurisdiction over motor carriers, domestic water transportation, and the rates and services of pipelines that are not regulated by the Federal Energy Regulatory Commission.[22]

From a logistics perspective, the economic deregulation of transportation is important because it has allowed transportation companies much greater freedom with respect to pricing and service options—two attributes that are at the heart of the tailored logistics concept that was presented in Chapter 1. In addition, the economic deregulation that occurred in the United States has been the catalyst for economic deregulation of transportation in Canada and some European nations.[23]

LEGAL CLASSIFICATION OF CARRIERS

Although there has been a dramatic reduction in U.S. economic regulation since the late 1970s, the legal classification of carriers continues to be relevant. More specifically, transportation carriers are classified as either for hire or private, and for-hire carriers can be further subdivided into common, contract, and exempt carriers. The legal classification of carriers is important because of the vary-ing levels of economic regulation that are applicable to the different carriers (e.g., common carriers have more extensive economic regulation than contract carriers). However, all carriers, regardless of their legal classification, must comply with the relevant environmental and safety regulations.

The key factor that separates a **common carrier** from other forms of transportation is that the common carrier has agreed to serve the general public. To ensure that the general public is adequately serviced, common carriers assumed four specific obligations: to serve, to deliver, to charge reasonable rates, and to avoid discrimination in pricing and service. The service obligation means that common carriers are supposed to serve all customers who request service, so long as the commodity and origin/destination are within a carrier's scope of service. For example, a motor carrier that specializes in dry van, general freight service would not be expected to transport a ship-ment of liquid chemicals. Even though a company might not want to carry certain types of freight, its undesirability (see Figure 12-4) is not a legitimate reason to avoid the obligation to serve. To this end, in recent years the major U.S. freight railroads have tried to convince the STB to waive their common carrier obligations associated with the transportation of hazardous chemicals such as chlorine.[24]

The obligation to deliver requires that a carrier provide timely pickup and delivery as well as ensuring that the delivered shipment is in the same condition as the picked up shipment (i.e., the avoidance of lost or damaged freight). The obligation to charge reasonable rates has long been viewed as offering protection for both carriers and users; the idea of reasonable rates guards against rates so low that carriers are unable or unwilling to carry freight, and it guards against rates so high that users are unwilling or unable to tender freight to carriers. The obliga-tion to avoid discrimination in pricing and service suggests that similarly situated customers (e.g., customers that ship the same product, customers that ship to the same origin and destina-tion point) should receive identical treatment. One of the key provisions of the ICC Termination Act of 1995 was the elimination of the reasonable rate obligation (hence also the obligation to avoid discrimination in pricing and service) for many types of motor carriers.

A **contract carrier** offers a specialized service to customers on a contractual basis, and the contract specifies the compensation to be received, the services to be provided, and the type of equipment to be used, among others. Unlike the common carrier, the contract carrier is under no obligation to render services to the general public and only has to serve customers with whom it has contracts. Moreover, the contract carrier is under no obligation to treat its customers on an equal basis. Because each contract can be tailored to the specifications of

[22] *http://www.stb.dot.gov/stb/about/overview.html.*
[23] John J. Coyle, Edward J. Bardi, and Robert A. Novack, *Transportation*, 6th ed. (Mason, OH: South-Western, 2006).
[24] John D. Boyd, "A Toxic Rate Battle," *The Journal of Commerce*, June 22, 2009, 62.

"IT'S CARRYING A LOAD OF FERTILIZER."

FIGURE 12-4 Undesirable Cargo

Source: Reproduced by permission of *Jet Cargo News*.

individual customers, contract carriage is viewed as offering many of the advantages of private transportation (e.g., control over service) while avoiding many of the disadvantages of private transportation (e.g., the hiring of drivers and owning equipment).

Exempt carriers are for-hire carriers that have been exempted from economic regulation through provisions in various pieces of legislation; the appropriate rates and services must be negotiated directly between the carrier and user. For example, the Transportation Act of 1940, which brought domestic water carriers under economic regulation, exempted liquid bulk commodities from economic regulation, as well as dry-bulk commodities, so long as no more than three dry-bulk commodities were moved in a particular tow.[25] In a similar fashion, the Motor Carrier Act of 1935, which brought motor carriers under economic regulation, exempted unprocessed agricultural commodities from economic regulation; the Motor Carrier Act of 1980, which lessened economic regulation for motor carriers, exempted agricultural seeds and plants from regulation.[26]

Private carriers, which are exempt from any economic regulation, are companies whose primary business is other than transportation and provide their own transportation service by operating trucks, railcars, barges, ships, or airplanes. Private transportation is most prevalent in the trucking industry, accounting for over 50 percent of the U.S. highway mileage for trucks.[27] Prominent private truckers in the United States include Wal-Mart, ExxonMobil, Kraft Foods, and Frito-Lay, among others.

One advantage to private transportation is that the equipment can serve as a rolling billboard that allows an organization to promote itself. Operational control is another advantage to private transportation, in part because shipments can move at a time convenient for the company, as opposed to a time that might be convenient for a for-hire carrier. Private transportation can also provide important competitive advantages to an organization. For example, many private truckers utilize their drivers as the organization's familiar and consistent face to their customers.[28]

---

[25] Harper, *Transportation in America.*
[26] Ibid.
[27] *http://www.nptc.org/index.php?option=com_content&task=view&id=45&Itemid=87.*
[28] Warren Payne, "Private Fleets Come Back," *World Trade*, June 2007, 20–24.

Although private transportation can be a cost-effective form of transportation, a key disadvantage is that it can be quite costly, in part because of the capital expenditures that are necessary to own or lease the relevant vehicles as well as regular expenditures to maintain the vehicles. Moreover, managerial costs are often ignored or underestimated; many private fleets require at least one full-time employee to manage the various responsibilities such as vehicle selection, vehicle maintenance, staffing, labor relations, regulatory compliance, and so on.

Summary

Transportation, the actual, physical movement of goods and people between two points, is pivotal to the success of any logistics or supply chain operation. The chapter started by comparing transportation infrastructures in several different countries and found dramatic infrastructural differences across the countries.

The chapter presented a discussion of the five modes of transportation in terms of each mode's capability, capacity, cost, flexibility, reliability, and speed. This mode-by-mode discussion was followed by a look at intermodal transportation, with a particular focus on containerization. The roles that can be played by transportation specialists such as freight forwarders and brokers were also examined.

The chapter discussed environmental regulation, safety regulation, and economic regulation as they apply to transportation. We learned that a number of U.S. federal agencies are responsible for transportation and also that the levels and types of regulation may not be consistent across modes. The chapter concluded with a look at the four legal classifications of carriers: common, contract, exempt, and private.

Questions for Discussion and Review

1. Why is transportation important to a firm's supply chain operations?
2. Why is it important to know about the characteristics of a country's transportation infrastructure?
3. Discuss the speed of airfreight transportation in terms of its line-haul and accessorial service.
4. Why is the reliability of airfreight transportation somewhat problematic?
5. How do truckload operations differ from less-than-truckload operations?
6. How do speed limits and hours-of-service rules potentially affect motor carrier service?
7. What are advantages and disadvantages to a pipeline's lack of vehicles?
8. What are pipeline slurry systems? How do they function?
9. Discuss the drawbacks to rail transportation.
10. How do weather conditions influence the reliability of inland water carriers?
11. Discuss the positive attributes of inland water transportation.
12. How do containers help to facilitate intermodal transportation?
13. What are freight forwarders? How do they function? What services do they perform?
14. What is a shippers' association?
15. Discuss the various options that are available to parcel shippers.
16. List several environmental regulations and describe their impact on transportation.
17. Pick three modes of transportation, name the federal agency responsible for safety regulation for each of the modes you've picked, and provide a safety-related role or responsibility for each mode.
18. Define what is meant by economic regulation. Why is transportation economic deregulation important?
19. How does a common carrier differ from a contract carrier?
20. Discuss advantages and disadvantages to private transportation.

Suggested Readings

Coyle, John J., Edward J. Bardi, and Robert A. Novack. *Transportation*. 6th ed. (Mason, OH: South-Western, 2006).

Farris II, M. Theodore, and Terrance L. Pohlen. "Evaluating the Private Fleet." *Transportation Journal* 47, no. 4 (2008): 51–66.

Hull, Bradley Z. "Oil Pipeline Markets and Operations." *Journal of the Transportation Research Forum* 44, no. 2 (2005): 111–127.

Hurst, D. Michael. "Surface Transportation's Regulatory Roller Coaster." *Journal of Transportation Law, Logistics and Policy* 73, no. 2 (2006): 180–219.

Koetse, Mark J., and Piet Rietveld. "The Impact of Climate Change and Weather on Transport: An Overview of Empirical Findings." *Transportation Research Part D* 14, no. 4 (2009): 205–221.

Levinson, Mark. *The Box: How the Shipping Container Made the World Smaller and the World Economy Bigger* (Princeton, NJ: Princeton University Press, 2006).

Lin, Pei-Chun, and Chia-Hui Lee. "How Online Vendors Select Parcel Delivery Carriers." *Transportation Journal* 48, no. 3 (2009): 20–31.

Medda, Francesca, and Gianni Carbonaro. "Growth of Container Seaborne Traffic in the Mediterranean Basin: Outlook and Policy Implications for Port Development." *Transport Reviews* 27, no. 5 (2007): 573–587.

Neiberger, Cordula. "The Effects of Deregulation, Changed Customer Requirements and New Technology on the Organisation and Spatial Patterns of the Air Freight Sector in Europe." *Journal of Transport Geography* 16, no. 4 (2008): 247–256.

Nordhaus, Robert R., and Emily Pitlick. "Carbon Dioxide Pipeline Regulation." *Energy Law Journal* 30, no. 1 (2009): 85–103.

Turner, Will, and Katrina Savitskie. "Freight Forwarding: Benefits and Implications for Managers." *IFCAI Journal of Supply Chain Management* 5, no. 2 (2008): 58–67.

Ullman, John E. "Railroad Safety: An Unfinished Investment." *Journal of Transportation Law, Logistics & Policy* 74, no. 1 (2007): 110–123.

CASE

CASE 12-1   HDT Truck Company

HDT Truck Company has been located in Crown Point, Indiana, since 1910. Its only products—large trucks—are built to individual customer specifications. The firm once produced automobiles but dropped out of the auto business in 1924. The firm nearly went out of business in the late 1930s, but by 1940 its fortunes were buoyed by receipt of several military contracts for tank retrievers—large-wheeled vehicles that can pull a disabled tank onto a low trailer and haul it to a location where it can be repaired.

Since World War II, HDT had manufactured only large off-road vehicles, including airport snowplows, airport crash trucks, oil-field drilling equipment, and the like. HDT purchased all components from small manufacturers that were still clustered in the Milwaukee–Detroit–Toledo–Cleveland area. Essentially, all HDT did was assemble components into specialized vehicles containing the combinations of frame, power plant, transmission, axles, cab, and other equipment necessary to do the job. The assembly line was relatively slow. After wheels were attached to the frame and axles, the night shift labor force would push the chassis along to its next station on the line so it would be in place for the next day's shift. By using one shift, two trucks could be assembled each day. If large orders for identical trucks were involved, it was possible to assemble three trucks per day. Quality declined whenever the pace became quicker. HDT officials had decided they could not grow and became satisfied with their niche in the very heavy–truck market. With only two exceptions, since 1970, HDT had always had at least a four-month backlog of orders. In the 1960s, its best market had been airports, but since 1980 its best market had been for oil-field equipment, first

for the North Slope in Alaska and then for the Middle East. The U.S. military was also a regular customer.

In late 2002, HDT received an order for 50 heavy trucks to be used in the oil fields of Saudi Arabia. The terms of sale were delivery on or before July 1, 2003, at the Port of Doha, Saudi Arabia. Specifically, HDT would receive $172,000 per truck in U.S. funds FAS (free alongside ship) at the discharging vessel in Doha, which meant that HDT was responsible for all transportation costs up until the time and point the trucks were discharged from the ship's tackle at Doha. Once each truck was unloaded, HDT would be paid for it.

Chris Reynolds, production manager at HDT, estimated that production could start approximately April 1, 2003, and the order would take 18 working days to complete. Because weekends were involved, all 50 trucks would be completed by April 20–25. Reynolds thought that May 1, 2003, was a more realistic completion date because he had always found it difficult to restrict the assembly line to constructing trucks for only one account. The reason for this was that Vic Guillou, HDT's sales manager, liked to have trucks being built for as many accounts as possible on the assembly line at any one time. Prospective buyers frequently visited the plant and were always more impressed when they could see a diverse collection of models being built for a wide range of uses.

Norman Pon, HDT's treasurer, wanted to give priority to building trucks that were being sold on an FOB plant basis because that would improve his cash flow position. At the time the $172,000 price had been set on the truck sale to Saudi Arabia, Pon had argued (unsuccessfully) that the price was too low. Guillou, on the other hand, argued that the sale was necessary because the Arab world represented a growth market by anyone's definition, and he wanted HDT trucks there. HDT's president, Gordon Robertson, had sided with Guillou. Robertson thought that Pon was a good treasurer but too much of a worrier when it came to making important decisions. Pon, in turn, thought that Robertson had yet to shed the image he had acquired in the 1980s when his late father was president of HDT. Pon had lost count of the number of times the elder Robertson had needed cash to buy his son's way out of some embarrassing situation. Guillou was young Robertson's fraternity roommate in college, and Pon thought the two of them shared a similar love of life in the fast lane. At the time the order was signed in 2002, Guillou argued that the FAS destination port represented the best terms of sale because ocean charter rates were declining as a result of an oversupply of tonnage. Guillou predicted that by mid-2003 charter rates would be so low that the cheapest method of transport would be to load all 50 trucks on one vessel. Pon countered that HDT should try to make a profit only from the manufacture of trucks because nobody in the firm knew much about ocean shipping. Robertson, who was a gambler at heart, disagreed.

In March 2003, Reynolds had the 50-truck order scheduled to be on the line from April 2 to April 29, which represented 2.5 trucks per working day. Other work was scheduled for the assembly line at the same time, so the production schedule was considered firm. Component parts for the oil-field trucks and for the other trucks were already arriving. Orders were backlogged for over seven months, the highest figure since 1989. This was due, almost in total, to Guillou's additional sales of oil-field equipment to Arab producers. Three separate orders were involved and totaled 115 trucks.

Robertson and Guillou left Crown Point for an industry convention in San Diego. Robertson phoned from San Diego that he and Guillou had decided to vacation in Mexico for a while before returning to Crown Point. Robertson knew that HDT could function in his absence and knew that with Pon overseeing operations, the company's assets would be safe. Several days later, a Mexican postcard postmarked in Tijuana arrived, saying that both were enjoying Mexico and would stay longer than initially planned.

Pon was relieved to learn that Guillou and Robertson would be gone for a longer time and immediately began wondering what types of bills they were accumulating in Mexico and for which ones they would want company reimbursement. Both had several credit cards belonging to the company. Based on experience, Pon also expected Robertson to phone on his cell phone for a cash advance or transfer about once a week. (Robertson did not want charge records generated for some of his expenses.) As usual, Pon started wondering how paying for the Robertson and Guillou vacation venture would affect HDT's cash flow. Pon looked at his cash flow projections, which were always made up for six weeks in advance, in this case through the first of April, when some of the bills for components of the oil-field trucks would come due. In fact, if Reynolds's schedule were adhered to, all the components would be on hand by April 10 and, if HDT were to receive the customary discounts, all of the components would have to be paid for in the period between April 8 and April 20 (HDT received a 1 percent discount for goods paid for within 10 days of actual or requested receipt, whichever came later). For a moment, Pon thought that the worst might happen: The component bills would be due at the same time as Robertson's and Guillou's request for a hefty cash advance. He called the Crown Point Bank and Trust Company, where HDT had a line of credit, and learned that the current rate was 8 percent per annum. He then asked Bob Vanderpool, who was HDT's traffic manager, when the oil-field trucks would arrive in Saudi Arabia.

"I don't know," was Vanderpool's reply. "I assumed that Guillou had arranged for transportation at the time you decided to charge $172,000 per truck, but I'll check further." He did and phoned back to tell Pon that Guillou's secretary could find nothing in the files to indicate that Guillou had checked out charter rates. "That figures," muttered Pon. "Would you mind doing some checking?" Vanderpool said he *would* mind doing some checking. Pon then suggested to him that there were several other newer orders also destined for the Arab countries so Vanderpool should start thinking about widening his area of expertise. Vanderpool reluctantly agreed, and Pon heard nothing until Vanderpool passed him in the hall a few days later and said the assignment was much more time consuming than he had imagined. One week later, Vanderpool said he had done as much as he could and would turn the figures over to Pon. Vanderpool also said that he did not have the authority to charter a ship and suggested that Pon determine who could do so in Robertson's absence. Later that day, Vanderpool came to Pon's office with a thick file.

"It looks like you've been doing a lot of figuring," said Pon.

"No, not me," said Vanderpool, "but two outsiders. One is Bob Guider, an international freight forwarder in Chicago whom we use for our export parts shipments. And he put me in touch with Eddie Quan, a New York ship broker who is on top of the charter market. We have two alternatives."

"What are they?" asked Pon.

"Well," answered Vanderpool, "the St. Lawrence Seaway will open in mid-April, so we could use it. The problem is that the Seaway route is circuitous, especially to reach the Arab countries. Also, there aren't many scheduled Seaway sailings to that area, and because the Seaway will just be opening again, cargo space is hard to come by. Therefore, if we're not going to charter a ship, the best bet is to use Baltimore."

"What about chartering a ship?" asked Pon. "Why not use Baltimore for that?"

"In theory, we could," answered Vanderpool. "But Quan says the size of ship we want is rather small and not likely to be sailing into Baltimore. We could arrange to share a ship with another party, but many bulk cargoes are pretty dusty and might not be compatible with our vehicles. Quan says there is one foreign vessel entering the Great Lakes in April that is still looking for an outbound charter. Seaway vessels, you know, are smaller because of the lock size restrictions. If we want to charter that vessel, we'll have to move quickly, because if somebody else charters her, she's gone."

"What kind of vessel is it?" asked Pon.

"The vessel's name is the *Nola Pino*, the same name as a French movie actress of the 1960s. You may recall that some Greek shipping magnate named the vessel after her, but his wife made him give up both Nola Pino the actress and *Nola Pino* the ship. At present, it's scheduled to be in Chicago the last week in April with a load of cocoa beans and ready for outbound loading May 1. Quan thinks we could charter it for $2,400 per day for 30 days, which would be enough time for it to load, transit the Seaway, reach Doha, and discharge the trucks by May 29 or 30."

"Tell me about the alternative," said Pon.

"Baltimore has fairly frequent sailings to the area we want to reach," said Vanderpool. "We could load two trucks per day on railcars here and send them to Baltimore. Two ships a week are scheduled from Baltimore to Doha. It would take the trucks an average of 4 days to reach Baltimore, where they would wait an average of 3 days to be loaded aboard ship. The figure should be 3.5 days, but the railroad will hustle if it knows we're trying to connect with an outgoing sailing. Sailing time to Doha averages

15 days—a little more, a little less, depending on the amount of cargo to be handled at ports in between."

"That averages 22 days per truck," stated Pon, who had been putting the figures in his calculator. "What are the charges?"

Vanderpool answered, "It costs $120 to load and block two trucks on a flatcar, which is, of course, $60 apiece as long as they move in pairs. Sticking to pairs, the rail rate for two on a flatcar totals $1,792 to Baltimore. Handling at Baltimore is $200 per truck, and ocean freight rate from Baltimore to Doha is $1,440 per truck. We also have to buy insurance, which is about $150 per truck."

"That totals $2,790," said Pon, after consulting his calculator. "What are the costs if we charter the *Nola Pino*? You said it could be $72,000 for the vessel. What else is involved?"

"There are two ways of getting the trucks to port," said Vanderpool. "The loading and blocking would be only $40 per truck because we'd be doing all 50 at one time. The rail rate per truck would average out to $180 each, and it would take 1 day for them to reach Chicago and another day to be loaded. We'd be tying up a wharf for 1 day, and the wharfage charge runs $2 per foot, and the *Nola Pino* is 535 feet long. We'd be responsible for loading and stowing the cargo, and this would cost $4,000 for all 50 trucks. The Seaway tolls are $1.80 cents per ton or, in our case, $54 per truck. At Doha, the unloading costs will be $4,200 for the entire vessel. Marine insurance will be $210 per truck."

"Are there any other alternatives?" asked Pon.

"The only other one that comes close is to drive the trucks from here to Chicago," answered Vanderpool. "We would need temporary licenses and a convoy permit and pay to have the fuel tank on each truck drained before it is loaded. The problem is that the convoy would cross state lines, and we would need temporary licenses and permits in Illinois as well. We'd also need 50 drivers and have to pay for their time and for their trips back home."

"Do me one favor," said Pon. "Please call Frank Wood, our outside counsel, and ask him what steps we have to go through to charter a ship. Tell him I'm especially concerned about the liability. Give him Quan's phone number. I want to make sure there are no more costs involved. If Robertson's fooling around is on schedule, he'll be phoning me asking that I cable cash. I'd really appreciate it if you would summarize what you've told me in two columns, with the charter costs on the left and the overland Baltimore cost column on the right. Then when Robertson calls, I can ask him to decide."

EXHIBIT 12-A   **Map of the Northeastern United States**

"One question," asked Vanderpool.

"Shoot," responded Pon.

"Why should the charter figures be on the left?"

"Because on a map (see Exhibit 12-A), Chicago is to the left of Baltimore and that's the only way I'll keep them straight when I'm talking on the phone."

Questions

1. Assume you are Vanderpool. Draft the comparison Pon just requested.
2. Which of the two routing alternatives would you recommend? Why?
3. Assume that the buyer in Saudi Arabia has made other large purchases in the United States and is considering consolidating all its purchases and loading them onto one large ship, which the buyer will charter. The buyer contacts HDT and, although acknowledging its commitment to buy FAS Doha, asks how much HDT would subtract from the $172,000 per truck price if the selling terms were changed to FOB HDT's Crown Point plant. How much of a cost reduction do you think HDT should offer the buyer? Under what terms and conditions?
4. Answer Question 3 with regard to changing the terms of sale to delivery at port in Baltimore. The buyer would unload the trucks from the railcars.
5. Is there an interest rate that would make HDT change from one routing to another? If so, what is it?
6. Assume that the cost to HDT of borrowing money is 12 percent per year. Because the buyer will pay for trucks as they are delivered, would it be advantageous for HDT to pay overtime to speed up production, ship the trucks as they are finished via the Port of Baltimore, and collect its payment earlier? Why or why not?

13 | TRANSPORTATION MANAGEMENT

Key Terms

- Amodal shipper
- Bill of lading
- Class rate system
- Commodity rate
- Concealed loss or damage
- Demurrage
- Density

- Detention
- Documentation
- Expediting
- FOB destination
- FOB origin
- Freight bill
- Freight claims

- Rate
- Routing
- Routing guide
- Stowability
- Tracing
- Transportation management
- Weight break

Learning Objectives

- To learn about contemporary transportation management
- To understand how rates are determined
- To learn about modal and carrier selection
- To distinguish among various transportation documents
- To understand select activities associated with making and receiving shipments
- To learn about transportation service quality

The transportation manager's job is much different today than when the first edition of this text was published in the 1970s, in part because of globalization and changes in regulation. With respect to globalization, consider that in the 1970s the People's Republic of China (China) was in the midst of the Cultural Revolution, a movement that severely restricted the country's economic development as well as trade with other countries. Today, by contrast, China has the second-largest economy in the world (based on gross domestic product) and is a key source of manufactured products for many countries. The transportation requirements associated with a shipment of, say, toys, from Shanghai, China, to Des Moines, Iowa, are noticeably different than those for a shipment of toys from Cleveland, Ohio, to Des Moines.

As for changes in regulation, Chapter 12 pointed out that a reduction of economic regulation in the United States began in the late 1970s, and with it came greater options in terms of both pricing and service. These pricing and service options meant that transportation managers have morphed from a reactive to a proactive focus; rather than simply accepting the available pricing and service packages that were established by economic regulation (reactive), today's transportation manager can play an active role (proactive) in blending the appropriate pricing and service packages for an organization.

For our purposes, **transportation management** will refer to the buying and controlling of transportation services by either a shipper or consignee.[1] Today more than ever before, organizations are concerned about transportation management because transportation represents a major expense item. In general terms, freight transportation accounts for approximately 6 percent of U.S. gross domestic product. Moreover, as we've emphasized throughout, transportation is the most costly logistics activity for many organizations, and as pointed out in Chapter 12, transportation is pivotal to the successful operation of any supply chain.

Similar to Chapter 12, the discussion in this chapter will be approached from the perspective of the transportation manager in the United States. Again, it's important for readers to understand that a particular country's transportation system, along with the degree of government involvement in transportation, will influence the nature of transportation management in that country. For example, in some countries, there may be only one government-run transportation company in a particular mode; thus the transportation manager wouldn't need to be concerned with carrier selection considerations for that particular mode.

Although the majority of this chapter will focus on several of the transportation manager's key responsibilities, it should be pointed out that transportation managers are also involved with many other operations of the firm. They can assist marketing by quoting freight rates for salespeople, suggesting quantity discounts that can be based on transportation savings, and selecting carriers and routes for reliable delivery of products. Transportation managers can help manufacturing by advising on packaging and materials handling and making certain that an adequate supply of transportation is available when it is needed. Transportation managers can aid the outbound shipping process by providing simplified shipping or routing guides, drawing up transportation documents, and encouraging shipment consolidations. Finally, they can help purchasing by advising about methods to control the costs and quality of inbound deliveries and by tracing and expediting lost or delayed shipments of important inputs.

Our discussion in the remainder of the chapter will focus on some of a transportation manager's primary responsibilities. We'll first analyze rate (pricing) considerations, with a particular emphasis on rate determination. Next, the chapter will discuss modal and carrier selection, and this will be followed by a discussion of documentation considerations. The chapter also looks at making and receiving shipments and concludes with an examination of transportation service quality.

RATE (PRICING) CONSIDERATIONS

Rate Determination

As we've seen throughout this text, logistics has discipline-specific terminology, and to this end, one key responsibility of transportation managers involves rate considerations, with **rate** being the logistics term that signifies the price charged for freight transportation ("fare" refers to the prices charged for passenger transportation). When the first edition of this book was published in the 1970s, all rates appeared in tariffs (a book that contained published freight rates), and it wasn't uncommon to have to refer to multiple tariffs to find the applicable rate. Rate determination is essential to calculating the appropriate transportation cost, according to the following formula:

$$\text{Weight} \times \text{rate} = \text{transportation charge}$$

The changes in economic regulation discussed in Chapter 12 have had a profound impact on rate determination. Tariff requirements have been greatly relaxed, if not eliminated altogether; as a result, carriers, users, and transportation specialists can exchange pricing data via electronic

---

[1] John J. Coyle, Edward J. Bardi, and Robert A. Novack, *Transportation*, 6th ed. (Mason, OH: South-Western, 2006).

means, including electronic data interchange (EDI) and e-mail. In many cases, transportation rates are now available on carrier Web sites.

Although the rate determination process today is vastly different than in the 1970s, it continues to be based on long-standing freight rate determination practices. More specifically, transportation rates are based on three primary factors—product, weight, and distance— which will be discussed next:

- Relationships between *different products*, in terms of their handling characteristics, for example, the difference between carrying 2,000 pounds of ballpoint pens and 2,000 pounds of live chickens
- Relationships between shipments of *different weights*, for example, shipments of 10 pounds each versus shipments of 1,000 pounds each versus shipments of 10,000 pounds each
- Relationships between *different distances* the products are carried, for example, from Boston, Massachusetts, to Albany, New York, versus from Atlanta, Georgia, to Spokane, Washington

Rate determination has to define all three relations in numeric form and then has to devise methods of tying those numbers into a rate for a specific shipment. The three relationships just mentioned are of continual importance to the transportation manager because if they are altered, the total transportation charges will be altered.

One approach to rate making is to determine one specific rate for every possible combination of product, weight, and distance—in other words, a **commodity rate**. Although a commodity rate is very good for dealing with demand-specific situations, the number of commodity rates quickly becomes overwhelming (and potentially counterproductive) when you consider how many different products, weights, and distances exist. For example, because there are over 30,000 "important" shipping and receiving points in the United States, in the commodity rate system there would need to be separate rates for all possible combinations of shipping and receiving points—a number that is in the trillions of trillions![2]

When you consider that the transportation rate structure dates to the time of economic regulation in the late 1800s—a time when "office automation" might have meant a *manual typewriter*—it becomes clear that the transportation community needed a way to simplify rate determination. This was accomplished through the **class rate system**, which simplified each of the three primary rate factors—product, weight, and distance. One widely used system for simplifying the number of products is the National Motor Freight Classification (NMFC), which has 18 separate ratings, or classes, from 50 to 500[3]; the higher the rating, the greater the relative charge for transporting the commodity. Classification numbers are very important because they are code words that describe cargo in a manner that carriers and shippers understand, and classification descriptions also specify the packaging that must be used and that carriers require. Figure 13-1 shows a page of the NMFC; note the detail. *NOI* stands for "not otherwise indexed by number" (i.e., one cannot find a definition that fits more closely). Packages are referred to by number; they are described in great detail in the classification document.

Four factors are used to determine a product's freight classification, namely, *density, stowability, ease of handling*, and *liability to damage and theft*. **Density**, which refers to how heavy a product is in relation to its size, is viewed as the primary factor for setting a product's classification, in part because of the opportunity costs associated with it. That is, a product with low density (i.e., low weight per cubic foot), such as foam rubber, can easily fill a vehicle's usable capacity (cubing out) before the reaching the maximum weight (weighing out). As a result, low-density products are assigned a higher classification; for example, at the time of this book's publication, products with densities of less than one pound per cubic foot are assigned to Class 400.[4]

[2] Ibid.
[3] *http://www.nmfta.org/Pages/Nmfc.aspx.*
[4] *http://www.nmfta.org/Documents/CCSB/CCSB%20Policies%202009.pdf.*

NATIONAL MOTOR FREIGHT CLASSIFICATION 100-AB

ITEM	ARTICLES	CLASS
	GLASS: subject to item 86500	
86700	**Glass,** flat, see Note, item 86736, NOI:	
86720	Bent, NOI, in boxes or crates:	
Sub 1	220 united inches or less; when in shipments weighing less than 30,000 pounds, see Note, item 86512	85
Sub 2	Exceeding 220 united inches but not exceeding 15 feet in length nor 9 feet in breadth; when in shipments weighing less than 24,000 pounds, see Note, item 86512.	100
Sub 3	Exceeding 15 feet in length or 9 feet in breadth; when in shipments weighing less than 24,000 pounds, see Note, item 86512	250
86730	Not bent, see Note, item 86731, in boxes, crates or Packages 195, 198, 235, 785, 2008, 2025, 2147, 2149, 2160, 2239, 2245, 2281 or 2497; when in shipments weighing less than 40,000 pounds, see Note, item 86512:	
Sub 1	220 united inches or less, see Note, item 86737	65
Sub 2	Exceeding 220 united inches but not exceeding 15 feet in length nor 9 feet in breadth	100
Sub 3	Exceeding 15 feet in length or 9 feet in breadth.	200
86731	NOTE—Flat glass, not bent, may also be cut to size, edges beveled or ground, or holes cut or drilled.	
86736	NOTE—The term 'flat' applies to glass known as sheet, plate, polished prism, rolled, window or float glass, whether or not polished, laminated, colored, opalescent, opaque, chipped, decorated, wired, etched, figured, acid dipped, ground, sandblasted, metalized (sprayed with atomized metal while glass is hot) or tempered, but not when silvered for mirrors, nor flashed, nor framed or leaded (set in or framed by lead or other metal).	
86737	NOTE—Provisions will also apply on shipments weighing 40,000 pounds or more when glass is shipped on its flat surface in wooden boxes on pallets.	
86750	**Glass,** leaded, see Note, item 86752; when in shipments weighing less than 24,000 pounds, see Note, item 86512:	
Sub 1	With landscape, pictorial or religious designs, packed in boxes	200
Sub 2	With curved, angled or straight line patterns, or with designs other than landscape, pictorial or religious, in boxes	100
86752	NOTE—The term 'leaded glass' means glass either colored or clear, set in lead or in other metal.	
86770	**Glass,** microscopical slide or cover, see Note, item 86771, in boxes; when in shipments weighing less than 36,000 pounds, see Note, item 86512	70
86771	NOTE—Does not apply on microscope slides or slide cover glasses. Applies only on the glass from which these articles are manufactured.	
86830	**Glass,** rolled, overlaid with aluminum strips with metal terminals attached, in boxes or crates; when in shipments weighing less than 30,000 pounds, see Note, item 86512.	77.5
86840	**Glass,** rolled, overlaid with aluminum strips, NOI, in boxes or crates; when in shipments weighing less than 36,000 pounds, see Note, item 86512	70
86900	**Glass,** silvered for mirrors, not framed, nor backed nor equipped with hangers or fastening devices:	
Sub 1	Shock (window glass, silvered), in boxes, see Note, item 86902; when in shipments weighing less than 30,000 pounds, see Note, item 86512	85
Sub 2	Other than shock glass, in packages shown:	
Sub 3	Bent; when in shipments weighing less than 24,000 pounds, see Note, item 86512:	
Sub 4	Not exceeding 15 feet in length nor 9 feet in breadth, in boxes	100
Sub 5	Exceeding 15 feet in length or 9 feet in breadth, in boxes	250
Sub 6	Not bent, see Package 785:	
Sub 7	120 united inches or less, in boxes, crates or Packages 198 or 235; when in shipments weighing less than 30,000 pounds, see Note, item 86512	70
Sub 8	Exceeding 120 united inches but not exceeding 15 feet in length or 9 feet in breadth, in boxes or crates; when in shipments weighing less than 40,000 pounds, see Note, item 86512	100
Sub 9	Exceeding 15 feet in length or 9 feet in breadth, in boxes or crates; when in shipments weighing less than 40,000 pounds, see Note, item 86512	200
86902	NOTE—Glass, silvered for mirrors, which has been framed or backed, or equipped with hangers or fastening devices, is subject to the classes for mirrors, NOI.	
86940	**Glass,** window, other than plate, with metal edging other than sash or frames, in boxes; when in shipments weighing less than 30,000 pounds, see Note, item 86512.	77.5
86960	**Glazing Units,** glass, not in sash, see Note, item 86966, in boxes, crates or Packages 2149 or 2281; when in shipments weighing less than 30,000 pounds, see Note, item 86512	70
86966	NOTE—Applies on units consisting of sheets of glass separated by air or vacuum, sealed at all edges with same or other materials.	
87100	**Glass Factory Flattening Stones, Floats, Gathering Rings or Pot Rings or Glasshouse Pots,** clay; in boxes, crates, drums or on skids; or loose when weighing each 2,500 pounds or more packed in packing material and securely braced	85
87500	**GLASSWARE GROUP:** Articles consist of Glassware or Glass Articles, see Note, item 87512, as described in items subject to this grouping.	
87512	NOTE—All articles of glassware which are plated, mounted or trimmed with gold or silver will be subject to the provisions provided for glassware, gold or silver deposit, gold or silver mounted or gold or silver trimmed.	
87520	**Ampoules (Ampuls),** in boxes, drums or Package 2362	100
87540	**Aquariums or Terrariums,** capacity over ½ gallon, see Note, item 87552, in boxes, crates or drums:	
Sub 1	Each in individual fibre box, two or more smaller sizes nested within one larger.	85
Sub 2	NOI.	150
87550	**Aquariums or Terrariums,** NOI, capacity ½ gallon or less, see Note, item 87552, in boxes, crates or drums	100
87552	NOTE—Applies only on aquariums or terrariums constructed with metal or plastic frames.	
87560	**Aquariums or Terrariums,** glass, with plastic frames, disassembled into panels, in boxes	70
87570	**Ballotini (Decorative Glass Globules),** in boxes	85
87590	**Balls,** lightning rod, in boxes or drums.	85

Only participants in the NMFC at the time the transportation occurs may use this publication.
For explanation of abbreviations and reference marks, see last page of this Classification. ©ATA 2001

422

FIGURE 13-1   Page from National Motor Freight Classification
Source: Reprinted from the National Motor Freight Classification © ATA 2002.

Stowability refers to how easy the commodity is to pack into a load, and possible considerations involve the commodity's ability to be loaded with hazardous materials and ability to load freight on top of the commodity. *Ease or difficulty of handling* refers to challenges to handling that might be presented by a commodity's size, weight, and so on. Finally, the *liability for loss and* *damage* considers, among others, a commodity's propensity to damage other freight, its perishability, and its value.[5]

Just as the freight classification is used to simplify the number of commodities, shipment weight is simplified through weight groups (e.g., less than 500 pounds; 500–999 pounds; 1,000–1,999 pounds). The rate for shipments weighing less than 500 pounds will be higher than that for shipments between 500–999 pounds, and so on. Distances are simplified in a similar fashion; historically, distances were classified according to a rate basis number, and the higher the rate basis number, the greater the distance between origin and destination. Increasingly, rate basis numbers are being replaced by the zip codes of a particular shipment's origin and destination.

An example of rate determination using the class rate system is presented in Table 13-1. Before proceeding with a discussion of the class rate system, note that the rates are expressed in terms of hundredweight (100 pounds), rather than per pound. Shipment 1 in Table 13-1 will serve as our reference point for looking at changes in commodity classification, weight, and distance.

As shown in Table 13-1, the commodity classification is the only difference between Shipment 1 (class 100) and Shipment 2 (class 200). As pointed out earlier, a higher class rating takes a higher rate, and Shipment 2's rate per hundredweight ($386.42) is exactly twice as much as Shipment 1's rate. With respect to the class rate system and weight, Shipment 1 weighs 500 pounds versus 1,500 for Shipment 3, and the rate per hundredweight is lower for Shipment 3 than for Shipment 1. Finally, Shipments 1 and 4 differ in terms of the destination zip code, and because Shipment 4 is traveling much further than Shipment 1, Shipment 4's rate per hundredweight is substantially higher.

A commodity's freight classification is developed and maintained by the Commodity Classification Standards Board, which consists of at least three but no more than seven full-time employees of the National Motor Freight Traffic Association. There is often a natural tension between shippers and carriers with respect to a product's classification; shippers tend to prefer a lower classification number (which translates into a lower rate), whereas carriers tend to prefer a higher classification number. Transportation managers can appeal a commodity's classification; Figure 13-2 shows an excerpt from a proposal to adopt new classifications for sparkplugs. The present classification is described first in the figure, and then the proposal is shown. Figure 13-3 shows an applicant's completed worksheet for submission to the classification committee.

Note that Figure 13-2 contains the notations "LTL," "TL," and "MW," and each has a number underneath it. If we look at the first listing in Figure 13-2, Item 177080 Sub 1, we see the number 100 associated with less-than-truckload (LTL), the number 55 associated with truckload (TL), and the number 24 associated with minimum weight (MW). This indicates that the product is Class 100 for LTL shipments and Class 55 for TL shipments. The number 24 indicates that the TL rate can be applied at a shipment weight of 24,000 pounds.

TABLE 13-1 Example of the Class Rate System

Shipment	Commodity Classification	Weight (pounds)	Distance (using zip codes)	Rate Per Hundredweight (cwt)[a]
1	Class 100	500	44023 to 32169	$193.21
2	Class 200	500	44023 to 32169	$386.42
3	Class 100	1,500	44023 to 32169	$163.57
4	Class 100	500	44023 to 90210	$592.15

[a]Rates are representative as of late 2009.

Source: Data derived from a sample rate calculator for Con-Way Freight, *https://www.con-way.com/webapp/rating_p_app/RatingOptions.jsp?timeout=.*

[5] Ibid.

PROPOSED

PRESENT CLASSIFICATION: (Show specific NMFC item number and description under which commodity is now being classified.)

ITEM NO.	DESCRIPTION	LTL	TL	MW

PRESENT

ITEM NO.	DESCRIPTION	LTL	TL	MW
177080	**Spark Plugs**, NOI, in boxes:			
Sub 1	Card mounted, blister packed or skin packed	100	55	24
Sub 2	Other than card mounted, blister packed or skin packed	85	45	30

PROPOSED AMENDMENTS: (Show description, classes and MW exactly as you propose them to be established in the Classification.)

ITEM NO.	DESCRIPTION	LTL	TL	MW

PROPOSED

ITEM NO.	DESCRIPTION	LTL	TL	MW
177080	**Spark Plugs**, NOI, in boxes:			
Sub 1	Card mounted, blister packed or skin packed	100	55	24
Sub 2	Other than card mounted, blister packed or skin packed :			
>Sub 3	Density less than 30 pounds per cubic foot; or actual value exceeding $6.00 per pound; or where no density or value is shown at time of shipment	85	45	30
>Sub 4	Density in pounds per cubic foot of 30 or greater, and actual value not exceeding $6.00 per pound, see Note, item NEW	70	37.5	36
NEW	NOTE -- Shipper must certify on shipping orders and bills of lading at time of shipment that density is 30 pounds or greater per cubic foot and that the actual value per pound does not exceed $6.00.			

JUSTIFICATION: Due to the density, value per pound and ease of handling of the involved commodities, the proposed changes are warranted.

_____

_____

_____

If you have any questions regarding the proper execution of these forms or require technical assistance please contact our staff at (703) 838-1869.

FIGURE 13-2 **Motor Carrier Classification Docket Proposal for Changing the Classification of Sparkplugs**

Source: Permission to reproduce this material has been granted by the National Motor Freight Traffic Association, Inc.

The fact that the LTL classification number is higher than the TL classification number means that the LTL rate will be higher than the corresponding TL rate. When combined with an MW requirement, this suggests that it is possible to reduce transportation costs by sending an LTL shipment as if it met the minimum requirement for a TL rate. This illustrates the **weight break** concept, that is, the shipment size that equates transportation charges for different rates and weight groups. Although typically applied to the LTL and TL trade-off, the weight break concept can be applied whenever rates differ by volume and an MW is specified for the higher volume classification.

The formula for calculating the weight break is as follows:

$$\text{Higher volume rate} \times \text{minimum weight} = \text{lower volume rate} \times \text{weight break}$$

Suppose, for example, that the LTL rate is $1.25 per cwt (hundredweight), the TL rate is $.80 per cwt, and the TL minimum is 25,000 pounds. The weight break is

$$\$.80 \text{ per cwt} \times 250 \text{ cwt} = \$1.25 \text{ per cwt} \times \text{weight break}$$
$$\$200 = \$1.25 \text{ per cwt} \times \text{weight break}$$
$$160 \text{ cwt} = \text{weight break}$$

TRANSPORTATION CHARACTERISTICS

I. **DENSITY:** (Please base your calculations on the exterior dimensions and the shipping weight of the commodity as packaged for shipment.)

Model	Description of Package	Length	Width	Height	Weight	Density*
Spark	packaged individually,	38"	38"	42"	1280 #	36.5
plugs	then packaged into cartons					
(boxed)	of 10, then packaged into					
	cartons of 100. Shipped					
	in master cartons on skids.					

*To determine the density (pounds per cubic foot), multiply the three dimensions of the article as packed for shipment. If the result is in cubic inches, divide by 1728 to convert to cubic feet. Then divide the weight by the cubic feet. To determine the cubic feet of space occupied by a drum, pail, or other cylindrical container, square the greatest diameter and multiply that result by the height or length. If the package is of irregular shape, use the greatest dimensions, including all projections.

II. **LIABILITY**

1) Claim value per package (Please match the models with those reported under **DENSITY**)

Model	Description of Package	Weight	Dollar Amount	Value Per Pound
Spark	packaged individually,	1280 #	$7200	$5.63
plugs	then packaged into cartons			
(boxed)	of 10, then packaged into			
	cartons of 100. Shipped			
	in master cartons on skids.			

2) Does the commodity require temperature control? __NO__

3) Is the commodity subject to U.S. Department of Transportation Regulations governing hazardous materials?
Yes ___ No _XX_ If yes, what HMT commodity description and label are required?
_____

4) Does commodity have protruding edges? __NO__

5) Is commodity liquid _NO_ dry _NO_ paste _NO_

FIGURE 13-3 Worksheet for Motor Carrier Classification Docket Proposal for Changing the Classification of Sparkplugs

Source: Permission to reproduce this material has been granted by the National Motor Freight Traffic Association, Inc.

In other words, the transportation costs ($200) for the LTL and TL rates are equal at 160 cwt, or 16,000 pounds. As such, if the actual shipment weight is less than 16,000 pounds, then the LTL rate should be applied, while shipments weighing between 16,000 and 24,999 pounds should be sent at the TL weight of 25,000 pounds.

Although the freight classification system might appear to be arcane and ill-suited to today's highly computerized world, approximately 950 motor carriers, ranging from nationwide truckers to local delivery companies, currently use the NMFC. Moreover, even though today's transportation pricing system is much different than that existed under economic regulation, the NMFC can provide a starting point for price negotiations between carriers and shippers.[6]

Rate and Service Negotiations

As pointed out earlier in the chapter, the contemporary transportation manager is much less constrained by rate and service regulations and thus has the opportunity to assume a proactive role in rate and service negotiations. Today's transportation manager can craft rate and service packages that best meet an organization's logistical needs, and these rate and service packages can conceivably vary from product to product, location to location, or customer to customer.

The rate and service flexibility afforded by economic deregulation allows transportation managers to take advantage of trade-offs between price and service, and these price and service trade-offs are limited only by the transportation manager's creativity and ingenuity. Consider the following two examples from the railroad industry. In one case, the shipping organization agreed to pay the railroad a premium for each railcar that was delivered on a precise, previously agreed-upon schedule. In the second case, an organization agreed to ship six million pounds of intermodal freight each year between Houston and Chicago. The shipper agreed to pay the railroad an additional $75 per trailer when at least 90 percent of the trailers completed the rail movement within 96 hours. Although these two examples illustrate situations where monetary premiums were paid for meeting predetermined service standards, the rate and service negotiations can also include *monetary penalties* for failure to achieve predetermined service standards.

It is not possible to present a comprehensive list of all possible rate and service items that might by negotiated by shippers and carriers. However, Table 13-2 contains a representative list of items that might be used in the negotiation process.

TERMS OF SALE

One consideration in rate and service negotiations involves the terms of sale, or when the freight charges are paid for a particular domestic shipment. Free on board (FOB) is followed by either "origin" or "destination," and this location specifies the point at which the title and control of a shipment passes from buyer to seller. With **FOB origin**, the buyer assumes title and

TABLE 13-2	Representative Rate and Service Items in the Carrier–Shipper Negotiation Process	
Adjustment to rates	Arbitration	Articles and commodities covered
Audit rights	Basis for charges	Billing procedures
Carrier equipment and drivers	Carrier insurance	Carrier notification requirements
Detention time	Duration of agreement	Estimated transportation volume
How loss and damage claims are handled	Lead times	Pallet loading
Proof of delivery	Renegotiation and reopening of contract	Schedule of rates and charges
Termination of agreement	Transportation service level	Waiver of terms

---

[6] Ibid.

control of a shipment at the point of pickup, while with **FOB destination** the seller retains title and control of a shipment until it is delivered.

FOB origin and FOB destination are typically qualified by modifying terms, the most common of which are *freight collect, freight prepaid*, and *freight prepaid and charged back.* Using FOB origin and FOB destination in conjunction with these modifiers results in six possible payment options (terms of sale), which are described below.[7]

- *FOB origin, freight collect:* The buyer pays freight charges and owns the goods in transit.
- *FOB origin, freight prepaid:* The seller pays the freight charges, but the buyer owns the goods in transit.
- *FOB origin, freight prepaid and charged back:* The seller pays the freight charges in advance but bills the buyer for them. The buyer owns the goods in transit.
- *FOB destination, freight prepaid:* The seller pays the freight charges and also owns the goods in transit.
- *FOB destination, freight collect:* The buyer pays the freight charges when the goods arrive, and the seller owns the goods while they are in transit.
- *FOB destination, freight prepaid and charged back:* The seller owns the goods in transit, prepays the freight charges, and bills the buyer for the freight charges.

In addition to establishing the point at which title for a shipment passes from buyer to seller, the FOB location term also establishes which party is responsible for arranging transportation for a shipment as well as which party is responsible for filing freight claims (a topic that will be discussed later in this chapter). More specifically, under FOB origin the buyer is responsible for arranging transportation as well as for filing freight claims; under FOB destination, the seller is responsible for arranging transportation as well as for filing freight claims.

The transportation responsibilities associated with FOB origin and FOB destination have important implications for transportation management. For example, an advantage of FOB destination from the seller's perspective is that the seller controls transportation and can assure a more uniform transportation outcome for each buyer. Alternatively, a disadvantage of FOB destination from a seller's perspective is that the seller's organization must have a thorough knowledge of transportation management (e.g., rate and service negotiations, modal and carrier selection), and this knowledge is not learned in a short period of time.

TRANSPORTATION COST ANALYSIS

Another consideration in rate and service negotiation involves transportation cost analysis, which can be especially valuable in the shipment consolidation decision. Because transportation costs tend to be lower per unit of weight for larger shipments, there is a natural motivation to consolidate smaller shipments into larger ones. Having said this, shipment consolidation decisions affect other logistical activities such as warehousing and inventory management.

Transportation cost analysis continues to be facilitated by advances in information technology. Some trucking companies, for example, can examine inbound or outbound deliveries for a representative period of time using data gathered from a customer's paid freight bills. This can allow both the carrier and the customer to determine whether individual shipments or shipment patterns can be improved. Moreover, it's also possible to conduct sensitivity analysis to determine the transportation costs for varying levels of transportation service. Although sensitivity analysis can provide insights about potential transportation cost savings if shifting from one service level to another, the sensitivity analysis does not estimate other relevant costs (e.g., unhappy customers because of slower transportation service).

---

[7] Ray Bohman, "Know the Terms of Sale," *Logistics Management*, October 2006, 26.

MODAL AND CARRIER SELECTION

Transportation managers have long been responsible for both modal and carrier selection; conceptually, modal and carrier selection is a two-step process where the transportation manager first determines the appropriate mode, or modes, to use and then selects a particular carrier, or carriers, within the chosen mode(s). At a minimum, an understanding of the modal characteristics presented in Chapter 12 would be helpful in the modal selection process.

Unfortunately, the carrier selection procedure is more challenging than that for modal selection, in part because there can be tens, hundreds, or even thousands of carriers from which to choose in a particular mode. It might not be realistic to expect a transportation manager to be aware of every possible carrier in a particular mode or to know about each carrier's service and operating characteristics.

Carrier selection is also less straightforward due to a lack of agreement on the number of relevant factors that might be used in carrier selection. For example, the number of carrier selection factors evaluated in academic research studies has ranged from less than 10 to over 150. As was the case with rate and service negotiation, it's not possible to provide a comprehensive list of all possible factors that might be used in the carrier selection decision. Table 13-3 contains a list of 20 characteristics that were evaluated in one academic study of carrier selection.

Modal and carrier selection has become even murkier in recent years with the rise in what we'll call the **amodal shipper**. An amodal shipper refers to a transportation manager who purchases a prespecified level of transportation service (e.g., two-day delivery for a particular price) and is indifferent to the mode(s) and/or carrier(s) used to provide the actual transportation service. Indeed, research indicates that shippers are exhibiting more interest in transportation metrics such as transit time and transit time dependability than in transportation modes. One reason for the growth of amodalism is that nonasset-based third-party logistics companies have the ability to develop multimodal solutions to a client's transportation problems.[8] Amodalism is also aided by companies such as UPS and FedEx that own companies that provide different types of transportation services (e.g., air, expedited, LTL, parcel).

TABLE 13-3 Possible Carrier Selection Characteristics

Characteristic	Characteristic
Consistent dependable transit times	Billing accuracy
Competitive pricing	Action and follow-up on service complaints
Communication of service disruptions	Equipment availability
Knowledge and problem-solving skills	Quality of drivers of contact personnel
General reputation for quality and integrity	Financial stability
Proactive monitoring of delivery appointments	Ability to provide expedited service
Ability to handle all transportation needs	Satellite tracing and communications
Traditional EDI capabilities	Internet tracking
Internet POD	Ability to implement fuel surcharge
Internet freight posting services	Internet pricing

Source: John L. Kent and Carlo D. Smith, "Carrier Selection Criteria: Differences among Truckload Motor Carrier Offerings," *Journal of Transportation Management* 16, no. 2 (2005): 48–59.

---

[8] "Transport Buying Shifts from Mode to Metrics," *Transportation and Distribution*, January 2006, 34–35.

DOCUMENTATION

The definition of logistics presented in Chapter 1 refers to the *management of information*, and the documents associated with transportation shipments, or **documentation**, are one important source of logistics information. Transportation documentation serves a practical function (e.g., what, where, and how much is being transported) as well as potentially providing legal recourse if something goes awry with a particular shipment. Our discussion here will focus on the documents associated with domestic shipments; the documentation for international shipments is presented in Chapter 14.

The transportation department is responsible for completing all the documents needed to transport the firm's products. Today, many carriers provide software that enables the shipper to use computers to generate all the commonly used documents. Some shippers also have their own order processing software that is capable of generating transportation documents.

Bill of Lading

The most important single transportation document is the **bill of lading**, which is the basic operating document in the industry. The bill of lading functions as a delivery receipt when products are tendered to carriers. On receipt of the freight, the carrier signs the bill of lading and gives the original to the shipper. The signed original of the bill of lading is the shipper's legal proof that the carrier received the freight. The bill of lading is a binding contract, specifying the duties and obligations of both carrier and shipper. The bill of lading contract for surface carriers is basically standardized by law and greatly simplifies the transportation manager's job because it specifies exactly the duties of the shipper and carrier.

There are two types of bills of lading: the straight bill of lading and the order bill of lading. On a *straight bill of lading*, which is printed on white paper, the name of the consignee is stated in the appropriate place, and the carrier is under a strict legal obligation to deliver the freight to the named consignee and to no one else. Ownership of the goods is neither stated nor implied. On the *order bill of lading*, which is printed on yellow paper, the name of the consignee is not specified. For example, assume that a lumber company in Washington state has loaded a boxcar of plywood that it has not yet sold. It would use an order bill and tender the shipment to the Burlington Northern Railroad, which would start the car moving toward Chicago. Once a buyer for the plywood is found, the shipper would send the original copy of the order bill by mail to a bank near the buyer and would also tell the buyer which bank had possession of the order bill. The buyer would go to the bank and pay for the plywood, and the bank would give the original copy to the buyer. The buyer would take it to the railroad, and the railroad would deliver the carload of plywood. Order bills can also be used when faced with slow-paying customers because the order bill guarantees that the customer must pay for the products prior to receipt.

An additional classification for bills of lading is the specific form: long, short, or preprinted. The *long-form bill of lading*, which may be either an order or straight bill, contains the standard information on the face of the bill (see Figure 13-4), and on the reverse side it contains the entire contract between carrier and shipper. The reverse side is printed in extremely small print. Because of the difficulty of reading the long-form contract and the printing costs of including the contract on all bills, in 1949 the railroads and motor carriers adopted the short-form bill of lading. The short form has the following statement on its face: "Every service to be performed hereunder shall be subject to all the terms and conditions of the Uniform Domestic Straight Bill of Lading."

Another kind of bill of lading—which may be long, short, order, or straight—is preprinted. In theory, the bill of lading is prepared and issued by the carrier. In fact, however, most shippers buy their bills of lading and then have them preprinted with a list of the products they regularly ship. Figure 13-5 illustrates a *preprinted short-form bill of lading*. Shippers go to the expense of

FIGURE 13-4   A Long-Form Bill of Lading

buying and printing their own bills because, in practice, they frequently prepare them prior to calling the carrier. The preprinted bill can be prepared more rapidly and with less chance of error; for example, the shipper can insert the correct classification rather than letting the carrier determine it.

A few shippers are adopting their own bills of lading, which carriers may be reluctant to accept because the carriers may be subject to new liabilities specified in the documents. Carriers are advised to supply their drivers with stickers to place on the bills of lading, indicating that the drivers' signature means only that they have picked up the freight.

FIGURE 13-5 A Preprinted Short-Form Bill of Lading

Freight Bill

Another basic document that the transportation manager must be familiar with is the **freight bill**, which is an invoice submitted by the carrier requesting to be paid. Often, the transportation manager must approve each freight bill before it is paid, and carriers must be paid within a specific number of working days. In an attempt to meet these time limits, many transportation managers now participate in automated *freight bill-paying services*. Once the transportation manager initiates the program with the payment service, the carriers submit their freight bills directly to the service. The payment service treats the freight bills as checks drawn on the shipper's freight account and then pays the carriers.

One continuing issue with freight bills involves companies being charged too much (overcharges) for transportation services. To detect current errors that result in overcharges and to correct these errors in the future, shippers conduct *internal audits* (work is performed by employees of the company) of their freight bills. Some shippers also conduct *external audits* (work is performed by an independent third party) of their freight bills. Figure 13-6 is an example of a form used by a freight-bill auditor to request that a common carrier reimburse the auditor (on behalf of the auditor's client) for the carrier's overcharges.

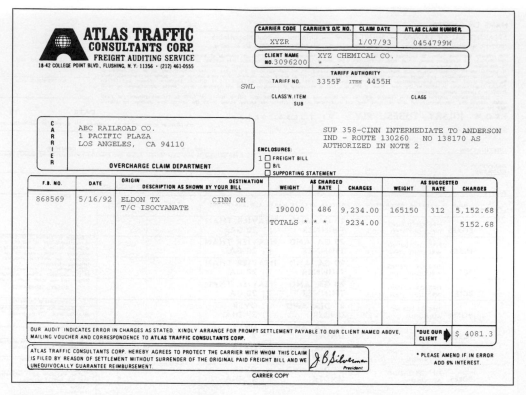

FIGURE 13-6 An Overcharge Claim Form

Source: Courtesy of Atlas Traffic Consultants Corporation, Flushing, NY.

Freight Claims

Another key documentation issue involves **freight claims**, which refers to a document that notifies a carrier of wrong or defective deliveries, delays, or other delivery shortcomings.[9] Filing claims against carriers is a routine matter, and many carriers post filing information and sample claim forms on their Web sites. The following are representative of freight claims information that might be found on a carrier Web site: "Who can file a claim? What is the time limit for filing a claim? How do I file a claim? What documents do I need to file a freight claim? What should I expect to happen after the freight claim has been filed? What should I do with damaged goods?"[10] You should be aware that there are time limitations—nine months from the delivery date—within which a freight claim must be filed.

Although shippers and carriers often satisfactorily adjudicate freight claims, on some occasions the two parties disagree in terms of claim settlement. The Transportation Arbitration Board (TAB) was formed by shippers and carriers as a means of settling claim disputes. When a carrier and a shipper (or consignee) agree to submit their case to TAB, they both pay a fee that is currently $150 per party. The shipper (consignee) prepares the claim file, including a written statement explaining why it is believed that the claim should be paid. This is sent to the carrier, which adds its file and contentions to the claim file. The claim file is then returned to the claimant, who has a final opportunity to offer a rebuttal brief, with a copy of the rebuttal going to the carrier. The claimant then sends the entire file to TAB, where a decision is made.

One of the most difficult and challenging aspects of claim work is the determination of the exact dollar amount of the damage. The law states that the common carrier is responsible for the

---

[9] *Logistics Dictionary,* 2005, accessed at *www.tntfreight.com.*
[10] *http://works.pittohio.com/mypittohio/onlinetools/ot_formsusa.asp?sessionid=F0A5C6D7-8277-401F-98F1-C88977CC74B1.*

full actual loss sustained by the shipper or consignee. But what is meant by "full actual loss?' Assume, for example, that a retailer owned the products shipped via a common carrier and that they were damaged beyond repair. The question arises, "Should the retailer recover the wholesale price or the retail price?" If the products destroyed were going into a general inventory replacement stock, the retailer would recover the wholesale price plus freight costs (if they had been paid) because the retail price has not been earned. Assume, instead, that a product is ordered especially for a customer. When the product arrives, it is damaged, and the retailer's customer states that he or she will wait no longer and cancels the order. In this situation, the retailer is entitled to the retail price because the profit would have been earned if the carrier had properly performed its service.

Another difficult area for shippers and carriers alike involves **concealed loss or damage**, which refers to a situation where loss or damage is not apparent until after a shipment has been unpacked and inspected. Carriers may be reluctant to pay concealed loss and damage claims for two reasons. First, if the shipment came through the transportation process with no exterior damage, then there is a strong possibility that the product was improperly protected on the inside. If this is the case, the carrier is exempted from liability because improper packaging is the fault of the shipper. Second, the possibility exists that the consignee's employees damaged or stole the products in question. The potential delicateness of concealed loss or damage claims is the balancing act between a carrier (1) not wanting to pay claims caused by shipper or consignee errors and (2) upsetting a shipper or consignee by seemingly implicating them in the loss or damage.

Since transportation deregulation, the volume of claims activity has dropped because, during the negotiation process, the shipper may agree to hold the carrier less liable for claims in return for lower transportation charges. In addition, the transportation deregulation acts have reduced carrier liability. The Staggers Act of 1980, which lessened railroad economic regulation, and the Motor Carrier Act of 1980, which pertained to trucks, permitted railroads and motor carriers, respectively, to establish released value rates (wherein the shipper agrees that a commodity is worth no more than so many dollars per hundred pounds in case a claim is filed, in return for a lower rate).

MAKING AND RECEIVING SHIPMENTS

Another key area of decision making in transportation management involves making and receiving shipments, which refers to tactical planning and control of shipments along with supervision of freight loading and unloading.[11] A number of activities are associated with making and receiving shipments, and we'll discuss some of them in the paragraphs that follow.

Consolidating Small Shipments

Small shipments, often defined as those that weigh more than 150 pounds and less than 500 pounds, represent one of the most challenging situations faced by the transportation manager. As mentioned in Chapter 12, the nature of transportation costs is that it costs less on a per-pound basis to ship a larger quantity because certain costs (fixed, administrative, or terminal) are the same per shipment. When the shipment is larger, such costs can be allocated over a larger weight. The transportation manager faces the decision of whether and when to consolidate large numbers of small shipments into small numbers of large shipments. Some shipment consolidation activities are shown in Figure 13-7.

Smaller shipments are problematic for several reasons. From a carrier perspective, there may be reluctance to accept small shipments because they tend to require a high degree of manual labor, thus increasing labor costs. In addition, there is a belief by some carriers that they lose money on small shipments because the revenues from them don't sufficiently reflect cost considerations. From

---

[11] John E. Tyworth, Joseph L. Cavinato, and C. John Langley, *Traffic Management: Planning, Operations, and Control* (Prospect Heights, IL: Waveland Press, 1991).

Truckload shipments of a single product directly from supplier to customer, bypassing warehouse.

A truckload made up of products from suppliers and plants goes from warehouse to customer.

Truckload of single product directly from plant to customer.

Customers

Warehouse

Truckload of railcar lots from supplier and plants to warehouse.

Outside supplier 3

Outside supplier 2

Outside supplier 1

Plant 3

Plant 2

Plant 1

FIGURE 13-7 The Transportation Manager Consolidates Shipments Whenever Possible a transportation manager's perspective, a large number of small shipments means that there needs to be an information system capable of keeping track of each shipment's status; as a general rule, it's easier to keep track of, say, 1 shipment of 10 units than to keep track of 10 shipments of 1 unit apiece. However, it could take some time to accumulate 10 units, and the increased time could result in poorer service to the final customer. Moreover, although a 10-unit shipment might yield transportation cost savings, there would be inventory carrying cost considerations in the sense that it's more costly to hold 10 units of product than to hold 1 unit of product.

Potential solutions for consolidating small shipments involve consolidation across time or place.[12] Continuing with the 10-unit example from the previous paragraph, and supposing that 2 units are available for shipment each day, consolidation across time could be accomplished through volume guidelines (e.g., minimum shipment of 8 units, which would mean a shipment on the fourth day) or time guidelines (e.g., ship every third day, in which case the shipment volume would be 6 units). In consolidation across place, the transportation manager looks to build volume with shipments going to a similar destination or similar destinations, and this often involves looking outside one's firm. Transportation specialists such as freight forwarders, shippers' associations, and transportation brokers (each of which was discussed in Chapter 12) can be helpful in achieving consolidation across place.

Demurrage and Detention

Demurrage is a penalty payment made by the shipper or consignee to a railroad for keeping a railcar beyond the time when it should be released back to the carrier. Demurrage is also collected by inland water carriers if their barges are kept by the shipper or consignee for a longer period than allowed. Pipelines are involved with demurrage if oil stored in tanks at destination is not removed within specified time limits. **Detention** is basically the same concept as demurrage, except that it usually refers to the trucking industry. Users of containers owned by the airlines are subject to similar charges. With both demurrage and detention, carriers are concerned that their equipment is idle and unproductive—a less-than-optimal situation for a revenue-generating asset. From the shipper or consignee perspective, idle transportation vehicles such as a rail car or truck trailer can act as temporary (and potentially inexpensive) warehousing.

Both demurrage and detention operate on a "free-time" principle; that is, shippers or consignees are permitted a specified amount of time to load or unload freight before monetary penalties are levied. For example, a number of U.S. freight railroads currently allow 24 hours of free time for loading railcars and 48 hours of free time for unloading railcars. As of late 2009, the Union Pacific Railroad's penalties for demurrage violations were $80 per day per car, except for refrigerated units, which were charged at $175 per day per car.[13] By contrast, the CSX Railroad's demurrage charges in late 2009 were $90 per day per car, except for refrigerated units where the charge was $150 per day per car.[14]

Many carriers currently offer averaging agreements, where an accounting system of debits and credits is established, for demurrage and detention. A credit is received every time the shipper or consignee releases a piece of equipment early, and a debit is recorded each time a piece of equipment is surrendered to a carrier late. These averaging agreements are typically one month in duration, and at the end of a month, credits and debits are totaled, and the particular demurrage account is settled. If the total demurrage days exceed the total credit days, then demurrage charges are equal to: (total demurrage days minus total credit days) times the applicable demurrage rate. Alternatively, if the total credit days exceed the total demurrage days, then no demurrage charges are paid. As a general rule, credits are not allowed to be carried over from one month to another.

---

[12] Ibid.

[13] Information derived from the Union Pacific Railroad's Accessorial Tariff UP 6004, *http://www.uprr.com/customers/myterms.shtml*.

[14] *http://www.csx.com/share/customers/tariff/docs/A_quick_guide_for_managing_demurrage-REF10310.pdf*.

Routing

Routing can be defined as the process of determining how a shipment will be moved between consignor and consignee or between place of acceptance by the carrier and place of delivery to the consignee.[15] One example of routing is a **routing guide**, which is a document that can provide a variety of shipment-related information such as shipment preparation, freight invoicing, a list of preferred carriers, and a list of which carrier or carriers to use for shipments moving between two points.

As an example, Nordstrom's (a high-end retail department store) routing guide contains information that lists which distribution center is to supply a particular retail location (e.g., the Nordstrom's in Spokane, Washington, is supplied from the Nordstrom's distribution center in Portland, Oregon). In addition, Nordstrom's routing guide also indicates which carriers are to be used to transport shipments to Nordstrom's distribution centers. For example, a 40-pound shipment using surface transportation from Cleveland, Ohio, to the Portland, Oregon, distribution center is to move via UPS Ground. In a similar fashion, a 5,000-pound shipment using surface transportation from Cleveland to the Portland distribution center is to move via Norcon, Ltd.[16]

An increasingly important routing issue involves the transportation of hazardous materials, and hazmat routing has become particularly contentious issue since the terrorist attacks of September 11, 2001. As mentioned earlier in the text, some large U.S. metropolitan areas are seeking bans on railroad movement of hazardous materials through major cities. These proposed bans have the potential to create significant transportation problems in the sense that railroads have a common carrier obligation to transport hazardous materials. If these shipments are prohibited from moving through major cities, they will be rerouted through other, less-populated areas—but it's not likely that these areas will be happy with this situation. Moreover, rerouting will add to transit times and transport costs, and the railroads' costs of hauling hazardous materials have increased dramatically in recent years because of higher insurance premiums associated with transporting hazardous materials.[17]

The potential danger involved in the transportation of hazardous materials has been recognized for some time; the U.S. federal government began regulating its transport in 1838, and since then hundreds of changes have been made to federal statutes dealing with the transportation of hazardous materials. Currently, the Office of Hazardous Materials Safety (part of the Pipeline and Hazardous Materials Safety Administration) is responsible for the transportation of hazardous materials moving by air, highway, rail, and water. The Office of Pipeline Safety (also part of the Pipeline and Hazardous Materials Safety Administration) is responsible for the transportation of hazardous materials moving by pipeline.

Transportation managers working for firms that handle hazardous materials have several important responsibilities. While the hazardous materials are under the managers' control, they must see that the materials are moved safely. An organization is required to know, track, and record the location of all hazardous materials that it owns, controls, or generates. Originating shippers' documents must include a telephone number that will be answered 24 hours a day.

In addition, federal requirements prescribe the training of personnel to handle the materials, the packaging of the product, the marking and labeling of the packages, the placarding of the vehicles that transport the materials, and the information required on shipping documents. The colors, symbols, and numbers of the diamond-shaped placards seen on truck trailers, containers, and railcars identify the hazardous properties of the products being carried. Figure 13-8 shows a

---

[15] *Logistics Dictionary,* 2005.
[16] *www.nordstromsupplier.com.*
[17] R. G. Edmonson, "Not in My Backyard," *Journal of Commerce,* July 24, 2006, 34–36.

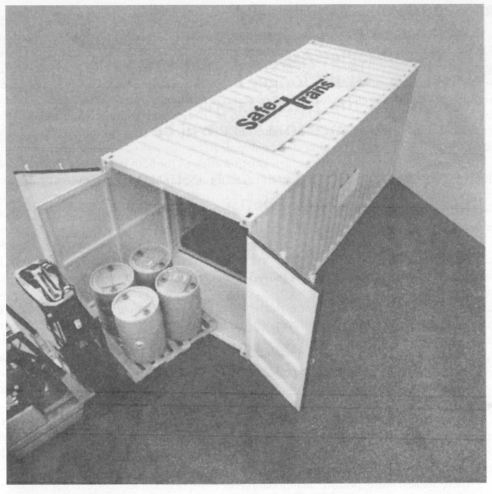

FIGURE 13-8   Specialized Container with Sump to Capture Hazardous Waste Leaks from Barrels
Source: Safety Storage, Inc.

container designed specifically for carrying drums of hazardous materials; should one rupture, it would drain into a sump.

Tracing and Expediting

Tracing refers to determining a shipment's location during the course of its move, and the ability to trace shipments directly affects **expediting**, which involves the need to rapidly move a shipment to its final destination. Today many transportation carriers have information systems that provide real-time information about shipment status, and this information is widely available to customers through the Internet, thus making it fast and easy to trace shipments. Moreover, where expediting historically involved shipments by air transportation, in recent years expediting has seen an increasing use of motor carriers. We know from Chapter 12 that motor carriers are less expensive than air transportation, and because expedited motor carriers can often dedicate one truck to one shipment, expedited shipment by motor carriage can provide *faster and more reliable* service than expedited shipments involving air transportation.[18]

---

[18] Aaron Kapp, "Advantage Ground," *Air Cargo World*, August 2005, 26–30.

TRANSPORTATION SERVICE QUALITY

We'll conclude this chapter with a look at transportation service quality. Chapter 7 pointed out that macroenvironmental changes, such as globalization and advances in technology, have caused organizations to demand higher levels of service quality, and this is particularly true for transportation services. For example, the combination of real-time information systems and global positioning systems now allows for virtually instantaneous tracking of a shipment. In addition, this tracking information can be directly provided to the transportation manager at his or her computer or smart phone—as opposed to the "old days," where the transportation manager had to contact the carrier for information about a shipment.

As pointed out earlier, economic deregulation allowed for both price and service competition among carriers, and this resulted in the need for organizations to measure their carriers' performance. To this end, some transportation managers utilize performance scorecards that contain a list of relevant attributes (perhaps the same attributes used to select carriers) and an evaluation of each carrier on every attribute.

Table 13-4 illustrates how a carrier performance scorecard might work; in this example, the transportation manager has selected seven performance attributes that will be used to evaluate individual carriers. The transportation manager assigns each attribute an importance rating, such as 25 percent for "service performance improvement." The transportation manager also assigns a gross score for each attribute that signifies the manager's assessment of a particular carrier's performance on that attribute; 4.5 is the gross score assigned to "service performance improvement." "Net weighted score" is calculated by multiplying each attribute's importance rating by its gross score; for example, the 1.125 for "service performance improvement" comes from its 25 percent importance multiplied by its 4.5 gross score. The net weighted scores for all seven attributes are summed (4.05 in Table 13-4) and divided by the maximum possible gross score (5.00) to yield the "performance score."

The performance scorecard can be used as a diagnostic tool; if an individual carrier's performance is rated as lower than, say, 70, then the carrier might be put on probation for a certain time period. Moreover, if performance does not exhibit satisfactory improvement during the probationary period, then the carrier might be fired.

There are also more "positive" manifestations of transportation service quality. A number of organizations now officially recognize (e.g., a press release, an awards recognition dinner, a plaque) transportation carriers that provide superior service. In addition, some of the logistics trade publications annually recognize transportation service excellence. For example, *Logistics Management* annually conducts its "Quest for Quality," in which users of transportation services are asked to rate transportation companies on five dimensions: on-time performance, value, customer service,

TABLE 13-4	Example of a Carrier Performance Scorecard		
Attribute	**Importance (%)**	**Gross Score (0–5)**	**Net Weighted Score**
Service performance improvement	25	4.5	1.125
Continued cost savings	20	3	0.6
Driver performance	15	5	0.75
Sales representative responsiveness	15	3.5	0.525
Loss/damage claims	10	4.5	0.45
Customer complaints	10	4.5	0.45
Inbound deliveries by 9:00 A.M.	5	3	0.15
Sum			4.05
Performance score			81.00%

Source: Rob Martinez, "Shipper Scorecard," *Multichannel Merchant*, August 2008, 49.

information technology, and equipment and operations. Individual carriers receive a "Quest for Quality" award when their overall rating on the five dimensions exceeds their industry average, and many of these carriers prominently feature this award on their Web sites.

Summary

This chapter covered transportation management, which refers to the buying or selling of transportation services by a shipper or consignee. A transportation manager's job has changed dramatically over the past 35 years, and this chapter analyzes several of a transportation manager's primary responsibilities. Rate considerations are one prominent responsibility, particularly in terms of rate determination. A transportation manager is also responsible for modal and carrier selection, and an emerging selection trend involves a focus on transportation metrics as opposed to transportation mode.

Documentation is another responsibility of a transportation manager, and the chapter discussed key documents such as the bill of lading, freight bill, and freight claims. Another key area of decision making in transportation management is making and receiving shipments, which includes activities such as shipment consolidation, demurrage, and detention, among others. The chapter concluded by looking at transportation service quality.

Questions for Discussion and Review

1. How is the transportation manager's job different today than when the first edition of this book was published in the 1970s?
2. Discuss how transportation managers could be involved with other operations of the firm.
3. How does the class rate system simplify with respect to product, weight, and distance?
4. Discuss the four factors used in determining a product's freight classification.
5. Explain the weight break concept.
6. Discuss how a transportation manager might take advantage of the trade-offs between price and service.
7. List and describe the payment options (terms of sale) that can be applied to domestic U.S. shipments.
8. Why is the carrier selection process less straightforward than the modal selection process?
9. Define what is meant by an amodal shipper, and discuss the factors that have contributed to its growth.
10. The bill of lading is the single most important document in transportation. Discuss some of the basic functions it performs.
11. Distinguish between the straight bill of lading and the order bill of lading.
12. What is a freight bill? Why should each freight bill be audited?
13. Explain how the Transportation Arbitration Board functions.
14. Discuss the basic issues, conflicts, and problems involved in concealed loss and damage claims.
15. Explain why smaller shipments are challenging to transportation managers.
16. Discuss the basic idea of demurrage and detention and how averaging agreements can be helpful in this area.
17. Explain how a routing guide might be used by a transportation manager.
18. What challenges might occur if rail movements of hazardous materials are banned from going through major cities?
19. Distinguish between tracing and expediting. Why are motor carriers being used to a greater extent in expediting?
20. What is a carrier performance scorecard? How might it be used by transportation managers?

Suggested Readings

Albright, Dan. "Transportation Management's Role in Supply Chain Excellence." *Supply Chain Management Review* 13, no. 7 (2009): S52–S62.

Bohman, Ray. "New LTL Pricing: Thinking Inside the Cube." *Logistics Management* 46, no. 10 (2007): 39–42.

Clair, Lee A., and Steven D. Fox. "Time to Simplify Trucking Tariffs." *Supply Chain Management Review* 8, no. 3 (2004): 36–42.

Holter, Andreas R., David B. Grant, James Ritchie, and Nigel Shaw. "A Framework for Purchasing Transport Services in Small and Medium Size Enterprises." *International Journal of Physical Distribution & Logistics Management* 38, no. 1 (2008): 21–38.

Martinez, Rob. "Inside Real-Life Carrier Negotiations." *Multichannel Merchant* 5, no. 7 (2009): 36–37.

Maynard, Jill L., John E. Bell, and Alan W. Johnson. "Frustrated Hazardous Material: Military and Commercial Training Implications." *Transportation Journal* 47, no. 1 (2008): 30–42.

Meixell, Mary J., and Mario Norbis. "A Review of the Transportation Mode Choice and Carrier Selection Literature." *International Journal of Logistics Management* 19, no. 2 (2008): 183–211.

Poli, Patricia M., and Carl A. Scheraga. "A Balanced Scorecard Framework to Assessing LTL Motor Carrier Quality Performance." *Transportation Quarterly* 57, no. 3 (2003): 105–130.

Sykes, Scott, Matthew Menner, and Vincent Chiodo. "7 Steps to Transportation Management Excellence." *Outsourced Logistics* 1, no. 1 (2008): 30–41.

Zsidisin, George A., M. Douglas Voss, and Matt Schlosser. "Shipper-Carrier Relationships and Their Effect on Carrier Performance." *Transportation Journal* 46, no. 2 (2007): 5–18.

CASE

CASE 13-1   Chippy Potato Chip Company

Located in Reno, Nevada, since 1947, the Chippy Potato Chip Company manufactured potato chips and distributed them within a 100-mile radius of Reno. It used its own trucks for delivery in the Reno, Carson City, and Lake Tahoe areas and common carrier trucking for all other outgoing shipments. All of its motor carrier shipments were on an LTL basis. The applicable motor carrier freight rating, or classification, for LTL potato chips was 200. This classification was high, although potato chips are often given as textbook examples of bulky freight that will cause a truck to cube out. Even after much of the motor carrier industry was deregulated, Chippy had difficulty finding contract truckers interested in negotiating specific contract rates. This was because potato chips—as a result of their bulk—were not a desirable cargo from the truckers' point of view.

The potato chips were packed in bags containing 8 ounces of chips. Twenty-four 8-ounce bags were packed in cartons that were 12 inches by 12 inches by 36 inches. The packed carton weighed 14 pounds. The 8-ounce bags of chips wholesaled FOB plant for 40 cents each and retailed at 59 cents.

Recently the Chippy firm acquired rights to produce a new type of chip, made from powdered potatoes, yielding chips of identical shape that could be packed in tubular containers. A 5-ounce paper tube of chips would wholesale (FOB plant) at 40 cents and retail for 59 cents. The new chips were much less bulky: Twenty-four 5-ounce containers could be packed in a carton measuring one cubic foot. The filled carton weighed 10 pounds. (The difference between the weight of chips and that of cartons is due to packaging materials. The carrier is paid on the basis of carton weight.)

Chippy management believed that because the new chips were less bulky, the LTL classification of 200 was too high. Management decided to ask the motor carrier classification bureau for a new, lower classification. (Motor carrier rates for a movement are the classification multiplied by a distance factor. If the classification were lowered, the rate would be lowered proportionally for all shipments.)

Questions

1. If you worked for Chippy, what new classification would you ask for? Give your reasons.
2. Classifications are based on both cost and value of service. From the carrier's standpoint, how has cost of service changed?
3. Given the existing LTL classification of 200, how has value of service to the customer changed?
4. The new tubular containers are much sturdier. If you worked for Chippy, how—if at all—would you argue that this factor influences classification?
5. You work for the motor carrier classification bureau and notice that the relationship between the weight of potato chips and the weight of packaging has changed. How, if at all, should this influence changes in the product's classification?
6. One of Chippy's own trucks, used for local deliveries, has two axles and an enclosed body measuring (inside) 7 feet by 8 feet by 20 feet and is limited by law to carrying a load of no more than 8,000 pounds. Because the truck is not supposed to be overloaded, what combinations, expressed in terms of cartons of both new- and old-style chips can it legally carry? (*Hint:* Use a piece of graph paper.)

14 INTERNATIONAL LOGISTICS

Key Terms

- Balance of payments
- Cargo preference
- Certificate of origin
- Commercial invoice
- Embargoes
- Export management company
- Export packers
- Import quota
- Incoterms

- International freight forwarders
- International logistics
- Letter of credit
- Load centers
- Logistics Performance Index (LPI)
- Macroenvironmental influences
- Methods of payment
- Nontariff barriers
- Nonvessel-operating common carrier (NVOCC)

- Ocean carrier alliances
- Open account
- Open skies agreement
- Shipper's export declaration (SED)
- Shipper's letter of instruction (SLI)
- Shipping conferences
- Short-sea shipping
- Tariffs
- Terms of sale

Learning Objectives

- To understand macroenvironmental influences on international logistics
- To examine documentation as well as terms of sale and methods of payment for international shipments
- To distinguish among the unique activities of international trade specialists

- To examine transportation and inventory considerations in international distribution
- To introduce you to the Logistics Performance Index

An understanding of international logistics is vital due to the tremendous increase in global trade during the first decade of the twenty-first century. Although world trade likely experienced a pullback during 2009 due to the worldwide recession, the value of world merchandise exports grew from approximately $6.2 trillion in 2000 to approximately $16.2 trillion in 2008, or an increase of $10 trillion![1] From a relative perspective, the ratio of merchandise exports to world domestic product [i.e., the gross domestic product (GDP) of all countries] grew from approximately 14 percent in 2000 to approximately 26 percent in 2008.[2]

---

[1] World Trade Organization, *International Trade Statistics*, 2001 and 2009.
[2] Calculated from data in the World Trade Organization, *International Trade Statistics*, 2001 and 2009 as well as The *CIA World Factbook*, 2001 and 2009.

International logistics—logistics activities associated with goods that are sold across national boundaries—occurs in the following situations:

1. A firm exports a portion of a product made or grown—for example, paper-making machinery to Sweden, wheat to Russia, or coal to Japan.
2. A firm imports raw materials—such as pulpwood from Canada—or manufactured products—such as motorcycles from Italy or Japan.
3. Goods are partially assembled in one country and then shipped to another, where they are further assembled or processed. For example, a firm stamps electronic components in the United States. It ships them to a free trade zone in the Far East, where low-cost labor assembles them, and then the assembled components are returned to the United States to become part of the finished product.
4. The firm is *global* in outlook and sees almost all nations as being markets, sources of supply, or sites for markets or for assembly operations.
5. Because of geography, a nation's domestic commerce crosses foreign borders, often in bond. For example, goods moving by truck between Detroit and Buffalo or between the Lower 48 states and Alaska, through Canada, travel in bond, which means that the carrier handling them has a special legal obligation to keep them sealed and to make certain that they are not released for sale or use within the country through which they are traveling. Products shipped in bond are not subject to normal duties of the country through which they are passing.

This chapter begins with a discussion of macroenvironmental influences on international logistics, and this is followed by a look at three key transaction-related considerations in international logistics, namely, documentation, terms of sale, and methods of payment. Next is a discussion of key international trade specialists, including international freight forwarders and export packers. The chapter then looks at transportation considerations in international logistics, followed by a discussion on international trade inventories. The chapter concludes by looking at a new international logistics concept, the Logistics Performance Index.

MACROENVIRONMENTAL INFLUENCES ON INTERNATIONAL LOGISTICS

Macroenvironmental influences refer to the uncontrollable forces and conditions facing an organization and include cultural, demographic, economic, natural, political, and technological factors.[3] While these macroenvironmental factors provide various challenges in an organization's domestic market, they provide even greater challenges when doing business outside of one's home market. For example, many countries have regulations and laws pertaining to air pollution; however, the nature of these regulations and laws as well as the degree of enforcement of them is not uniform from country to country.

A comprehensive discussion of the influences of all six environmental factors on international logistics is beyond the scope of this text. However, to give you a sense as to how macroenvironmental factors can impact international logistics, we'll look at three such influences, namely, political, economic, and cultural factors.

Political Factors

Political restrictions on international trade can take a variety of forms. Many nations ban certain types of shipments that might jeopardize their national security; for example, the United States does not ship military equipment or strategic materials to certain nations. Likewise, individual nations may band together to pressure another country to not be an active supplier of materials that could be used

---

[3] *http://www.marketingpower.com/_layouts/Dictionary.aspx?dLetter=M.*

to build nuclear weapons. Some nations restrict the outflow of currency because a nation's economy will suffer if it imports more than it exports over a long term. These regulations are not concerned with specific commodities; rather, they are concerned with restricting the outflow of money. All imports require advance approval, and goods that arrive without prior approval are not allowed to enter.

A relatively common political restriction on trade involves **tariffs**, or taxes that governments place on the importation of certain items. Tariffs are often established to protect local manufacturers, producers, or growers, and once tariff barriers are built, they are not easily torn down. Sometimes, the tariff the importing nation charges differs according to the nation from which the good is coming, and from an international sourcing standpoint, this could influence the choice of a production site.

Another group of political restrictions on trade can be classified as **nontariff barriers**, which refer to restrictions other than tariffs that are placed on imported products.[4] One type of nontariff barrier is an **import quota**, which limits the amount or product (either in units or by value) that may be imported from any one country during a period of time. The health and safety of a country's population often provides "convenient" reasons for applying nontariff barriers. Many nations are concerned with stopping the spread of plant and animal diseases and therefore inspect various commodities or products to make certain that they do not contain these problems. If material is found to be infested, it cannot enter the country until it is cleaned. Entry of other products may be prohibited because they do not meet safety standards. For example, because of the danger of earthquakes in Japan, upright refrigerators must be built so that they will remain upright, even when tilted as much as 10 degrees.

Embargoes, or the prohibition of trade between particular countries, are another political restriction on trade and generally result from political tensions. For example, U.S. trade with Cuba has been banned since the late 1950s (corresponding to Fidel Castro's rise as Cuban prime minister and installation of a communistic government). In a similar fashion, because of long-standing political tensions, Israel and several Arab nations do not trade with each other, and this embargo has been extended to include nations that are sympathetic, or provide support, to Israel.

Yet another political consideration that influences international logistics is the degree of federal government involvement in cross-border trade. Businesses involved in foreign trade find that a federal government's role is more significant than in domestic transactions, and as a result the buying and selling parties are not always free to contract the terms to suit their needs. In part, this is because most firms are first developed in domestic markets and take all existing governmental controls as a given factor. As a firm expands beyond its domestic markets, it finds requirements that differ for each nation with which the firm wishes to trade.

Figure 14-1 is from a guidebook prepared by an international airline that outlines, in general terms, the various restrictions that apply when shipping to the African nations of Senegal and Sierra Leone. The information in Figure 14-1 identifies a number of challenges that companies might face when importing products into nondomestic markets. Note that the documentation requirements for importing into Senegal involve a commercial invoice that must contain a declaration written in French. Alternatively, the documentation requirements for importing into Sierra Leone involve a combined certificate of value and origin written in English. In addition, whereas Senegal prohibits *all goods* of Portuguese or South African origins, Sierra Leone is more selective and prohibits arms and ammunition from Liberia as well as shaving brushes from Japan.

Businesses that engage in international logistics also learn that federal governments are often more involved in international transportation than they are in domestic transportation. One reason for this is that ocean carriers and international airlines can operate as extensions of a nation's economy, and most of the revenues they receive flow into that nation's economy. To that nation, international carriage functions as an export with favorable effects on the nation's **balance of payments** (system of accounts that records a country's international financial transactions[5]). However, to the nation on the other end of the shipment, the effect is

---

[4] Philip R. Cateora, Mary C. Gilly, and John L. Graham, *International Marketing*, 14th ed. (New York: McGraw-Hill Irwin, 2009).
[5] Ibid.

SENEGAL

GOVERNMENT REPRESENTATION

The Republic of Senegal is represented in the United States by an Embassy at 2112 Wyoming Ave., N.W., Washington, D.C. and a United Nations Mission at 51 East 42nd St., New York. Both also act for Canadian affairs.

GENERAL INFORMATION

Customs Airports: Dakar, Saint Louis and Ziguinchor.
Collect Service acceptable to Dakar and Saint Louis only.
COD Service not acceptable.
Free House Delivery not acceptable.

DOCUMENTATION

Commercial consignments—2 commercial invoices containing the following declaration: "Nous certifions que les marchandises denommees dans cette facture sont de fabrication et d'origine (country of origin) et que les prix indiques ci-dessus s'accordent avec les prix courants sur le marche d'exportation."
Sample consignments—Without commercial value: No documents. With commercial value: same as for commercial consignments.
Gift consignments—no documentary requirements.

RESTRICTIONS

Live animals: Health certificate.
Dogs and other domestic animals: Health certificates issued not later than 3 days before shipment and stating that the animals originate from an area free from contagious diseases of the species for the preceding 6 weeks, and in case of cats and dogs, that no rabies has been detected for the same period.
PROHIBITED: Hares and rabbits.
Live plants and plant material: Health certificate.
Arms and ammunition: Special import permit.

PROHIBITIONS

All goods of Portuguese or South African origin; skins of hares and rabbits; beetroot sugar; blankets; cloth of textile fibers; cotton cloth; fibres; flower pots, stoneware, pottery, clay products, matches, ornamental bricks and other clay products for building purposes; outwear, shirts, except shirts over CFA 1700. value; shoes, except fashionable shoes over CFA 400. value; trousers under CFA 1900. value; sisal carpets and rugs; sugar cane, yarn and thread; cotton, apéritifs of alcohol or wine basis; digestives.

IMPORT AND EXCHANGE REGULATIONS

Liberalized items may be imported without quantitative restrictions on the basis of an import certificate, which is made out by the importer, endorsed by the Customs on clearance of the merchandise and delivered to an authorized bank for visa by the Exchange Control Office.
Non-liberalized goods require an import license, issued by the Director General for Economic Services and visaed by the Exchange Control Office. Validity of certificate and license is 6 months.
The currency exchange is obtained through the authorized banks on strength of import certificate or import license. No tolerance in value or quantity shown on import certificate or import license is permitted.
The importation of goods competitive with locally produced items may be prohibited from time to time.
Rate of exchange: 247 C.F.A. Francs = $1.00

SIERRA LEONE

GOVERNMENT REPRESENTATION

Sierra Leone is represented in the United States by an Embassy at 1701 19th Street, N.W., Washington, D.C. and a United Nations Mission at 30 East 42nd St., New York. Both also act for Canadian affairs.

GENERAL INFORMATION

Customs Airport: Freetown.
Collect Service acceptable.
COD Service not acceptable.
Free House Delivery not acceptable.

DOCUMENTATION

Commercial consignments—4 combined certificates of value and origin in English bearing the supplier's letterhead and his seal or stamp against his signature or that of his representative. In case of occasional shipment, when overprinting of the letterhead is prohibitive, the combined certificate must be accompanied with the supplier's own invoice duly signed against his seal or stamp, and containing the certification: "We hereby declare that this commercial invoice is in support of the attached certificate invoice No. . . . and that the particulars shown on the certified invoice are true and correct in every detail."

RESTRICTIONS

Live animals: Import authorization from Veterinary Dept.
Dogs: Additional health and rabies vaccination certificate in English.
Live plants and plant material: Import authorization from Agricultural Department.
PROHIBITED: Aniseed and Indian hemp.
Medicines and narcotics: Import license from Director of Medical services.

PROHIBITIONS

Arms and ammunition from Liberia, obscene photographs, shaving brushes from Japan, traps for night hunting.

IMPORT AND EXCHANGE REGULATIONS

Most goods may be freely imported under "Open General License." Specific import license required for a short list of specified items only . . . issued by the Import Licensing Authority of the Ministry of Commerce and Industry; the validity is generally 12 months.
Exporters should avoid overshipment of goods covered by specific import licenses. No tolerances are permitted.
The currency exchange is obtained through authorized banks. No exchange permit is required. An import license, whether specific or open, automatically entitles the importer to buy the relative foreign exchange.
Rate of exchange: 1 Leone = $1.20

FIGURE 14-1   Examples of Restrictions of Exporting to Other Nations
Source: Courtesy of Sabena Belgian World Airlines.

opposite because it must import the transport service, and this has an adverse impact on its balance-of-payments position. Some nations with very weak balance-of-payments positions issue an import license, or permit, on the condition that the goods move on a vessel or plane flying that nation's flag, which means it is importing only the goods, not the transportation service required to carry them.[6] Situations such as this dictate carrier choice.

Another aspect of federal government involvement in cross-border trade is that many nations provide subsidies, train their own merchant marine officers, absorb portions of the costs

---

[6] As used here, flying a nation's flag is synonymous with being owned by private or public entities in that nation.

of building commercial vessels, and engage in other activities to promote their own merchant fleets. Governments also support their own carriers through **cargo preference** rules, which require a certain percentage of traffic to move on a nation's flag vessels.

Historically, many international airlines were owned and operated by their national government; examples include Air India, Air China, and Alitalia (owned by the Italian government). However, over the past 25 years some government-owned international carriers have moved to the private sector, a process called privatization. For example, British Airways (formerly British Overseas Airways Corporation, or BOAC) was privatized by the British government in the late 1980s, and Kenya Airlines was privatized by the Kenyan government in the mid-1990s.

Economic Factors

A number of different economic factors—currency fluctuations, market size, income, infrastructure, and economic integration, among others—impact international trade, and in turn, international logistics. Consider currency fluctuations, or changes in the relative value of currencies. When one country's currency is weak relative to other currencies, it becomes more costly to import products, but exports often surge; when one country's currency is strong relative to other currencies, the reverse occurs.

Population is one proxy for market size, and you might recall from Chapter 9 that China and India are the world's two most populous countries. Indeed, China and India each have populations in excess of 1.1 billion people, and the two countries combined account for about one-third of the world's population. From a population perspective, China and India might be potentially attractive markets because of their absolute and relative size.

While both China's and India's GDP have been rapidly expanding over the past 15 years, China's GDP per capita is approximately $6,000, and India's GDP per capita is approximately $2,900.[7] GDP per capita figures have potential implications in terms of the products that are available in particular countries. One strategy for marketing in countries with relatively low GDP per capita, such as India, involves single-use packets of products, called *sachets*, because people may not be able to afford to buy products in larger quantities. From a logistical perspective, single use packets require different packaging and are easier to lose and more prone to theft than products sold in larger quantities.

A country's logistics infrastructure is another economic factor that can impact international logistics. We learned in Chapter 12 that the transportation infrastructures in Brazil, China, Germany, Nigeria, and the United States are quite different, and these differences have important implications for cross-border commerce. A lack of 10,000-foot airport runways, for example, could limit a country's ability to participate in long-haul international movements of higher-value products. Warehousing, another key logistics infrastructure component, also varies tremendously across countries. In India, for example, warehouses are rarely larger than 25,000 square feet, dirt floors are not uncommon, and mechanized materials handling equipment is rare.[8]

Economic integration is the final economic factor that we'll discuss in terms of international logistics. Varying degrees of economic integration exist, ranging from a free trade area (such as the North American Free Trade Agreement), which focuses on removing trade barriers among participant countries, to an economic union (such as the European Union), which integrates economic policies among member nations and allows the free movement of goods, services, and factors of production among member nations.[9]

[7] World Trade Organization, *The CIA World Factbook*, 2009.

[8] Pakmini Madarapakan Pagadala and Steven Mulaik, "Now's the Time for an India Strategy," *CSCMP Supply Chain Quarterly*, Quarter 1, 2009.

[9] Michael R. Czinkota and Ilkka A. Ronkainen, *International Marketing*, 9th ed. (Mason, OH: Cengage Learning, 2010), Chapter 4.

While a comprehensive discussion of economic integration is beyond the scope of this text, many countries continue to explore the different types of economic integration. For example, at the time of publication, the United States has signed free trade agreements with Colombia, South Korea, and Panama, but these agreements have yet to be officially ratified by the U.S. Congress. In addition, Croatia, Macedonia, and Turkey have applied for admission to the European Union, and their candidacies are in various stages of review. Potential logistical implications of economic integration include reduced documentation requirements, reduced tariffs, and the redesign of distribution networks. For example, you might recall from Chapter 9 that Poland and the Czech Republic have become favorite distribution sites with the eastward expansion of the European Union.

Cultural Factors

Cultural considerations will be the final macroenvironmental influence on international logistics to be discussed, and cultural influences include religion, values, rituals, beliefs, and language. We'll look at three cultural factors—language, national holidays, and time orientation—and their potential implications for international logistics.

With respect to language, cargo handlers may not be able to read and understand the language of the exporting country, and it would not be unusual for cargo handlers in some countries to be illiterate. Hence, cautionary symbols, rather than writing, must be used (see Figure 14-2). Cargo moving aboard ocean vessels has distinct markings that identify the shipper, consignee, destination point, and piece number (in multipiece shipments). Some cartons and crates moving internationally are marked with what looks like a cattle brand, which is a shipper's mark, and a drawing of the mark also appears on the documentation. The shipper's mark is for use in areas in which dockworkers cannot read but need a method to keep documents and shipments together.

As with domestic cargo, care must be taken so that pilferable items are not identified. This may include changing the symbols every few months. Figure 14-3 shows a package with the various markings required for movement in cross-border commerce. The bill of lading,

FIGURE 14-2   Some of the Symbols Used for Packing Export Shipments

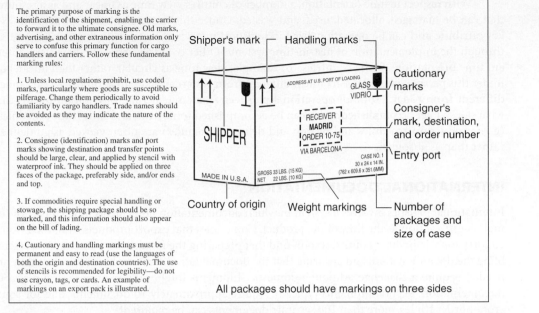

The primary purpose of marking is the identification of the shipment, enabling the carrier to forward it to the ultimate consignee. Old marks, advertising, and other extraneous information only serve to confuse this primary function for cargo handlers and carriers. Follow these fundamental marking rules:

1. Unless local regulations prohibit, use coded marks, particularly where goods are susceptible to pilferage. Change them periodically to avoid familiarity by cargo handlers. Trade names should be avoided as they may indicate the nature of the contents.

2. Consignee (identification) marks and port marks showing destination and transfer points should be large, clear, and applied by stencil with waterproof ink. They should be applied on three faces of the package, preferably side, and/or ends and top.

3. If commodities require special handling or stowage, the shipping package should be so marked, and this information should also appear on the bill of lading.

4. Cautionary and handling markings must be permanent and easy to read (use the languages of both the origin and destination countries). The use of stencils is recommended for legibility—do not use crayon, tags, or cards. An example of markings on an export pack is illustrated.

All packages should have markings on three sides

FIGURE 14-3   A Package Marked for Export

Source: From *Ports of the World*, 15th ed., a publication of CIGNA Property & Casualty.

packing list, letter of credit, and other documents pertaining to a shipment must contain similar markings. Note that markings on the box are in both inches and meters. Both weight and dimensions are given because density is a factor in determining international transportation charges.

National holidays are another cultural aspect that can affect the effectiveness and efficiency of international logistics. Consider, for example, the Chinese New Year that, unlike the New Year that many of you are familiar with, does not take place on January 1. Rather, because the Chinese New Year is based on the lunar calendar, it has a different starting date each year (see Table 14-1). Moreover, the Chinese New Year is characterized by a 15-day celebration period when many businesses shut down—a situation that affects shipments within, into, and out of China during that period.

TABLE 14-1	Beginning Dates for the Chinese New Year, 2011–2018
Year	**Beginning Date**
2011	February 3
2012	January 23
2013	February 10
2014	January 31
2015	February 19
2016	February 8
2017	January 28
2018	February 16

Source: www.apples4theteacher.com/holidays/chinese-new-year/when-is-chinese-new-year.html.

With respect to time orientation, a number of cultures view time as linear and as a resource that can be managed, allocated, used, and wasted. Under this time orientation, punctuality is a key attribute and can be operationalized in logistical metrics such as on-time service as well as through the implementation of just-in-time systems. Other countries, however, have very different time orientations. Some countries, for example, view time as circular, rather than linear, and under this perspective, today isn't much different from yesterday; similarly, tomorrow isn't much different from today. From an operational perspective, a circular time orientation means that what doesn't get accomplished today can be accomplished tomorrow, and thus "time schedules" (e.g., production schedules and pickup and delivery schedules) are often viewed as guidelines, rather than as absolutes.

INTERNATIONAL DOCUMENTATION[10]

International logistics involves a system in which documentation flows are as much a part of the main logistical flow as the flow of the product. Companies that export products from their home country for sale in other countries soon find that preparing the requisite documentation, assembling the documentation, and ensuring that the documentation arrives where and when they are needed is quite a challenge. Although domestic shipments might only require several pieces of documentation, export shipments typically require approximately 10 documents, and for some cross-border trades, more than 100 separate documents can be required!

Documentation can act as a nontariff barrier in the sense that all the necessary documents are required at the point of importation. Failure to do this can cause delays or, in some cases, result in the shipment being seized by the customs authority of the importing country. Moreover, simply having all required documentation is often just a starting point; the exporting organization may be given specific instructions, such as the relevant languages as well as appropriate font types and sizes, for completing the documentation.

Given the vast array of documents that can be used for international shipments, it's only possible to discuss several of the most commonly used, and we'll look at certificates of origin, commercial invoices, shipper's export declaration, and shipper's letter of instruction. A **certificate of origin** specifies the country(ies) in which a product is manufactured and can be required by governments for control purposes or by an exporter to verify the location of manufacture. A **commercial invoice** is similar in nature to a domestic bill of lading in the sense that a commercial invoice summarizes the entire transaction and contains (should contain) key information to include a description of the goods, the terms of sale and methods of payment (to be discussed in the next section), the shipment quantity, the method of shipment, and so on.

A **shipper's export declaration** (**SED**) contains relevant export transaction data such as the transportation mode(s), transaction participants, and description of what is being exported. SEDs often serve as the basis for a country's official export statistics. A **shipper's letter of instruction** (**SLI**) often accompanies an SED and provides explicit shipment instructions. For example, an SLI might indicate which parties should receive which documents, the method or route of shipment, what types of insurance to purchase, and which insurance company(ies) to use.

Before concluding our discussion of the documentation requirements associated with international shipments, mention should be made about free trade agreements. Although some free trade agreements have led to a decrease in documentation requirements, others actually result in an *increase* in documentation, which could defeat the primary purpose of these agreements, namely, facilitating trade between participating countries.

---

[10] This material in this section is drawn from Donald F. Wood, Anthony Barone, Paul R. Murphy, and Daniel L. Wardlow, *International Logistics*, 2nd ed. (New York: Amacom, 2002), Chapter 12.

Consider, for example, the U.S. and Central America Free Trade Agreement (CAFTA), which went into effect in 2005. To receive the favorable tariffs specified in this agreement, organizations provide extensive documentation, beginning with a detailed certificate of origin that is supported by sworn affidavits from various supply chain participants such as suppliers and producers. By contrast, much less documentation is required for products imported from China.[11]

TERMS OF SALE[12]

Choosing the **terms of sale** involves parties working within the negotiations channel, looking at the possible logistics channels, and determining when and where to transfer the following between buyer and seller:

1. The physical goods (the logistics channel)
2. Payment for the goods, freight charges, and insurance for the in-transit goods (the financing channel)
3. Legal title to the goods (the ownership channel)
4. Required documentation (the documentation channel)
5. Responsibility for controlling or caring for the goods in transit, say, in the case of livestock (the logistics channel).

Transfer can be specified in terms of calendar time, geographic location, or completion of some task. One must think in terms of both time and location.

In the 1930s, the International Chamber of Commerce developed, and then has periodically revised, terms of sale for international shipments. In the recent past, these terms of sale, commonly referred to as **Incoterms**, were revised at the beginning of a new decade, such as Incoterms 1990 and Incoterms 2000. However, the next Incoterms revision will not be effective until 2011 at the earliest, and this revision is likely to reflect changes in global trade caused by the September 11, 2001, terrorist attacks and the growth of electronic commerce, among other factors.[13]

Although Incoterms use is not mandatory, they are generally accepted by legal authorities as well as buyers and sellers worldwide. All Incoterms begin with the letters C, D, E, or F, and for each of the terms, the respective responsibilities of the seller's and the buyer's logistics managers change. The product and added services are listed in the following paragraphs, and from the seller's viewpoint, they are the different locations, or stages, for quoting a price to an overseas buyer.

EXW (Ex-Works)

In this most basic transaction, the seller transfers all risk of loss and all responsibility for expenses to the buyer at the seller's loading dock. In an Ex-Works transaction, goods are made available for pickup at the seller's factory or warehouse. *Example:* EXW Toledo Incoterms 2000.

FCA (Free Carrier)

In this type of transaction, the seller is responsible for arranging transportation to a specific carrier at a named place. For example, a shipper (seller) located in Milwaukee may sell FCA Chicago. In this transaction, the seller arranges to deliver goods to an agreed-upon carrier in Chicago. The goods are "delivered" when they are receipted by the buyer's carrier, and all risk of loss transfers to the seller at that point. *Example:* FCA Chicago Incoterms 2000.

---

[11] Alan M. Field, "Too Complex?" *The Journal of Commerce*, May 16, 2005, 16–18.
[12] The material in this section is drawn from Wood et al., *International Logistics*, Chapter 11.
[13] Alan M. Field, "Incoterms Revisited," *The Journal of Commerce*, November 2, 2009, 36.

FAS (Free Alongside Ship)

In this transaction, the seller must arrange for delivery, and assume all risks, up to the ocean carrier at a port. Unofficial usage understands delivery to be "within reach of the ship's tackle." Freight costs up to alongside vessel, risk of loss, and costs of export clearance are borne by the seller. *Example:* FAS Savannah Incoterms 2000.

FOB (Free on Board)

Incoterms limit the use of FOB to carriage by water and define the point of title transfer as occurring when the goods have passed over the ship's rail. In other words, freight to a vessel, loading aboard, and export clearance are the seller's responsibilities. Once the goods are loaded, the risk of loss and costs of transport revert to the buyer. *Example:* FOB Rotterdam Incoterms 2000.

CFR (Cost and Freight)

The "cost" portion of CFR refers to the merchandise. The "freight" portion refers to all the freight, including export clearance, up to the foreign port of unloading. What is not included is cargo insurance from the port of loading. Indeed, risks are shared in a CFR transaction. The seller must deliver over the ship's rail, so any loss up to that point is the seller's responsibility. Once loaded, the risk transfers to the buyer. This term is only used on waterborne shipments. *Example:* CFR Hong Kong Incoterms 2000.

CPT (Carriage Paid To)

This term is similar to CFR, but it can be used for any mode of transport, including air. CPT means that the seller will pay all freight costs all the way to the foreign port and that the buyer assumes all risk of loss beyond the loading port. *Example:* CPT Paris Incoterms 2000.

CIF (Cost, Insurance, and Freight)

A CIF transaction includes the costs of freight and the costs of insurance. The seller retains the risk of loss up to the foreign port of unloading. This term is used on waterborne shipments. *Example:* CIF Miami Incoterms 2000.

CIP (Carriage and Insurance Paid To)

This term is similar to CIF except that it is primarily used in multimodal transactions where the place of receipt and place of delivery may be different from the port of loading or place of unloading. *Example:* CIP Zurich Incoterms 2000.

DES (Delivered Ex Ship)

In this type of transaction, the seller must pay all the costs and bear all the risks of transport up to the foreign port of unloading, except the cost or risk of unloading the cargo from the ship. In the case of large pieces of equipment, or bulk cargoes, the costs of unloading can exceed the cost of the main freight. *Example:* DES Long Beach Incoterms 2000.

DEQ (Delivered Ex Quay)

This is the same as DES except that the terms provide for the seller to pay the costs of unloading the cargo from the vessel and the cost of import clearance. *Example:* DES New York Incoterms 2000.

DAF (Delivered at Frontier)

In DAF, the seller's responsibility is to deliver goods to a named frontier, which usually means a border crossing point, and to clear the transaction for export. The buyer's responsibility is to arrange for pickup of the goods after they are cleared for export, to carry them across the border, to clear them for importation, and to pay any duties. *Example:* DAF Laredo Incoterms 2000.

DDP (Delivered Duty Paid)

This is a term mainly used in intermodal transactions whereby the seller undertakes all the risks and costs from origin to the buyer's warehouse door, including export and import clearance and import customs duties. Essentially, the seller pays everything in a DDP transaction and passes on all related costs in the merchandise price. *Example:* DDP Baltimore Incoterms 2000.

DDU (Delivered Duty Unpaid)

This is the same as DDP except that duty is not paid. Because the importer is generally better informed about local customs, a DDU transaction is used when the buyer wants to avoid transportation and insurance issues. *Example:* DDU Milan Incoterms 2000.

METHODS OF PAYMENT[14]

With respect to international transactions, **methods of payment** refer to the manner by which a seller will be paid by a buyer; methods of payment are much more challenging in international logistics than in domestic logistics. The goals of international buyers and sellers are pretty much the same as those for domestic buyers and sellers—buyers want to receive the product that was paid for, and sellers want to get paid. However, the vagaries of international trade, such as delayed transportation and the economic and political riskiness of particular countries, impact the likelihood of successfully achieving these goals. Moreover, incorrect documentation for international shipments as well as documentation with incorrect information can cause sellers not to be paid by buyers.

Four distinct international methods of payment exist—cash in advance, letters of credit, bills of exchange, and the open account—and similar to terms of sale, the different payment methods offer varying amounts of risk to the involved parties. For example, although cash in advance is of minimal risk to the seller, it is extremely risky to the buyer—what if the paid-for product is never received? Alternatively, an **open account**, where a seller sends the goods and all documents directly to the buyer and trusts the buyer to pay by a certain date, involves tremendous potential risk for the seller and minimal risk for the buyer.

The worldwide economic slowdown that began in 2007 resulted in a dramatic reduction in credit availability for open account financing and generated renewed usage of letters of credit as an international payment method.[15] A **letter of credit** is issued by a bank and guarantees payment to a seller provided that the seller has complied with the applicable terms and conditions of the particular transaction. A sample letter of credit appears in Figure 14-4; note the specific terms such as duplicate certificates of origin and duplicate packing lists, among others.

The method of payment for international shipments should be established at the time that a shipment price is decided upon; the payment method can be influenced by key factors such as the country the product is to be sold in and the seller's assessment of buyer risk. For example,

---

[14] The material in this section is largely drawn from Jim Sherlock and Jonathan Reuvid, eds., *The Handbook of International Trade* (Edinburgh, UK: GMB Publishing, 2005), Part 8.
[15] Bernie Hart, "Risks and Rewards," *Gulf Shipper*, January 12, 2009, 58–60.

FIGURE 14-4 Letter of Credit
Source: Courtesy of Wells Fargo Bank.

with respect to the country the product is to be sold in, buyers located in countries characterized by political and/or economic instability would likely need to pay via cash in advance. The seller's assessment of buyer risk can be based on previous experience with the buyer, references from other companies that trade with the buyer, and the buyer's credit rating, if available.

INTERNATIONAL TRADE SPECIALISTS

Few companies involved in international logistics rely solely on in-house personnel to manage all shipping operations. Specialist firms have developed, and most companies involved in international trade eventually use one or more services that these specialists provide. Several of the more visible international trade specialists will be discussed in this section.

International Freight Forwarders

International freight forwarders specialize in handling either vessel shipments or air shipments, yet their functions are generally the same. Some of their principal functions are discussed in the following paragraphs.

ADVISING ON ACCEPTANCE OF LETTERS OF CREDIT

When a client receives a letter of credit, the document contains many conditions that the seller must meet. The forwarder determines whether the client can meet these conditions and, if it cannot, will advise the client that the letter of credit must be amended. The buyer and buyer's bank must be notified before the order can be processed further.

BOOKING SPACE ON CARRIERS

Space is frequently more difficult to obtain on international carriers than on domestic carriers for several reasons. Vessel or aircraft departures are less frequent, and the capacities of planes or ships are strictly limited. Connections with other carriers are more difficult to arrange, and the relative bargaining strength of any one shipper with an international carrier is usually weaker than it is with respect to domestic carriers. Forwarders are experienced at keeping tabs on available carrier space, and because they represent more business to the carrier than an individual shipper does, they have more success when finding space is difficult.

PREPARING AN EXPORT DECLARATION

An export declaration is required by the U.S. government for statistical and control purposes and must be prepared and filed for nearly every shipment.

PREPARING AN AIR WAYBILL OR BILL OF LADING

The international air waybill is a fairly standardized document; the ocean bill of lading is not. The latter may differ between ocean lines, coastal areas through which the shipments are moving, and for a variety of other circumstances. Ocean bills of lading are frequently negotiable, which means that whoever legally holds the document may take delivery of the shipment. Because nearly every ocean vessel line has its own bill of lading, a forwarder's expertise is necessary to fill it out accurately.

OBTAINING CONSULAR DOCUMENTS

Consular documents involve obtaining permission from the importing country for the goods to enter. Documents are prepared that the importing country uses to determine duties to be levied on the shipment as it passes through customs.

ARRANGING FOR INSURANCE

Unlike domestic shipments, international shipments must be insured. Either the individual shipment must be insured or the shipper (or forwarder) must have a blanket policy covering all shipments. International airlines offer insurance at nominal rates. Rates on vessel shipments are higher, and the entire process is complex because of certain practices that are acceptable at sea. For example, if the vessel is in peril of sinking, the captain may have some cargo jettisoned (thrown overboard) to keep the vessel afloat. The owners of the surviving cargo and the vessel owner must then share the costs of reimbursing the shippers whose cargo was thrown overboard.

PREPARING AND SENDING SHIPPING NOTICES AND DOCUMENTS

The financial transaction involving the sale of goods is carefully coordinated with their physical movement, and rather elaborate customs and procedures have evolved to ensure that the seller is paid when the goods are delivered. The international freight forwarder handles the shipper's role in the document preparation and exchange stages, and it is necessary to have certain documents available as the shipment crosses international boundaries.

SERVING AS GENERAL CONSULTANT ON EXPORT MATTERS

Questions continually arise when dealing with new products, terms of sale, new markets, or new regulations, and a good international freight forwarder knows the answers or how to find them. A conscientious forwarder also advises a shipper as to when certain procedures, such as similar shipments to the same market, become so repetitive that the shipper can handle the procedures in its own export department at a cost lower than the fees charged by the forwarder.

International freight forwarders' income comes from three sources. Similar to domestic forwarders, they buy space wholesale and sell it retail. By consolidating shipments, they benefit from a lower rate per pound. In addition, most carriers allow the forwarders a commission on shipping revenues they generate for the carriers. Also, forwarders charge fees for preparing documents, performing research, and the like. Figures 14-5 and 14-6 show forms used by forwarders. Figure 14-5 is used to prepare cost estimates for the client to use when quoting a price to a potential overseas buyer, while Figure 14-6 is the form that a forwarder uses to bill a client for handling a shipment.

Nonvessel-Operating Common Carriers

Another international logistics intermediary, the **nonvessel-operating common carrier** (**NVOCC**), is often confused with the international freight forwarder, because both intermediaries consolidate freight from different shippers and leverage this volume to negotiate favorable transportation rates from ocean carriers. The United States requires both NVOCCs and international freight forwarders to be licensed as ocean transportation intermediaries by the Federal Maritime Commission. According to the Federal Maritime Commission, NVOCCs are common carriers and thus have common carrier obligations to serve and deliver, among others. From the shipper's perspective, an NVOCC is a carrier; from an ocean carrier's perspective, an NVOCC is a shipper.

Although a company can simultaneously hold both NVOCC and international freight forwarder licenses, it cannot act as an NVOCC and international freight forwarder on the same shipment. Currently, three key factors differentiate NVOCCs from international freight forwarders: (1) NVOCCs can issues their own bills of lading; (2) NVOCCs can set their own rates for ocean and intermodal shipments; (3) NVOCCs can enter into service contracts with ocean carriers to purchase transportation services.[16]

Export Management Companies

Sometimes the manufacturer seeking to export retains the services of an **export management company** (**EMC**), a firm that acts as the export sales department for a manufacturer. EMCs can provide a variety of value-added activities, including marketing research in prospective countries, developing appropriate distribution channels, handling sales correspondence in foreign languages, and ensuring that foreign labeling requirements are met, among others. When

---

[16] James E. Devine, Jr., "10 Steps for FMC Licensing as an OTI," *Florida Shipper*, February 18, 2008, 11, 74.

EXPORT QUOTATION WORKSHEET

DATE_____ REF/PRO FORMA INVOICE NO._____
COMMODITY_____ EXPECTED SHIP DATE_____
CUSTOMER_____ PACKED DIMENSIONS_____
COUNTRY_____ PACKED WEIGHT_____
PAYMENT TERMS_____ PACKED CUBE_____

PRODUCTS TO BE SHIPPED FROM_____
                             TO_____

SELLING PRICE OF GOODS: $_____

SPECIAL EXPORT PACKING:
   $_____   quoted by_____
   $_____   quoted by_____
   $_____   quoted by_____ $_____

INLAND FREIGHT:
   $_____   quoted by_____
   $_____   quoted by_____
   $_____   quoted by_____ $_____

   Inland freight includes the following charges:
   ☐ unloading   ☐ pier delivery   ☐ terminal   ☐ _____

OCEAN FREIGHT			AIR FREIGHT		
	quoted by	tariff item		quoted by	spec code
$_____	_____	#_____	$_____	_____	#_____
$_____	_____	#_____	$_____	_____	#_____
$_____	_____	#_____	$_____	_____	#_____

Ocean freight includes the following surcharges: Air freight includes the following surcharges:

☐ Port congestion   ☐ Heavy lift   ☐ Fuel adjustment
☐ Currency adjustment ☐ Bunker   ☐ Container stuffing
☐ Container rental   ☐ Wharfage   ☐ _____
☐ _____   ☐ _____

☐ INSURANCE   ☐ includes war risk   ☐ INSURANCE   ☐ includes war risk
rate:_____ per $100 or $_____   rate:_____ per $100 or $_____

TOTAL OCEAN CHARGES $_____   **TOTAL AIR CHARGES** $_____ $_____
notes: notes:

FORWARDING FEES: $_____
Includes: ☐ Courier Fees ☐ Certification Fees ☐ Banking Fees ☐ _____

CONSULAR LEGALIZATION FEES: $_____

INSPECTION FEES: $_____

DIRECT BANK CHARGES: $_____

OTHER CHARGES: _____ $_____
                _____ $_____

TOTAL: ☐ FOB_____   ☐ C & F_____
         ☐ FAS_____   ☐ CIF_____ $_____

Form 10-020 Printed and Sold by *UNZ&CO* 190 Baldwin Ave., Jersey City, NJ 07306 • (800) 631-3098

FIGURE 14-5 A Forwarder's Export Quotation Sheet Showing Factors to Include When Determining the Price to Quote a Potential Buyer of a Product

Source: Reprinted with permission of Unz & Co., 190 Baldwin Ave., Jersey City, NJ.

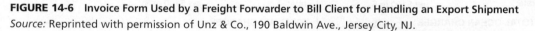

				INVOICE NO.
				DATE
				YOUR REF. NO.

CONSIGNEE:

FROM:				CARRIER:
TO:	☐ AIR		☐ OCEAN	B/L OR AWB NO.

INLAND FREIGHT/LOCAL CARTAGE	$
EXPORT PACKING	
AIR FREIGHT CHARGES	
OCEAN FREIGHT/TERMINAL CHARGES	
CONSULAR FEES	
INSURANCE/CERTIFICATE OF INSURANCE	
CHAMBER OF COMMERCE	
BROKERAGE FEES	
FORWARDING	
HANDLING AND EXPEDITING	
DOCUMENT PREPARATION	
MESSENGER FEES	
POSTAGE	
TELEPHONE	
CABLES	
CERTIFICATE OF ORIGIN	
BANKING: (LETTER OF CREDIT/SIGHT DRAFT)	
MISCELLANEOUS	

As amended by the United States Shipping Act of 1984.

	TOTAL	$

_____ has a policy against payment, solicitation, or receipt of any rebate, directly or indirectly, which would be unlawful under the United States Shipping Act, 1916, as amended

FIGURE 14-6   Invoice Form Used by a Freight Forwarder to Bill Client for Handling an Export Shipment
Source: Reprinted with permission of Unz & Co., 190 Baldwin Ave., Jersey City, NJ.

handling the overseas sales for a U.S. firm, the export management firm either buys and sells on its own account or provides credit information regarding each potential buyer to the U.S. manufacturer, which can judge whether to take the risk.

EMCs often specialize by product (products) or by country (regions). For example, Five Star LLC was founded solely to market U.S.-manufactured health care, beauty care, and food products in Mexico. To this end, Five Star represents U.S. manufacturers like Newman's Salad Dressings and Mrs. Fields Cookies, whose products are sold in prominent Mexican retailers such as Gigante and Walmart de Mexico.[17]

Export Packers

Export packers custom pack shipments when the exporter lacks the equipment or the expertise to do so itself. Export packaging involves packaging for two distinct purposes, in addition to the sales function of some packaging. The first is to allow goods to move easily through customs. For a country assessing duties on the weight of both the item and its container, this means selecting lightweight packing materials. For items moving through the mail, it might mean construction of an envelope with an additional small flap that a customs inspector could open and look inside

---

[17] *http://www.soldinmexico.com/.*

without having to open the entire envelope. For crated machinery, this might involve using open slats rather than completely closed construction (the customs inspectors would likely satisfy their curiosity by peering and probing through the openings between the slats).

The second purpose of export packing is to protect products in what almost always is a more difficult journey than they would experience if they were destined for domestic consignees. For many firms, the traditional ocean packaging method is to take the product in its domestic pack and enclose it in a wooden container. Ocean shipments are subject to more moisture damage and more extreme temperature variations than are domestic shipments. For example, because canned goods moving through hot areas sweat, causing the cans to rust and the labels to become unglued, Campbell's Soup adds desiccants to its cartons of soup, otherwise specks of rust will appear on the cans during their sea voyage.[18]

TRANSPORTATION CONSIDERATIONS IN INTERNATIONAL LOGISTICS

In many cases the distances associated with international shipments are often much greater than those associated with domestic shipments. Because these increased distances often mean that the buyer or seller must choose water or air transportation, we'll take a somewhat detailed look at ocean shipping and international air transportation in this section. This will be followed by a discussion of surface transportation in international logistics.

Before beginning our discussion, you should recognize the rather commonsense notion that international transportation can't be effective or efficient without fairly identical handling equipment being in place at each end of the trip. For example, containerization isn't feasible unless both the origin and destination ports are equipped with the appropriate container handling equipment. Having said this, even today there are countries where grain and sugar are still stowed or unloaded by stevedores carrying individual bags on their shoulders (or heads!) and walking up and down gangplanks. Although this manual loading and unloading is inefficient because of the increased loading or unloading times, the nations in which this practice occurs are often very poor, and manual cargo handling can be a means for providing jobs (and thus income) to many people.

Ocean Shipping

If you don't live near a seaport, you might not have an appreciation for the importance of water transportation in international trade; a frequently cited statistic is that approximately 60 percent of cross-border shipments moves by water transportation. Another example of the importance of water transportation in international trade can be seen in Table 14-2, which provides data on the world's 10 busiest container ports in 2008, as measured by TEU (20-foot equivalent units) throughput. As pointed out in Table 14-2, Singapore, the world's busiest container port, handled nearly 30 million TEUs in 2008; moreover, 8 of the 10 busiest container ports are located in Asia, with 6 of the ports located in China. Note that only 1 European port, and no U.S. ports, ranks among the 10 busiest container ports.

In addition, you might not be aware of the variety of ship types available for transporting international shipments by water. For example, dry-bulk cargoes, such as grain, ores, sulfur, sugar, scrap iron, coal, lumber, and logs, usually move in complete vessel-load lots on chartered vessels; a bulk carrier is shown in Figure 14-7. There are also large, specialized dry cargo ships that are often owned by shippers. Nissan Motor Company of Japan, for example, owns auto-carrying ships, which can carry between 1,200 and 1,900 vehicles. Liquid bulk cargoes, such as petroleum,

---

[18] *American Shipper*, September 2001, 26.

TABLE 14-2	World's Busiest Container Ports (2008)	
Port	**Country**	**TEU Throughput**
Singapore	Singapore	29,918,200
Shanghai	China	27,980,000
Hong Kong	China	24,248,000
Shenzhen	China	21,423,888
Pusan	South Korea	13,425,000
Dubai	United Arab Emirates	11,827,299
Ningbo	China	11,226,000
Guangzhou	China	11,001,300
Rotterdam	The Netherlands	10,783,825
Qingdao	China	10,320,000

Source: www.hafen-hamburg.de/en/content/container-throughput-world-wide-container-ports.

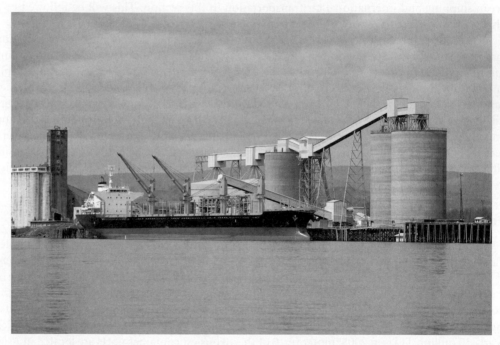

FIGURE 14-7 An Ocean Bulk Carrier Being Loaded with Export Coal Carried by a Mechanical Device at Far Left
Source: Shutterstock Photo.

are transported by tankers that are either owned by oil companies or leased (chartered) by them from individuals who invest in ships.

Another type of vessel that combines aspects of several vessel types is the parcel tanker, which has over 50 different tanks, ranging from 350 to 2,200 cubic meters. Each can carry a different liquid and is loaded and unloaded through a separate piping system. The tanks have different types of coating; some are temperature controlled. Some of the vessels go on round-the-world voyages and carry palm oil, coconut oil, chemicals, and refined petroleum products.

Finally, containerships dominate the traffic between Europe and the United States, Europe and Asia, and the United States and Asia. Shippers or forwarders tender full containers, and if a shipper tenders a less-than-container lot, the vessel operator must load all the less-than-container lots into containers so that the cargo can be loaded aboard the containership. In large container-ships, some of the containers are carried above the level of the deck, which increases the vessel's cubic carrying capacity.

We pointed out in an earlier chapter that the carrying capacity of containerships continues to increase, and this increased vessel size is one contributor to the growth of **load centers**, or major ports where thousands of containers arrive and depart each week. As vessel sizes increase, it becomes more costly to stop (call) at multiple ports in a geographic area, and, as a result, oper-ators of larger containerships prefer to call at only one port in a geographic area. Load centers might affect the dynamics of international transportation in the sense that some ports will be relegated to providing feeder service to the load centers. In addition, load centers might affect supplemental transportation providers, such as truck and rail, particularly if the existing road and rail infrastructure is insufficient to accommodate the higher volumes that will be associated with the megaports.

Shipping Conferences and Alliances

Beginning in the mid-1860s, ocean rates were determined by **shipping conferences**, or cartels of all ocean vessel operators operating between certain trade areas such as Asia and Europe. Historically, shipping conferences provided both rate stability and guaranteed space availability due in large part to the ability of member carriers to collectively set rates and service levels without fear of antitrust prosecution.

The relationship between buyers (shippers) and sellers (carriers) and groups of sellers (conferences or alliances) has changed dramatically over the last 20 years, and these relationships are currently very fluid. In certain regions, this commercial relationship has moved from a tightly regulated environment to a largely unregulated environment wherein shippers and carriers are free to work out whatever commercial relationship best suits them in confidential contractual agreements.

In particular, the influence of shipping conferences has been on the wane in the United States and Europe since the late 1990s. For example, although the U.S. Ocean Shipping Reform Act (OSRA) of 1998 did not explicitly prohibit shipping conferences, it allowed ocean shippers and carriers to negotiate confidential contracts—which severely undermined conferences' power and lessened their appeal. Moreover, in late 2008, the European Union (EU) removed the shipping conferences' antitrust immunity for collective ratemaking for ocean shipments between EU countries. This dissolution of European shipping conferences has caused shippers worldwide to push for the end of shipping conferences in their particular regions. However, early indications are that the intra-Asia, Asia-U.S., and Asia–Europe conference systems will continue to operate.[19]

In the mid-1990s, **ocean carrier alliances**, in which carriers retain their individual identities but cooperate in the area of operations, began forming in the container trades. There are presently three major ocean carrier alliances: the Grand Alliance [consisting of Hapag-Lloyd, Nippon Yusen Keisha (NYK) Line, Orient Overseas Container Line (OOCL)]; the New World Alliance [consisting of American President Lines (APL), Hyundai Merchant Marine, Mitsui O.S.K. Lines (MOL)]; and the CYKH Alliance [consisting of China Ocean Shipping Company (Cosco), Hanjin, "K" Line, Yang Ming]. These alliances provide two primary benefits to participating members, namely, the sharing of vessel space and the ability to offer shippers a broader service net-work (i.e., ports of call). For example, in early 2010, the Grand Alliance added Vietnam to a liner route that runs from Southeast Asia through the Suez Canal to the North American East Coast and

---

[19] Peter T. Leach, "Carriers' New Math," *The Journal of Commerce*, March 24, 2008, 12–15.

back.[20] Although alliances are not conferences, their size allows the alliances to exercise considerable clout in their dealings with shippers, port terminal operators, and connecting land carriers.

International Airfreight

Three types of international airfreight operations exist: chartered aircraft, integrated air carriers that specialize in carrying parcels, and scheduled air carriers. Chartering an entire aircraft is, of course, expensive, but sometimes the expense can be justified. For example, chartered aircraft have been used in the transport of livestock sold for breeding purposes, and one shipment involved carrying 7,000 cattle from Texas to southern Chile. Nineteen flights were involved, each lasting 15 hours. The comparable time by sea was 20 days, and past experience showed that the sea journey was hard on the cattle, causing either lung damage or long delays before the animals could be bred.

A second type of international airfreight focuses on parcel services offered by well-known carriers such as UPS, FedEx, and DHL International. These companies provide land pickup and delivery services for documents and small parcels and are called *integrated carriers* because they own all their vehicles and the facilities that fall in between. These parcel services are of special significance to international logistics because they often provide the fastest service between many major points. They are also often employed to carry the documentation that is generated by—and is very much a part of—the international movement of materials, although many international trade documents can now be transferred electronically. The integrated carriers also handle documentation services for their clients.

The principal function of scheduled airlines is to carry passengers; freight tends to be a secondary consideration and is often carried in the bellies of passenger aircraft. Having said this, some scheduled airlines use all-freight aircraft (called *freighters*) in certain markets. For example, Lufthansa, a German airline, flies freighters between Frankfurt (Germany) and Beijing (China), as well as between Frankfurt and Delhi (India) among other city pairs.

Historically, the routes of scheduled international air carriers were established by negotiations between nations, and these negotiations generally involved two countries (called *bilateral agreements*). The types of issues that could be negotiated in these bilateral agreements included the number of flights between the two nations, the types of aircraft to be used, the total number of seats to be offered, the regions or cities to be served, and the carriers that were to serve particular regions or city pairs, among others.

While the traditional bilateral air agreements provided an important stimulus to international air transportation, these agreements tended to be quite restrictive in nature, as illustrated in the previous paragraph. To this end, **open skies agreements**, which liberalize international aviation opportunities and limit federal government involvement, have become increasingly popular in the twenty-first century. Perhaps the most prominent open skies treaty is the Open Aviation Area agreement between the United States and 27 EU member states that went into effect in March 2008. A key provision of this agreement is that any EU airline as well as any U.S. airline can fly between any point in the EU and any point in the United States.[21] Moreover, Japan and the United States agreed to an open skies agreement in December 2009, which if ratified by both countries would reduce Fed Ex's long-standing dominance in Japan's air cargo market by allowing UPS to expand its Japanese operations.[22]

Surface Transport Considerations

While ocean shipping and air transportation play a key role in international trade, particularly among shipments that move long distances, an understanding of surface transportation considerations is

---

[20] Peter T. Leach, "Grand Alliance Adds Vietnam Stop," *JOC Online*, December 14, 2009, 4.

[21] Cathy Buyck, "A Slow Opening," *Air Transport World*, March 2008, 24–30.

[22] No author, "US, Japan Taxi to Open Skies," *The Journal of Commerce*, December 21–28, 2009, 8.

also important. For example, highway freight transportation is accomplished by trucks (motor carriers) in certain countries; alternatively, highway freight transportation can be provided by bicycles or some type of animal and cart combination in certain countries.

Surface transportation considerations in international logistics include an understanding of both a country's infrastructure and its modal operating characteristics. As an example of infrastructure characteristics, the United States ranks first in the world in terms of highway mileage (approximately 6.5 million kilometers), followed by India (approximately 3.3 million kilometers) and China (approximately 1.9 million kilometers). However, only 2,000 kilometers of Indian highways are classified as expressways, compared to 75,000 for the United States and 41,000 kilometers for China.[23]

The relative paucity of expressways in India suggests that motor carrier transit times might be slower than in other countries, and indeed one study suggests that a 1,000-mile truck shipment from Kolkata (formerly Calcutta) to Mumbai (formerly Bombay) can take between 7 and 10 days in part because of poor road conditions.[24] By comparison, several major U.S. motor carriers can provide two-day service for a shipment moving from Cleveland, Ohio, to Orlando, Florida, a distance of approximately 1,050 miles.

In addition to infrastructure characteristics, it's also important to understand a country's modal operating characteristics for surface transportation. For example, a motor carrier shipment from Cleveland, Ohio, to Orlando, Florida, experiences virtually no delays when moving across state borders (e.g., from Ohio into West Virginia and from West Virginia into Virginia). Alternatively, multistate motor carrier shipments in other countries can be subject to lengthy delays when moving across state borders. One source of delays is that certain countries limit a motor carrier's operations to within a particular state's borders; as a result, multistate shipments must be transferred from one company's vehicle to another company's vehicle whenever crossing into another state. Another source of delays is that certain countries conduct inspections of trucks as they move from one state to another. This can include physical counting and inspection of all shipments, inspection of documentation, vehicle inspection, as well as driver inspection. Keep in mind that delays, whatever their source, result in slower transit times and increased costs.

Service performance is another important modal operational characteristic associated with surface transportation in other countries. For example, freight is given lower priority than passengers in rail transportation in China. Railroad transportation in China is also plagued by poor handling techniques, resulting in higher damage than if shipments moved by truck. In addition, the theft of rail freight is quite common in China, and in some cases shippers provide their own security guards on trains to protect their goods from theft![25]

An alternative to surface transport in some nations is **short-sea shipping (SSS)**, which refers to waterborne transportation that utilizes inland and coastal waterways to move shipments from domestic ports to their destination.[26] SSS is more widely accepted and practiced in Europe (see Figure 14-8), and the EU has championed a Motorways of the Sea concept that specifies four well-defined SSS lanes involving EU member nations. Potential benefits to SSS include reduced rail and truck congestion, reduced highway damage, a reduction in truck-related noise and air pollution, and improved waterways utilization. Although the short-sea concept is receiving increased attention in North America, with a particular focus on the Great Lakes and the Atlantic Coast, currently SSS is only marginally used in North America due to regulatory and operational factors.[27]

---

[23] Highway data taken from *The CIA World Factbook*, 2009.
[24] Pagadala and Mulaik, "Now's the Time for an India Strategy."
[25] Christina Wu, "China Logistics Profile," *USDA Foreign Agricultural Service GAIN Report*, 2003.
[26] www.marad.dot.gov.
[27] Marc-André Roy and James Frost, "Unprecedented Opportunities to Promote Short-Sea Shipping in Canada," *Canadian Sailings*, February 9, 2009, 16–17.

FIGURE 14-8 **Ports in Europe and in the Mediterranean That Are Connected to Antwerp by "Short-Sea" Water Transport**

Source: Drawing copyright PUBLITRA, Belgium. Reprinted with permission.

INTERNATIONAL TRADE INVENTORIES

Even under the best conditions, the movement of products in an international supply chain is never as smooth as a comparable domestic movement. Because greater uncertainties, misunderstandings, and delays often arise in international movements, safety stocks must be larger. In addition, inventory valuation is difficult because of continually changing exchange rates. If goods are valued in the currency of where they are produced, that value can fluctuate with respect to the currency value of where the product is being stored. When a nation's (or the world's) currency is unstable, investments in inventories often rise because they are believed to be less risky than holding cash or securities.

Firms involved in international trade must give careful thought to their inventory policies, in part because inventory available for sale in one nation may not necessarily serve the needs of markets in nearby nations. Consider, for example, that electrical voltages, electrical plugs, and electrical sockets differ across countries. As a result, a 120-volt electrical product designed for use in the United States would need both a voltage converter and a plug adapter in order to be used in Europe.

Product return (reverse logistics) policies are another concern with respect to international inventory management. One issue is that, unlike the United States where products can be returned for virtually any reason, some countries don't allow returns unless the product is defective in some respect. A second challenge with international returns is that it may be unreasonable or impractical to tell buyers to return a defective item to the country where it was produced.

Warehousing is another inventory-related consideration associated with international logistics. Whereas warehousing facilities in economically developed countries have been developed to meet the requirements of contemporary logistics systems (e.g., high ceilings and sufficient lighting), warehousing facilities in other countries can be more problematic. Inefficient warehousing practices can affect inventory carrying costs through increased storage, handling, obsolescence, or shrinkage costs. In China, for example, the combination of poor warehousing facilities and unskilled warehousing management has led to high levels of inventory loss, damage, and deterioration.[28]

LOGISTICS PERFORMANCE INDEX[29]

We'll conclude this chapter with a look at a relatively new international logistics concept, the **Logistics Performance Index** (**LPI**), which was first introduced in 2007 and updated in early 2010. The LPI was created in recognition of the importance of logistics in global trade and measures a country's performance across six logistical dimensions (seven logistical dimensions were evaluated in 2007):

- Efficiency of the clearance process (i.e., speed, simplicity, and predictability of formalities) by border control agencies, including customs;
- Quality of trade- and transport-related infrastructure (e.g., ports, railroads, roads, and information technology);
- Ease of arranging competitively priced shipments;
- Competence and quality of logistics services (e.g., transport operators and customs brokers);
- Ability to track and trace consignments;
- Timeliness of shipments in reaching the destination within the scheduled or expected delivery time.

The LPI incorporates data for approximately 155 countries; Table 14-3 lists the five highest- and five lowest-rated countries in terms of their overall LPI score (i.e., score on all seven dimensions).

TABLE 14-3	Highest- and Lowest-Rated Countries Based on Overall LPI Score		
Highest Rated	**LPI Score**	**Lowest Rated**	**LPI Score**
Germany	4.11	Rwanda	2.04
Singapore	4.09	Namibia	2.02
Sweden	4.08	Sierra Leone	1.97
The Netherlands	4.07	Eritrea	1.70
Luxembourg	3.98	Somalia	1.34

Note: 1 = lowest possible score; 5 = highest possible score

Source: Connecting to Compete: Trade Logistics in the Global Economy (Washington, DC: The World Bank, 2010).

---

[28] John Kerr, "10 Key Challenges for the Chinese Logistics Industry," *Logistics Management*, February 2005, S64–S68.
[29] The material in this section is based on *Connecting to Compete: Trade Logistics in the Global Economy* (Washington, DC: The World Bank, 2010).

The LPI is a potentially valuable international logistics tool because the data can be analyzed from several different perspectives. First, the LPI can be analyzed for all countries according to the overall LPI score (see Table 14-3) as well as according to scores on each of the six dimensions. For example, while Singapore ranks second in terms of overall LPI score, it ranks first in terms of the "ease of arranging competitively priced shipments" dimension.

Second, the LPI can be analyzed in terms of an individual country's performance relative to its geographic region and income group. For example, one can compare Argentina's overall and dimension-specific LPI scores to Latin American and Caribbean countries as well as to upper-middle income countries. Third, the overall and dimension-specific LPI scores can be compared for up to 20 countries. For example, one can compare the LPI scores among the BRIC (Brazil, Russia, India, and China) nations.

Summary

This chapter covered various aspects of international logistics, which differs from domestic logistics in many respects, such as by having a requirement for numerous documents as well as by greater distances between origin and destination points. Macroenvironmental influences can provide significant challenges for international logistics; the chapter discussed three specific macroenvironmental factors—political, economic, and cultural.

From a political perspective, we learned that international trade can be influenced through tariff and nontariff barriers and that federal governments are actively involved in cross-border trade. The chapter also mentioned that different economic factors, such as currency fluctuations and economic integration, can impact international logistics. In terms of culture, a country's time orientation can influence the use of schedules as well as the emphasis placed on on-time performance.

The chapter also looked at three key operational issues—documentation, terms of sale, and methods of payment—in international logistics. Several key pieces of international documentation, including the certificate of origin and shipper's export declaration, were examined, and international terms of sale—Incoterms—were discussed. And because international logistics is complex, many firms rely on specialists, such as international freight forwarders and export packers, to help with export and import transactions.

The chapter also examined transportation and inventory considerations in international distribution. We looked at ocean shipping, international airfreight, and surface transportation, and we learned that the greater uncertainties associated with international shipments necessitate higher inventory levels. The chapter concluded with a discussion of a new international logistics concept, the Logistics Performance Index.

Questions for Discussion and Review

1. Discuss some of the key political restrictions on cross-border trade.
2. How might a particular country's government be involved in international trade?
3. Discuss how a nation's market size might impact international trade and, in turn, international logistics.
4. How might economic integration impact international logistics?
5. How can language considerations impact the packaging and labeling of international shipments?
6. What is a certificate of origin, a commercial invoice, and a shipper's export declaration?
7. Pick, and describe, one C Incoterm, one D Incoterm, one E Incoterm, and one F Incoterm.
8. Name the four methods of payment for international shipments. Which method is riskiest for the buyer? For the seller?
9. Discuss four possible functions that might be performed by international freight forwarders.
10. What is an NVOCC?
11. What are the two primary purposes of export packing?
12. Discuss the importance of water transportation for international trade.
13. Explain the load center concept. How might load centers affect the dynamics of international transportation?
14. Discuss the role of ocean carrier alliances in international logistics.
15. How do integrated air carriers impact the effectiveness and efficiency of international logistics?
16. How do open skies agreements differ from bilateral agreements?
17. Discuss the potential sources of delays in certain countries with respect to motor carrier shipments that move across state borders.
18. Define what is meant by short-sea shipping (SSS), and discuss some advantages of SSS.
19. What are some challenges associated with inventory management in cross-border trade?
20. What is the Logistics Performance Index? How can it be used?

Suggested Readings

Banomyong, Ruth, P. Cook, and P. Kent. "Formulating Regional Logistics Development Policy: The Case of ASEAN." *International Journal of Logistics: Research & Applications* 11, no. 5 (2008): 359–379.

Ghijsen, Paul W. Th., Janjaap Semeijn, and Herman Van Der Linden. "Rail Freight in Europe: Different Perspectives on Achieving Higher Service Levels." *Transportation Journal* 46, no. 4 (2007): 42–57.

Kilgore, Mike, Abraham Joseph, and Jeff Metersky. "The Logistical Challenges of Doing Business in India." *Supply Chain Management Review* 11, no. 7 (2007): 36–43.

Kwan, Clarence, and Kris Knutsen. "China's New Transport Corridor: The Yangtze." *Supply Chain Management Review* 10, no. 9 (2006): 16–21.

Lorentz, Harri, Chee Yew Wong, and Olli-Pekka Hilmola. "Emerging Distribution Systems in Central and Eastern Europe." *International Journal of Physical Distribution & Logistics Management* 37, no. 8 (2007): 670–697.

Markides, Vassilis, and Matthias Holweg. "On the Diversification of International Freight Forwarders: A UK Perspective." *International Journal of Physical Distribution & Logistics Management* 36, no. 5 (2006): 336–359.

Paixao Casaca, Ana. C. "Motorway of the Sea Port Requirements: The Viewpoint of Port Authorities." *International Journal of Logistics: Research & Applications* 11, no. 4 (2008): 279–294.

Ryu, Sungmin, and Martha Cook. "The Effect of LTO Culture on International Supply Chain Contracts." *Journal of Applied Business Research* 21, no. 4 (2005): 95–105.

Sohail, M. Sadiq, Rohit Bhatnagar, and Amrik S. Sohal. "A Comparative Study on the Use of Third Party Logistics Services by Singaporean and Malaysian Firms." *International Journal of Physical Distribution & Logistics Management* 36, no. 9 (2006): 690–701.

Volwes, Timothy M., and Sean Tierney. "The Geographic Impact of 'Open Skies' Policies on Trans-Tasman Air Passenger Service." *Asia Pacific Viewpoint* 48, no. 3 (2007): 344–354.

Wagner, Stephan M. "Innovation Management in the German Transportation Industry." *Journal of Business Logistics* 29, no. 2 (2008): 215–231.

Yap, Wei Yim, Jasmine Lam, and Theo Notteboom. "Developments in Container Port Competition in East Asia." *Transport Reviews* 26, no. 2 (2006): 167–188.

CASE

CASE 14-1   Nürnberg Augsburg Maschinenwerke (N.A.M.)

The Nürnberg Augsburg Maschinenwerke, one of Germany's most successful manufacturing companies, enjoys a long tradition. It dates from 1748, when the St. Antony Iron Mill opened in Oberhausen (located in the heart of the Ruhrgebiet industrial region) during the beginning years of German industrialization. The owners soon founded additional iron and coal mills, then established the firm as Gute Hoffungshuette (GHH). Shortly following, in Augsburg and Nürnberg, several companies joined together to form Nürnberg Augsburg Maschinenwerke (N.A.M.). These two firms, GHH and N.A.M., would ultimately merge in the early twentieth century. In the interim, N.A.M. had distinguished itself through the work of Rudolf Diesel, who invented his famous engine and then brought it to N.A.M. late in the nineteenth century. The diesel engine competed with the internal combustion engine in early automotive design and today powers heavy trucks, turbines, railroad engines, and ships. Based on this success, N.A.M. swiftly expanded manufacturing operations and distribution across the globe, only to have its foreign operations compromised by international politics on two occasions. First, N.A.M. lost most of its foreign property in the wake of World War I, a setback that, among other adjustments, encouraged its merger with GHH

in 1920. Second, N.A.M. lost all of its foreign property again after World War II and had to rebuild and restructure much of its domestic operation as well. In 1955, the company opened a truck unit in Munich, which would later become the new company headquarters.

By 2003, the company had reclaimed its preeminence as a global player in heavy truck and bus design, engineering, and manufacturing, as well as in print technology and rocket and energy science. It had reestablished both its plants and sales offices across the globe. It is one of the largest diesel engine makers in the world. Karl Huber was the N.A.M. regional vice president of sales for South America. He supervised a team of local sales representatives in the countries of that continent, plus a small group of people in the Munich headquarters.

On August 15, Huber received an e-mail from Leopold Escabar in Caracas, who had just returned from an important meeting with local authorities in charge of redesigning the local public transportation systems for the Brazilian cities of São Paulo and Rio de Janeiro. Escabar had attended the meeting along with salespeople from competing truck and bus companies. Escabar gave Huber some good news and some bad news. Escabar had been told N.A.M. was favored to receive an order for 224 N.A.M. class #4-G two-section articulated buses (or "accordion" buses, as Escabar liked to call them), with the possibility of securing a contract for an additional 568 buses. To win the business, however, N.A.M. would have to meet cost and timing guarantees.

The customers first required that N.A.M. must match or beat the total price per unit, including shipping, that N.A.M. had received for a shipment of 233 buses to the transit district of Buenos Aires, six months earlier. That price was Eurodollar (€)124,500 per bus. Huber had built in a small extra profit margin on the Buenos Aires deal, so he felt confident that to meet their pricing demand he could shave profit a little, if necessary, in this case.

The second guarantee, however, was more worrisome: The Brazilian authorities were feeling political heat because they were badly behind schedule in implementing their transportation plan and needed proof to show the public that their new programs were underway. So they had made this offer to N.A.M. on strict condition that the company could ensure delivery of the first 25 buses to Santos, the port that serves São Paulo, by November 15 (only three months away). If N.A.M. delivered this initial 90-day order on time, the company would receive a contract for the remaining 199 vehicles to be delivered in full within the following 15 months. The follow-on order for 568 more vehicles was, essentially, contingent on meeting terms of the initial contract to the letter, with regard to the 224 buses. All buses were to be delivered to Santos, a principal Brazilian port.

Huber whistled softly to himself as he read Escabar's e-mail. This would be a major order. In a single stroke, it could move him ahead of his regional sales targets for several quarters to come. Huber immediately sent back an e-mail, instructing Escabar to tentatively accept the offer, assuring the local authorities that they'd have their 25 buses in 90 days and the rest within 18 months. N.A.M. would formally agree to the proposal within five working days. Then he scratched his head and tried to figure out how. Huber had four days before the next managing director's meeting, at which time he would present the project and, with the vice president for production, propose a plan to accomplish it. Huber lunged for the phone and, scarcely glancing at the number pad, his fingers automatically dialed 4823.

Dieter Berndsen, the production vice president, listened as his old friend Huber described the opportunity, jotting down notes as he went. He explained to Huber that the factory in Munich was already producing to its limits, and the two other German facilities were also facing a backlog of orders through the fourth quarter. So Berndsen offered two immediate possibilities. First, he considered wait-listing a 40-bus order from the Thai military at the Munich plant. He said he was reluctant to do this, however, because the Thais had ordered several product modifications, and the Munich line had been already set up to handle them. Second, Berndsen suggested sending the new Brazil order to N.A.M.'s Prague facility. Prague was the smallest of all the European plants and had the oldest, slowest assembly lines, but they were just finishing up manufacture of an order of #4-G's and, due to a recent order cancellation, would now be working at only 70 percent capacity through year-end. Within eight weeks, figured Berndsen, Prague could easily handle the order for Brazil's first 25 buses.

Huber eagerly agreed, as Berndsen decided to recommend Prague for this assignment. The problem was that this facility could not produce fast enough to fulfill more than 20 percent of the rest of the contract (for the 224 buses), which meant that he would have to coordinate production and delivery on the rest of this order from other plants. Sighing audibly over the phone line, Berndsen said, "Thanks a lot for the new headache, Hubie. Let me mull this one over for a bit before I call you back. But don't worry, we'll make your deadline—and you will make your bonus. Just remember to cut me in for a piece."

Huber chuckled, thanked him, and hung up.

Berndsen decided to split the full order (224 buses) among the factories in Prague and the much larger plant in Munich. To finalize both scheduling and pricing, he now needed to estimate the time it would take to fulfill the order, as well as the cost of transportation. He was inclined to use the Deutsche Bundesbahn to transport the buses by train to the North Sea Port of Bremerhaven, but he wasn't sure that this was the best solution for each of the plants involved.

Berndsen's immediate problem was the first shipment of buses, which would be ready to leave Prague on October 15. Berndsen asked Marcus Weiss, his supply-chain analyst, to create a worksheet that would show all costs and times required to get the buses from the Prague factory to the Port of Bremerhaven, and he also asked Weiss to identify viable alternatives. (Europe possesses an extensive network of rivers and channels that connect together its network of commercial waterways. Barges represent alternatives to the road and railroad. The European Green movement continually asked shippers to use the water routes and, occasionally, would attempt to publicly embarrass shippers who used trucks rather than water.) Consequently, the Prague plant sometimes transported buses on barges via the Elbe, north to Hamburg.

EXHIBIT 14-A   Map of Central Europe

The German plants occasionally shipped north to Bremerhaven or Hamburg, via a network of industrial waterways, or westward, over the River Rhein, to the Port of Rotterdam in the Netherlands. (See Exhibit 14-A.)

Following is some of the information Weiss assembled for Berndsen:

- By train, the geographic distances between plants and ports were as follows: Prague to Hamburg 490K, Prague to Rotterdam 640K.
- N.A.M. would need three days to get the buses from the factories in Prague to the Port of Bremerhaven or Hamburg by train and four or five days to reach Rotterdam. The advantage of Rotterdam comes, however, in the shipping time from there to Santos, which saves a day versus Bremerhaven or Hamburg, and ocean shipping charges are 5 percent less.
- The Czech railway could transport the load to the border with Germany, where the Deutsche Bundesbahn would take over the flatcars, which carry two buses each. The Bundesbahn quotes a price of €1,643 per flatcar from Prague to Hamburg, which includes the service by its Czech partner. If rail were used from Prague to Rotterdam, the cost per flatcar would be €1,943. In either port, it costs another €45 per bus to have it unloaded and driven to alongside the vessel. The vessel line can load and pack 20 buses per day, charging €25 per bus and up to 30 buses with overtime charges. The overtime

charges would amount to an additional €15 per bus (for buses 21, 22, etc.). All charges per bus included detaching the two halves.
- Using the waterways instead of trains to reach the Hamburg port from Prague would decrease the transportation cost by €48 per bus. Waterway transportation would increase the transport time necessary by three days to Hamburg.
- For transoceanic shipping on any of these routes, N.A.M. works with Hapag-Lloyd AG. Hapag-Lloyd is able to offer a cheap and flexible commodity cost, through its alliance with NYK, and OOCL, for the ocean transport of the buses. One vessel could carry up to 125 buses as deck cargo, but they would have to be disassembled at their accordion junctions and then reassembled again at their destination.
- The cost per bus (in shipments of 20 buses or more) from Bremerhaven or Hamburg to Santos is quoted at €6,000, and the trip requires 18 days. Hapag-Lloyd indicates that deck space is available for the initial shipment of 25 buses on vessels departing Hamburg on October 24, October 27, October 31, and November 3. Hapag-Lloyd also has space on vessels leaving from Rotterdam to Santos on October 23, October 28, and November 2.
- Handling (unloading) in Santos is estimated to cost another €94 per bus, and this includes reattaching the two halves.
- The interest for N.A.M.'s line of credit is 10 percent.

Questions

1. Assume that you are Weiss. How many viable alternatives do you have to consider regarding the initial shipment of 25 buses?
2. Which of the routing alternatives would you recommend to meet the initial 90-day deadline for the 25-bus shipment? Train or waterway? To which port(s)? What would it cost?
3. What additional information would be helpful for answering Question 2?
4. How important, in fact, are the transport costs for the initial shipment of 25 buses?
5. What kinds of customer service support must be provided for this initial shipment of 25 buses? Who is responsible?
6. The Brazilian buyer wants the buses delivered at Santos. Weiss looks up the International Chamber of Commerce's Incoterms and finds two categories of "delivered" at a receiving port:

- *DES (Delivered Ex Ship).* In this type of transaction, the seller must pay all the costs and bear all the risk of transport up to the foreign port of unloading but not including the cost or risk of unloading the cargo from the ship.
- *DEQ (Delivered Ex Quay).* This is the same as DES, except that the terms provide for the seller to pay the costs of unloading the cargo from the vessel and the cost of import clearance.

How should he choose? Why?

7. Would you make the same routing recommendation for the second, larger (199 buses) component of the order, after the initial 90-day deadline is met? Why or why not?
8. How important, if at all, is it for N.A.M. to ship via water to show its support of the Green movement's desires?

GLOSSARY

ABC analysis of inventory Concept that recognizes that because inventories are not of equal value to a firm, they should not be managed in the same way.

Accessorial service Transportation service that is supplemental to line-haul transportation.

Accumulating (bulk-making) Bringing together inventory from different sources.

Activity-based costing (ABC) A technique that seeks to better understand the cost of a product by identifying what activities drive particular costs.

Agglomeration (industry cluster) Refers to the net advantage which can be gained by a sharing of common locations by various enterprises.

Agile supply chain Focuses on an organization's ability to respond to changes in demand with respect to volume and variety.

Allocating (bulk-breaking) Breaking larger quantities into smaller quantities.

Amodal shipper A transportation manager who purchases a pre-specified level of transportation service and is indifferent to the mode(s) or carrier(s) used to provide the actual transportation service.

Application-specific software Refers to software that has been developed for managers to deal with specific logistics functions or activities (e.g., transportation management systems).

Asset turnover In the Strategic Profit Model, asset turnover measures the efficiency of capital employed to generate sales.

Assets Are what a company owns and include current assets and long-time assets.

Assorting Building up a variety of different products for resale to a particular customer.

Back order Placing an order for an item that is out of stock.

Balance of payments Systems of accounts that records a country's international financial transactions.

Balance sheet Reflects an organization's assets, liabilities, and owners' equity at a given point in time.

Balanced Scorecard (BSC) A strategic planning and performance management system that evaluates a business from four distinct perspectives: customers, internal business processes, learning and growth, and financial.

Barge Flatboard boat used to transport heavy products.

Benchmarking Using measures of another organization's performance to judge one's own performance.

Bill of lading The most important single transportation document that is the basic operating document in the industry.

Bribes Money paid before an exchange.

Broker A company that helps both shipper and carrier achieve lower freight rates and more efficient utilization of carrier equipment. Brokers also help match carriers to loads.

Brownfields Locations that contain chemicals or other types of industrial wastes.

Building-blocks concept Combining smaller packages into larger units that can be more efficiently handled at one time.

Bullwhip effect Characterized by variability in demand orders among supply chain participants.

"C-level" position Refers to corporate officers such as a chief executive officer (CEO), chief operating officer (COO), or chief financial officer (CFO).

Cargo preference Requires a certain percentage of traffic to move on a nation's flag vessels.

Cause and effect (associative) forecasting Assumes that one or more factors are related to demand, and the relationship between cause and effect can be used to estimate future demand.

Center-of-gravity approach An approach for locating a single facility that minimizes the distance to existing facilities.

Centralized logistics organization An organization maintains a single logistics department that administers the related activities for the entire company from the home office.

Certificate of origin Specifies the country(ies) in which a product is manufactured.

Class rate system A system that simplifies each of the three primary rate factors—product, weight, and distance.

Closed-loop systems Refers to systems that consider the return flow of products, their reuse, and the marketing and distribution of recovered products.

Collaborative planning, forecasting, and replenishment (CPFR) Retail industry initiative where trading partners share planning and forecasting data to better match supply and demand.

Commercial invoice A document used in cross-border trade that summarizes the entire transaction and contains key information such as a description of the goods, the terms of sale and payment, and so on.

Commodity rate A specific rate for every possible combination of product, weight, and distance.

Common carrier Transportation carrier that has agreed to serve the general public and assumes four legal obligations: service, delivery, reasonable rates, and avoidance of discrimination.

Complementary products Inventories that are used or distributed together (e.g., razor blades and razors).

Concealed loss or damage Loss or damage that is not apparent until after a shipment has been unpacked and inspected.

Consignee The receiver of a shipment.

Container Security Initiative (CSI) An agreement in which the world's ports agree to allow U.S. customs agents to identify and inspect high-risk containers bound for the United States before they are loaded onto ships.

Containers A uniform sealed reusable metal "box" in which goods are shipped.

Contract carrier A contract carrier provides specialized service to each customer based on a contractual arrangement.

Contract (third-party) warehousing A type of contract logistics that focuses on providing unique and specially tailored warehousing services to particular clients.

Cost leadership strategy Requires an organization to pursue activities that will enable it to become the low cost producer in an industry for a given level of quality.

Cost trade-offs Changes to one logistics activity cause some costs to increase and others to decrease.

Cross-docking A process where product is received in a facility, occasionally married with product going to the same destination, then shipped at the earliest opportunity, without going into long-term storage.

Cubes out Occurs when a cargo takes up a vehicle's or a container's cubic capacity before reaching its weight capacity.

Current ratio A financial ratio that measures how well an organization can pay its current liabilities by using only current assets.

Customer profitability analysis (CPA) Refers to the allocation of revenues and costs to customer segments or individual customers to calculate the profitability of the segments or customers.

Customer service The ability of logistics management to satisfy users in terms of time, dependability, communication, and convenience.

Customs Trade Partnership Against Terrorism (C-TPAT) A program in which public and private organizations work together to prevent terrorism against the United States through imports and transportation.

Cycle (base) stock Inventory needed to satisfy demand during an order cycle.

Data Facts or recorded measures of certain phenomena.

Data mining Utilizes sophisticated quantitative techniques to find hidden patterns in large volumes of data.

Data warehouse A central repository for all relevant data collected by an organization.

Dead inventory (dead stock) Product for which there is no demand.

Decentralized logistics organization Logistics-related decisions are made separately at the divisional or product group level and often in different geographic regions.

Demand management The creation across the supply chain and its markets of a coordinated flow of demand.

Demurrage A charge assessed by rail carriers to users that fail to unload and return vehicles or containers promptly.

Density A measure of how heavy a product is in relation to its size.

Department of Transportation (DOT) U.S. federal government body with primary responsibility for transportation safety regulation.

Detention A payment from a shipper or consignee to a truck carrier for having kept the carrier's equipment too long.

Differentiation strategy Entails an organization developing a product and/or service that offers unique attributes that are valued by customers and that the customers perceive to be distinct from competitor offerings.

Dimensional (dim) weight Considers a shipment's density (the amount of space occupied relative to weight) to determine a shipment's billable weight.

Disintermediation The removal of levels (layers) from a channel of distribution.

Distribution center A warehouse with an emphasis on quick throughput, such as is needed in supporting marketing efforts.

Documentation The documents associated with transportation shipments.

Dunnage Material that is used to block and brace products inside carrier equipment to prevent the shipment from shifting in transit and becoming damaged.

Economic order quantity (EOQ) An order size that minimizes the sum of carrying and ordering costs.

Economic utility Refers to the value or usefulness of a product in fulfilling customer needs and wants.

Electronic data interchange (EDI) Computer-to-computer transmission of business data in a structured format.

Electronic procurement (e-procurement) Uses the Internet to make it easier, faster, and less expensive for an organization to purchase goods and services.

Embargoes Prohibition of trade between particular countries.

Enterprise resource planning (ERP) system Lets a company automate and integrate the majority of its business processes, share common data and practices across the enterprise, and produce and access information in a real-time environment.

Ergonomics The science that seeks to adapt work or working conditions to suit the abilities of the worker.

Excess capacity Unused available space.

Excess (surplus) materials Stock that exceeds the reasonable requirements of an organization.

Exempt carrier For-hire carriers that have been exempted from economic regulation through provisions in various pieces of legislation.

Expatriate workers Employees who are sent to other countries for extended periods of time.

Expediting The need to rapidly move a shipment to its final destination.

Expenses (costs) Provide a dollar value for the costs incurred in generating revenues during a given period of time.

Export management company Firm that acts as the export sales department for a manufacturer.

Export packers An international logistics specialist that custom packs shipments when the exporter lacks the equipment or expertise to do so itself.

Facility closing A company discontinues operations at a current site because the operations are no longer needed or can be absorbed by other facilities.

Facility location Refers to choosing the locations for distribution centers, warehouses, and production facilities to facilitate logistical effectiveness and efficiency.

Facility relocation A firm must move operations to another facility to better serve suppliers or customers.

Fast supply chain Emphasizes a speed or time component.

Fixed order interval system Inventory is replenished on a constant, set schedule and is always ordered at a specific time; the quantity ordered varies depending on forecasted sales before the next order date.

Fixed order quantity system Inventory is replenished with a set quantity every time it is ordered; the time interval between orders may vary.

Fixed slot location Each product is assigned a specific location in a warehouse and is always stored there.

Flexibility An organization's ability to address unexpected operational situations.

FOB destination A transportation term that signifies that the seller retains title and control of a shipment until it is delivered.

FOB origin A transportation term that signifies that the buyer assumes title and control of a shipment at the point of pickup.

Focus strategy Concentrates an organization's effort on a narrowly defined market to achieve either a cost leadership or differentiation advantage.

Form utility Refers to a product's being in a form that (1) can be used by the customer and (2) is of value to the customer.

Fourth-party logistics (lead logistics provider) General contractor that ensures that third-party logistics companies are working toward relevant supply chain goals and objectives.

Fragmented logistics structure Logistics activities are managed in multiple departments throughout an organization.

Free trade zone An area, usually near a port or an airport, where goods can be stored or processed before entering through the importing nation's customs inspections.

Freight bill An invoice submitted by a transportation carrier requesting to be paid.

Freight claims A document that notifies a transportation carrier of wrong or defective deliveries, delay, or other delivery shortcoming.

Freight forwarder Consolidates freight shipments and buys transportation services in volume rates.

Global positioning systems (GPS) Use satellites that allow companies to compute vehicle positions, velocity, and time.

Global procurement (sourcing) Refers to buying components and inputs anywhere in the world.

Global Supply Chain Forum (GSCF) model A framework that identifies eight relevant processes, such as customer relationship management, demand management, and order fulfillment, associated with supply chain management.

Globally Harmonized System of Classification and Labeling of Chemicals (GHS) An effort by the United Nations to classify and label hazardous materials that provides three key pieces of information: 1) a symbol; 2) a signal word; and 3) a hazard statement.

Grid systems A location technique utilizing a map or grid, with specific locations marked on the north–south and east–west axes. Its purpose is to find a location that minimizes transportation costs.

Hazardous material(s) Any item or agent (biological, chemical, physical) which has the potential to cause harm to humans, animals, or the environment, either by itself or through interaction with other factors.

Import quotas Absolute limits to the quantity of a product that can be imported into a country during a particular time period.

Importer Security Filing (ISF) rule Also known as "10 + 2;" a regulation that stipulates that importers are required to file 10 pieces of information, and carriers two pieces of information, before cargo is loaded at non-U.S. water ports.

Income statement Shows revenues, expenses, and profit for a period of time.

Incoterms Terms of sale for international transactions that represent, from the seller's viewpoint, the different locations, or stages, for quoting a price to an overseas buyer.

Information A body of facts in a format suitable for decision making.

Intermodal competition Refers to the number of transportation modes available to prospective users.

Intermodal transportation Using a container that can be transferred from the vehicle of one mode to a vehicle of another, and with the movement covered under a single bill of lading.

International freight forwarders An international trade specialist that can handle either vessel shipments or air shipments and that offers a number of different functions such as booking space on carriers, obtaining consular documents, and arranging for insurance, among others.

International logistics Refers to logistical activities associated with goods that move across national boundaries.

Intramodal competition Refers to competition among carriers within a particular mode.

Inventory Stocks of goods and materials that are maintained for many purposes.

Inventory carrying (holding) costs The costs of holding an inventory, such as interest on investment, insurance, deterioration, and so on.

Inventory shrinkage Refers to the fact that more items are recorded entering than leaving warehousing facilities.

Inventory tax Analogous to personal property taxes paid by individuals, an inventory tax is based on the value of inventory that is held by an organization on the assessment date.

Inventory turnover The number of times an inventory is used or replaced each year.

Investment recovery Identifies opportunities to recover revenues or reduce costs associated with scrap, surplus, obsolete, and waste materials.

ISO 9000 A set of generic standards used to document, implement, and demonstrate quality management and assurance systems.

Judgmental forecasting Refers to forecasting that involves judgment or intuition and is preferred in situations where there is limited, or no, historical data.

Just-in-time (JIT) approach Seeks to minimize inventory by reducing (if not eliminating) safety stock, as well as having the required amount of materials arrive at the production location at the exact time they are needed.

Kickbacks Money paid after an exchange.

Land bridge services Refers to a combination of water transportation and surface transportation between an origin and destination port.

Landed costs Price of the product at its source plus transportation costs to its destination.

Leagility Combines agility and leanness as a way to focus part of one's supply chain on a timely response to customer orders and/or product variety and another part of the supply chain on leveling out the planning requirements to smooth production output.

Lean manufacturing (lean) Focuses on the elimination of wastes and the increase of speed and flow.

Lean Six Sigma Integrates the goals and methods of the lean and Six Sigma approaches and recognizes that organizations cannot focus only on quality or speed.

Lean supply chain Focuses on eliminating all waste, including time, and ensuring a level schedule.

Less-than-truckload (LTL) carrier Shipments that range from about 150 to 10,000 pounds; they are often too big to handle manually, yet they do not fill an entire truck.

Letter of credit An international payment option that is issued by a bank and guarantees payment to a seller provided that the seller has complied with the applicable terms and conditions of the particular transaction.

Liabilities Financial obligations that a company owes to another party.

Line-haul Terminal-to-terminal movement of freight or passengers.

Load center A major port where thousands of containers arrive and depart per week. These ports specialize in the efficient handling of containers.

Locavore strategy Refers to food companies that purchase locally grown or produced foods.

Lock Raises or lowers barges so that they can meet the river's level as they move upstream or downstream.

Logistics According to the Council of Supply Chain Management Professionals, that part of supply chain management that plans, implements, and controls the efficient, effective forward and reverse flow and storage of goods, services, and related information between the point of origin and the point of consumption to meet customers' requirements.

Logistics information system (LIS) People, equipment, and procedures to gather, sort, analyze, evaluate, and distribute needed, timely, and accurate information to logistics decision makers.

Logistics Performance Index (LPI) An index that is designed to measure a country's performance across six logistical dimensions.

Logistics social responsibility Refers to corporate social responsibility issues that relate directly to logistics.

Macroenvironmental influences The uncontrollable forces and conditions facing an organization and include cultural, demographic, economic, natural, political, and technological factors.

Make-to-order Products are produced after receiving a customer order.

Make-to-stock Products are produced prior to receiving a customer order.

Malcolm Baldrige National Quality Award Established in the late 1980s to recognize U.S. organizations for their achievements in quality and performance.

Maquiladora plants Manufacturing plants that exist just south of the U.S.–Mexican border.

Marketing channels A set of institutions necessary to transfer the title to goods and to move goods from the point of production to the point of consumption and, as such, which consists of all the institutions and all the marketing activities in the marketing process.

Mass logistics A one-size-fits-all approach in which every customer gets the same type and levels of logistics service.

Materials handling (material handling) The short-distance movement of material between two or more points.

Materials management The movement and storage of materials into a firm.

Methods of payment With respect to international transactions refers to the manner by which a seller will be paid by a buyer.

Multichannel marketing systems Refers to separate marketing channels to serve customers.

Multiclient warehousing Mixes attributes of public and contract warehousing; services are more differentiated than a public facility but less customized than in a contract facility.

Multiple sourcing A procurement philosophy that suggests that by having more than one supplier increased amounts of competition, greater supply risk mitigation and improved market intelligence can arise.

Net profit margin Measures the proportion of each sales dollar that is kept as profit.

Nontariff barriers Restrictions other than tariffs that are placed on imported products.

Nonvessel-operating common carrier (NVOCC) In international trade, a firm that provides carrier services to shippers but owns no vessels itself.

Obsolete materials Refer to materials that are not likely to ever be used by the organization that purchased it.

Occupational Safety and Health Administration (OSHA) A U.S. federal agency that regulates workplaces to ensure the safety of workers.

Ocean carrier alliances Refers to an alliance in the container trades in which ocean carriers retain their individual identities but cooperate in the area of operations.

On-demand software (software-as-a-service) Refers to software that users access on a per-use basis instead of software they own or license for installation.

Open account A method of payment for international transactions where a seller sends the goods and all documents directly to the buyer and trusts the buyer to pay by a certain date.

Open skies agreement Refers to an agreement between two or more countries that liberalize international aviation opportunities and limit federal government involvement.

Order cycle Elapsed time between when a customer places an order and when the goods are received.

Order delivery The time from when a transportation carrier picks up the shipment until it is received by the customer.

Order fill rate The percentage of orders that can be completely and immediately filled from existing stock.

Order management The management of the various activities associated with the order cycle.

Order picking and assembly Includes all activities from when an appropriate location is authorized to fill an order until goods are loaded aboard an outbound carrier.

Order processing The time from when the seller receives an order until an appropriate location is authorized to fill the order.

Order to cash cycle The length of time it takes an organization to receive payment for an order.

Order transmittal The time from when the customer places or sends the order to when the seller receives it.

Order triage Classifying orders according to preestablished guidelines so that a company can prioritize how orders should be filled.

Ordering costs The costs associated with ordering inventory, such as order costs and setup costs.

Owners' equity Difference between what a company owns and what it owes at any particular point in time.

Packaging Materials used for the containment, protection, handling, delivery, and presentation of goods.

Pallet (skid) A small platform (made of plastic, steel, or wood) on which goods are placed for handling by mechanical means.

Paperless warehousing Generates and uses few or no paper documents and relies on technology to accomplish the relevant tasks.

Parcel carriers Companies that specialize in transporting parcels.

Part-to-picker system The pick location is brought to the picker (e.g., carousels).

Partnerships Positive, long-term relationships between supply chain participants.

Perfect order An order that simultaneously achieves relevant customer metrics.

Physical distribution Storage of finished product and movement to the customers.

Pick-to-light technology The orders to be picked are identified by lights placed on shelves or racks.

Picker-to-part system An order picker goes to where the product is located (e.g., a forklift).

Piggyback transportation Truck trailers on flatcars, also referred to as TOFC.

Pilferage Employee theft.

Pipeline (in-transit) stock Inventory that is in route between various nodes in a logistics system.

Place utility Having products available where they are needed by customers.

Possession utility Refers to the value or usefulness that comes from a customer being able to take possession of a product.

Postponement The delay of value-added activities such as assembly, production, and packaging to the latest possible time.

Power retailer Retailers that are characterized by large market share and low prices.

Private carrier Companies whose primary business is other than transportation provide their own transportation service by operating truck, railcars, barges, ships, or airplanes.

Private warehousing A warehousing facility that is owned by the firm using it.

Process Classification Framework (PCF) A framework that is organized around twelve cross-enterprise operating and management processes, including developing vision and strategy and developing and managing human capital.

Procurement (purchasing) Raw materials, component parts, and supplies brought from outside organizations to support a company's operations.

Procurement cards (p-cards) Are similar to credit cards for personal use, only p-cards are used for organizational purchases.

Productivity The amount of output divided by the amount of input.

Psychic stock Inventory that stimulates demand in the sense that customer purchases are stimulated by inventory that they can see.

Public warehousing Serves all legitimate users and has certain responsibilities to those users.

Pure materials Materials that lose no weight in processing.

Quality Conformance to mutually agreed upon requirements.

Quality-of-life considerations Their intent is to incorporate nonbusiness factors (e.g., cost of living, crime rate, educational opportunities) into the decision of where to locate a plant or distribution facility.

Radio-frequency identification (RFID) The use of radio frequency to identify objects that have been implanted with an RFID tag.

Rail gauge The distance between the inner sides of two parallel rail tracks.

Rate The price charged for freight transportation.

Regrouping function Involves rearranging the quantities and assortment of products as they move through the supply chain.

Relevancy Satisfying current and emerging customer needs.

Reorder (trigger) point (ROP) The level of inventory at which a replenishment order is placed.

Responsiveness The degree to which an organization can accommodate unique or unplanned customer requests.

Return on assets (ROA) Indicates what percentage of every dollar invested in the business ultimately is returned to the organization as profit.

Revenues (sales) A dollar value of all the products and/or services an organization provides to their customers during a given period of time.

Reverse auction A buyer invites bids from multiple sellers, and the seller with the lowest bid is often awarded the business.

Reverse logistics Goods that flow from the consumer to the manufacturer (e.g., product recalls and product recycling).

Right-to-work laws State laws that specify that a worker does not have to join the union to work permanently at a facility.

Routing The process of determining how a shipment will be moved between consignor and consignee or between place of acceptance by the carrier and place of delivery to the consignee.

Routing guide Provides guidance in terms of a preferred list of carriers for shipments moving between two points.

Safety (buffer) stock Inventory that is held in addition to cycle stock to guard against uncertainties in supply and/or lead time.

Scrap materials These are materials that are no longer serviceable, have been discarded, or are a by-product of the production process.

Service parts logistics Involves designing a network of facilities to stock service parts, deciding upon inventory ordering policies, stocking the required parts, and transporting parts from stocking facilities to customers.

Service recovery A process for returning a customer to a state of satisfaction after a service or product has failed to live up to expectations.

Shipper's export declaration (SED) Contains relevant export transaction data such as the transportation mode(s), transaction participants, and description of what is being exported.

Shipper's letter of instruction (SLI) Often accompanies an SED and provides explicit shipment instructions.

Shippers' associations Nonprofit membership cooperatives that perform basically the same function as freight forwarders.

Shipping conferences Cartels of all ocean vessel operators operating between certain trade areas.

Short-sea shipping Refers to waterborne transportation that utilizes inland and coastal waterways to move shipments from domestic ports to their destination.

Shrink-wrap Plastic wrapping that when heated shrinks in size to form a cover over the product.

Simulation A technique that models a real-world system, typically using mathematical equations to represent the relationships among components of the real-world system.

Single sourcing A procurement philosophy that consolidates purchase volume with a single supplier with the hopes of enjoying lower costs per unit and increased cooperation and communication in the supply relationship.

Six Sigma A practice that emphasizes the virtual elimination of business errors that strives to achieve 3.4 defects, deficiencies, or errors per one million opportunities.

Slip sheet A flat sheet of either fiberboard material or plastic that is placed under the unit load.

Slurry systems Transport products that are ground into a powder, mixed with water, and then shipped in slurry form through a pipeline.

Socially responsible procurement Procurement activities that meet the ethical and discretionary responsibilities expected by society.

Sorting function Bridges the discrepancy between the assortment of goods and services generated by the producer and the assortment demanded by the customer.

Sorting out Separating products into grades and qualities desired by different target markets.

Speculative stock Inventory that is held for several reasons such as seasonal demand, projected price increases, and potential product shortages.

Stock-keeping units (SKU) Each separate type of item that is accounted for in an inventory.

Stockout Being out of an item at the same time there is a willing buyer for it.

Stockout costs The costs to a seller when it is unable to supply an item to a customer ready to buy.

Stowability Refers to how easy a commodity is to pack into a load.

Strategic Profit Model Provides the framework for conducting return on assets analysis by incorporating revenues and expenses to generate a net profit margin, as well as an inclusion of assets to measure asset turnover.

Substitute products Products that customers view as being able to fill the same need or want as another product.

Supplier development (reverse marketing) A degree of aggressive procurement involvement not normally encountered in supplier selection.

Supplier parks Key suppliers locate on, or adjacent to, automobile plants, which helps reduce shipping costs and inventory carrying costs.

Supply chain All activities associated with the flow and transformation of goods from the raw material stage, through to the end user, as well as the associated information flows.

Supply chain analytics Combines technology with manual employee effort to identify trends, perform comparisons and highlight opportunities in supply chain processes, even when large amounts of data are involved.

Supply chain collaboration Cooperative, formal or informal supply chain relationships between manufacturing companies and their suppliers, business partners, or customers, developed to enhance the overall business performance of both sides.

Supply chain management (SCM) According to the Council of Supply Chain Management Professionals, SCM encompasses the planning and management of all activities involved in sourcing and procurement, conversion, and all logistics management activities. Importantly, it also includes coordination and collaboration with channel partners, which can be suppliers, intermediaries, third-party service providers, and customers. In essence, supply chain management integrates supply and demand management within and across companies.

Supply Chain Operations Reference-Model (SCOR) A framework that identifies five key processes—plan, source, make, deliver, return—associated with supply chain management.

Supply management A relational exchange approach involving a limited number of suppliers.

Surface Transportation Board (STB) A U.S. government agency with primary responsibility for regulating railroad pricing and service.

Sustainable products Refers to products that meet present needs without compromising the ability of future generations to meet their needs.

Sweatshops Organizations that exploit workers and that do not comply with fiscal and legal obligations toward employees.

Systems approach A company's objectives can be realized by recognizing the mutual interdependence of the major functional areas of the firm, such as marketing, production, finance, and logistics.

Tachograph A recording instrument that is installed inside a truck and produces a continuous, timed record of the truck, its speed, and its engine speed.

Tailored logistics Groups of customers with similar logistical needs and wants are provided with logistics service appropriate to those needs and wants.

Tariffs Taxes that governments place on the importation of certain items.

TEU Twenty-foot equivalent unit; a measure of the number of 20-foot containers that are used or handled.

Terminal A carrier or public facility where freight (or passengers) is shifted between vehicles or modes.

Terms of sale For international transactions, refers to determining when and where to transfer between buyer and seller, the physical goods, the payment for goods, legal title, required documentation as well as responsibility for controlling and caring for goods while in transit.

Theft (stealing) Taking and removing personal property with the intent to deprive the rightful owner of it.

Third-party logistics (logistics outsourcing; contract logistics) The general idea behind these concepts is that one company (e.g., a manufacturer) allows a specialist company to provide it with one or more logistics functions (e.g., warehousing, outbound transportation).

Throughput Refers to the amount of product entering and leaving a facility in a given time period.

Time series forecasting A group of forecasting techniques that is based on the idea that future demand is solely dependent on past demand.

Time utility Having products available when they are needed by customers.

Ton miles The number of tons times the number of miles.

Total cost approach Concept that suggests that all relevant activities in moving and storing products should be considered as a whole (i.e., their total cost), not individually.

Tracing A carrier's attempt to determine a shipment's location during the course of its move.

Transportation Actual physical movement of goods and people between two points.

Transportation management The buying and controlling of transportation services by either a shipper or consignee.

Transportation management system (TMS) A software package that automates the process of building orders, tending loads, and tracking shipments, audits, and payments.

Transportation Worker Identification Credential (TWIC) A common credential that is used to identify workers across all modes of transportation.

Truckload (TL) carrier A motor carrier that focuses on shipments of greater than 10,000 pounds.

Unified logistics structure Multiple logistics activities are combined into, and managed as, a single department.

Unit load (unitization) Consolidation of several units (cartons or cases) into larger units to improve efficiency in handling and to reduce shipping costs.

Unit load devices (ULD) An alternative name for airfreight containers.

Variable slot location A system in which products are stored wherever there is empty space available in a warehouse.

Vendor-managed inventory (VMI) A system in which the size and timing of replenishment orders into a retailer's system are the manufacturer's responsibility.

Voice-based order picking The use of speech to guide order-picking activities.

Warehouse Emphasize the storage of products and their primary purpose is to maximize usage of available storage space.

Warehouse management systems (WMS) Software packages that control the movement and storage of materials within a warehousing facility.

Warehousing That part of a firm's logistics system that stores products at and between points of origin and point of consumption.

Waste materials These are materials that have been spoiled, broken, or otherwise rendered unfit for further use or reclamation.

Weighing out Cargo reaches a vehicle's or a container's weight capacity without filling its cubic capacity.

Weight break The shipment size that equates transportation charges for different rates and weight groups.

Weight-gaining product characteristics A product that gains weight in processing; the processing point should be close to the market.

Weight-losing product characteristics A product that loses weight during the production process; the processing point should be as near to its origin as possible.

Wireless communication Refers to communication without cables and cords, and includes infrared, microwave, and radio transmissions.

NAME INDEX

SUBJECT INDEX

Note: The letters '*f*' and '*t*' following the locators refers to figures and tables cited in the text.